DATA PROTECTION AND PRIVACY

This book brings together papers that offer conceptual analyses, highlight issues, propose solutions, and discuss practices regarding privacy, data protection and Artificial Intelligence. It is one of the results of the thirteenth annual International Conference on Computers, Privacy and Data Protection (CPDP) held in Brussels in January 2020.

The development and deployment of Artificial Intelligence promises significant breakthroughs in how humans use data and information to understand and interact with the world. The technology, however, also raises significant concerns. In particular, concerns are raised as to how Artificial Intelligence will impact fundamental rights.

This interdisciplinary book has been written at a time when the scale and impact of data processing on society – on individuals as well as on social systems – is becoming ever starker. It discusses open issues as well as daring and prospective approaches and is an insightful resource for readers with an interest in computers, privacy and data protection.

Computers, Privacy and Data Protection

2017

Data Protection and Privacy: (In)visibilities and Infrastructures
Editors: Ronald Leenes, Rosamunde van Brakel, Serge Gutwirth, Paul De Hert
ISBN: 978-3-319-56177-6 (Print) 978-3-319-50796-5 (Online)

Previous titles in this series (published by Hart Publishing)

2018

Data Protection and Privacy: The Age of Intelligent Machines
Editors: Ronald Leenes, Rosamunde van Brakel, Serge Gutwirth, Paul De Hert
ISBN: 978-1-509-91934 5 (Print) 978-1-509-91935-2 (EPDF) 978-1-509-91936-9 (EPUB)

2019

Data Protection and Privacy: The Internet of Bodies
Editors: Ronald Leenes, Rosamunde van Brakel, Serge Gutwirth, Paul De Hert
ISBN: 978-1-509-92620-6 (Print) 978-1-509-92621-3 (EPDF) 978-1-509-9622-0 (EPUB)

2020

Data Protection and Privacy: Data Protection and Democracy
Editors: Dara Hallinan, Ronald Leenes, Serge Gutwirth, Paul De Hert
ISBN: 978-1-509-93274-0 (Print) 978-1-509-93275-7 (EPDF) 978-1-509-93276-4 (EPUB)

Data Protection and Privacy

Data Protection and Artificial Intelligence

Edited by

Dara Hallinan,
Ronald Leenes
and
Paul De Hert

·HART·
OXFORD · LONDON · NEW YORK · NEW DELHI · SYDNEY

HART PUBLISHING

Bloomsbury Publishing Plc

Kemp House, Chawley Park, Cumnor Hill, Oxford, OX2 9PH, UK

1385 Broadway, New York, NY 10018, USA

29 Earlsfort Terrace, Dublin 2, Ireland

HART PUBLISHING, the Hart/Stag logo, BLOOMSBURY and the Diana logo are
trademarks of Bloomsbury Publishing Plc

First published in Great Britain 2021

First published in hardback, 2021
Paperback edition, 2022

A catalogue record for this book is available from the British Library.

Library of Congress Cataloging-in-Publication Data

Names: Computers, Privacy and Data Protection (Conference) (13th : 2020 : Brussels, Belgium) |
Hallinan, Dara, editor. | Leenes, Ronald, editor. | Hert, Paul De, editor.

Title: Data protection and privacy : data protection and artificial intelligence / edited by Dara Hallinan,
Ronald Leenes, and Paul De Hert.

Description: Gordonsville : Hart Publishing, an imprint of Bloomsbury Publishing, 2021. |
Series: Computers, privacy, and data protection; vol 13 |
Includes bibliographical references and index.

Identifiers: LCCN 2020049885 (print) | LCCN 2020049886 (ebook) |
ISBN 9781509941759 (hardback) | ISBN 9781509946228 (paperback) |
ISBN 9781509941766 (pdf) | ISBN 9781509941773 (Epub)

Subjects: LCSH: Data protection—Law and legislation—Congresses. |
Privacy, Right of—Congresses. | Artificial intelligence—Law and legislation—Congresses.
Classification: LCC K3264.C65 C653 2020 (print) | LCC K3264.C65 (ebook) |
DDC 343.09/88—dc23

LC record available at https://lccn.loc.gov/2020049885

LC ebook record available at https://lccn.loc.gov/2020049886

ISBN: HB: 978-1-50994-175-9
PB: 978-1-50994-622-8
ePDF: 978-1-50994-176-6
ePub: 978-1-50994-177-3

Typeset by Compuscript Ltd, Shannon

To find out more about our authors and books visit www.hartpublishing.co.uk. Here you will find
extracts, author information, details of forthcoming events and the option to sign up for our newsletters.

PREFACE

It is early September 2020 as we write this foreword. Over the past year, data protection has shown itself to be more relevant than ever. It seems there are now few matters of social significance which can be disentangled from information processing, and few forms of information processing which can truly be disentangled from data protection. The COVID-19 pandemic is a prime example. Whilst all agree that the search for ways to disrupt virus transmission, for cures and for vaccines are essential, all also agree that such ends should only be pursued within an information processing framework which respects data protection principles.

The prominence and prevalence of data protection discussion, however, does not necessarily define how the data protection landscape will look in future. In light of the increasing embeddedness of data protection in matters of social debate, there are now critical choices to be made by data protection stakeholders – academics, civil society, industry and supervisory authorities alike – as to, for example, which challenges data protection answers, what the content of data protection law should look like, how data protection principles should be balanced against other legitimate interests and as to how data protection enforcement should best function.

In the meantime, the international privacy and data protection crowd gathered in Brussels for the thirteenth time to participate in the international Computers, Privacy and Data Protection Conference (CPDP) – between 22 to 24 January 2020. An audience of over 1,000 people had the chance to discuss a wide range of contemporary topics and issues with over 400 speakers in more than 80 panels, during the breaks, side events and at ad-hoc dinners and pub crawls. Striving for diversity and balance, CPDP gathers academics, lawyers, practitioners, policymakers, computer scientists and civil society from all over the world to exchange ideas and discuss the latest emerging issues and trends. This unique multidisciplinary formula has served to make CPDP one of the leading data protection and privacy conferences in Europe and around the world.

The conference was again a hive of activity and discussion. Conversations naturally dealt with data protection law. However, conversations also addressed much broader themes. Amongst these themes, the impact of AI on fundamental rights and social structures – the core theme of the conference – featured prominently. Also heavily discussed were cross-cutting issues emerging around the practice, difficulty and future of enforcing rights in a changing world – the topic of next year's conference.

The conference is definitely the place to be, but we are also happy to produce a tangible spin-off every year: the CPDP book. Papers in the book are cited frequently and the series has a broad readership. The book cycle starts with a call for papers in the summer preceding the conference. Submissions are then peer reviewed and authors whose papers are accepted present their work in the various academic panels at the conference. After the conference, speakers are also invited to submit papers based on panel discussions. All papers submitted on the basis of both calls are then (again) double-blind peer reviewed. This year, we received twelve papers in the second round of submissions, of which eight were accepted for publication. It is these eight papers that are found in this volume, complemented by the conference closing speech traditionally given by the EDPS (Wojciech Wiewiórowski).

The conference addressed numerous topics concerning privacy and data protection in its 80 plus panels. These naturally included panels dealing with AI, but also included panels dealing with numerous other topics, such as Adtech, facial recognition, children's privacy, the implementation and enforcement of the GDPR, interoperability in the AFSJ and international data protection laws. The conference covered far too many topics to list them all here. For more information, we refer the interested reader to the conference website: www.cpdp-conferences.org.

Whilst extensive, the current volume offers but a fraction of what is available across the whole conference. Nevertheless, the editors consider the volume to consist of an important set of papers addressing both contemporary and prospective privacy and data protection issues.

All of the chapters in this book have been peer reviewed and commented on by at least two referees with expertise and interest in the relevant subject matter. Since their work is crucial for maintaining the scientific quality of the book, we would like to take this opportunity to thank all the CPDP reviewers for their commitment and efforts: Aaron Martin, Alessandro Mantelero, Ana Fernandez Inguanzo, Andres Chomczyk Penedo, Andrew Adams, Arnold Roosendaal, Ashwinee Kumar, Bart Van der Sloot, Bettina Berendt, Claudia Diaz, Claudia Quelle, Colette Cuijpers, Daniel Le Métayer, Dennis Hirsch, Diana Dimitrova, Eduard Fosch Villaronga, Eleni Kosta, Eleonora Nestola, Els Kindt, Evelyn Wan, Franziska Boehm, Gabriela Zanfir-Fortuna, Georgios Bouchagiar, Gergely Biczók, Gianclaudio Malgieri, Gianluigi Maria Riva, Giorgio Monti, Giovanni Livraga, Gloria González Fuster, Hellen Mukiri-Smith, Henrik Junklewitz, Hideyuki Matsumi, Hiroshi Miyashita, Ian Brown, Inge Graef, Ioulia Konstantinou, Irene Kamara, Ivan Szekely, Joanna Kulesza, Juraj Sajfert, Katerina Demetzou, Kees Stuurman, Kristina Irion, Lina Jasmontaite, Lucas Jones, Magda Brewczynska, Maria Grazia Porcedda, Marit Hansen, Masa Galic, Massimo Durante, Matthieu Peeters, Maurizio Borghi, Maximilian von Grafenstein, Merel Noorman, Michael Birnhack, Mistale Taylor, Nicholas Martin, Nicolo Zingales, Nora Ni Loideain, Oliver Vettermann, Orla Lynskey, Paulus Meessen, Raphael Gellert, Robin Pierce, Sara Roda, Sascha van Schendel, Shaz Jameson, Simone Van Der Hof,

Stefano Fantin, Stephanie von Maltzan, Tal Zarsky, Tineke Broer, Tjaša Petročnik and Yung Shin Van Der Sype.

As is now customary, the conference concluded with some closing remarks from the European Data Protection Supervisor, Wojciech Wiewiórowski. He was appointed as Supervisor on the 5 December 2019 – just shortly before the conference. We are very happy and honoured that he was willing to continue the tradition and we look forward to more of his closing speeches in future.

Dara Hallinan, Ronald Leenes and Paul De Hert
8 September 2020

CONTENTS

LIST OF CONTRIBUTORS

Ala'a Al-Momani is a researcher and a PhD candidate at the Institute of Distributed Systems at Ulm University, Germany.

Vibeke Binz Vallevik is Deputy Director and Principal Researcher at the DNV GL Precision Medicine research program.

Christoph Bösch is a postdoctoral researcher at the Institute of Distributed Systems at Ulm University, Germany.

Tiago Sérgio Cabral is a researcher and Master in European Union Law. He is also a member of the AI Team at Vieira de Almeida and Associados.

Davit Chokoshvili is Regulatory Affairs and Bioethics Manager at Megeno S.A., a genomics and health data analytics company based in Luxembourg.

Diana Dimitrova is a Research Associate in the Intellectual Property Law Unit at FIZ Karlsruhe and a PhD student at LSTS/Vrije Universiteit Brussel (VUB), focusing on data subject rights in the context of the AFSJ.

Serge Egelman is the Research Director of the Usable Security and Privacy group at the International Computer Science Institute and holds a research appointment in the Department of Electrical Engineering and Computer Sciences at the University of California, Berkeley. He is also CTO and co-founder of AppCensus, Inc.

Álvaro Feal is a third-year PhD student working on Android privacy and regulatory compliance topics at the IMDEA Networks Institute in Madrid, Spain.

Eduard Fosch-Villaronga is a Marie Skłodowska-Curie Postdoctoral Researcher at the eLaw Centre for Law and Digital Technologies at Leiden University, Netherlands.

Julien Gamba is a fourth-year PhD student in Android security and privacy at the IMDEA Networks Institute in Madrid, Spain.

Marcello Ienca is a Senior Researcher at the Department of Health Sciences and Technology at ETH Zurich, Switzerland.

Yordanka Ivanova is a joint PhD candidate at the Law Faculty of Sofia University 'St. Kliment Ohridski' (Bulgaria) and Vrije University Brussels (VUB).

Irene Kamara is a PhD researcher at the Tilburg Institute for Law, Technology and Society, affiliate researcher at the Vrije Universiteit Brussel and attorney-at-law.

Frank Kargl is a Professor for Distributed Systems at Ulm University, where he investigates privacy-preserving automotive systems.

Robin L Pierce specialises in regulation and governance of digital technologies for health at the Institute for Law, Technology, Markets and Society at Tilburg Law School.

Teresa Quintel is a PhD candidate in Law at the University of Luxembourg, Faculty of Law, Economics and Finance, in collaboration with Uppsala University, Sweden.

Joel Reardon is an Assistant Professor in Computer Science at the University of Calgary, as well as a co-founder and forensic lead at AppCensus, Inc.

Alfred Rossi is a Research Scientist at Immuta, and a Senior Lecturer in the Ohio State University Department of Computer Science and Engineering.

Sophie Stalla-Bourdillon is Senior Privacy Counsel and Legal Engineer at Immuta, and a Professor at the University of Southampton Law School, where she co-directs the Web Science Institute.

Juan Tapiador is Professor of Computer Science at Universidad Carlos III de Madrid, Spain, where he leads the Computer Security Lab.

Narseo Vallina-Rodriguez is an Assistant Research Professor at IMDEA Networks, part-time Research Scientist at the International Computer Science Institute (ICSI) at UC Berkeley, and co-founder of AppCensus, Inc.

Primal Wijesekera is a staff research scientist at the Usable Security and Privacy research group at ICSI and also holds an appointment in the Department of Electrical Engineering and Computer Sciences at the University of California, Berkeley.

1

Don't Accept Candy from Strangers: An Analysis of Third-Party Mobile SDKs

ÁLVARO FEAL[1], JULIEN GAMBA[2], JUAN TAPIADOR[3], PRIMAL
WIJESEKERA[4], JOEL REARDON[5], SERGE EGELMAN[6] AND NARSEO
VALLINA-RODRIGUEZ[7]

Abstract

Mobile application (app) developers often include third-party Software
Development Kits (SDKs) in their software to integrate services and features
offered by other companies, like online payments or social network integration, or
to monetise their apps through advertisements. As a result, SDKs play a key role
in the software supply chain. Their integration in apps is practically mandatory
if developers aim at producing software that integrates smoothly in the current
ecosystem of internet services. Unfortunately, these common software development practices might come at a privacy cost to end users since many third-party
library providers implement data-driven business models that allow them to offer
their services to developers free of monetary payment. In this chapter, we provide
an overview of the third-party library ecosystem for the Android platform and we
discuss its privacy implications for mobile end users due to limitations present
in the permission system of today's mobile platforms, and the overall lack of
transparency in the industry. We apply software analysis techniques and manual
analysis to: (1) compare the effectiveness and limitations of state-of-the-art SDK
detection tools; (2) manually classify SDKs by their purpose and compare the
classification capabilities of current auditing tools; and (3) gain empirical insights
about their behaviour and data collection practices. We discuss different ways to
tackle the limitations present in current detection tools to increase developers'

[1] IMDEA Networks Institute, Universidad Carlos III de Madrid.
[2] IMDEA Networks Institute, Universidad Carlos III de Madrid.
[3] Universidad Carlos III de Madrid.
[4] ICSI, U.C. Berkeley.
[5] AppCensus Inc., University of Calgary.
[6] ICSI, U.C. Berkeley, AppCensus Inc.
[7] IMDEA Networks Institute, ICSI, AppCensus Inc.

awareness and regulatory enforcement through the design and development of new software analysis tools. We also discuss potential solutions to mitigate the limitations found in the current permission model in order to enhance user awareness and control.

Keywords

Android, Privacy, Third-party SDKs.

I. Introduction

In the last decade, smartphones have evolved from rare gadgets to indispensable and powerful tools ubiquitously carried by billions of users everywhere and nearly at all times. Modern smartphones have a variety of sensors such as the camera, GPS, and microphone that allow application developers to access personal information and details about their environment. These capabilities have enabled a rich ecosystem of innovative and 'smart' mobile apps that help users in all types of online activities, including social networking, banking, shopping, entertainment, and augmented reality applications.

Yet, developing profitable and innovative mobile applications can turn into a complex and costly process. As in the case of web and desktop software development, most app developers rely on already developed components (libraries or SDKs) offered by other companies or organisations (third parties), to integrate desired functionalities in their products, such as online payments, bug reporting, analytics or advertising and graphics support, among many others. The ability to reuse well-tested and well-maintained code in their software – which is often available for free – allows developers to speed up the development process and, ultimately, reduce development costs and time. Moreover, using such libraries constitutes a best practice in the software engineering discipline since these libraries are modular and reusable. This is particularly important in the case of security-critical code, such as cryptographic libraries, which can be implemented once and reused, making the code more robust and bug free.

The use of third-party SDKs may come at a privacy cost for end users, especially when developers integrate proprietary SDKs offered by data-driven organisations like analytics and advertising companies. The ubiquitous nature of smartphones and their capacity to access sensitive and behavioural data, along with the innovations enabled by the 'Big Data' revolution, provide many SDK providers with easy access to an unprecedented volume of high-quality data thanks to developers integrating their components in to millions of apps. Regulatory efforts such as the General Data Protection Regulation (GDPR)[8] and California's Consumer

---

[8] 'The general data protection regulation', Council of the European Union, www.consilium.europa.eu/en/policies/data-protection-reform/data-protection-regulation/ (last accessed April 2020).

Protection Act (CCPA),[9] enforce transparency by forcing software developers to declare the types of data that general categories of third parties may collect or receive from the app and obtain informed user consent (provided that there is no other legal basis for such collection). Nevertheless, regulation without strict enforcement seems to be insufficient to protect end users' privacy in digital products as previous academic studies have revealed.[10,11,12]

Mobile operating systems such as Android and iOS implement a permission model to enable user control and prevent unwanted or unauthorised access to sensitive data at the application level. However, these security mechanisms are insufficient when SDKs are embedded in an app. This happens because current mobile operating systems allow third-party code to run in the same context and with the same privileges as the app itself. This makes it difficult for users to identify whether a given permission will be used for the primary purposes of the app or for secondary usages such as user profiling or advertising. These inherited privileges, along with the fact that the specific behaviours of these third-party libraries are generally opaque to end-users and developers alike, constitute severe transparency and privacy issues. Users can only rely on the information disclosed by application developers in their privacy policies, which are typically incomplete and inaccurate.[13]

New regulatory frameworks make application developers liable for any personal data collection malpractice incurred by the third-party libraries embedded in their products. Yet, most SDKs do not open their code for inspection, leaving developers with no choice but to trust the SDK providers' claims and disclosures (ie, privacy by trust). Developers should investigate whether their third-party components are (or claim to be) compliant with privacy regulations.[14,15]

In this book, we aim to shed light on the issues and challenges that third-party SDKs bring to the mobile ecosystem from a privacy, transparency, and regulatory compliance standpoint. Our main contributions are:

- We provide an overview and a taxonomy of the SDKs available in the mobile ecosystem.

---

[9] 'California Consumer Privacy Act (CCPA)', State of California Department of Justice, oag.ca.gov/privacy/ccpa (last accessed April 2020).

[10] Hu, Xuehui, and Nishanth Sastry, 'Characterising Third Party Cookie Usage in the EU after GDPR', *Proceedings of the 10th ACM Conference on Web Science.*

[11] Sanchez-Rola et al, 'Can I Opt Out Yet? GDPR and the Global Illusion of Cookie Control', *Proceedings of the 2019 ACM Asia Conference on Computer and Communications Security.*
Jannick Sørensen and Sokol Kosta, 'Before and after gdpr: The changes in third party presence at public and private european websites', *The World Wide Web Conference.*

[12] Janis Wong and Tristan Henderson, 'How Portable is Portable? Exercising the GDPR's Right to Data Portability', *Proceedings of the 2018 ACM International Joint Conference.*

[13] Okoyomon et al., 'On the ridiculousness of notice and consent: Contradictions in app privacy policies', *Workshop on Technology and Consumer Protection (ConPro).*

[14] Razaghpanah et al, 'Apps, trackers, privacy, and regulators: A global study of the mobile tracking ecosystem', *The Network and Distributed System Security Symposium.*

[15] Reardon et al, '50 Ways to Leak Your Data: An Exploration of Apps' Circumvention of the Android Permissions System', *28th USENIX Security Symposium.*

- We discuss existing approaches to detect the presence of SDKs in mobile apps and compare the features provided by state-of-the-art SDK detection tools.

- We combine static, dynamic, and manual analysis to classify the SDKs present in the top 50 most popular apps on Google Play according to their claimed features, and compare the result to the classification provided by current auditing tools.

- We demonstrate the privacy and security risks derived from the data collection practices observed in third-party SDKs embedded in the corpus of 50 apps.

- We conclude by discussing possible solutions to the issues that SDKs bring from a privacy and regulatory compliance standpoint, such as educating developers, joint efforts for auditing SDKs, and improvements to the current permission model.

II. Background

Several studies focusing on code reuse in the Android platform have reported on the rich and diverse ecosystem of SDKs available for app developers and how their use is often perceived as a reflection on software engineering best practices.[16,17,18,19] Most mobile app developers use SDKs to integrate external features, components, and services in their software – eg, integrating game engines, handling online payments – but also for advertisement and analytics purposes.[20]

Previous work has shown the presence of third-party libraries in all kind of applications[21] regardless of their audience,[22,23] origin[24,25] or price.[26] Empirical

---

[16] Michael Backes, Sven Bugiel and Erik Derr, 'Reliable third-party library detection in android and its security applications', *Proceedings of the 2016 ACM SIGSAC Conference on Computer and Communications Security*.

[17] Theodore Book, Adam Pridgen, and Dan S Wallach, 'Longitudinal analysis of android ad library permissions', *arXiv preprint arXiv:1303.0857*.

[18] Mojica et al, 'A large-scale empirical study on software reuse in mobile apps', *IEEE software*.

[19] Ruiz et al, 'Understanding reuse in the android market', *IEEE International Conference on Program Comprehension*.

[20] Han et al, 'The Price is (Not) Right: Comparing Privacy in Free and Paid Apps', *Proceedings on Privacy Enhancing Technologies Symposium*.

[21] Razaghpanah,' Apps, trackers' (n 14).

[22] Reyes et at, '"Won't somebody think of the children?" Examining COPPA compliance at scale' *Proceedings on Privacy Enhancing Technologies*.

[23] Junia Valente and Alvaro A Cardenas, 'Security and privacy in Smart Toys', *Workshop on Internet of Things Security and Privacy*.

[24] Gamba et al, 'An Analysis of Pre-installed Android Software', *IEEE Symposium on Security and Privacy*.

[25] Wang et al, 'Beyond google play: A large-scale comparative study of chinese android app markets', *Proceedings of the Internet Measurement Conference*.

[26] Han, 'Comparing Free and Paid apps' (n 20).

evidence shows that mobile applications contact on average six domains related to advertisement and tracking SDKs,[27] typically offered by different companies. The use of SDKs in the mobile software supply chain is so extended that even apps that come preinstalled on the phone are packaged with third-party advertising and analytics libraries.[28]

Despite their central role in the app development process, we barely understand the mobile SDK ecosystem and their privacy risks. An app developer might include third-party code in their software without realising that this is potentially harmful for users' privacy. Developers making SDK choices based on the service offered by the third-party library might render ineffective. The boundaries between many SDK categories are unclear, and SDK providers tend to offer more than one product to app developers. For instance, analytics and advertising services have become extremely entangled since most AdTech companies integrate both functionalities in the same SDK, potentially using the data gathered by the analytics service for user profiling or advertising.[29] Unfortunately, there are no reliable methods to accurately quantify their personal data collection practices and their purpose at scale.

The lack of information and transparency in the use of SDKs by mobile app developers has consumer protection implications, too. Marketplaces and app stores allow users to download apps and understand what type of feature they provide, whether they cost money, the number of users that they have and the legal documents in which data collection is explained. However, there is not enough transparency about the presence and data collection practices of SDKs embedded in the apps. Developers, users, and regulators could benefit from the existence of technologies to study the functioning and purpose of third-party libraries, ideally in a publicly available observatory.

A. The Mobile SDK Landscape

There are a broad range of third-party SDK providers that specialise in offering one or multiple features, services, or technologies to application developers. The type of services they offer range from SDKs offering UI support, to SDKs that collect user data in order to generate revenue. To illuminate this ecosystem, we rely on public information from hundreds of SDKs detected by previous research[30,31]

---

[27] Razaghpanah, 'Apps, Trackers' (n 14).
[28] Gamba, 'Pre-installed Android Software' (n 24).
[29] Ruiz, 'Reuse on Android' (n 19).
[30] Razaghpanah,' Apps, trackers' (n 14).
[31] Ma et al, 'LibRadar: fast and accurate detection of third-party libraries in Android apps', *Proceedings of the 38th international conference on software engineering companion*.

to create a more comprehensive classification of mobile SDKs by their offered functionality:

i. Development Support

These are libraries which help developers adding support features to their code, such as widgets, UI features or JavaScript Object Notation (JSON) and XML formatters. Examples of this category include the Android Support Library and GSON (Google's JSON implementation). These libraries are expected to be found in many applications and, assuming that they have not been tampered with to include malicious code, they should be harmless to users' privacy since they do not collect personal data. Therefore, a-priori they do not need to be included in documents such as the privacy policy. Nevertheless, some development SDKs might engage in personal data collection, like Google's Firebase[32] and Unity3D,[33] a library that supports the development of games but also includes analytics and advertisement capabilities. In this case, their ability to collect sensitive data will vary from one application to another, depending on how application developers integrate these services in their mobile products. It is possible to identify multiple subcategories of development support libraries, depending on their intended purpose:

Networking and protocol support: These libraries offer support for implementing network protocols such as HTTP/HTTPS or Google's QUIC.

Database support: These SDKs provide developers with code to manage and store data, implementing well known database solutions like SQL.

Cryptography support: These libraries help developers implementing cryptographic solutions for data storage or secure communications.

Cloud integration and support: The SDKs in this group allow for the integration of cloud services capabilities into applications, for instance Amazon Web Services[34] or Google's Firebase.[35]

Browser support: These SDKs provide functionalities to open web content, such as Android's WebView which allows applications to render webpages.

Cross-platform development: While application code in Android is developed using one of the two languages supported by the platform (Kotlin and Java), there are several SDKs that allow to include code in other languages for cross-platform development. One example is Facebook Hermes,[36] which allows to include React

---

[32] 'Google Mobile Services', Android, www.android.com/gms/ (last accessed April 2020).

[33] 'Unity for all', Unity, https://unity.com/ (last accessed April 2020).

[34] 'Getting Started with Android', Amazon AWS, accessed April 2020, https://aws.amazon.com/developers/getting-started/android/ (last accessed April 2020).

[35] 'Firebase', Google, https://firebase.google.com/ (last accessed April 2020).

[36] 'GitHub: Hermes', Facebook, https://github.com/facebook/hermes (last accessed April 2020).

code in Android and iOS apps, or Apache Cordova,[37] which allows using web development techniques to build mobile apps.

ii. Push Notifications/Consumer Engagement

Push notifications are small server-to-client messages used to reach mobile audiences anywhere and anytime. This technology is at the core of companies offering 'customer engagement' services to create a direct communication channel between an external stakeholder (consumer) and an organization (often a company, developer, advertiser, or brand). Many of the companies offering these services also offer analytics and advertisement. This is the case of Google, which offers its own cross-platform service – Firebase Cloud Messaging (FCM)[38] – JPush[39] or airPush.[40]

iii. Online Payments

Several SDK providers like AliPay[41] and Google Pay[42] allow developers to include online payment services. Many mobile applications, especially mobile games, no longer implement advertising-based monetisation models. Solutions like Fortumo[43] allow developers to explore alternative sources of revenues by requesting users to pay a small fee for unlocking premium features or purchasing virtual goods.

iv. Maps and Location Services

SDKs like the Google Maps SDK,[44] Here.com[45] or Baidu Maps[46] allow application developers to add maps, geo-location, and navigation capabilities to their products. The set of features and services offered by maps and location providers is very broad. While some offer pure mapping services, others like Google Maps provide data-driven added value like location-based business searches, geo-coding and even Augmented Reality (AR) services.[47]

---

[37] 'Apache Cordova', Apache, https://cordova.apache.org/ (last accessed April 2020).
[38] 'Firebase Cloud Messaging', Firebase, https://firebase.google.com/docs/cloud-messaging (last accessed April 2020).
[39] 'Product Introduction of JPush', JiGuang Docs, https://docs.jiguang.cn/en/jpush/guideline/intro/ (last accessed April 2020).
[40] 'The future of Mobile Advertising', airpush, https://airpush.com/ (last accessed April 2020).
[41] 'Trust makes it simple', Alipay, https://intl.alipay.com (last accessed April 2020).
[42] 'Google Pay', Google Developers, https://developers.google.com/pay (last accessed April 2020).
[43] 'Global direct carrier billing platform', Fortumo, https://fortumo.com/ (last accessed April 2020).
[44] 'Overview', Google Maps Platform, https://developers.google.com/maps/documentation/android-sdk/intro (last accessed April 2020).
[45] 'Homepage', HERE Technologies, www.here.com/ (last accessed April 2020).
[46] 'Android SDK', Baidu, lbsyun.baidu.com/index.php?title=androidsdk.
[47] 'Introducing Live View', Google Maps Help, https://support.google.com/maps/thread/11554255?hl=en (last accessed April 2020).

v. Authentication

These are services that allow application developers to protect parts of the application's functionality from unauthorised access using an online identity or two-factor authentication mechanisms. Examples of these SDKs are OAuth and Google's Firebase (Google Login).

vi. Social Networks

These SDKs allow developers to include functionality from social networks, such as login capabilities and the ability to share content with a list of friends. One remarkable example is the Facebook Graph SDK, which also provides analytics and advertisement services. As we will discuss in Section IV, applications integrating these libraries might be able to harvest personal data from the social network profile of the user.

vii. Analytics

Many companies provide analytics tools to understand how users interact with their app, find, and solve bugs and crashes, optimise user engagement, and generate revenue with highly detailed data about customers. Therefore, analytics SDKs could be broken down into several subcategories, with some SDKs providing more than one functionality to the app, including bug reporting (eg, Crashlytics),[48] A/B testing (eg, Firebase A/B testing),[49] and user engagement or CRM (eg, StartApp).[50]

viii. Advertisement

Advertisement SDKs are used by app developers to show ads to users, generating revenue for the developer. Because of targeted advertisement, many of these libraries also collect personal data in order to generate user profiles to better understand the type of content that a given user is interested on. Examples of these libraries are Google's AdMob,[51] Unity3D[52] or Twitter's MoPub.[53]

---

[48] 'Firebase crashlytics', Firebase, https://firebase.google.com/docs/crashlytics (last accessed April 2020).
[49] 'Firebase A/B Testing', Firebase, https://firebase.google.com/docs/ab-testing (last accessed April 2020).
[50] 'Mobile, Fulfileld', StartApp, www.startapp.com/ (last accessed April 2020).
[51] 'AdMob', Google Developers, https://developers.google.com/admob (last accessed April 2020).
[52] 'Monetize your game', Unity, https://unity.com/solutions/unity-ads (last accessed April 2020).
[53] 'Powerful app monetization', MoPub, www.mopub.com/ (last accessed April 2020).

Table 1 Examples of SDKs for each category

Type	Examples
Development support	Android Support, GSON, Unity3D
Network support	OKHTTP, Facebook Fizz, jmDNS
Database support	ORMLite, Android Wire, Firebase
Crypto support	Jasypt, Bouncy Castle
Browser support	HTML TextView, Chromium
Cloud integration and support	Google Firebase (Google Cloud)
Cross Platform Development	Apache Cordova, Facebook Hermes
Push notifications/Consumer engagement	Firebase Cloud Messaging, JPush, airPush
Online payments	AliPay, Fortumo
Social Networks	Facebook, Twitter, VK
Authentication	Google Firebase (2FA)
Maps/Location services	Google Maps, MapsForge, Baidu Maps
Analytics	Firebase, Baidu, Flurry
Advertisement	Unity, Google Ads, Amazon Mobile Ads

As we have seen, many SDKs offer multiple capabilities to app developers in a single library. This impedes attributing a single label in most cases. Table 1 provides examples for each of these types, showing how the same SDK can be labelled differently depending on its behaviour. The screenshot in Figure 1, shows one remarkable example which is Google's Firebase SDK. This SDK unifies analytics services, bug reporting, two-factor-authentication, services for integrating apps with Google cloud, and more. While we acknowledge that this taxonomy might not be complete, we believe that it offers a representative overview of the most common solutions that can be found in today's mobile applications.

B. Privacy Risks: Privilege Piggybacking

Both Android and iOS implement a permission model to protect sensitive system resources and data from abusive, malicious, or deceptive apps. Whenever a user installs an app from the app store, the OS forces the app to declare their access to protected resources. Only when the user consents to this – either at runtime or when installing the app, depending on the sensitivity of the permission and the OS policies – can the app access such protected resources. This app-centric permission model presents fundamental limitations to properly inform users

Figure 1 Screenshot from Firebase documentation page, showing the different products that it provides

Firebase by product

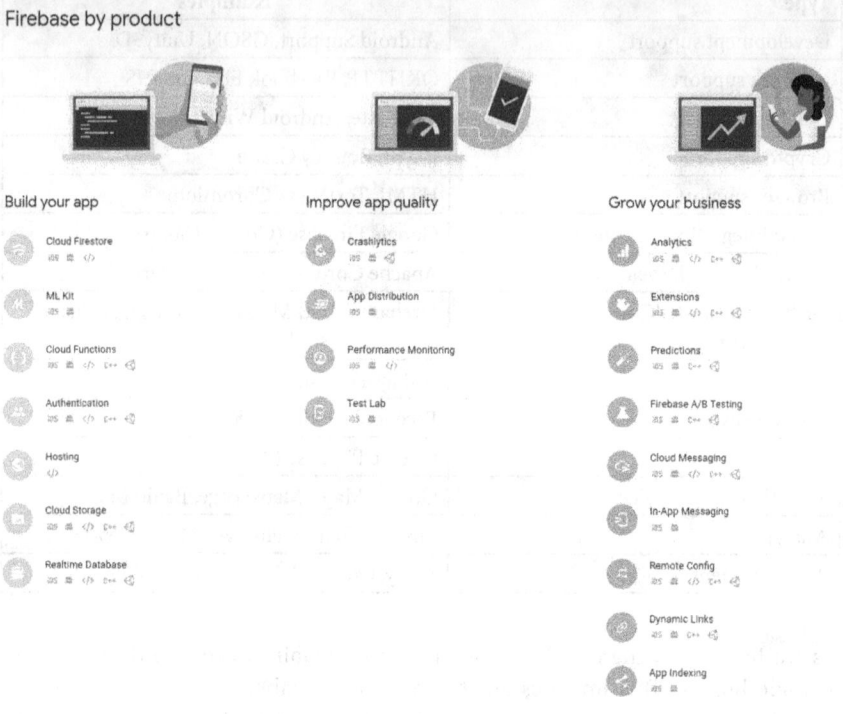

about the access to sensitive data by embedded SDKs. These run with the same privileges and permissions as the host app, as shown in Figure 2.

Many mobile users might trust the app developer when they give the app access to a piece of sensitive data such as location. However, they might not necessarily trust opaque third-party SDKs embedded in the product, particularly when the user is not even aware of their presence or is not familiar with the company, its business, and the way they will process their data.

Unfortunately, mobile operating systems and platforms fail to inform users about the SDKs that might be embedded in an app and whether they access sensitive data (unless the developer voluntarily discloses this list on their privacy policy). According to Google, the inclusion of privacy policies in mobile apps is not mandatory except when the application collects sensitive data or is aimed at children.[54] Furthermore, Google does not detail what review process it is followed to actively look for apps violating such a policy. Despite provisions in relevant privacy regulation like GDPR, CCPA, and others whose purpose is protecting

---

[54] 'Privacy, Security and Deception', Google Play, https://play.google.com/about/privacy-security-deception/ (last accessed April 2020).

Figure 2 Permission scalation in Android: SDKs can leverage the same permissions as the host application to access protected resources. In this example, the app has access to unique identifiers, location information and the external storage. Both embedded SDKs (Google and Facebook) could access those resources without requesting the appropriate permission to do so

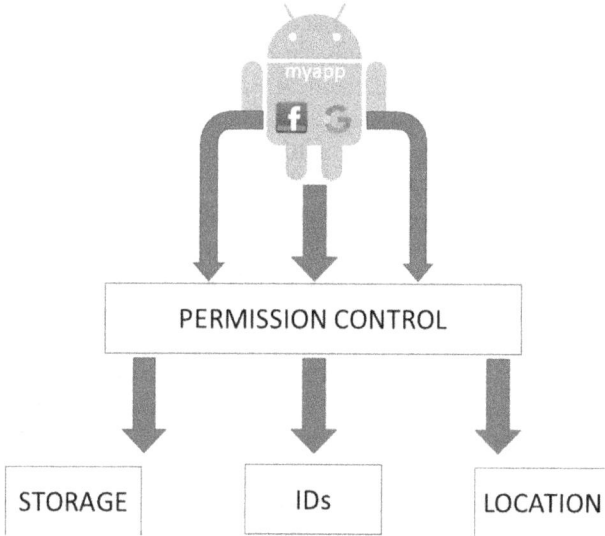

children's privacy like the Children's Online Privacy Protection Act (COPPA) in the US, developers can decide not to add a comprehensive and complete privacy policy when uploading an app to Google Play (see the screenshot of the process shown in Figure 3).

C. Transparency and Privacy Regulation

The GDPR regulates the way in which personal data from European citizens can be accessed, processed, and shared. All European users have the right to

Figure 3 Developers can decide not to include a privacy policy when uploading an app to Google Play

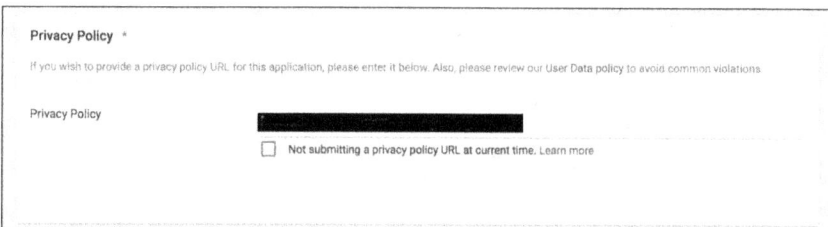

Privacy Policy *

If you wish to provide a privacy policy URL for this application, please enter it below. Also, please review our User Data policy to avoid common violations.

Privacy Policy

☐ Not submitting a privacy policy URL at current time. Learn more

be informed about data collection practices by online services (such as apps) and – unless grounds such as legitimate interest exist – no data collection should be allowed before the user has granted explicit consent.

In most cases, app publishers (the controllers, according to the rule) are responsible for informing users about the presence of third-party libraries, the type of personal data that they collect and their treatment. Developers could be liable for any privacy malpractice inflicted by third-party SDKs present in their products. However, the SDK itself could be considered as the controller or joint controller of the data if the host application has nothing to do with the data collection process of the SDK. One example of this situation would be a third-party SDK that collects data in an application and uses it for different purposes than those originally intended, thus deciding the objectives and means of processing.[55]

As we discussed previously, Google Play only requires some applications to have a privacy policy link in the app profile in Google Play,[56] namely those falling in the Designed for Families (DFF) program and those that require access to permissions labelled as 'Dangerous' by Android's official documentation.[57] Dangerous permissions are those protecting the access to especially sensitive data, such as location or unique identifiers. On the other hand, DFF apps are those that target children and thus should be complaint with COPPA and GDPR provisions for children data usage.[58] However, there seems to be no control over the completeness and accuracy of the privacy policy content.[59] Moreover, it is possible for apps using non-dangerous permissions to also collect personal data that fall outside of the permission model of Android. This is the case of apps exploiting side channels and covert channels to circumvent the permission model, and those that collect personal data directly introduced by the user in the UI without accessing dangerous permissions.[60]

In the case of iOS, Apple recommends permissions only be requested when they are necessary for the correct functioning of the app, and that the permission request prompt comes with a clear text description of why a permission is needed.[61] Furthermore, in their app store guidelines, Apple states that all applications must include an easy-to-access link to their privacy policy, and that this policy must be complete and define all data collection and sharing practices.[62]

---

[55] 'Facebook loses Belgian privacy case, faces fine of up to $125 million', Reuters, www.reuters.com/article/us-facebook-belgium/facebook-loses-belgian-privacy-case-faces-fine-of-up-to-125-million-idUSKCN1G01LG (last accessed April 2020).

[56] 'Privacy, Security and Deception', Google Play, https://play.google.com/about/privacy-security-deception/ (last accessed April 2020).

[57] 'Permissions Overview', Android Developers, https://developer.android.com/guide/topics/permissions/overview (last accessed April 2020).

[58] 'Families', Google Play, https://play.google.com/about/families/ (last accessed April 2020).

[59] Okoyomon, 'Ridiculousness of Notice and Consent' (n 13).

[60] Reardon, '50 ways' (n 15).

[61] 'Requesting Permission', Apple Developer, https://developer.apple.com/design/human-interface-guidelines/ios/app-architecture/requesting-permission/ (last accessed April 2020).

[62] 'App Store Review Guidelines', App Store, https://developer.apple.com/app-store/review/guidelines/ (last accessed April 2020).

i. Vulnerable Populations

The GDPR has special provisions for protecting the privacy of children under the age of 16. In the US, the COPPA[63] regulates data collection practices for minors under the age of 13. Both rules require the app to gather verifiable parental consent before collecting any personal or behavioural data from children. There are different ways in which SDKs handle these special provisions. Some libraries directly state in their Terms of Service (ToS) that they are not suitable to be used by apps targeting a children audience,[64] while others integrate switches to adapt their behaviour when the developer states that the application is directed at children. There are several resources available for developers to choose libraries that respect legislation specific to children data. One remarkable example is Google's list of self-certified suitable for children libraries.[65] Unfortunately, it has been proven[66] that self-certification does not guarantee that SDKs are indeed complying with current legislation without external auditing and enforcement. Likewise, Apple provides recommendations for developers of applications that collect, store and process children data. Apple recommends that these applications avoid including third-party analytics and advertisement SDKS. If this were not possible, the developer must ensure that that embedded SDKs comply with any applicable privacy laws.[67]

III. Methods for Detecting the Presence of Third-Party Services

When installing an application, most mobile users do not realise that the app publisher might not be the only actor potentially collecting personal data from them. Previous research has shown that Android apps embed, on average, between six and nine third-party libraries.[68,69] In order to detect SDKs in mobile apps and analyse the behaviour, the research community has primarily used the following two methods.

---

[63] 'Children's Privacy', Federal Trade Commission, www.ftc.gov/tips-advice/business-center/privacy-and-security/children%27s-privacy (last accessed April 2020).

[64] Reyes, 'Think of the children' (n 22).

[65] 'Participate in the Families Ads Program', Google Support, https://support.google.com/googleplay/android-developer/answer/9283445?hl=en (last accessed April 2020).

[66] Reyes, 'Think of the children' (n 22).

[67] 'App Store Review Guidelines', App Store, https://developer.apple.com/app-store/review/guidelines/ (last accessed April 2020).

[68] Zhang et at, 'Detecting third-party libraries in Android applications with high precision and recall', *IEEE 25th International Conference on Software Analysis, Evolution and Reengineering.*

[69] Razaghpanah, 'Apps, Trackers' (n 14).

A. Static Analysis

These techniques do not rely on running the software on a system but rather on analysing the code itself. This means that the analysis is generally easier to scale but also prone to failure due to code obfuscation and dynamic code loading.[70,71] Static analysis helps provide a higher bound on the data collection techniques of apps and SDKs, since it identifies every possible behaviour of a piece of software. Nevertheless, when the application is run with real user stimuli, it is possible that not every code path is executed or that pieces of the code are unreachable, thus generating a false positive. This often happens due to unfinished functionalities, dead and legacy code, and snippets copied from the internet and online development fora.[72] Examples of SDK detection tools that rely on static analysis are LibRadar, LibScout and LibPecker.[73,74,75] The problem with this approach is that it will be difficult to identify SDKs in applications using code obfuscation techniques. Many of these tools rely on fingerprinting SDKs to be able to detect them in APKs. Nevertheless, SDKs are in constant evolution[76,77] and, therefore, these fingerprints must be updated and maintained, or else the tool will become obsolete. Another detection tool that uses static analysis is Exodus,[78] which relies on matching code packages names and URLs found with the list of packages names and domains related to a given SDK provider (ie, the package com.crashlytics and the domain crashlytics.com would be matched to the Crashlytics SDK).

B. Dynamic Analysis

Tools based on dynamic analysis rely on running the software on an instrumented device to analyse the tested software's behaviour. Some tools rely on the analysis of information flows,[79] while others rely on intercepting and analysing the traffic generated by the software being tested.[80] While dynamic analysis provides actual

---

[70] Continella et al, 'Obfuscation-Resilient Privacy Leak Detection for Mobile Apps Through Differential Analysis', *The Network and Distributed System Security Symposium*.

[71] Faruki et al, 'Evaluation of android anti-malware techniques against dalvik bytecode obfuscation', *IEEE 13th International Conference on Trust, Security and Privacy in Computing and Communications*.

[72] Felt et al, 'Android permissions demystified', *ACM conference on Computer and communications security*.

[73] Ma, 'LibRadar' (n 31).

[74] Backes et al, 'Reliable third-party library detection' (n 16).

[75] Zhang et al, 'Detecting third-party' (n 68).

[76] Calciati et al, 'What did really change with the new release of the app?', *Proceedings of the 15th International Conference on Mining Software Repositories*.

[77] Ren et al, 'Bug fixes, improvements, and privacy leaks', *Proceedings of Network and Distributed Systems Security Symposium*.

[78] 'What Exodus Privacy does', Exodus Privacy, https://exodus-privacy.eu/en/page/what/ (last accessed April 2020).

[79] Enck et al, 'TaintDroid: an information-flow tracking system for realtime privacy monitoring on smartphones', *ACM Transactions on Computer Systems*.

[80] Razaghpanah et al, 'Haystack: In situ mobile traffic analysis in user space', *arXiv preprint arXiv:1510.01419*.

evidence of software behaviour (and, therefore, personal data dissemination), it is harder to automatise and test at scale due to the need to stimulate the device in order to thoroughly test the software.[81,82] Nevertheless, in the case of Android applications, there are tools for simulating user's interaction such as Apium,[83] Culebra Tester,[84] or the Android exerciser Monkey.[85] One instance of dynamic analysis used to detect SDK presence is the Appcensus platform, which runs apps in a highly instrumented version of Android and monitors access to personal data, permission usage and network traffic in order to understand what kind of personal data an app collects and who is responsible for such data collection.[86,87,88] While this solution only reports actual evidence of SDKs present in an app, it will not identify SDKs that do not generate traffic (such as UI, development support or cryptography libraries).

We note that there is a dearth of tools for studying SDKs present in iOS applications. Most of the academic efforts have been directed at understanding privacy aspects of Android applications. This situation is aggravated by the fact that many SDKs offer cross-platform support (Android, iOS, IoT, web), which gives them the ability to monitor users across all their device, and ubiquitously.[89,90]

IV. Comparison of SDK Analysis Tools

We perform a qualitative and quantitative analysis of the capabilities and limitations of four popular SDK analysis tools: three based on static analysis (LibRadar,[91] LibScout,[92] and Exodus[93]) and one based on dynamic analysis (AppCensus[94]). We focus on their ability to detect, classify and characterise SDKs embedded in the 50 most popular mobile applications published in Google Play.[95] Table 2 summarises the four detection tools and the capabilities that they implement.

---

[81] Reardon, '50 ways' (n 15).
[82] Reyes, 'Think of the children' (n 22).
[83] 'Mobile App Automation Made Awesome', Appium, appium.io/ (last accessed April 2020).
[84] 'Android UI Testing Simplified', CulebraTester, culebra.dtmilano.com/ (last accessed April 2020).
[85] 'UI/Application Exerciser Monkey', Google Developers, https://developer.android.com/studio/test/monkey (last accessed April 2020).
[86] Han, 'Comparing Free and Paid apps' (n 20).
[87] Reyes, 'Think of the children' (n 22).
[88] Reardon, '50 ways' (n 15).
[89] Brookman et al, 'Cross-device tracking: Measurement and disclosures', *Proceedings on Privacy Enhancing Technologies*.
[90] Zimmeck et al, 'A privacy analysis of cross-device tracking', *USENIX Security Symposium*.
[91] Ma, 'LibRadar' (n 31).
[92] Backes et al, 'Reliable third-party library detection' (n 16).
[93] 'What Exodus Privacy does', Exodus Privacy, https://exodus-privacy.eu.org/en/page/what/ (last accessed April 2020).
[94] Reyes, 'Think of the Children' (n 22).
[95] We acquired this list on 25 September 2019.

Table 2 Comparison of features in different SDK detection tools. ATS stands for 'Advertising and Tracking Services', and indicates that these methods group together these services in a single category.

	Analysis method	SDK Detection	SDK Classification	Detects personal data dissemination
LibRadar	Static	Yes	Yes	No
LibScout	Static	Yes	No	No
Exodus	Static	Yes	ATS	No
AppCensus	Dynamic	Yes	ATS	Yes

A. SDK Detection

LibRadar and LibScout detect SDKs at the code-level regardless of their purpose. LibRadar can identify 60 unique SDKs, while LibScout found 29. However, as discussed in Section III, the fact that a given library is detected using static analysis does not imply that it is causing privacy damage to end users. Consequently, in order to understand the privacy risk that a given SDK might pose it is important to distinguish between libraries potentially disseminating sensitive data from those that are simply making the development process of the application easier. It is, therefore, necessary to manually inspect and validate its output to eliminate false positives.

Exodus and AppCensus, instead, report those SDKs with hostnames associated to advertising and tracking services (ATS). More concretely, Exodus reports 67 seven libraries while AppCensus finds network flows attributed to 20 SDKs. This property makes these two options more suitable for privacy and regulatory auditing of Android apps. However, Exodus can still identify libraries that might be present on the code but not necessarily invoked at runtime, thus potentially rendering false positives.

B. SDK Classification

Only LibRadar aims to classify SDKs by their purpose. It considers the following categories: App Market, Development Aid, Development Framework, Game Engine, GUI Components, Map/LBS, Payment, Utility, Advertisement, Digital Identity, Mobile Analytics and Social Network. The classification performed by LibRadar is relatively complete, but it fails to capture the multi-purpose nature of many SDKs as we discussed in Section II B. In fact, most of the libraries that LibRadar can detect are classified as development aid (around 60 per cent), when many of them also provide analytics and advertising services as in the case of Unity 3D and Google's Firebase. Similarly, Facebook Graph's SDK is labelled as Social Networking, when it also allows app developers to integrate Facebook's ads and leverage their analytics services. Exodus and AppCensus do not offer any classification. Instead, they report SDKs associated with advertising, analytics, marketing and tracking services.

To compare the accuracy of the categories offered by LibRadar, we identified and visited the websites of each provider to manually identify their purpose according to the taxonomy introduced in Section II A. Unfortunately, we could not find any information for 20 per cent of libraries found by LibRadar (ie, LibRadar sometimes does not find the whole package name of libraries, making it impossible to match google.com to the appropriate Google SDKs or service included in the app) or we were not able to find the homepage of the library. To minimise human errors, several authors reviewed the output of this process, also putting it into the context of state-of-the-art research on Android privacy and third-party SDKs behaviour.

According to our classification, the majority (43 per cent) of the SDKs detected by LibRadar in our dataset of 50 applications can be classified as development support. This is followed by Analytics SDKs (12 per cent), Social Networking SDKs (7 per cent), Networking SDKs (5 per cent), Advertisement SDKS (4 per cent), and Online Payments (3 per cent). However, as we can see in Table 3 for the most popular SDKs detected by Exodus privacy,[96] LibRadar fails to capture the multi-purpose nature of many SDKs, including those collecting personal data which could be associated with advertising and tracking purposes. The most notable differences are Firebase, which is only labelled as Mobile Analytics by LibRadar, Facebook Ads, which is labelled as Social Network despite also being an advertisement network, and several analytics and advertisement services that are not included in LibRadar's fingerprints.

Table 3 Categories for the 20 most popular SDKs detected by Exodus Privacy across the 50 apps, and according to our manual classification

SDK Name	Category			
	Manual	LibRadar	Exodus	AppCensus
Firebase	Analytics, Development support, Database, Cloud, Push notifications, Authentication	Development Aid	Tracker	ATS
Crashlytics	Analytics, Development Support	Mobile Analytics	Tracker	ATS
Facebook SDK	Social network, Authentication	Social Network	Tracker	ATS

(continued)

---

[96] We use the results for Exodus because they only include tracker related SDKs, which are more relevant from a privacy and regulatory compliance point of view.

Table 3 *(Continued)*

SDK Name	Category			
	Manual	**LibRadar**	**Exodus**	**AppCensus**
Google Ads	Advertisement	Advertisement	Tracker	ATS
Google Analytics	Analytics	Mobile analytics	Tracker	ATS
DoubleClick	Analytics, Advertisement	Not found	Tracker	ATS
Appsflyer	Analytics	Mobile Analytics	Tracker	ATS
Google Tag Manager	Analytics	Mobile Analytics	Tracker	ATS
Facebook Ads SDK	Advertisement	Social Network	Tracker	ATS
Adjust	Analytics	Mobile Analytics	Tracker	ATS
Braze	Analytics	Not found	Tracker	ATS
Amazon Mobile Ads	Advertisement	Advertisement	Tracker	ATS
Appnexus	Analytics	Not found	Tracker	ATS
Moat	Analytics	Not found	Tracker	ATS
ComScore	Analytics, Advertisement	Mobile Analytics	Tracker	ATS
Mapbox	Maps	Not found	Tracker	ATS
Microsoft appcenter crashes	Development support, Analytics	Not found	Tracker	ATS
HelpShift	Analytics	Not found	Tracker	ATS
Demdex	Analytics	Not found	Tracker	ATS
MoPub	Analytics, Advertisement	Advertisement	Tracker	ATS

C. Understanding SDK's Data Collection Practices

In Section II, we discussed that the permission model of both iOS and Android fail to inform users on whether a given permission is requested by secondary purposes related to those of the SDK provider, including advertising and analytics. These two categories of SDK, together with Social Networks, account for 23 per cent of the total third-party components found by LibRadar.

In this section, we look beyond the limitations of mobile system permission models and discuss other potential privacy risks associated with each one of these categories. To do that, we leverage data from AppCensus, which reports the type of data collection by third-party SDKs in each app.

i. Social Networks

These SDKs represent a threat to privacy as they give social networks the ability to monitor users' activities outside of their own mobile applications. This means that social networks can potentially leak user data to the application developer or other third parties present in the app. For example, Facebook, through its own permission model, grants access to data such as the list of friends of the user or the pages that the user has liked on the platform.[97] Likewise, Twitter4J[98] allows developers to interact directly with the user's profile on the platform and Spotify allows gaining access to user data like gender, email account, or age. Cases such as the Cambridge Analytica scandal,[99] in which a political consulting firm got access to data from millions of Facebook users through a third-party app, highlights how dangerous social media data can become if it falls in the wrong hands.

ii. Analytics

Analytics SDKs serve different purposes and, as a result, their privacy risks can vary greatly depending on how app developers integrate them into their solutions. Some analytics libraries are used for user engagement; thus, they collect behavioural data that could be linked to a given user profile. Another example are A/B testing libraries, which rely on showing two different versions of an app component to different users and measuring which of the versions receives more positive interactions, which could reveal cognitive disabilities of the user.[100] All of these uses of analytics tools are legitimate and both apps and users might benefit from them, but the collection of such behavioural data linked to sensitive data (eg, particularly unique identifiers) should be informed to and consented by the user.

Some analytics SDKs allow developers to collect events defined by the application developer, known as 'custom events'. For instance, the developer of a medical app might want to monitor in their analytics dashboard the number of users showing certain symptoms in a geographical area. One library that allows for this kind of behaviour is Firebase, in which developers can register any event that they want to track even if it's not part of the events reported by the SDK by

[97] 'Facebook Graph API', Facebook Developers, accessed April 2020, https://developers.facebook.com/docs/graph-api/ (last accessed April 2020).

[98] 'Homepage', Twitter4J, twitter4j.org/en/.

[99] 'Revealed: 50 million Facebook profiles harvested for Cambridge Analytica in major data breach', *The Guardian*, www.theguardian.com/news/2018/mar/17/cambridge-analytica-facebook-influence-us-election.

[100] Dekelver et al, 'Design of mobile applications for people with intellectual disabilities', *Communications in Computer and Information Science*.

Figure 4 Example of a custom event declaration with Firebase

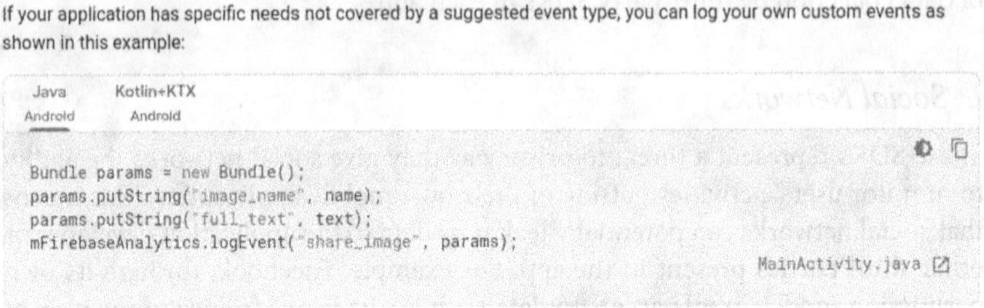

If your application has specific needs not covered by a suggested event type, you can log your own custom events as shown in this example:

```
  Java        Kotlin+KTX
  Android     Android

  Bundle params = new Bundle();
  params.putString("image_name", name);
  params.putString("full_text", text);
  mFirebaseAnalytics.logEvent("share_image", params);
                                                   MainActivity.java
```

default (see Figure 4 for a screenshot of this feature). This level of detail gives SDKs the ability to track users' every move and constitute a danger for their privacy, especially when analytics services collect information that can identify users uniquely. Using AppCensus data, we find 11 providers collecting different types of persistent unique identifiers (eg, AppsFlyer, Branch, Facebook, StartApp, Taplytics). While the majority (63 per cent) of them collect the AAID, a resettable user ID recommended by Google's policies, we find that four SDKS collect persistent identifiers like the IMEI or the Hardware ID. This behaviour is against Google's best practices[101] and defeat any privacy purpose of resettable IDs.

iii. Advertisement

Advertisement libraries collect personal data in order to show highly targeted advertisements to users and maximise revenue.[102] This brings severe privacy implications to users, with a high number of mobile SDKs collecting user data to create profiles and with the appearance of companies like data brokers,[103] which specialise in selling these types of profiles. Furthermore, because the advertisement model is highly distributed and dynamic, multiple ad publishers bid for the ability to show an ad to a given user depending on the personal characteristics of such a user.[104] This might result in user data being broadcasted to multiple organisations without the user knowing or consenting to as pointed out by ICO. Using AppCensus data, we observed seven advertisement libraries (including Verizon Ads and MoPub) collecting user identifiers (the AAID and the

---

[101] 'Best practices for unique identifiers', Android developers, https://developer.android.com/training/articles/user-data-ids (last accessed April 2020).

[102] Michael Plotnick, Charles Eldering, and Douglas Ryder, 'Behavioral targeted advertising', *U.S. Patent Application 10/116,692*.

[103] 'Time to Build a National Data Broker Registry', *The New York Times*, accessed April 2020, https://www.nytimes.com/2019/09/13/opinion/data-broker-registry-privacy.html (last accessed April 2020).

[104] Shuai Yuan, Jun Wang, and Xiaoxue Zhao, 'Real-time bidding for online advertising: measurement and analysis', *Proceedings of the Seventh International Workshop on Data Mining for Online Advertising*.

persistent Android ID) as well as location data. As in the case of mobile analytics, targeted advertisement is not necessarily against the user's privacy if the user has consented to such data collection and if there are appropriate mechanisms in place so that the user can exercise the associated data rights.

V. Mitigating the Privacy Risks of SDKs

We discuss several steps that can be taken in order to mitigate the privacy risks of third-party SDKs discussed in the previous sections.

A. Improving Auditing Tools

As shown in Table 2, the current arsenal of tools for SDK auditing presents several shortcomings. Identifying and classifying SDKs by their purpose, while monitoring their behaviour and data collection practices, is indeed a challenging task. This is particularly challenging when analysing applications at scale. Even in this study, we were unable to match 20.5 per cent of the library code packages found just in 50 apps. This state-of-affairs puts users at a vulnerable position. Those users that want to exercise their data rights lack mechanisms to identify the organisations that have access to their personal data within their apps. Users have to rely on application developers accurately disclosing this information on their privacy policies (assuming that the SDK is fully transparent to the developer). Nevertheless, previous work has shown that these policies are often inaccessible, incomplete, and written in such a way that they are difficult to understand by the average user.[105,106]

There is, indeed, a need for more accurate software analysis tools to catch up with the evolving adTech industry and mobile technologies. These methods must be able to attribute observations to the responsible organisation at scale. Technical tools such as LibRadar,[107] Exodus[108] and Appcensus[109] have made positive steps to provide transparency in this complex and opaque ecosystem. They are important for users, app developers, regulators, and even privacy advocates because they ease the detection and understanding of the SDKs embedded in mobile apps, even for users without much technical expertise. Yet, they present many limitations as discussed in Section IV. We believe that static and dynamic

---

[105] Carlos Jensen and Colin Potts, 'Privacy policies as decision-making tools: an evaluation of online privacy notices', *Proceedings of the SIGCHI conference on Human Factors in Computing Systems*.

[106] Okoyomon, 'Ridiculousness of Notice and Consent' (n 13).

[107] Ma, 'LibRadar' (n 31).

[108] 'What Exodus Privacy does', Exodus Privacy, https://exodus-privacy.eu/en/page/what/ (last accessed April 2020).

[109] Reyes, 'Think of the children' (n 22).

analysis techniques could be combined to develop more comprehensive, accurate and effective analysis tools, capable of overcoming the limitations inherent to each technique when used in isolation.

B. Application Developers and SDK Providers

Intuitively, an app developer will select the third-party SDK that provides the best functionality, but the question remains whether the SDK's resources usage or data sharing practices are ever considered in that decision-making process. It is imperative that developers understand the risks that many SDKs might bring to users' privacy. Application developers are liable for any regulatory violation that occurs within their application, even those inflicted by third-party components. With new legislation such as the GDPR, the fines can add up to €20 million or four per cent of the company's worldwide annual revenue from the preceding financial year, whichever is higher.[110]

It is critical that developers play a more central role in taking responsibility for their decisions to bundle third-party SDKs and that they follow the privacy-by-design principles. For that, it is necessary to also put SDK providers under scrutiny, demanding more transparency about their data collection practices and purposes and about their business models. This could be complemented with contractual agreements between app developers and SDK providers allowing developers to have additional legal guarantees and a better understanding of the privacy implications associated with a given SDK.

C. Stricter App Store Policies

Mobile platform providers should strive to audit applications and SDKs in order to improve and safeguard users' privacy. The Google Play store has checks in place to improve the privacy of applications. In early 2019, Google forced applications requesting call and SMS permission to either be the default messaging or calling app or to submit a special form explaining why such permissions are necessary for the app.[111] Furthermore, in newer Android versions (Android 10) Google has added restrictions for using unique non resettable identifiers (such as the IMEI) and for accessing alternate methods to infer location without requesting the appropriate permission.[112]

---

[110] 'What are GDPR fines?', GDPR.eu, https://gdpr.eu/fines/ (last accessed April 2020).
[111] 'Reminder SMS/Call Log Policy Changes', Android Developers Blog, https://android-developers.googleblog.com/2019/01/reminder-smscall-log-policy-changes.html (last accessed April 2020).
[112] 'Privacy in Android 10', Android Developer, https://developer.android.com/about/versions/10/privacy (last accessed April 2020).

Google has also published a list of self-certified third-party SDKs suitable for children's applications.[113] This list is a great resource for developers of children-oriented applications, as it reduces the search scope before making the decision to bundle a third-party SDK in their application. In this case, as these SDKs are self-certified, developers must trust that those components do indeed comply with existing regulation. There is no public information on whether Google verifies the claims made by each provider. Similarly, it is still possible to find applications that do not carry a privacy policy and examples of incomplete policies.[114] While we acknowledge that a thorough privacy analysis of all applications submitted to the market is a technically complex and costly task, we believe that these enforcement mechanisms could benefit from including some of the auditing techniques developed by the research community.

These policies are not specific to Android. Apple's App Store provides very exhaustive recommendations for app developers to minimize privacy damage to users.[115] These recommendations are focused on helping developers successfully pass their strict app review process prior to publication. In addition to minimum quality checks and recommendations – eg, releasing bug-free software and offering appropriate content – these guidelines also discuss the need for including complete privacy policies (data access, and third-party SDKs, data minimisation, and access to user data, among many others).

D. Changes in the Permission Model

Current permission models are app-centric by design so there is no separation between SDKs or apps accessing a given permission. Application developers only need to declare the permission in the app manifest file. Therefore, when a user grants the application permission to access a resource, the user has no information about whether an SDK or the app itself will exercise this permission. This goes in the opposite direction of current legislation, which is making strides towards better transparency and informing users about data collection and sharing practices, including the recipients of such data.

Android mentions the use of an explanation before requesting a permission as a best practice but does not enforce it in published apps.[116] If developers had to justify the inclusion of a permission request, users could make a more informed decision on whether to grant such permission or not. Additionally, the operating

---

[113] 'Participate in the Families Ads Program', Google Support, https://support.google.com/googleplay/android-developer/answer/9283445?hl=en (last accessed April 2020).
[114] Okoyomon, 'Ridiculousness of Notice and Consent' (n 13).
[115] 'App Store Review Guidelines', App Store, https://developer.apple.com/app-store/review/guidelines/ (last accessed April 2020).
[116] 'App permissions best practices', Android developers, https://developer.android.com/training/permissions/usage-notes (last accessed April 2020).

system could monitor and inform users whenever a protected method has been invoked by the actual application or an embedded SDK, and whether this has been disseminated to a server hosted on the internet. Unless users know which company is collecting personal data in an app, they will not be able to exercise their data rights per current legislation.

E. Certifying Bodies and Regulatory Actions

Trusted certification authorities could independently validate and certify the data collection practices of SDK providers. Article 42 and recital 81 and 100 of the GDPR propose ways to ensure compliance by controllers and processors through certification mechanisms and data protection seals or marks.[117] However, previous certification attempts such as COPPA's Safe Harbor have proven ineffective. As revealed by academic research, many applications certified by certification authorities still incur into potential violations of the COPPA law.[118]

It is unclear whether certification mechanisms can be effective in preventing deceptive behaviours and malpractices by third-party SDKs. The success of any certification scheme largely depends on the quality and depth of the certification process – ie, the length for which the process is going to make sure that the SDKs are in compliance with any regulations and for how long they will be able to bring out any potential violations. The use of auditing tools could play a fundamental role in the validation of the claims made by SDK providers from a technical standpoint.

Additionally, regulators must stay diligent and continue investigating any privacy malpractice on mobile applications. The FTC has previously acted towards SDK providers,[119,120] contributing to hold companies accountable when they do not respect users' privacy. These actions also have a valuable educational component. Once a regulatory action shows that a given company's behaviour constitutes privacy malpractice, other companies with similar policies might take additional precautions to protect their brands, reputation, and business, and avoid regulatory scrutiny and fines.

---

[117] 'Certification', Article 42, GDPR, www.privacy-regulation.eu/en/article-42-certification-GDPR.htm (last accessed April 2020).

[118] Reyes, 'Think of the Children' (n 22).

[119] 'Video Social Networking App Musical.ly Agrees to Settle FTC Allegations That it Violated Children's Privacy Law', Federal Trade Commission, www.ftc.gov/news-events/press-releases/2019/02/video-social-networking-app-musically-agrees-settle-ftc (last accessed April 2020).

[120] 'Mobile Advertising Network InMobi Settles FTC Charges It Tracked Hundreds of Millions of Consumers' Locations Without Permission', Federal Trade Commission, www.ftc.gov/news-events/press-releases/2016/06/mobile-advertising-network-inmobi-settles-ftc-charges-it-tracked (last accessed April 2020).

VI. Conclusion

In this chapter, we have discussed the privacy risks and open challenges that SDKs bring to the mobile ecosystem. To illustrate our main points, we compared the SDK detection and classification capabilities of state-of-the-art tools in a group of 50 popular apps from Google Play. We show that, depending on their analysis methodology, auditing tools have different results in terms of the type and number of libraries that they detect. Furthermore, we show that there is a need to manually inspect results in order to better understand the nature and risks of these libraries. We argue that auditing techniques can benefit from the mixing of static and dynamic analysis in order to be more resilient against code obfuscation and attribution problems. We also show that most tools do not focus on classifying these libraries by their purposes and that those that do lack the ability to correctly classify third-party libraries that offer more than one similarity (eg, Unity 3D and Google's Firebase). We also showed empirical evidence of data collection by social networks, analytics, and advertisement third-party SDKs. We find 20 libraries collecting different type of personal and behavioural data (such as unique identifiers and location information). We argue that the collection of personal data by third-party SDKs can often be opaque for the end user. Therefore, we argue that the lack of understanding and awareness around the presence and data sharing practices of SDKS embedded in apps prevents users from making informed decisions. We conclude by discussing open regulatory and technological challenges and propose measures to alleviate this situation. Examples of these measures are modifying current permission models to accommodate SDK resource accesses, educating app developers on the importance of data minimisation, building more complete and robust auditing tools, having better auditing efforts from app stores and creating certifying bodies. These measures could help increasing transparency both for app developers, who would make better informed decisions when bundling third-party SDKs, and for end users, who would have more information at their disposal to decide whether they want to use a given application or not.

Acknowledgements

The authors would like to thank our anonymous reviewers for their valuable feedback that helped us to prepare the final version of this book chapter. This project is partially funded by the US National Science Foundation (grant CNS-1564329), the European Union's Horizon 2020 Innovation Action program (grant Agreement No. 786741, SMOOTH Project), the Spanish MINECO grant (TIN2016-79095-C2-2-R) and the Comunidad de Madrid co-financed by European Structural Funds ESF and FEDER (grant P2018/TCS-4566). The authors would also like to acknowledge the support and feedback provided by the Agencia Española de Protección de Datos (AEPD).

References

Backes, Michael, Sven Bugiel, and Erik Derr. 2016. 'Reliable third-party library detection in android and its security applications.' *Proceedings of the 2016 ACM SIGSAC Conference on Computer and Communications Security.* 356–367.

Brookman, Justin, Phoebe Rouge, Aaron Alva, and Christina Yeung. 2017. 'Cross-device tracking: Measurement and disclosures.' *Proceedings on Privacy Enhancing Technologies.* 133–148.

Calciati, Paolo, Konstantin Kuznetsov, Xue Bai, and Alessandra Gorla. 2018. 'What did Really Change with the new Release of the App?' *Proceedings of the 15th International Conference on Mining Software Repositories.* 142–152.

Continella et al, 'Obfuscation-Resilient Privacy Leak Detection for Mobile Apps Through Differential Analysis', *The Network and Distributed System Security Symposium.*

Dekelver, Jan, Marina Kultsova, Olga Shabalina, Julia Borblik, Alexander Pidoprigora, and Roman Romanenko. 2015. 'Design of mobile applications for people with intellectual disabilities.' *Communications in Computer and Information Science.* 823–836.

Enck, William, Peter Gilbert, Seungyeop Han, Vasant Tendulkar, Byung-Gon Chun, Landon P. Cox, Jaeyeon Jung, Patrick McDaniel, and Anmol N Sheth. 2014. 'TaintDroid: an information-flow tracking system for realtime privacy monitoring on smartphones.' *ACM Transactions on Computer Systems (TOCS)* (ACM) 32: 5.

Felt, Adrienne Porter, Erika Chin, Steve Hanna, Dawn Song, and David Wagner. 2011. 'Android permissions demystified.' *Proceedings of the 18th ACM conference on Computer and communications security.* 627–638.

Faruki et al, 'Evaluation of android anti-malware techniques against dalvik bytecode obfuscation', *IEEE 13th International Conference on Trust, Security and Privacy in Computing and Communications.*

Gamba, J, M Rashed, A Razaghpanah, J Tapiador, and N Vallina-Rodriguez. 2020. 'An Analysis of Pre-installed Android Software.' *S&P.*

Han et al, 'The Price is (Not) Right: Comparing Privacy in Free and Paid Apps', *Proceedings on Privacy Enhancing Technologies Symposium.*

Hu, Xuehui, and Nishanth Sastry. 2019. 'Characterising Third Party Cookie Usage in the EU After GDPR.' *Proceedings of the 10th ACM Conference on Web Science.* New York, NY, USA: ACM. 137–141. doi:10.1145/3292522.3326039.

Jensen, Carlos, and Colin Potts. 2004. 'Privacy policies as decision-making tools: an evaluation of online privacy notices.' *Proceedings of the SIGCHI conference on Human Factors in Computing Systems.* 471–478.

Ma, Ziang, Haoyu Wang, Yao Guo, and Xiangqun Chen. 2016. 'LibRadar: fast and accurate detection of third-party libraries in Android apps.' *Proceedings of the 38th international conference on software engineering companion.* 653–656.

Mojica, Israel J, Bram Adams, Meiyappan Nagappan, Steffen Dienst, Thorsten Berger, and Ahmed E Hassan. 2013. 'A large-scale empirical study on software reuse in mobile apps.' *IEEE software* (IEEE) 31: 78–86.

Okoyomon, Ehimare, Nikita Samarin, Primal Wijesekera, Amit Elazari Bar On, Narseo Vallina-Rodriguez, Irwin Reyes, Álvaro Feal, and Serge Egelman. 2019. 'On The Ridiculousness of Notice and Consent: Contradictions in App Privacy Policies.' *Workshop on Technology and Consumer Protection (ConPro).*

Plotnick, Michael, Charles Eldering, and Douglas Ryder. 2002. 'Behavioral targeted advertising.' *Behavioral targeted advertising.* Google Patents, 11.

Razaghpanah, Abbas, Narseo Vallina-Rodriguez, Srikanth Sundaresan, Christian Kreibich, Phillipa Gill, Mark Allman, and Vern Paxson. 2015. 'Haystack: In situ mobile traffic analysis in user space.' *arXiv preprint arXiv:1510.01419* 1–13.

Razaghpanah, Abbas, Rishab Nithyanand, Narseo Vallina-Rodriguez, Srikanth Sundaresan, Mark Allman, Christian Kreibich, and Phillipa Gill. 2018. 'Apps, trackers, privacy, and regulators: A global study of the mobile tracking ecosystem.'

Reardon, Joel, Álvaro Feal, Primal Wijesekera, Amit Elazari Bar On, Narseo Vallina-Rodriguez, and Serge Egelman. 2019. '50 Ways to Leak Your Data: An Exploration of Apps' Circumvention of the Android Permissions System.' *28th {USENIX} Security Symposium ({USENIX} Security 19).* 603–620.

Ren, Jingjing, Ashwin Rao, Martina Lindorfer, Arnaud Legout, and David Choffnes. 2016. 'Recon: Revealing and controlling pii leaks in mobile network traffic.' *Proceedings of the 14th Annual International Conference on Mobile Systems, Applications, and Services.*

Ren, Jingjing, Martina Lindorfer, Daniel J. Dubois, Ashwin Rao, David Choffnes, and Narseo Vallina-Rodriguez. 2018. 'Bug fixes, improvements, … and privacy leaks.'

Reyes, Irwin, Primal Wijesekera, Joel Reardon, Amit Elazari Bar On, Abbas Razaghpanah, Narseo Vallina-Rodriguez, and Serge Egelman. 2018. '"Won't Somebody Think of the Children?" Examining COPPA Compliance at Scale.' *Proceedings on Privacy Enhancing Technologies* (De Gruyter Open) 2018: 63–83.

Ruiz, Israel J Mojica, Meiyappan Nagappan, Bram Adams, and Ahmed E Hassan. 2012. 'Understanding reuse in the android market.' *2012 20th IEEE International Conference on Program Comprehension (ICPC).* 113–122.

Sanchez-Rola, Iskander, Matteo Dell'Amico, Platon Kotzias, Davide Balzarotti, Leyla Bilge, Pierre-Antoine Vervier, and Igor Santos. 2019. 'Can I Opt Out Yet?: GDPR and the Global Illusion of Cookie Control.' *Proceedings of the 2019 ACM Asia Conference on Computer and Communications Security.* New York, NY, USA: ACM. 340–351. doi:10.1145/3321705.3329806.

Sørensen, Jannick, and Sokol Kosta. 2019. 'Before and After GDPR: The Changes in Third Party Presence at Public and Private European Websites.' *The World Wide Web Conference.* New York, NY, USA: ACM. 1590–1600. doi:10.1145/3308558.3313524.

Valente, Junia, and Alvaro A Cardenas. 2017. 'Security & Privacy in Smart Toys.' *IoTS&P '17.* ACM.

Wang, Haoyu, Zhe Liu, Jingyue Liang, Narseo Vallina-Rodriguez, Yao Guo, Li Li, Juan Tapiador, Jingcun Cao, and Guoai Xu. 2018. 'Beyond google play: A large-scale comparative study of chinese android app markets.' *Proceedings of the Internet Measurement Conference 2018.* 293–307.

Wong, Janis, and Tristan Henderson. 2018. 'How Portable is Portable?: Exercising the GDPR's Right to Data Portability.' *Proceedings of the 2018 ACM International Joint Conference and 2018 International Symposium on Pervasive and Ubiquitous Computing and Wearable Computers.* New York, NY, USA: ACM. 911–920. doi:10.1145/3267305.3274152.

Yuan, Shuai, Jun Wang, and Xiaoxue Zhao. 2013. 'Real-time bidding for online advertising: measurement and analysis.' *Proceedings of the Seventh International Workshop on Data Mining for Online Advertising.* 3.

Zhang, Yuan, Jiarun Dai, Xiaohan Zhang, Sirong Huang, Zhemin Yang, Min Yang, and Hao Chen. 2018. 'Detecting third-party libraries in Android applications with high precision and recall.' *25th International Conference on Software Analysis, Evolution and Reengineering (SANER).* IEEE.

Zimmeck, Sebastian, Jie S Li, Hyungtae Kim, Steven M Bellovin, and Tony Jebara. 2017. 'A privacy analysis of cross-device tracking.' *USENIX Security Symposium.* 1391–1408.

2

AI and the Right to Explanation: Three Legal Bases under the GDPR

TIAGO SÉRGIO CABRAL[1]

Abstract

In this chapter we shall examine the existence of a right to explanation regarding decisions by Artificial Intelligence (AI)-based systems in the General Data Protection Regulation (GDPR). In our analysis we will explore some preliminary questions such as the value of recitals under European Union law and which types of decisions fall within the scope of application of article 22 of the General Data Protection Regulation. We will conclude that several articles of the GDPR may serve as possible legal bases for the right to explanation, namely the right to information, the right to access and the right not to be subject to automated individual decision-making. In addition, the nature of the required explanation may vary depending on when it is provided to the data subject. If an explanation is provided before processing operations it will cover system functionality, however, if it is provided after processing operations it should cover the specific decision affecting the data subject in question.

Keywords

Artificial Intelligence, Data Protection, GDPR, Right to Explanation.

I. Introduction

In this chapter we will address the issue of the existence of a right to explanation regarding decisions by Artificial Intelligence-based systems in Regulation 2016/679/EU of the European Parliament and of the Council of 27 April 2016 on the protection of natural persons with regard to the processing

[1] Researcher at the Research Centre for Justice and Governance – EU Law (University of Minho, Portugal). Member of the AI Team at Vieira de Almeida and Associados.

of personal data and on the free movement of such data, and repealing Directive 95/46/EC, generally known as the GDPR. Throughout this chapter we will take a logical and analytical approach to the analysis of the GDPR's provisions and aim for its application to AI in a manner that is both realistic and respects the spirit of the law and European legal framework in general.

Our chapter differs from current literature in that it offers a two-step approach under which the nature of the required explanation may vary depending on when it is provided to the data subject. In addition, our analysis concludes that explanation for AI-based decisions may be required not just under one legal basis under the GDPR, but, at least under three (right to information, access and not to be subject to automated decision-making) and provides independent analysis to each of these legal bases. While the chapter aims to argue and prove the existence of a right to explanation under the three abovementioned bases, each could probably stand on its own. In our opinion, this strengthens the case for explanation under the GDRP and safeguards it from eventual challenges under specific provisions of each of the legal bases.[2] Further, we hope to offer a deeper analysis regarding key concepts and certain preliminary questions that must be understood before offering an answer to the main issue. This will be achieved through a more complete study of the GDPR's objectives and preparatory work and/or of key matters in EU law that, are sometimes, not adequately covered in sectorial literature, even if they are key to the discussion, such as the value of recitals in EU law.

II. References within the GDPR

Regulation of AI has been a widely discussed topic between legal scholars in the last few years. The European Union (hereinafter, 'EU'), in particular, is making an effort to establish itself as the world standard-setter for AI regulation, as it did with data protection. While preliminary documentation from the EU, including the Communications from the Commission and deliverables from the High-Level Expert Group on Artificial Intelligence may offer a glimpse of the future EU AI policy, transforming those ideas into a proposal and then into law might still take some time.[3] However, some of the main topics under discussion, such as the existence of a right to explanation, are, partially, already addressed in the EU's body of legislation. In fact, the GDPR already provides a number of rights to data subjects when AI processes personal data including, as we will show below, a right to explanation of AI decisions.

It is possible to find relevant references to the right to explanation in three different sets of provisions of the GDPR: the right to information (Articles 13 and 14

---

[2] For example, the controversy around what are adequate safeguards under Art 22 or whether information under Art 15 should mirror those of Arts 13 and 14.

[3] Aimee van Wynsberghe, 'Artificial Intelligence: From Ethics to Policy' (European Parliamentary Research Service), www.europarl.europa.eu/RegData/etudes/STUD/2020/641507/EPRS_STU (2020)641507_EN.pdf (last accessed 20 June 2020).

of the GDPR); the right to access (Article 15 of the GDPR); and the right not to be subject to automated individual decision-making, including profiling (Article 22 of the GDPR).

As an introduction, it is necessary to go into the different provisions and see how they might differ.

In accordance with the mandatory information to be provided to data subjects under the GDPR, the data subject has the right be informed of 'the existence of auto-mated decision-making, including profiling, referred to in Article 22(1) and (4)[4] and, at least in those cases, meaningful information about the logic involved, as well as the significance and the envisaged consequences of such processing for the data subject'.

The right to access states that 'the data subject shall have the right to obtain from the controller confirmation as to whether or not personal data concerning him or her are being processed, and, where that is the case, access to the personal data and the following information' including 'the existence of automated decision-making, including profiling, referred to in Article 22(1) and (4) and, at least in those cases, meaningful information about the logic involved, as well as the significance and the envisaged consequences of such processing for the data subject'. On this matter, Article 15 is further complemented by Recital 63 according to which:

> every data subject should therefore have the right to know and obtain communication in particular with regard to the purposes for which the personal data are processed, where possible the period for which the personal data are processed, the recipients of the personal data, the logic involved in any automatic personal data processing and, at least when based on profiling, the consequences of such processing.

In accordance with Article 22 of the GDPR, data subjects have the right not to be subjected to a decision based solely on automated processing which produces legal effects concerning him or her or, similarly, significantly affects him or her. There are three exceptions to this rule: (i) explicit consent;[5] (ii) when such processing is neces-sary for entering into or performing a contract, where the controller and data subject are parties, or; (iii) it is authorised by European Union or Member State law. In every case suitable safeguards must be implemented and, at least in the context of consent or contract, the data subject must be able to obtain human intervention. Further restrictions are in place for special categories of personal data, in this case it is only admissible when there is specific consent or reasons of substantial public interest (and, of course, pursuant to abovementioned suitable safeguards). Recital 71 complements

---

[4] General prohibition on certain types of automated decision-making.

[5] While we will not develop significantly this issue, do take note that for consent to be valid under the GDPR, it must be a 'freely given, specific, informed and unambiguous indication of the data subject's wishes'. For consent to be freely given, there must be no clear imbalance of power. It is important to point out that information asymmetry may equally give rise to a case of power imbalance. If the differ-ence in information is excessive it may hinder the validity of consent as a whole. Thus, data controllers when using this legal basis should be extra careful when providing the data subject with the necessary information. Additionally, if information is not accessible or understandable data subjects' consent may not be valid due to not being informed. EDPB, 'Guidelines 05/2020 on Consent under Regulation 2016/679', https://edpb.europa.eu/sites/edpb/files/files/file1/edpb_guidelines_202005_consent_en.pdf (last accessed 10 June 2020).

this provision with the following: 'such processing should be subject to suitable safeguards, which should include specific information to the data subject and the right to obtain human intervention, to express his or her point of view, to obtain an explanation of the decision reached after such assessment and to challenge the decision.'

III. Finding a Legal Basis for the Right to Explanation under the GDPR

A. Preliminary Question: What is a Decision based Solely on Automated Processing?

Before diving into the question of the possible legal basis for the right to explanation under the GDPR we should, first, clarify some concepts regarding automated individual decision-making. Decisions by AI-based systems will be, by design, automated decisions and, if they fall within the scope of Article 22, will be subject to the restrictions and high level of protection enshrined in the GDPR for decisions that are based solely on automated processing and which produce legal effects concerning the data subject or similarly significantly affect the data subject.[6,7]

First, there is some controversy about what should be interpreted as 'based solely on automated decision' that we should address. In trilogue[8] negotiations the EP had proposed a broader formulation which included 'solely or predominantly'. The apparently restrictive final choice has been the source of some degree of confusion. Did the European legislator intend to enshrine a regime where the mere fact that a human participating in the decision-making excludes the application of Article 22? Even if said human was only rubber-stamping the conclusions of the machine?

From the outset, that interpretation did not seem acceptable. The use of the adverb 'solely' implies that a decision does not involve anyone or anything else. That is to say it exclusively derived from the machine's decision. 'Predominantly', on the other hand, would make Article 22 applicable to any decision where 51 per cent of the final result was due to the machine's decision. That is to say, using the word predominantly could give rise to undesirable situations. Imagine that there is a human supervising the algorithm,[9] said human has perfect knowledge

---

[6] Including Art 13, n 2, f), Art 14, n 2, g) and Art 15, n 1, h).

[7] Machine learning is a subset of AI development, where the machine is capable of learning by itself. The learning can happen either based on a dataset that is previously fed to the machine and/or by the machine collecting information from its surroundings. Most papers on AI nowadays are, in fact, about machine learning since it is the most popular and shows the most potential in the development of AI. Ours is no exception. Our analysis focuses on the decisions by machine learning-based AI systems, though it should be applicable, for example, to programmable AI with minor adjustments.

[8] Tiago Sérgio Cabral, 'A Short Guide to the Legislative Procedure in the European Union', (2020) 6 *UNIO – EU Law Journal* 161–80.

[9] The difference between an algorithm and a model is purely technical and not necessarily consistent across works in this field. Therefore, and due to the fact that it does not affect the scope of our chapter

of the rules to be applied and of the algorithm's working and possesses the power to change its decision if he/she decides to do so. For argument's sake, said human actor is working diligently in supervising the algorithm. Under the 'predominantly' formulation, Article 22 would still be applicable, since most of the work would still be done by the algorithm.[10] The result of such an option could be that a much higher number of data processing activities would be restricted under Article 22, causing significant problems for data controllers, potentially even regarding the legal basis for data processing activities.[11] Further, it would probably remove all incentive to have a human actor 'controlling' the algorithmic decisions and may even be counterproductive. In fact, if Article 22 was always applicable data controllers could think that they might as well cut costs and go for entirely automated means.

As it is possible to conclude, quite a few problems could appear by using the word 'predominantly' and those, by themselves, justify its suppression. It does not mean that the European legislator intended to apply an ultra-restrictive approach to human intervention. In fact, if the legislator intended to do so, there are other redactions that would be far more effective[12] or, in alternative, the general prohibition could be suppressed since it would lose all its effectiveness.

'Solely' implies, realistically, that the power to make the decision rests exclusively in the program. If the person who is supervising it does not have the power to override or does not understand its functioning in a manner that would allow him/her to detect errors[13] and correct them, said power still sits solely with the program and, thereby, Article 22 is applicable.[14]

In its Guidelines on Automated Individual Decision-Making and Profiling, the Article 29 Data Protection Working Party[15] (hereinafter 'WP29') clarified its opinion about what it understood by human involvement. In line with the above, it considers that data controllers cannot fabricate human involvement to avoid the application of Article 22. According to the Guidelines 'to qualify as human involvement, the controller must ensure that any oversight of the decision is meaningful, rather than just a token gesture. It should be carried out by someone who has the

---

and to avoid constant sentences like 'the AI model created by the AI algorithm' we will frequently use the term 'algorithm' to encompass the entire procedure from learning to result, as in to model that when inputted new situations can make a prediction.

[10] It is unlikely that the human can review by doing the same amount of calculations, the human actor will probably try to find mistakes in the algorithm's inner workings and look for nuances that the algorithm did not understand.

[11] You would never be able to rely on the legitimate interests of the data controller for any processing activity where an algorithm was used for a pre-assessment, even if a human had key intervention at a second stage.

[12] Something along the line of 'data subjects have the right not to be subjected to a decision based on automated processing, save if any type of human overlook is established'.

[13] In fact, the person should be able to detect errors, at least, at the level of someone who is reasonably familiarised with the program and is reasonably diligent.

[14] The analysis should be, as with the establishment of the legal position of the parties as data processor or controller, based on the situation de facto and not de jure.

[15] Replaced by the European Data Protection Board (EDPB), under the GDPR.

authority and competence to change the decision. As part of the analysis, they should consider all the relevant data.'[16] While decisions from the WP29 are not binding, they represent the shared opinion of data protection supervisory authorities across the EU. We find unlikely that, if called upon to do so, the European Court of Justice (hereinafter, 'ECJ'), would opt to disagree with what appears to be a very adequate and balanced opinion by the supervisory authority. The controversy seems to have been put to rest.[17,18]

B. Preliminary Question: What is a Decision that Produces Legal Effects Concerning Him or Her or Similarly Significantly Affects Him or Her

Likewise, the GDPR offers no definition about what should be considered as a decision producing legal or similarly significant effects. Recital 71 offers the example of 'automatic refusal of an online credit application or e-recruiting practices without any human intervention' but it is not possible to find further clarification of the legal text.

Again, the input of the WP29 is invaluable to provide some degree of clarity. In accordance with its Guidelines on Automated Individual Decision-Making, a decision shall be considered having legal effects when it affects a person's legal rights, legal status or rights under a contract. The Information Commissioner's Office[19] adds that to trigger the application of Article 22 and the general

---

[16] Nonetheless, in accordance with the Norwegian Data Protection Authority (Datatilsysnet), even in these cases there may be a right to some type of similar explanation. Datatilsysnet states that 'even though there is no right to an explanation when a decision is not automated, the transparency principle requires that the data controller should give an explanation similar to those given for automated decisions'. Datatilsynet, 'Artificial Intelligence and Privacy', www.datatilsynet.no/globalassets/global/english/ai-and-privacy.pdf (last accessed 20 May 2019).

[17] See, Paul Voigt and Axel von dem Bussche, *The EU General Data Protection Regulation (GDPR)* (Cham, Springer International Publishing, 2017), 181ff, https://doi.org/10.1007/978-3-319-57959-7; WP29, 'Opinion 1/2010 on the Concepts of "Controller" and "Processor"', https://ec.europa.eu/justice/article-29/documentation/opinion-recommendation/files/2010/wp169_en.pdf (last accessed 10 June 2019); WP29, 'Guidelines on Automated Individual Decision-Making and Profiling for the Purposes of Regulation 2016/679', https://ec.europa.eu/newsroom/article29/document.cfm?action=display&doc_id=49826 (last accessed 10 June 2019).

[18] While the ECJ does not defer to the EDPB on matters of data protection, it's undeniable that the Board's opinions have persuasive authority over both the Court and the opinions of the Advocate Generals, which are frequently followed by the Court. We provide below a few examples where the guidelines or opinions were cited by the Court or (more frequently) by Advocate Generals. Further, to our knowledge, there is no single instance where the ECJ contradicted the EDPB or its previous itineration, the WP29, to establish a rule that protected data subjects in a minor degree. See, *Tietosuojavaltuutettu v Jehovan todistajat – uskonnollinen yhdyskunta*, No C–15/17 (ECJ 10 July 2019); *Parliament v Council*, No Joined Cases C-317/04 and C-318/04 (ECJ 30 June 2006). As abovementioned, the situation is more frequent for AG opinions, with 16 references. See, de Sousa Costa Rita, *A Realização Do Direito Da Protecção de Dados Da União Europeia Através Das Fontes Não-Legislativas: Dos Grandes Temas Jurisprudenciais Aos Desafios Do Soft Law, No Contexto Da Aplicação Do Regulamento Geral Sobre a Protecção de Dados* (Lisbon, Universidade Católica Portuguesa, 2019).

[19] The British Data Protection Authority.

prohibition, said legal effects have to be adverse to the data subject. However, and as reasonable as this seems at first glance, one has to note that it can be rather troublesome. What is an adverse effect on the legal rights of the data subject? If there are three job openings for a position at a company, and the company uses an algorithm to select candidates, the one that got third place did not suffer an adverse effect *stricto sensu*, but there may be some interest in, for example, obtaining human intervention if the candidate feels like he/she should have been seriated first.

The definition of an effect that is similar is slightly more difficult and must be accessed on a case-by-case basis. According to the Guidelines on Automated Individual Decision-Making, the threshold should be that those effects should affect the data subject in a similar manner as the legal effects. The WP29 establishes three criteria: the decision must have the potential to: (i) 'significantly affect the circumstances, behaviour or choices of the individuals concerned'; (ii) 'have a prolonged or permanent impact on the data subject' or; (iii) 'at its most extreme, lead to the exclusion or discrimination of individuals'.[20] A similarly significant effect can arise from situations created by third parties and not necessarily by the data subject. The WP29 gives the example of credit card company reducing a customer's credit card limit based on the financial history of people in the same residential area.

While a considerable amount of discussion is still possible regarding what should be considered as having a similarly significant effect on specific cases we deem this to be a reasonable interpretation, do not consider it to be likely to be struck down (at least in the near future) and, therefore, following it seems the most reasonable choice.[21]

C. Preliminary Question: Recitals under EU Law

Article 296 of the Treaty on the Functioning of the European Union (hereinafter, 'TFEU') states that EU acts 'shall state the reasons on which they are based and shall refer to any proposals, initiatives, recommendations, requests or opinions required by the Treaties'. Thereby, recitals (and citations) are mandatory for EU legal instruments and in their absence the Act is void. The requirement is applicable to every act from EU institutions, bodies, offices or agencies that are intended

---

[20] The WP29 gives a few examples of decisions that should be considering as meeting this threshold such as:

  (a) 'decisions that affect someone's financial circumstances, such as their eligibility to credit;
  (b) decisions that affect someone's access to health services;
  (c) decisions that deny someone an employment opportunity or put them at a serious disadvantage;
  (d) decisions that affect someone's access to education, for example university admissions'.

[21] See, WP29, 'Guidelines on Automated Individual Decision-Making and Profiling for the Purposes of Regulation 2016/679' (n 17); Information Commissioner's Office, *Guide to the General Data Protection Regulation* (London, ICO, 2019).

to produce legal effects in relation to third parties. The ECJ has previously stated that the raison d'être of this disposition is to allow the Court itself exercise its power of review and Member States and parties concerned to understand the manner in which the institutions have applied the Treaties (the central question seems to be compliance with the principle of subsidiarity).[22]

Now that the reason behind the existence of recitals is explained, what is their value in interpretation? It is widely accepted by the ECJ's case law that recitals are not binding. In fact, the Court states that 'the preamble to a Community act has no binding legal force and cannot be relied on as a ground for derogating from the actual provisions of the act in question'.[23]

Recitals cannot derogate operative provisions. They can, however, provide clarification on certain aspects of those provisions, including their scope or purposes.[24] Thus, if a recital contains a rule that is not reflected in any of the

---

[22] See, Tadas Klimas and Jūratė Vaičiukaitė, 'The Law of Recitals in European Community Legislation' (2008) 15(1) *ILSA Journal of International & Comparative Law* 1–31; Ingrid Opdebeek and Stéphanie De Somer, 'The Duty to Give Reasons in the European Legal Area a Mechanism for Transparent and Accountable Administrative Decision-Making? – A Comparison of Belgian, Dutch, French and EU Administrative Law' (2016) 2 *Rocznik Administracji Publicznej* 97–148; Manuel Lopes Aleixo, 'Anotação Ao Art.º 296.º Do TFUE', in Manuel Lopes Porto and Gonçalo Anastácio (eds) *Tratado de Lisboa Anotado e Comentado*, (Coimbra, Almedina, 2012), 1060–62.

The ECJ had long recognised that the reasoning behind acts is a mandatory formality, including the statement of the legal basis pursuant to which the act is adopted. See, *Fonderie Acciaierie Giovanni Mandelli v Commission of the European Communities*, No C-3/67 (ECJ 8 February 1968); *France v Commission*, No C-325/91 (ECJ 16 June 1993).

[23] See, *Nilsson and others*, No C-162/97 (ECJ 19 September 1998).

[24] See, *C.*, No C-435/06 (ECJ 27 September 2007).

'51. The term "civil matters" must be interpreted as capable of extending to measures which, from the point of view of the legal system of a Member State, fall under public law.'

'That interpretation is, moreover, supported by Recital 10 in the preamble to Regulation No 2201/2003, according to which that regulation is not intended to apply "to matters relating to social security, public measures of a general nature in matters of education or health …." Those exceptions confirm that the Community legislature did not intend to exclude all measures falling under public law from the scope of the regulation.'

The Queen v Secretary of State for Trade and Industry, ex parte Broadcasting, Entertainment, Cinematographic and Theatre Union, No C-173/99 (ECJ 26 June 2001).

'37. As regards, first, the purpose of Directive 93/104, it is clear both from Article 118a of the Treaty, which is its legal basis, and from the first, fourth, seventh and eighth recitals in its preamble as well as the wording of Article 1(1) itself, that its purpose is to lay down minimum requirements intended to improve the living and working conditions of workers through approximation of national provisions concerning, in particular, the duration of working time.

38. According to those same provisions, such harmonisation at Community level in relation to the organisation of working time is intended to guarantee better protection of the health and safety of workers by ensuring that they are entitled to minimum rest periods and adequate breaks.

39. In that context, the fourth recital in the preamble to the directive refers to the Community Charter of the Fundamental Social Rights of Workers adopted at the meeting of the European Council held at Strasbourg on 9 December 1989 which declared, in point 8 and the first subparagraph of point 19, that every worker in the European Community must enjoy satisfactory health and safety conditions in his working environment and that he is entitled, in particular, to paid annual leave, the duration of which must be progressively harmonised in accordance with national practices.'

legal instrument's enacting terms (the substantive provisions or articles) said rule will not have legal binding value. If a recital contains a provision that is clearly contradictory with the articles, the latter shall prevail. However, it is incorrect to think that recitals have no value. They may provide clarification 'on the interpretation to be given to a legal rule, [even if by themselves they] cannot constitute such a rule' as was established by the ECJ in its *Casa Fleischhandels* judgment. The Court was careful in stating that a 'recital cannot be relied upon to interpret [an Act] in a manner clearly contrary to its wording'. Thus, a contrario, a recital may be relied upon to interpret an Act in a manner that is not contradictory to its wording, giving them explanatory value. Thereby, it seems fair to argue, from the ECJ's case-law, that while not binding, recitals are a powerful tool for interpretation. Indeed, the recitals are frequently a direct line to the intentions behind the norm.[25]

Some authors even point out that recitals may play the role of supplementary normative tools, basing such an argument, in part on the Commission's Communication on guidance for better transposition and application of Directive 2004/38/EC. We cannot find a legal foundation neither in the Union's Constitutional law nor in the ECJ's case-law to support this position. In this specific case, the Commission's communication is far from clear (and stable) and, even if it was, its interpretation holds no special value in this matter.[26,27]

Gianclaudio Malgieri and Giovanni Comandé, 'Why a Right to Legibility of Automated Decision-Making Exists in the General Data Protection Regulation', (2017) 7(4) *International Data Privacy Law* 243–65, https://doi.org/10.1093/idpl/ipx019.

[25] See, Roberto Baratta, 'Complexity of EU Law in the Domestic Implementing Process', http://ec.europa.eu/dgs/legal_service/seminars/20140703_baratta_speech.pdf (last accessed 2 May 2019); Roberto Baratta, 'Complexity of EU Law in the Domestic Implementing Process' (2014) 2 *The Theory and Practice of Legislation* 2 293–308, https://doi.org/10.5235/12050-8840.2.3.293; Malgieri and Comandé, 'Why a Right to Legibility' (n 24); *Giuseppe Manfredi v Regione Puglia*, No C-308/97 (ECJ 25 November 1998); *Casa Fleischhandels v Bundesanstalt für landwirtschaftliche Marktordnung*, No C-215/88 (ECJ 13 July 1989).

[26] See, Klimas and Vaičiukaitė, 'The Law of Recitals in European Community Legislation' (n 22); Malgieri and Comandé, 'Why a Right to Legibility' o (n 24); Humphreys Llio et al., 'Mapping Recitals to Normative Provisions in EU Legislation to Assist Legal Interpretation', [2015] *Frontiers in Artificial Intelligence and Applications* 41–49, https://doi.org/10.3233/978-1-61499-609-5-41; Sandra Wachter, Brent Mittelstadt, and Luciano Floridi, 'Why a Right to Explanation of Automated Decision-Making Does Not Exist in the General Data Protection Regulation' (2017) 7(2) *International Data Privacy Law* 76–99, https://doi.org/10.1093/idpl/ipx005; Slaughter and May, 'Introduction to the Legislative Processes for EU Directives Matters and Regulations on Financial Services', www.slaughterandmay.com/what-we-do/publications-and-seminars/publications/client-publications-and-articles/i/introduction-to-the-legislative-processes-for-eu-directives-and-regulations-on-financial-services-matters.aspx (last accessed 5 July 2019); W Voermans, Maarten Stremler, and PB Cliteur, 'Constitutional Preambles: A Comparative Analysis' in Elgar (ed) *Monographs in Constitutional and Administrative Law* (Cheltenham, Edward Elgar Publishing, 2017); Giovanni Sartor, 'The Impact of the General Data Protection Regulation (GDPR) on Artificial Intelligence' (European Parliamentary Research Service), www.europarl.europa.eu/RegData/etudes/STUD/2020/641530/EPRS_STU(2020)641530_EN.pdf (last accessed 26 June 2020); European Commission, 'Communication from the Commission to the European Parliament and the Council on Guidance for Better Transposition and Application of Directive 2004/38/EC on the Right of Citizens of the Union and Their Family Members to Move

D. The Right to Explanation under the GDPR: The Right to Information

Legal scholars have been debating whether the data subject has the right to full explanation or just to information and if said explanation or information should cover the specific decisions or just system functionality.[28] In fact, the distinction between information and explanation is quite empty in this context, but we will address that below.[29]

The first two legal bases that we can find in the GDPR for the right to explanation are Articles 13 and 14.[30] Under these dispositions the data subject has the right to be informed of 'the existence of automated decision-making, including profiling, referred to in Article 22(1) and (4) and, at least in those cases, meaningful information about the logic involved, as well as the significance

---

and Reside Freely within the Territory of the Member States', https://eur-lex.europa.eu/legal-content/EN/TXT/PDF/?uri=CELEX:52009DC0313&from=EN (last accessed 3 May 2019); *Commission v Council*, No C-370/07 (ECJ 1 October 2009); *Club Hotel Loutraki v Commission*, No C-131/15 P (ECJ 21 December 2016); *France v Commission*, No C-325/91 (ECJ 16 June 1993); *Alexios Anagnostakis v Commission*, No T-450/12 (EGC 30 September 2015); *Alexios Anagnostakis v. Commission*, No C-589/15 P (ECJ 12 September 2017); *Germany v Commission*, No C-24/15 (ECJ 4 July 1963); *TWD Textilwerke Deggendorf GmbH v Commission*, No Joined Cases T-244/93 and T-486/93 (Court of First Instance 13 September 1995); *TWD Textilwerke Deggendorf GmbH v Commission*, No C-355/95 P (ECJ 15 May 1997); *Deutsches Milch-Kontor GmbH v Hauptzollamt Hamburg-Jonas*, No C-136/04 (ECJ 24 November 2005).

[27] While we admit that it is enticing, absent a proper sustaining argumentation calling upon a specific Commission's Communication is not persuasive. While having an institution defending this interpretation could be important, mainly because it has very competent professionals working for it and could successfully argue it in the ECJ, as far as we know the abovementioned communication is an isolated case and it does not seem inclined to defend this position in a consistent manner.

[28] We do note that after the writing of this chapter, ICO released the final version of its Explaining decisions made with Artificial Intelligence Guide. While said guide makes for an interesting read and the divisions adopted by ICO (namely, 'rationale explanation', 'responsibility explanation', 'data explanation', 'fairness explanation', 'safety and performance explanation' and 'impact explanation') may provide data controllers with some help at a second stage, the British data protection authority still does not assume a position regarding the question of system information against specific decisions (or, in ICO's wording, process-based against outcome-based). Unfortunately, as ICO itself appears to admit, this question of system information or specific decision (or both) precedes the detailed definition of the content of the information itself, where ICO's other divisions could be more useful. ICO and The Alan Turing Institute, 'Explaining Decisions Made with AI (Parts 1, 2 and 3)', https://ico.org.uk/for-organisations/guide-to-data-protection/key-data-protection-themes/explaining-decisions-made-with-ai/ last accessed 20 June 2020).

[29] While information, in a broad sense, could be read as the information that must be provided, for example, under Arts 13, 14 and 15 and that does not always entail an explanation (matters such as who is the data controller or the DPO's contacts) in this chapter we are mostly dealing with information regarding AI-based decisions. In this case, or rather information strictly speaking, providing information generally entails also providing an explanation, as it is possible to conclude our explanation below regarding what is meaningful information. Without doing so, neither would the information be meaningful nor would the data subject be really informed about the data processing operations and a data subject that is not informed cannot adequately use its rights under the GDPR, defeating one of the main purposes of the legislation.

[30] Specifically, Arts 13, n 2, f), and14, n 2, g).

and the envisaged consequences of such processing for the data subject'. There are a number of questions that must be addressed to understand this provision. First, not all automated decision-making is relevant, only when it falls within the scope of Article 22. That is to say, 'a decision based solely on automated processing, including profiling, which produces legal effects concerning him or her or similarly significantly affects him or her'. There is sound logic behind this choice, the legislator considers that there is a greater risk for the rights of the data subject in this type of processing. Clearly, if there are no relevant effects for the data subject's rights that greater risk disappears and, with it, the need for more protective rules. Imagine one of those 'which character from X TV show are you?' Apps that collect the users' birth data, favourite colour and a few other miscellaneous (not sensitive) information to provide them with an answer. There is automated decision-making and may even use AI, but provided that there is no further processing, its impact on the data subject is completely negligible and there is no reason to ask for the meaningful information about the logic involved or the significance and envisaged consequences of the processing.[31]

In our preliminary questions, we have already clarified what should be understood by 'based solely on automated processing and produces legal effects concerning him or her or similarly significantly affects him or her', so we refer to the previous points on these matters.

i. The Right to Information: Article 13

There is a reasonable degree of controversy surrounding the nature of the information (or explanation) that must be provided to the data subjects. Should it be information about the system functionality ('logic, significance, envisaged consequences and general functionality' of the system) or the specific decision ('the weighting of features, machine-defined case-specific decision rules, information about reference or profile groups')? Should it be provided *ex ante* (before the automated decision-making) or *ex post* (after the automated decision-making)?

Should these divisions even be adopted? The abovementioned were adopted by Wachter and others. The authors adhere to a very restrictive view of the right to explanation under the GDPR – the original paper is called 'Why a Right to Explanation of Automated Decision-Making Does Not Exist in the General Data

---

[31] The answer to the second and third question would be; 'there is no significance and no consequences are to be expected', the answer to the first one would be something in line with 'if you answer (c) more than Y times, you will be assigned character Z'. In fact, while it could be slightly more complicated, the argument still stands, there is no reason for more stringent rules. A different interpretation would be incoherent with the remaining provisions in the GDPR and with the legislator's intentions.

Protection Regulation.' Though we must point out that is not precisely what is defended by the authors.[32,33]

First, regarding the provision of meaningful information under the right to information we should separate Articles 13 and 14. For Article 13, information must be provided to the data subject when the personal data is collected. This moment is previous to the processing of the personal data for automated decision-making and thus, when data is collected the data controller still has no information about the specific decision. Thereby, it is only possible to provide information about the system functionality and not about a specific decision because there is none.

Andrew D Selbst and Julia Powles rightly draw attention to the fact that, due to AI's deterministic nature, it should be possible to generate an explanation of the specific decision immediately when you have the input data. While technically that is absolutely true, and you have to do no more than feeding the data to the model, reality is a bit more complicated. Even if the abovementioned authors are right and their theory aligns with GDPR's logic there are two main issues with it. First, Article 13 establishes the following sequence of events: (a) collection and provision of information and then; (b) further processing.[34] To apply Andrew D Selbst and Julia Powles's method, provision of information would have to be moved to after further processing. Doing so would be in clear contradiction with the wording of Article 13 (and with Recital 61 of the GDPR). Automated decisions also do not have to be made immediately when data is collected. For security, strategic or operational reasons, the system that collects data may not be the same as the one that makes the decisions and those may not be directly connected. Data may be pulled from one to the other to finish the operation. There is no guarantee that the same model is used for all data subjects (a different one may be used based on the region where the data subject lives for example). In fact, there may be a first model to decide which second model is adequate to deal with that specific data subject. Burdening the data controller with making an immediate decision would be extremely difficult and could, in fact, be counterproductive for operational or even security reasons.

---

[32] See, Wachter, Mittelstadt, and Floridi, 'Why a Right to Explanation' (n 26).

[33] Of course, their paper also does not appear in a vacuum, the discussion around this issue was popularised by Goodman and Flaxman who argued, in a short conference paper (presented at the 2016 ICML Workshop on Human Interpretability in Machine Learning), for the existence of a right to explanation under GDPR provisions back in 2016. See, Bryce Goodman and Seth Flaxman, 'European Union Regulations on Algorithmic Decision-Making and a "Right to Explanation"', 2016 ICML Workshop on Human Interpretability in Machine Learning, 2 October 2017, https://arxiv.org/pdf/1606.08813.pdf; Brian Casey, Ashkon Farhangi, and Roland Vogl, 'Rethinking Explainable Machines: The GDPR's "Right to Explanation" Debate and the Rise of Algorithmic Audits in Enterprise' (2019) 34 *Berkeley Technology Law Journal* 142–83.

[34] See, Andrew D Selbst and Julia Powles, 'Meaningful Information and the Right to Explanation' (2017) 7 *International Data Privacy Law* 233–242.

With this in mind, meaningful information must still merit the qualification as 'meaningful' even if it covers system functionality. The data controller does not have to disclose the full algorithm and, in fact, should avoid complex and non-understandable explanations about its inner workings. However, the data subject must be able to comprehend the basis for the decision that will be made about him or her. This could entail: (i) explaining the data that will inform the algorithm in its decision; (ii) the most relevant aspects for arriving at a decision;[35] (iii) standard scenarios to contextualise the data subject; (iv) measures to ensure that the algorithms used remain 'fair, effective and unbiased'; and (v) the right of the data subject to request human intervention and other relevant safeguards.

Regarding the significance and the envisaged consequences for the data subject, information about how the automated decision-making might affect the data subject using 'meaningful and understandable, real, tangible examples of the type of possible effects should be given' in line with the WP29's Guidelines on Automated Decision-Making. The information should be provided for current and subsequent processing operations.[36] We must note that the real tangible examples are in line with our suggestion for standard scenarios and may be built jointly to meet both requirements but are not the same. To meet the requirements of meaningful information about system functionality, you must build a standard scenario in which an individual ('A') with X characteristics provides Y data. With that data the model will produce Z result. For the significance and envisaged consequences what counts is the effect of the Z result on the individual. If the Z is a bad score, person A will not be provided with a loan.

ii. The Right to Information: Article 14

Article 14 shares most of the same limitations as Article 13, with one serious difference. Information according to Article 14 (when data is not obtained from the data subject) must be provided 'within a reasonable period after obtaining the personal data, but at the latest within one month, having regard to the specific circumstances in which the personal data are processed'.

This means that, in theory, the automated decision could have already been reached before information is provided to the data subject. Still, we argue that such a scenario will only manifest exceptionally. There are two main reasons for this fact, the first being the legal basis under which personal data can be processed for automated decision-making and, the second, the concept of 'reasonable period having regard to the specific circumstances'.

---

[35] Based on aggregated data of previous decisions if need be, or, if unavailable, the aggregated data from algorithmic testing.
[36] See, WP29, 'Guidelines on Automated Individual Decision-Making and Profiling for the Purposes of Regulation 2016/679' (n 17).

Personal data can be processed for automated decision-making under the following legal basis: (a) necessary for entering into or for the performance of a contract; (b) authorised by EU or Member State law or; (c) based on the data subject's explicit consent.

Explicit consent makes it impossible for data to be processed absent provision of information, since said consent would not be valid. Thus, the data controller may collect data but cannot process it for automated decision-making. If processing is compliant with the GDPR, there will never be a scenario where data is processed before information is provided grounded on the legal basis of consent.

Data that is necessary for entering into a contract or for the performance of a contract implies that there was a previous contact between the parties. Whether they already entered into a contract or are taking the necessary steps to do so, it is implied that both parties are aware of and willing to contract with each other. Thus, information should be provided in one of the previous instances where contact was established. Ideally, when the data controller first becomes aware that automated decision-making will be needed to enter or to perform said contract. Assuming that there is an available channel for communication between parties, processing of personal data for automated decision-making absence information also seems very unlikely or, at least, very rare.

Third, we have the option of the data processing being authorised by EU or Member State law, but even then, the same laws must also lay 'down suitable measures to safeguard the data subject's rights and freedoms and legitimate interests'. Under these suitable measures, there must be measures ensuring the provision of information to data subjects. In any case, it is expected that said measures will minimise the risk for data subjects' rights and interests, creating fewer issues than other types of processing. Still, this is the only one of the three scenarios where we can imagine processing for automated decision-making happening without previous information being provided. If this happens the information to be provided after will need to be evaluated on a case-by-case basis, but it is possible that it may encompass more than information about system functionality.

There is also the concept of 'reasonable period having regard to the specific circumstances'. The one-month deadline in Article 14 is absolute and may be restricted if it is not reasonable due to the specific circumstances of the processing.[37] How restricted depends on the case, but in its Guidelines on Transparency the WP29 points out that

> the principles of fairness and accountability under the GDPR require data controllers to always consider the reasonable expectations of data subjects, the effect that the processing may have on them and their ability to exercise their rights in relation to that processing, when deciding at what point to provide the Article 14 information.

---

[37] Or when Arts 14 (3) point (b) or (c) are applicable.

Data controllers must further be able to demonstrate the reasoning behind their decision. In fact, according to the WP29 'wherever possible, data controllers should, in accordance with the principle of fairness, provide the information to data subjects well in advance of the stipulated time limits'.[38] Thus, since this type of data processing activity is considered particularly 'sensitive' by the legislator, then, by nature, the processing will affect the data subject in a reasonably high manner thus making information yet more valuable, and taking into consideration other aspects that may arise in case, when possible, data controllers should inform data subjects before the processing activity (and automated decision-making) takes place.

Taking the abovementioned arguments into account, generally, information to be provided under Article 14 must follow the same rules as Article 13, that is, it must be on system functionality and have the aforementioned characteristics. When this proves false, and processing is done before the provision of information, a case-by-case analysis should be performed, but, in general, data controllers should then provide information about the specific decision also (in accordance with the rules about the right to access). If it is feasible and not disproportionate to do, the principle of transparency and fairness of processing will generally require data controllers to disclose information before processing in this type of situations.

E. The Right to Explanation under the GDPR: The Right to Access

i. Should Information given under Article 15 be the same as under Articles 13 and 14?

As a preliminary question, we must point out that in its Guidelines on Automated Decision-Making[39] the WP29 states that the data controller should already have provided the data subject with the information (Article 15 information) in line with its Article 13 obligations. However, in our opinion this does not mean that the information provided under Article 13 and Article 15 must be exactly the same. In fact, information under Article 15 can, and should at times, be more detailed than under Article 13, as we will elaborate in a matter of moments.[40]

As for the reasons serving as foundations to our conclusion, they are the following: in the Guidelines the WP29 is referring to compliance with the obligation

---

[38] See, WP29, 'Guidelines on Transparency under Regulation 2016/679', https://ec.europa.eu/news-room/article29/document.cfm?action=display&doc_id=51025 (last accessed 10 June 2019).

[39] See, WP29, 'Guidelines on Automated Individual Decision-Making and Profiling for the Purposes of Regulation 2016/679' (n 17).

[40] If information under Arts 13 (and 14) is 'A', information under the Right to Access will be 'A + X'.

of informing the data subject under Article 13 (and 14), namely the provision of information regarding:

(a) the existence of automated decision making, including profiling;
(b) meaningful information about the logic involved; and
(c) the significance and envisaged consequences of such processing for the data subject.

As mentioned above, under the right to information this would entail the provision of information about system functionality and not about the specific decision. Still, reading the legal norm and WP29's opinion in such a manner is both artificial and unrealistic. The WP29 states the information should have been previously provided in line with Article 13 obligations but it does not say that said obligations are the same as Article 15 obligations. The Guidelines themselves address this fact saying that 'by exercising their Article 15 rights, the data subject can become aware of a decision made concerning him or her'. Being made aware without having the tools to understand would not provide the data subject with more than a (possible) illusion of control. Therefore, it is unlikely that when the WP29 refers to it, it does so in a superficial manner. Awareness should be understood as covering both awareness of the decision and awareness of the reasons for the decision.

If we take into account the principle of transparency, it is also clear that, since the data controller has new information that will be helpful for the data subject to exercise his or her rights, it should be disclosed.

This is not a change in the information to be provided under Articles 13 and 14. As established, information to be disclosed under these Articles is restricted by the timing in which it must legally be provided. Therefore, if the mathematical model (the system) does not change, neither does the information about it. However, the right to access is not restricted by these timing aspects and, therefore, more information can be provided.[41]

Conceptually it would make no sense for the data subject to be provided with information about how the system works, the result of the system's computations (the conclusions or inferences) and not about how the system arrived at those results in his/her specific case.

According to the WP29 'the controller should provide the data subject with general information (notably, on factors taken into account for the decision-making process, and on their respective "weight" on an aggregate level) which is also useful for him or her to challenge the decision'.[42] Having this information is essential, but it is not enough to establish, for example, bias in algorithmic decisions and due to this fact, without specific information the data subjects will not be able to exercise their rights and the principle of fairness will not be realised (as we will explain below). Thereby, the Guidelines should not be read

---

[41] See, WP29, 'Guidelines on Transparency under Regulation 2016/679' (n 38).
[42] WP29, 'Guidelines on Automated Individual Decision-Making and Profiling for the Purposes of Regulation 2016/679' (n 17).

as restricting the provision of specific information, just establishing that general comparing information should also be provided.

ii. The Right to Access: Article 15

Rules will be slightly different under the right to access when compared to the ones regulating the right to information. In most cases, the processing for automated decision-making will have already taken place. As established above, information under the right to access does not have to be the same as information under the right to information and can be broader. Therefore, there is no technical reason to justify a restriction of explanation of the specific case to the right to access, in line with what we defended for the right to information. With this in mind, is there a right to explanation of the specific decision under the right to access or are any other reasons to argue that it does remain restricted to system functionality?

First, the division between information and explanation should be rejected as meaningless and artificial. As argued by Selbst and Powles 'if "meaningful" is to have any substance, that appears on its face to be a move in the direction of explanation of some type'.[43] In fact, for information about system functionality to be useful to the data subject it implies explanation (the data controller cannot just make available the technical guide for using the software/algorithm).

Providing information regarding the specific decision is, arguably, easier and less harmful for the interests of the data controller than providing general information about the system's inner workings. To provide system information, for example in an algorithm that is based on deep learning, the data controller must provide information on a model which will evaluate hundreds if not thousands of parameters and that, in fact, may not be fully understood. To provide information on a specific decision the data controller 'just' needs to provide information on the parameters (the weights) that were more relevant for that decision. If you are able to accomplish the first you will certainly be able to accomplish the second, but the opposite is not necessarily true. For data controllers the system working only interpretation offers a plethora of risks absent almost any advantage. Data controllers will have to build an explanation about the more challenging system functionality, and by not providing one relating to specific decisions, will be at the mercy of a possible restrictive interpretation by data protection supervisors and by the ECJ.[44]

---

[43] See, Selbst and Powles, 'Meaningful Information and the Right to Explanation' (n 34).

[44] In its guidelines regarding data processing for AI, AEPD, even if not decisively taking a position regarding the question of providing information about system functionally versus about the specific decision, does state some information that it considers as essential in these types of operations:

  (a) Detailed information about the subject's data used for decision-making regardless of the category, especially regarding with how old the subject's data under processing are.
  (b) The relative importance or weight of each data category in the decision making (official translation appears imprecise as the original refers to '*la importancia relativa que cada uno de ellos [datos empleados or used data] tiene en la toma de decision*'.)

Looking at the issue from another angle, is there a right to explanation of the specific decisions under the GDPR and, namely, under the right to access? To understand this issue, we must understand what the purpose of such a right is. The answer should be to ensure that the principles for the processing of personal data are complied with and that the data subject can exercise his or her rights under the GDPR (and under the EU's constitutional law).

Within these rights we may count access, erasure, rectification, restriction of processing, portability and right to object. However, the data subject also has the right to lodge a complaint with a supervisory authority (Article 78 GDPR), the right to an effective judicial remedy against a controller or processor (Article 79 GDPR) and the right to compensation or liability (Article 82 GDPR). Absent information about the specific decision it would be truly impossible for a data subject to prove damages and therefore pursue compensation in accordance with Articles 79 and 82 of the GDPR and Article 47 of the Charter. Even if a data processing operation is not fair, if its 'unfairness' did not cause damage to a specific citizen it is unlikely that compensation can be granted. The absence of a specific explanation would hinder severely the capacity of data subjects to exercise these rights in cases of algorithmic discrimination.[45] To accept such an interpretation would be entirely out of line with the general principles of the GDPR.

In addition, Recital 71 should not be ignored. Even if it has no binding authority and relates mainly to Article 22, it clearly demonstrates that the European legislator desired to enshrine a proper right to explanation of the specific situation. In fact, this interpretation avoids an unnecessary controversy on the nature of the adequate safeguards under Article 22. With a right to explanation under the previous Articles, the safeguard of explanation for a particular data subject is already ensured. It is our belief that this interpretation is the one that better reflects the legislator's thinking.

(c) The quality of training data and the type of patterns used.

(d) Profiling activities conducted and their implications.

(e) Error or precision values, according to the appropriate metrics used to measure the eligibility of the inference.

(f) Whether qualified human supervision is involved or not.

(g) Any reference to audits, especially on the possible deviation of inference results, as well as certification or certifications performed on the AI system. For adaptive systems or evolutive systems, the last audit conducted.

(h) If the AI system includes information referring to identifiable third-data subjects, prohibition of processing such information without legitimisation and of the consequences of doing so. See, AEPD, 'Adecuación al RGPD de Tratamientos Que Incorporan Inteligencia Artificial. Una Introducción', www.aepd.es/sites/default/files/2020-02/adecuacion-rgpd-ia.pdf (last accessed 25 February 2020), and the official English translation: AEPD, 'RGPD Compliance of Processings That Embed Artificial Intelligence. An Introduction', www.aepd.es/sites/default/files/2020-02/adecuacion-rgpd-ia-en_0.pdf.

[45] By nature, as explained by Wachter and others, detecting bias in AI decisions may be a significant challenge. See, Sandra Wachter, Brent Mittelstadt, and Chris Russell, 'Why Fairness Cannot Be Automated: Bridging the Gap Between EU Non-Discrimination Law and AI', *SSRN [Preprint]*, 2020. Nevertheless, we would argue that giving data subjects the tools to understand decisions regarding themselves could be of use in this endeavour.

The information to be provided should be enough to allow the data subject to exercise his or her rights and should reflect the requirements of the WP29 for general information, but applied to the specific situation, namely the factors taken into account for the decision-making process, and on their respective 'weight'. Standard scenarios should still be provided to the data subject to allow the data subject to compare his/her situation with the generality of users.

As a final note, according to Recital 63, the right to explanation should

> not adversely affect the rights or freedoms of others, including trade secrets or intellectual property and in particular the copyright protecting the software. However, the result of those considerations should not be a refusal to provide all information to the data subject.[46]

The situations where the right to data protection conflicts with rights of the data controller such as keeping trade secrets and intellectual property rights will have to be analysed case-by-case. This should not be seen, at all, like a (albeit non-binding) attempt to restrict data subjects' rights. In fact, the same conflict and result would arise if no recital existed. The wording of the recital actually appears to put the burden on the data controller, to find a manner to disclose the information without hurting its own rights. Of course, it also reinforces our considerations regarding how the controller does not need to disclose the source code or every single factor weighted by the algorithm in the decision (only the most important ones that are truly needed to guarantee the data subject's rights).[47]

F. The Right to Explanation under the GDPR: Automated Individual Decision-making

Having concluded that there is a right to an explanation of the specific decision under Article 15, we could have completely avoided the controversy around the specific safeguards of Article 22. However, there are good reasons not to do so. First, the wording of Article 22, in fact, reinforces our conclusions about Articles 13, 14, and 15. Second, even if our previous arguments were not accepted the right to explanation of the specific decision is also contained within Article 22's safeguards and, as a precaution, we intend to cover all of the possible scenarios.

Article 22 states that when processing is based on explicit consent or into its necessity for entering or performing a contract:

> the data controller shall implement suitable measures to safeguard the data subject's rights and freedoms and legitimate interests, at least the right to obtain human

---

[46] The concept of legibility defended by Malgieri and Comandé can provide an adequate starting point for compliance by data controllers, since it meets and may even exceed the necessary requirements. See, Malgieri and Comandé, 'Why a Right to Legibility' (n 24).

[47] Doing so would actually create confusion in the data subject and hurt the principle of transparency itself.

intervention[48] on the part of the controller, to express his or her point of view and to contest the decision.

This provision is complemented by Recital 71 where it is stated that

> processing should be subject to suitable safeguards, which should include specific information to the data subject and the right to obtain human intervention, to express his or her point of view, to obtain an explanation of the decision reached after such assessment and to challenge the decision.

One interesting question is whether 'the right to obtain human intervention, to express his or her point of view, to obtain an explanation of the decision reached after such assessment and to challenge the decision' is also applicable to automated decision making authorised by Union or Member State law to which the controller is subject (Article 22, nº2, (b)). On one side, Article 22 itself distinguishes between this type of exception to the general prohibition and one could argue that this was a deliberate attempt by the legislator to not establish these minimum requirements in this specific case. On the other side, Recital 71 does not distinguish and the wording of the recital is not in contradiction with the wording of the Article, as the right to obtain human intervention, express a point of view, obtain an explanation and challenge the decision can be considered one of the needed safeguards that are also referred in Article 22, n. 2, (b) even if they are not further developed. Furthermore, there is no reason to hold data processing based on Union or Member State law to a lower degree of scrutiny, especially if we take into account the difficulties of challenging a decision absent proper information. Uniform interpretation would also be in line with our interpretation regarding the existence of a right to explanation of the specific decision under other rights of the data subject, as we have established above. Thereby, we are inclined to think that when data processing is based on Union or Member State, data controllers are subject to the same requirements regarding explanation, human intervention and challenge as they would be for consent or contract.

By accepting our interpretation of Articles 13, 14, and 15, the suitable safeguard of obtaining an explanation in regard to the decision concerning him or her is, in fact, a legal requirement contained in both Articles 15 and 22. This position is in line with the interpretation contained in Recital 71, with the general principles of transparency and fairness in the processing of personal data and with the rights of the data subject. It also explains why the legislator did not feel the need to expressly state in Article 22 something that is already a requirement under Article 15. It is probably the solution that best reflects the philosophy behind the GDPR, the line of interpretation followed by the ECJ and data protection authorities (in our opinion), meanwhile managing to guarantee coherent application and not burdening the data controller with unrealistic requirements, such as asking for an explanation of the specific decision before a decision exists. Even if recitals

---

[48] We will study the question of human intervention below, for now we shall focus on the right to explanation.

are not binding, as explained in our section about their value in EU law, they are a highly valuable interpretative source and, the concept of meaningful information (and adequate safeguards also) are the type of open concepts where their guidance is most valuable. In our previous sections we also had the opportunity to rebuke argumentation that favoured ignoring the recital altogether

There is another key fact: in Article 22 it is stated clearly that data subjects have the right to express their point of view or to contest the decision. Explanation of their specific situation is clearly implicit in these ideas. Expressing their point of view should be interpreted as expressing their point of view in an informed manner, and it is only possible to express one's point of view in relation to a decision if one knows the arguments behind the decision. To think otherwise would be to concede that this right is no more than a placebo. The data subject can say that he/she does not agree but is not given 'the weapons'[49] to mount a proper response. Contesting the decision should be interpreted broadly, as contesting the decision to the data controller, but also to a supervisory authority or court of law. This is in line with the provisions of the GDPR which give the data subject all these rights. In fact, such diligences would not be possible (or at least could never succeed) without information. The aforementioned interpretation is clearly in line with our argumentation regarding the existence of a right to information regarding the specific decision contained within the right to access. Still, even if such a position is not adopted, a right to information regarding the specific decision would still be contained within Article 22, without the need to apply or consider directly provisions of a recital. It needs no more than a functional and realistic interpretation that respects the general principles of the GDPR.[50]

The diagram below presents a short summary of our position:

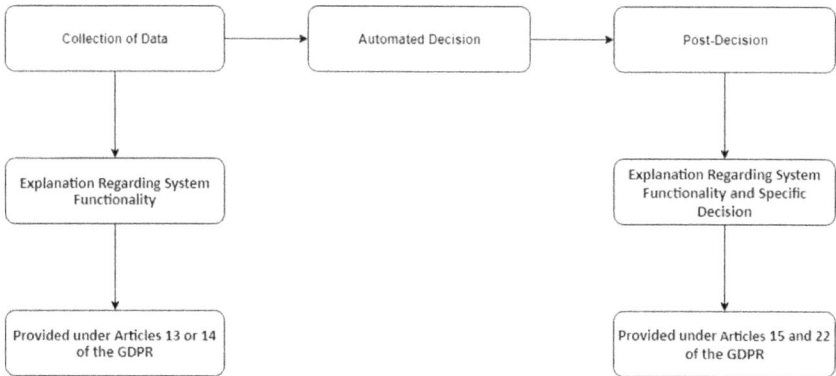

---

[49] The WP29 is clear in saying that 'The data subject will only be able to challenge a decision or express their view if they fully understand how it has been made and on what basis.' See, WP29, 'Guidelines on Automated Individual Decision-Making and Profiling for the Purposes of Regulation 2016/679' (n 17).

[50] The following general key sources regarding the issue of GDPR-based explanation of AI decisions: Wachter, Mittelstadt, and Floridi, 'Why a Right to Explanation' (n 26); Selbst and Powles, 'Meaningful Information and the Right to Explanation' (n 34); Malgieri and Comandé, 'Why a Right to Legibility of Automated Decision-Making Exists in the General Data Protection Regulation' (n 24);

The diagram is a generalisation and there are exceptions. One exception can arise when information under Article 14 is provided after the decision is made. However, as explained above that will be the exception and not the rule. Furthermore, both Articles 15 and 22 independently provide a right to an explanation of the specific decision; a stronger argument can be made by joining the provisions of both.

The solution for the issue of black box algorithms and lack of human explanation may be a technological one. Development of explainable AI (hereinafter 'XAI') solutions where the algorithm itself is able to produce and explanation for its decisions and that explanation is understandable by humans has been gaining traction and can, indeed, solve the conundrum. Of course, this does depend on how advanced the technology for providing an explanation is and if the explanation meets the current requirements mentioned above and future requirements that will certainly appear on AI-specific legislation. While XAI appears to have the potential to be a cornerstone of the European Trustworthy AI strategy and private companies such as IBM are already investing in it, if the EU is really serious about taking a leading role as the standard-setter for AI, it must provide adequate funding for XAI development and the necessary research, testing and development conditions for this technology to reach a degree of advancement where it can both provide adequate explanations and results similar in quality to 'black box AI'.[51,52]

Lilian Edwards and Michael Veale, 'Slave to the Algorithm? Why a Right to Explanationn Is Probably Not the Remedy You Are Looking For' (2017) 16(1) *Duke Law & Technology Review*: https://doi.org/10.2139/ssrn.2972855; Gianclaudio Malgieri, 'Automated Decision-Making in the EU Member States: The Right to Explanation and Other "Suitable Safeguards" in the National Legislations' (2019) 35(5) *Computer Law & Security Review*: 105327, https://doi.org/10.1016/j.clsr.2019.05.002; Goodman and Flaxman, 'European Union Regulations on Algorithmic Decision-Making' (n 33); Sandra Wachter, Brent Mittelstadt, and Chris Russell, 'Counterfactual Explanations Without Opening the Black Box: Automated Decisions and the GDPR' (2018) 31 *Harvard Journal of Law & Technology* 841–87; Mireille Hildebrandt, 'Privacy as Protection of the Incomputable Self: From Agnostic to Agonistic Machine Learning' (2019) 20(1) *Theoretical Inquiries in Law* 83–121, https://doi.org/10.1515/til-2019-0004; Margot E Kaminski, 'The Right to Explanation, Explained' (2019) 34(189) *Berkeley Technology Law Journal*: https://doi.org/10.2139/ssrn.3196985; Gianclaudio Malgieri, 'Trade Secrets v Personal Data : A Possible Solution for Balancing Rights' (2016) 6(2) *International Data Privacy Law* 102–16, https://doi.org/10.1093/idpl/ipv030; WP29, 'Guidelines on Transparency under Regulation 2016/679' (n 38); EDPB, 'Guidelines 05/2020 on Consent under Regulation 2016/679' (n 5); WP29, 'Guidelines on Automated Individual Decision-Making and Profiling for the Purposes of Regulation 2016/679' (n 17); Andrew Burt, '"Is There a Right to Explanation' for Machine Learning in the GDPR', 17 July 2019, https://iapp.org/news/a/is-there-a-right-to-explanation-for-machine-learning-in-the-gdpr; Isak Mendoza and Lee A Bygrave, 'The Right Not to Be Subject to Automated Decisions Based on Profiling', in Tatiana-Eleni Synodinou et al (eds) *EU Internet Law.* (Cham, Springer International Publishing, 2017) 77–98, https://doi.org/10.1007/978-3-319-64955-9_4.

[51] Unfortunately, the ML-techniques that are currently achieving the most impressive results such as Deep Learning, are also the most difficult to explain and, therefore, to develop an XAI solution for. Thus, adequate funding and conditions for research seem to be necessary to overcome this obstacle.

[52] See, Aleksandra Mojsilovic, 'Introducing AI Explainability 360', www.ibm.com/blogs/research/2019/08/ai-explainability-360 (last accessed 20 August 2019); Liya Ding, 'Human Knowledge in Constructing AI Systems – Neural Logic Networks Approach towards an Explainable AI' (2018) 126 *Procedia Computer Science* 1561–70, https://doi.org/10.1016/j.procs.2018.08.129; Robert R Hoffman, Gary Klein, and Shane T Mueller, 'Explaining Explanation For "Explainable Ai"' (2018) 62(1) *Proceedings of the Human Factors and Ergonomics Society Annual Meeting* 197–201, https://doi.org/10.1177/1541931218621047.

IV. Conclusion

The GDPR is a relatively recent legislative effort and well-designed data protection rules should be adaptable to the challenges arising from new technology. Of course, there is no such thing as fully 'future-proof' legislation since reality will always far exceed the legislator's capability to predict the future and legal interpretation is a flexible but not limitless solution. Nevertheless, on the specific issue under analysis in this chapter, we would argue that the GDPR passes the test.

From the perspective of the data subject, the GDPR offers strong protection and guarantees of transparency in the processing of personal data. As we have established above, it is possible to find, at least, three possible legal bases for the right to explanation under the GDPR. While a reasonable and reality-focused interpretation means that different information may be provided depending on if the data processing operations have already occurred or not, the GDPR offers the data subjects an explanation regarding both system functionality and the specific decision.[53]

We do note the potential challenges that data controllers may face when trying to meet these legal requirements under the GDPR. While we have proposed some solutions such as support for XAI solutions we would add that, to avoid a chilling effect in the development of AI in the EU, European Data Protection Authorities should adopt an educational approach and try to cooperate with data controllers before deploying the more severe weapons in their arsenal against breaches of the GDPR. When developing new technologies, breaches of data protection rules are frequently the result of not understanding how to comply with the legal framework, more than anything else.

Nevertheless, if it is needed, the GDPR does offer plenty of solutions for enforcement of the data subject's rights. These include (the widely known) fines that may go up to €20 million, or in the case of an undertaking, up to four per cent of the total worldwide annual turnover of the preceding financial year, whichever is higher. Accessory sanctions such as a temporary or definitive limitation including a ban on processing may be even more severe on a data controller's activities. The GDPR also offers solutions for private enforcement including the right to be compensated for any material or non-material damage that may result from breaching its rules. Data protection rules may, in this manner and if properly used by data subjects, prove themselves as highly useful tools against, for example, algorithm discrimination. and having a right to explanation will be key to achieve this.[54]

---

[53] This is in addition to the information/explanation requirements that could be extracted from the principle of transparency itself, and that were not under the scope of this chapter.

[54] Tiago Sérgio Cabral, 'O "Juiz Artificial": Breves Notas Sobre a Utilização de Inteligência Artificial Pelos Tribunais e a Sua Relação Com a Legislação Europeia de Proteção de Dados', in Joana Covelo de Abreu, Larissa Coelho, and Tiago Sérgio Cabral (eds) *O Contencioso Da União Europeia e a Cobrança Transfronteiriça de Créditos: Compreendendo as Soluções Digitais à Luz Do Paradigma Da Justiça Eletrónica Europeia (e-Justice)* (Braga: Universidade do Minho, 2020), in press.

Acknowledgements

The author would like to thank Alessandra Silveira, Iakovina Kindylidi and Rui Vieira for their precious inputs in writing this chapter.

References

AEPD. 'Adecuación al RGPD de Tratamientos Que Incorporan Inteligencia Artificial. Una Introducción'. Accessed 25 February 2020. www.aepd.es/sites/default/files/2020-02/adecuacion-rgpd-ia.pdf.

——. 'RGPD Compliance of Processings That Embed Artificial Intelligence. An Introduction'. Accessed 2 March 2020. www.aepd.es/sites/default/files/2020-02/adecuacion-rgpd-ia-en_0.pdf.

Aleixo, Manuel Lopes. 'Anotação Ao Art.º 296.º Do TFUE'. In Manuel Lopes Porto and Gonçalo Anastácio (eds) *Tratado de Lisboa Anotado e Comentado*, (Coimbra: Almedina, 2012) 1060–62.

Alexios Anagnostakis v Commission, No. T-450/12 (EGC 30 September 2015).

Alexios Anagnostakis v Commission, No. C-589/15 P (ECJ 12 September 2017).

Baratta, Roberto. 'Complexity of EU Law in the Domestic Implementing Process' (2014) 2(3) *The Theory and Practice of Legislation* 293–308. doi.org/10.5235/12050-8840.2.3.293.

——. 'Complexity of EU Law in the Domestic Implementing Process'. Accessed 2 May 2019. ec.europa.eu/dgs/legal_service/seminars/20140703_baratta_speech.pdf.

Burt, Andrew. "Is There a 'Right to Explanation' for Machine Learning in the GDPR', 17 July 2019. https://iapp.org/news/a/is-there-a-right-to-explanation-for-machine-learning-in-the-gdpr.

C., No. C-435/06 (ECJ 27 September 2007).

Cabral, Tiago Sérgio. 'A Short Guide to the Legislative Procedure in the European Union' (2020) 6(1) *UNIO – EU Law Journal* 161–80.

——. 'O 'Juiz Artificial': Breves Notas Sobre a Utilização de Inteligência Artificial Pelos Tribunais e a Sua Relação Com a Legislação Europeia de Proteção de Dados'. In Joana Covelo de Abreu, Larissa Coelho, and Tiago Sérgio Cabral (eds) *O Contencioso Da União Europeia e a Cobrança Transfronteiriça de Créditos: Compreendendo as Soluções Digitais à Luz Do Paradigma Da Justiça Eletrónica Europeia (e-Justice)*, in press. (Braga: Universidade do Minho, 2020).

Casa Fleischhandels v Bundesanstalt für landwirtschaftliche Marktordnung, No. C-215/88 (ECJ 13 July 1989).

Casey, Brian, Ashkon Farhangi, and Roland Vogl. 'Rethinking Explainable Machines: The GDPR's 'Right to Explanation' Debate and the Rise of Algorithmic Audits in Enterprise' (2019) 34 *Berkeley Technology Law Journal* 142–83.

Club Hotel Loutraki v Commission, No. C-131/15 P (ECJ 21 December 2016).

Commission v Council, No. C-370/07 (ECJ 1 October 2009).

Datatilsynet. 'Artificial Intelligence and Privacy'. Accessed 20 May 2019. www.datatilsynet.no/globalassets/global/english/ai-and-privacy.pdf.

Deutsches Milch-Kontor GmbH v Hauptzollamt Hamburg-Jonas, No. C-136/04 (ECJ 24 November 2005).

Ding, Liya. 'Human Knowledge in Constructing AI Systems – Neural Logic Networks Approach towards an Explainable AI' (2018) 126 *Procedia Computer Science* 1561–70. https://doi.org/10.1016/j.procs.2018.08.129.

EDPB. 'Guidelines 05/2020 on Consent under Regulation 2016/679'. Accessed 10 June 2020. https://edpb.europa.eu/sites/edpb/files/files/file1/edpb_guidelines_202005_consent_en.pdf.

Edwards, Lilian, and Michael Veale. 'Slave to the Algorithm? Why a Right to Explanationn Is Probably Not the Remedy You Are Looking For' (2017) 16(1) *Duke Law & Technology Review* 16. https://doi.org/10.2139/ssrn.2972855.

European Commission. 'Communication from the Commission to the European Parliament and the Council on Guidance for Better Transposition and Application of Directive 2004/38/EC on the Right of Citizens of the Union and Their Family Members to Move and Reside Freely within the Territory of the Member States'. Accessed 3 May 2019. https://eur-lex.europa.eu/legal-content/EN/TXT/PDF/?uri=CELEX:52009DC0313&from=EN.

Fonderie Acciaierie Giovanni Mandelli v Commission of the European Communities, No. C-3/67 (ECJ 8 February 1968).

France v Commission, No. C-325/91 (ECJ 16 June 1993).

France v Commission, No. C-325/91 (ECJ 16 June 1993).

Germany v Commission, No. C-24/15 (ECJ 4 July 1963).

Giuseppe Manfredi v Regione Puglia, No. C-308/97 (ECJ 25 November 1998).

Goodman, Bryce, and Seth Flaxman. 'European Union Regulations on Algorithmic Decision-Making and a 'Right to Explanation''. *2016 ICML Workshop on Human Interpretability in Machine Learning*, 2 October 2017. https://arxiv.org/pdf/1606.08813.pdf.

Hildebrandt, Mireille. 'Privacy as Protection of the Incomputable Self: From Agnostic to Agonistic Machine Learning' (2019) 20(1) *Theoretical Inquiries in Law* 83–121. https://doi.org/10.1515/til-2019-0004.

Hoffman, Robert R, Gary Klein, and Shane T Mueller. 'Explaining Explanation For 'Explainable Ai'' (2018) 62(1) *Proceedings of the Human Factors and Ergonomics Society Annual Meeting* 197–201. https://doi.org/10.1177/1541931218621047.

ICO, and The Alan Turing Institute. 'Explaining Decisions Made with AI (Parts 1, 2 and 3)'. Accessed 20 June 2020. Explaining decisions made with AI.

Information Commissioner's Office. *Guide to the General Data Protection Regulation*. London: ICO, 2019.

Kaminski, Margot E 'The Right to Explanation, Explained' (2019) 34(189) *Berkeley Technology Law Journal*. https://doi.org/10.2139/ssrn.3196985.

Klimas, Tadas, and Jūratė Vaičiukaitė. 'The Law of Recitals in European Community Legislation' (2008) 15(1) *ILSA Journal of International & Comparative Law* 1–31.

Llio, Humphreys, Santos Cristiana, di Caro Luigi, Boella Guido, van der Torre Leon, and Robaldo Livio. 'Mapping Recitals to Normative Provisions in EU Legislation to Assist Legal Interpretation'. *Frontiers in Artificial Intelligence and Applications*, 2015, 41–49. https://doi.org/10.3233/978-1-61499-609-5-41.

Malgieri, Gianclaudio. 'Automated Decision-Making in the EU Member States: The Right to Explanation and Other 'Suitable Safeguards' in the National Legislations' (2019) 35(5) *Computer Law & Security Review*: 105327. https://doi.org/10.1016/j.clsr.2019.05.002.

———. 'Trade Secrets v Personal Data: A Possible Solution for Balancing Rights'(2016) 6(2) *International Data Privacy Law* 102–16. https://doi.org/10.1093/idpl/ipv030.

Malgieri, Gianclaudio, and Giovanni Comandé. 'Why a Right to Legibility of Automated Decision-Making Exists in the General Data Protection Regulation' (2017) 7(4) *International Data Privacy Law* 7 243–65. https://doi.org/10.1093/idpl/ipx019.

Mendoza, Isak, and Lee A Bygrave. 'The Right Not to Be Subject to Automated Decisions Based on Profiling'. In Tatiana-Eleni Synodinou, Philippe Jougleux, Christiana Markou, and Thalia Prastitou (eds) *EU Internet Law* 77–98 (Cham: Springer International Publishing, 2017). https://doi.org/10.1007/978-3-319-64955-9_4.

Mojsilovic, Aleksandra. 'Introducing AI Explainability 360'. Accessed 20 August 2019. www.ibm.com/blogs/research/2019/08/ai-explainability-360.

Nilsson, No. C-162/97 (ECJ 19 September 1998).

Opdebeek, Ingrid, and Stéphanie De Somer. 'The Duty to Give Reasons in the European Legal Area a Mechanism for Transparent and Accountable Administrative Decision-Making? – A Comparison of Belgian, Dutch, French and EU Administrative Law' (2016) 2 *Rocznik Administracji Publicznej* 97–148.

Parliament v Council, No. Joined Cases C-317/04 and C-318/04 (ECJ 30 June 2006).

Rita, de Sousa Costa. *A Realização Do Direito Da Protecção de Dados Da União Europeia Através Das Fontes Não-Legislativas: Dos Grandes Temas Jurisprudenciais Aos Desafios Do Soft Law, No Contexto Da Aplicação Do Regulamento Geral Sobre a Protecção de Dados*. (Universidade Católica Portuguesa, 2019).

Sartor, Giovanni. 'The Impact of the General Data Protection Regulation (GDPR) on Artificial Intelligence'. European Parliamentary Research Service. Accessed 26 June 2020. www.europarl.europa.eu/RegData/etudes/STUD/2020/641530/EPRS_STU(2020)641530_EN.pdf.

Selbst, Andrew D, and Julia Powles. 'Meaningful Information and the Right to Explanation' (2017) 7(4) *International Data Privacy Law* 7, 233–42. https://doi.org/10.1093/idpl/ipx022.

Slaughter and May. 'Introduction to the Legislative Processes for EU Directives Matters and Regulations on Financial Services'. Accessed 5 July 2019. www.slaughterandmay.com/what-we-do/publications-and-seminars/publications/client-publications-and-articles/i/introduction-to-the-legislative-processes-for-eu-directives-and-regulations-on-financial-services-matters.aspx.

The Queen v Secretary of State for Trade and Industry, ex parte Broadcasting, Entertainment, Cinematographic and Theatre Union, No. C-173/99 (ECJ 26 June 2001).

Tietosuojavaltuutettu v Jehovan todistajat – uskonnollinen yhdyskunta, No. C–15/17 (ECJ 10 July 2019).

TWD Textilwerke Deggendorf GmbH v Commission, No. Joined Cases T-244/93 and T-486/93 (Court of First Instance 13 September 1995).

TWD Textilwerke Deggendorf GmbH v Commission, No. C-355/95 P (ECJ 15 May 1997).

Voermans, W, Maarten Stremler, and PB Cliteur. 'Constitutional Preambles: A Comparative Analysis'. Elgar *Monographs in Constitutional and Administrative Law* (Cheltenham, Edward Elgar Publishing, 2017).

Voigt, Paul, and Axel von dem Bussche. *The EU General Data Protection Regulation (GDPR)* (Cham, Springer International Publishing, 2017). https://doi.org/10.1007/978-3-319-57959-7.

Wachter, Sandra, Brent Mittelstadt, and Luciano Floridi. 'Why a Right to Explanation of Automated Decision-Making Does Not Exist in the General Data Protection Regulation' (2017) 7(2) *International Data Privacy Law* 76–99. https://doi.org/10.1093/idpl/ipx005.

Wachter, Sandra, Brent Mittelstadt, and Chris Russell. 'Counterfactual Explanations Without Opening the Black Box: Automated Decisions and the GDPR' (2018) 31 *Harvard Journal of Law & Technology* 841–87.

——. 'Why Fairness Cannot Be Automated: Bridging the Gap Between EU Non-Discrimination Law and AI'. *SSRN [Preprint]*, 2020.

WP29. 'Guidelines on Automated Individual Decision-Making and Profiling for the Purposes of Regulation 2016/679'. Accessed 10 June 2019. https://ec.europa.eu/ newsroom/article29/document.cfm?action=display&doc_id=49826.

——. 'Guidelines on Transparency under Regulation 2016/679'. Accessed 10 June 2019. https://ec.europa.eu/newsroom/article29/document.cfm?action=display&doc_id=51025.

——. 'Opinion 1/2010 on the Concepts of 'Controller' and 'Processor''. Accessed 10 June 2019. https://ec.europa.eu/justice/article-29/documentation/opinion-recommendation/ files/2010/wp169_en.pdf.

Wynsberghe, Aimee van. 'Artificial Intelligence: From Ethics to Policy'. European Parliamentary Research Service. Accessed 20 June 2020. www.europarl.europa.eu/ RegData/etudes/STUD/2020/641507/EPRS_STU(2020)641507_EN.pdf.

3

A Comparison of Data Protection Regulations for Automotive Systems

ALA'A AL-MOMANI, CHRISTOPH BÖSCH AND FRANK KARGL[1]

Abstract

Many artificial intelligence and machine learning applications pose threats to consumers' privacy. Organisations are collecting a vast amount of individuals' data to train and enhance their business models. The adoption of data protection regulations was necessary to regulate how and for what purpose consumers' data is collected, processed, and shared. Generally, organisations that collect, process, or share personal information of data subjects are required to comply with one (or more) data protection regulations. An example of such organisations include the automotive industry as their services may collect, process, and potentially share personal and sensitive information, such as identifiers and geolocation data of end-users. In this chapter, we compare the data protection regulations in major automotive industry markets around the world, ie, the European Union (EU), the United States of America (US), and Japan. In particular, we look at the General Data Protection Regulation (GDPR), the California Consumer Privacy Act (CCPA), and the Japanese Act on the Protection of Personal Information (APPI), respectively, and discuss the impact of these regulations on automotive services. Particularly, we consider an autonomous taxicab service as an example of automotive service and investigate how such a service can be designed in compliance with the previous regulations. We further highlight the challenge that a worldwide service provider faces when complying with all of the previous regulations at once as they may substantially differ in some aspects. Furthermore, we provide recommendations on how to design such a service in a way that considers the three regulations and provide an example of a service designed after considering the regulations.

[1] Institute of Distributed Systems, Ulm University, Germany: alaa.al-momani@uni-ulm.de; christoph.boesch@uni-ulm.de; frank.kargl@uni-ulm.de.

Keywords

Automotive Systems, Autonomous Taxicab, GDPR, CCPA, APPI.

I. Introduction

The European Data Protection Regulation (GDPR)[2] which became effective on 25 May 2018, made companies check and revise their privacy policies and practices. For many countries, concepts like the Data Protection Impact Assessment (DPIA) or mandatory Data Protection Officer (DPO) bring along major changes to established processes and practices. At the same time, there are open questions and uncertainties regarding GDPR that will only be clarified over time. This is evidenced by the fact sheet of the European Commission pointing out that a two-year-long transition period between introducing the GDPR in May 2016 and enforcing it in May 2018 was not enough.[3]

As the automotive industry is steadily transforming towards a digital industry that collects, stores, and processes a lot of Personal Information (PI) from, eg, connected or autonomous cars, they are also heavily affected by this change. A connected car may, for example, collect mobility data including geolocation data, along with an identifier of either the vehicle or the driver, and send such information to the manufacturer's backend systems. Very often, services offered to individual customers based on their (precise) locations, eg, routing services, are linked to privacy risks posed to the individuals using such services. For this reason, this chapter focuses on such individualised location-based services.

The trend towards automated driving will make vehicles collect and process even more data due to new services, more sensors, higher storage capacity, and enhanced processing power in vehicles. Vehicles are also becoming part of larger mobility solutions like car-sharing[4] or future self-driving taxicab services[5] which makes privacy analysis and data protection even more challenging. It is therefore mandatory for automotive service providers and car manufacturers to have a proper privacy regime in place to not violate consumer trust or data

[2] European Parliament and Council of the European Union, *General Data Protection Regulations* (Brussels: Official Journal of the European Union, 2016), 1-88, https://eur-lex.europa.eu/legal-content/EN/TXT/PDF/?uri=CELEX:32016R0679&from=EN (last accessed 25 April 2020).

[3] 'MYTHBUSTING: General Data Protection Regulation,' European Commission, https://ec.europa.eu/commission/sites/beta-political/files/100124_gdpr_factsheet_mythbusting.pdf (last accessed 26 March 2020).

[4] Brett Helling, '2017: The Year the Rideshare Industry Crushed the Taxi,' https://rideshareapps.com/2015-rideshare-infographic/ (last accessed 20 March 2020).

[5] Abhimanyu Ghoshal, 'Uber CEO: self-driving cabs will hit the streets by mid-2019,' https://thenextweb.com/insider/2018/01/24/uber-ceos-self-driving-cabs-will-hit-the-streets-by-mid-2019/ (last accessed 20 March 2020).

protection regulations. The automotive industry, including both service providers and manufacturers, is operating in a worldwide setting and is highly based on the division of labour. This raises the question of how automotive Information and Communication Technology (ICT) systems can be designed in a way compliant with data protection regulations in one market like Europe, and whether such an approach could even fulfill legal requirements in other major markets like the US and/or Japan. A joint approach to privacy engineering has economic and technical benefits, as unified systems can be designed and development can take place in global teams.

With this chapter, we want to investigate how automotive systems offering location-based services, like autonomous taxicab services, can be designed in a way that is compliant with worldwide data protection regulations. To this end, we look at data protection regulations in Europe, the US, and Japan. In particular, we investigate the GDPR in Europe, the CCPA as an example of a privacy act in the US, and the APPI in Japan. We exclude secondary legal sources in relation to these regulations in their respective territories such as, eg, the European Data Protection Board guidelines on GDPR,[6] from the scope of this chapter, and focus rather on the top-level instruments to investigate substantial differences.

We first describe the system model for our use-case, the autonomous taxicab service, before discussing the different data protection regulations and their consequences on the use-case. We then compare the different regimes and provide recommendations on how to approach worldwide data protection-compliant service.

II. The System Model

For our analysis, we consider an Autonomous Taxicab Service (ATS) as part of a bigger Intelligent Transportation System (ITS) which relies heavily on artificial intelligence and machine learning, eg, mobility pattern recognition. Recently, such services for driverless cabs have gained a lot of attention especially among ride-hailing and ride-sharing service providers.[7,8,9] We consider a simplified setting for such a service in which fully autonomous taxicabs can be requested on-demand to transport passengers to their desired destinations.

Requesting a transportation service includes providing a pick-up location and a destination for the trip, likely together with the desired time of pick up (or arrival). Additional personal preferences may be given, eg, features of the autonomous

---

[6] GDPR: Guidelines, Recommendations, Best Practices, https://edpb.europa.eu/our-work-tools/general-guidance/gdpr-guidelines-recommendations-best-practices_en (last accessed 28 June 28 2020).

[7] 'What is Easy Ride,' Easy Ride, https://easy-ride.com (last accessed 26 March 2020).

[8] Ghoshal, 'Uber CEO: self-driving cabs will hit the streets by mid-2019' (n 5).

[9] 'Our Journey', Journey, Waymo, https://waymo.com/journey/ (last accessed 22 April 2020).

taxicab such as available seating, driving style and many more. Ideally, the transportation system will provide a driverless taxicab in a matter of a few minutes. This either requires a very large fleet or a detailed analysis of past demand together with an accurate prediction capability based on large scale collection and processing of behavioural data. After the service is delivered, the autonomous taxicab vehicle may offer multiple payment options, including cash, credit cards, or a fully automatic payment based on a long-term contract.

Moreover, the provider of an autonomous taxicab service may wish to record a video of the trip, eg, to identify vandalism. Therefore, the autonomous taxicab may have a camera installed in the vehicle's main compartment. Furthermore, as premium customers may be eligible for special discounts and customer loyalty programs, the autonomous taxicab provider may also collect certain data for a longer duration, eg, all trips that were taken. This may also be helpful for tax declarations in case of business-related usage of the autonomous taxicab. Besides, some countries may have laws that require passengers to be identified and trip information to be held available for law enforcement and crime prevention.

Our simplified setting for ATS, shown in Figure 1, assumes four parties: a service provider (SP) dispatching autonomous taxicab vehicle (V) to a customer (C) of the service, ie, a data subject, and several third-party (3P) services. The SP may collect, process, and share data of customers to provide the requested service, and potentially offer additional features provided by 3Ps. Thus, 3Ps may also process and store the shared data from the SP to offer additional features such as navigating nearby places at the destination, or to learn the mobility patterns of users for the sake of, eg, traffic management in case the 3P is a traffic management authority.

Figure 1 A simplified system model of the ATS which consists of four parties; a customer (C), a service provider (SP), a third party (3P), and an autonomous taxicab vehicle (V)

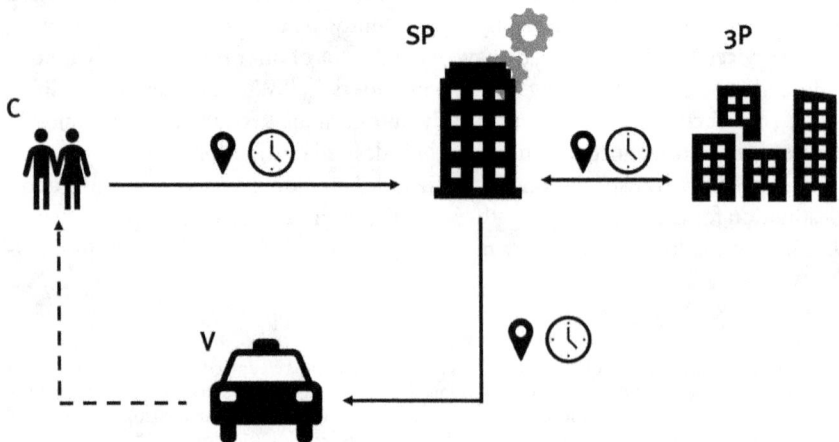

As mentioned earlier, offering such a transportation service inevitably implies collecting, processing, and sharing data about the whereabouts and the behaviour of customers. Such data may be used to infer further sensitive information about customers' activities, inter alia, sexual habits and orientation, drinking and social behaviour, physical or mental health, and religious or political beliefs.[10,11,12,13]

Therefore, we generally assume that ITS services fall under data protection regulations and need to consider how to process personal data in a compliant way and how to apply mechanisms to avoid collecting and processing superfluous personal data.

III. Data Protection Frameworks in Major Markets

With the era of Artificial Intelligence (AI) and big data, protecting personal data has become a must. Therefore, many legislators around the world have updated and implemented data protection regulations to address this. In this section, we discuss three of the recent and widely considered data protection frameworks, and further address their impact on the use case we presented earlier. In particular, we start by discussing the GDPR, followed by the CCPA, and finally the APPI. The previous three acts cover markets that are among the leaders in the automotive and its services sectors.

A. The European Union

i. GDPR Overview

The GDPR is a binding norm throughout the EU Member States that passed the European Parliament in 2016, but is directly applied only since 25 May 2018. Instead of the earlier Directive 95/46/EC, the GDPR does not require implementation in national law but is binding all by itself. Depending on the status of data protection regulation in individual Member States before GDPR, the actual changes in data protection practices in these states can range from small

---

[10] Colum Murphy, 'Uber Orders Drivers in China to Steer Clear of Taxi Protests,' [2015] *The Wall Street Journal*, www.wsj.com/articles/uber-orders-drivers-in-china-to-steer-clear-of-taxi-protests-1434181092 (last accessed March 2020).

[11] Owen Hughes, 'Uber employees "used tracking technology to stalk celebrities, politicians and ex-lovers", *International Business Times UK*, 2016, www.ibtimes.co.uk/former-uber-employee-reveals-drivers-used-tracking-technology-stalk-celebrities-politicians-1596263 (last accessed 20 March 2020).

[12] Kashmir Hill, 'God View': Uber Allegedly Stalked Users for Party-Goers' Viewing Pleasure,' *Forbes*, 2014, www.forbes.com/sites/kashmirhill/2014/10/03/god-view-uber-allegedly-stalked-users-for-party-goers-viewing-pleasure/ (last accessed 20 March 2020).

[13] Douglas Perry, 'Sex and Uber's "Rides of Glory": The company tracks your one-night stands and much more,' The Oregonian/Oregon Live, 2014, www.oregonlive.com/today/2014/11/sex_the_single_girl_and_ubers.html (last accessed 22 April 2020).

to substantial. Beyond, the GDPR governs data protection for non-EU entities, as long as personal data of data subjects who are in the EU are involved.
Major aspects discussed in the GDPR articles can be summarised as follow.
The *territorial scope* can extend beyond the limits of the EU as long as:
(1) personal data is processed in the context of the activities of an establishment in the Union, or; (2) personal data of data subjects who are in the
Union. *Sanctions* can, in severe cases, reach levels of up to four per cent of
the annual worldwide turnover of companies, making it prohibitive to accept
bad data protection practices. The definition of *personal data* in the GDPR
is broad and includes all data that can be linked to a person using all likely
reasonable means. However, this broad definition is very similar to the previous definition of personal data found in the GDPR predecessor, ie, the Data
Protection Directive 95/46/EC. The GDPR defines a special category of *sensitive data* (ie, special category of personal data) and prohibits the processing of
such data unless the processing falls under some stated exemptions. Examples
of such exemptions include that the data subject has given explicit consent to
the processing of such a special category of personal information, or that the
processing is necessary for reasons of substantial public interest. The GDPR
also foresees its own duties and *direct liability for data processors* independent
of the duties of the data controller, requiring clear definitions of mutual obligations between controller and supplier in contracts. The GDPR lists the so-called
data protection principles that remain largely intact from the earlier regulation
including data minimisation and storage limitation. *International transfer* of
personal data outside of the EU is also covered by the GDPR, requiring at
least comparable data protection on the receiving side or that the transfer is
subject to appropriate safeguards such as binding corporate rules according to
Article 47. The list of such countries that qualified to receive GDPR-protected
personal data[14] currently includes a dozen names. However, the cooperation with the US – until July 2020 where the European Court of Justice (ECJ)
declared it invalid – has been limited to the EU-US Privacy Shield agreement[15]
while adequacy with Japan has recently been recognised.[16] *Data breaches* that
affect personal data now require quick notifications within a maximum of
72 hours, in addition to other requirements such as a description of the breach,
its consequences and the contact point where more information can be obtained.
Individuals covered by the GDPR, in general, enjoy *considerable rights* such as
the right to access stored information and the right for changing the stored
data or even deleting them. Moreover, in many circumstances, a *data protection
officer (DPO)* needs to be appointed, which was already the case, for example,
in Germany but is now mandatory EU-wide. *Data-protection-by-design (DPbD)*

---

[14] https://ec.europa.eu/info/law/law-topic/data-protection/data-transfers-outside-eu/adequacy-
protection-personal-data-non-eu-countries_en.

[15] 'Welcome to the privacy shield,' International Trade Commission, 2016, www.privacyshield.gov/
(last accessed 20 March 2020).

[16] europa.eu/rapid/press-release_IP-18-4501_en.htm, www.ppc.go.jp/files/pdf/310123_pressstatement_
en.pdf.

and by-default implies that systems processing personal data will have to be developed with privacy in mind, including a *data protection impact assessment (DPIA)*. In addition, the GDPR states that technical and organisational measures have to be put in place to ensure state-of-the-art privacy protection. In conclusion, GDPR *raises the bar for lawful processing* of personal data that are even more severe for sensitive data like biometric or genetic data. In general, the lawful basis of processing, according to Article 6 Paragraph (1) of the GDPR, are either: (a) the data subjects have already given explicit consent for the processing, or the processing is necessary for; (b) the performance of a contract such like delivering a service; (c) compliance with legal obligations;(d) protecting vital interests of the data subject; (e) public interest matters, and; (f) legitimate interest of the data controller or third parties. In all cases, the data subject should be informed at the time their data are obtained about, among others, the purpose of the processing and the legal basis for such processing, and for how long the data is retained. For additional details on the information to be provided where personal data are collected, we refer the reader to Article 13 of the GDPR.

By the very nature of this extensive law, this discussion can only be incomplete and provide a brief overview. It is interesting to note that many international companies, including US-based companies, are taking GDPR as a baseline for their data protection practices.[17] The GDPR seems to set an example that reaches way beyond the EU itself.

ii. GDPR Implications on ATS

Considering the use case of the ATS in Section II, one can derive several conclusions. For instance, when designing such a system, one has to follow a clear data-protection-by-design and -default approach, documenting each of the activities. Such activities include conducting a data protection impact assessment, and implementing technical and organisational measures including privacy strategies like minimisation and having a clear data retention strategy. Furthermore, there should be appointed responsibilities and a DPO overseeing the process. The data subjects – ie, the customers in the ATS scenario – should be informed of any (new) processing purposes on their data other than the purposes they initially gave their informed consent to if the new purposes are incompatible with the initial purposes, and accordingly give their new consent assuming the personal data have been collected based on the data subject's consent. In the case of processing for a purpose for which the personal data was not collected based on the consent, the ATS provider has to ascertain that the new processing is for a lawful purpose as discussed earlier. We note that for countries that already had high privacy standards, like Germany, most of this was legally required anyway. However, for other countries, such implications would have been given before the GDPR only as *advice*. However, now that the

[17] www.statista.com/statistics/946800/steps-taken-companies-taken-comply-gdpr-usa/.

maximum penalties are substantially higher, and that obligations for controllers and processors are more sharply defined, a company offering an ATS *needs* to treat the previous aspects with high priority.

An important aspect of the GDPR is that it explicitly addresses profiling and automated decision making. Explicitly addressing the automated decision making is not new in the GDPR as its predecessor, the 95/46/EC Directive, addressed it already (see Article 15). However, addressing profiling of data subjects was rather implicitly addressed in the Directive, but the GDPR explicitly addresses this in addition to the automated decision making. Such processing is subject to additional obligations to the controller and to the processor such as, eg, the right to appeal to an individual for checking or requiring explicit (and informed) consent. Concerning the ATS use case, one may have a system in place that tracks individuals' mobility, or calculates individual fares based on the attributes of a person. As this constitutes profiling and automated decision making, one has to take appropriate precautions in the system design into account including the lawful basis for such automated decision making according to Article 22. Such lawful bases, in this case, might include, among others, that the decision is necessary for the performance of a contract between the user and the ATS provider, or that the ATS provider obtains the user's explicit consent for such automated-decision making.

On the positive side, one aspect includes that users now benefit from an extensive law to protect their data. Moreover, another aspect includes that there is now an EU-wide legal framework and clear legal allocation to the country of an organisation's primary installment, so companies can operate on safe ground.

We will now move on to discuss the legal situation in the US and Japan, and compare whether the advice given for the GDPR in the EU is sufficient to cover the legal requirements there.

B. The United States of America: The Case of California

As the data protection and privacy regulations differ among the States in the US, we focus on the State of California with its recently introduced privacy act which is considered the most comprehensive privacy law in the US.[18]

i. CCPA Overview

The CCPA[19] was introduced in January 2018 and went into effect on 1 January 2020. The CCPA grants Californian citizens and residents a broad *range of rights*

---

[18] Mitchell Noordyke, 'US state comprehensive privacy law comparison,' International Association of Privacy Professionals (IAPP), 2019, https://iapp.org/news/a/us-state-comprehensive-privacy-law-comparison/ (last accessed 20 March 2020).

[19] Ed Chau and Robert Hertzberg, 'Assembly Bill No. 375 CCPA,' California Legislative Information, 2018, https://leginfo.legislature.ca.gov/faces/billTextClient.xhtml?bill_id=201720180AB375 (last accessed 22 April 2020). ·

over their personal information. Such rights include the right to access and erase their information, information portability, and the right to opt-out of selling personal information. The *territorial scope* of CCPA applies to any organisation that annually obtains personal information of, at least, 50,000 Californians. Furthermore, additional conditions to consider whether an organisation falls under the CCPA includes that the annual gross revenue of that organisation is at least US$25 million; or that it receives 50 per cent of its annual revenue from selling Californians' personal information.

The CCPA has a broad definition of *personal information*. Personal information is defined by the Act as 'information that identifies, relates to, describes, is capable of being associated with, or could reasonably be linked, directly or indirectly, with a particular consumer or household'. More particularly, *identifiers* such as real name and postal code, *commercial information* such as records of personal property and purchased services, *biometric information, electronic network activity information* such as internet browsing or search history, and *geolocation data*, are all considered personal information in the CCPA. Another noteworthy point in this regard is that the CCPA also considers the information obtained from *inferences* and correlating the previous information together or with auxiliary information, eg, to create a profile of the subject, as personal information. However, the CCPA excludes personal information that falls under different privacy acts from its scope. For instance, the information covered by the Confidentiality of Medical Information Act (CMIA),[20] Health Insurance Portability and Accountability Act (HIPPA),[21] Gramm-Leach-Bliley Act (GLBA),[22] Driver's Privacy Protection Act (DPPA),[23] in addition to the publicly available personal information, are all excluded.

The CCPA oversees *sanctions* on violations, which can in severe (and intentional) cases, reach up to US$7,500 per violation. Furthermore, recovery of consumer's damage is included in the Act and it can reach up to US$750 per consumer per incident.

An example of such a case is a major breach or other systematic violation of the Act. Therefore, organisations can expect a large class of actions and claims representing all individuals affected by such a violation.

Moreover, an important remark concerning the CCPA is that *Data protection principles* such as data minimisation and limited storage are not explicitly stated. However, the CCPA broadly defines *collecting* and regulates the *selling* of personal information. *Collecting* refers to receiving consumers' information which could

---

[20] 'Confidentiality of Medical Information Act,' California Legislative Information, 1981, https://leginfo.legislature.ca.gov/faces/codes_displayexpandedbranch.xhtml?tocCode=CIV&division=1.&title=&part=2.6.&chapter=&article= (last accessed 21 March 2020).

[21] Nancy Kassebaum and Edward Kennedy, 'Health Insurance Portability and Accountability Act' US Government Publishing Office Website, 1996, www.govinfo.gov/content/pkg/PLAW-104publ191/pdf/PLAW-104publ191.pdf (last accessed 20 March 2020).

[22] Phil Gramm and Jim Leach, 'Gramm-Leach-Bliley Act' US Government Publishing Office website, 1999, www.govinfo.gov/content/pkg/STATUTE-113/pdf/STATUTE-113-Pg1338.pdf#page=1 (last accessed 21 March 2020).

[23] Jim Moran, 'Driver's Privacy Protection Act,' Cornell Law School website, 1994, www.law.cornell.edu/uscode/text/18/2725 (last accessed 21 March 2020).

be in either an *active* or a *passive* manner. However, consumers have the right to know what personal information is being collected about them. Somewhat surprisingly, the CCPA does not require a lawful ground for the collection of personal information and does not impose obtaining consumer's consent prior to the collection. *Selling* information, on the other hand, covers broad activities of releasing, disclosing, dissemination, making available, and transferring personal information to a third party. However, the CCPA does not specify any requirement for the international transfer or selling of personal information such as the adequacy requirement in the GDPR and the APPI. The CCPA does, however, require the provision of a clear option (ie, a uniform and recognisable opt-out logo) to opt-out of selling the subject's personal information.

Regarding *data breaches*, the California law specifies some elements as requirements for a data breach notification to be included, for example, the issuing authority of the notification, a general description of the breach, in addition to who is in charge of resolving the breach problem. It is worth noting that California's data breach notification requirements take into account the sectoral approach to privacy in the US. For example, an organisation covered under the HIPAA is required to comply with the notification requirements according to HIPAA. Thus, the breach notification requirements are rather sector-dependent and are not unified among California's organisations. California introduced a security breach notification law in 2002, implemented it in 2003, and was the first State to do so.[24] Nowadays, California is among 21 States to revise their existing security breach laws to expand the definition of personal information, shortening the time frame for breach reporting, and requiring, in some cases, reporting breaches to the attorney general. In particular, the pending Assembly Bills (ABs) – which are likely to be accepted due to the suitability with the CCPA – in California are the AB 1035 and the AB 1130. These Bills deal with setting the breach notification to be within 72 hours after the breach discovery and expand the personal information definition.[25]

The CCPA clearly defines *pseudonymisation* of processing in which personal information can no longer be attributed nor linked to an individual without the help of additional (auxiliary) information. It is also interesting to point out that recording processing activities is not mandatory under the CCPA.

The CCPA does not provide an obligation on the appointment of a *DPO*, nor forces the process of a *DPIA*. Thus, the notion of *data-protection-by-design and by-default* is not explicitly addressed in the CCPA. However, the act requires well-trained staff concerning the handling of consumers' inquiries about the organisation's privacy practices.

ii. CCPA Implications on ATS

The previous overview of CCPA shows that several aspects have to be considered when designing an ATS whenever Californian residents' information is involved.

---

[24] https://leginfo.legislature.ca.gov/faces/billTextClient.xhtml?bill_id=200120020SB1386.
[25] www.ncsl.org/default.aspx?tabid=/%2033382.

First, according to the use case description, such a system collects personal information – as stated by the CCPA's definition of personal information – including identifiers, biometric information, and geolocation data. Concerning the processing of any of the previous information, the system should employ technical measures to ensure the pseudonymisation of processing in a way to break the linkability between personal information and the identity of the consumer.

The geolocation data is of particular interest as the autonomous taxicab service, among other location-based services, depends mainly on geolocation data. We remind the reader that geo-location data is explicitly defined as personal information in the CCPA. Therefore, designers of an ATS should give particular attention to geolocation data at the collection, processing, and sharing phases, and ensure that those activities are done in a compliant way with the CCPA. This, inevitably, includes ensuring that the consumers are fully aware of the collection of such information and whether their information is sold or transferred to third parties. Geolocation data has a huge potential to be used to infer sensitive information about the consumers and build profiles of consumer's mobility patterns and consumer's points of interest. However, organisations are not free to perform such profiling of their consumers because the CCPA defines such profiles as personal information. Therefore, organisations are obliged to disclose the aim of such profiling including any profile-selling intentions to the consumer.

Thus, from a CCPA perspective, selling consumers' profiles to third parties is equivalent to selling any other personal information to third parties. In this regard, a clear option to opt-out should be provided to the consumer, such as the one suggested by the CCPA, ie '*don't sell my data*' link.

An organisation offering ATS should implement measures to avoid possible (and systematic) violations like data breaches to avoid not only hurting the company's reputation among its consumers, but also the financial sanctions we discussed earlier. Furthermore, the organisation should establish well-defined processes for breach notification according to the CCPA requirement in advance to meet the time requirement of the notification. Moreover, an organisation offering an ATS must ensure adequate staff training concerning the handling of the right of access whenever a consumer practices their right. Despite this, the CCPA does not mandates appointing a DPO.

C. Japan

i. APPI Overview

The APPI came into force in 2005 and was substantially amended in September 2015.[26] The amendments became effective in May 2017. It aims to protect an

---

[26]'Amended Act on the Protection of Personal Information (tentative translation),' Personal Information Protection Commission, Government of Japan, 2016, www.ppc.go.jp/files/pdf/Act_on_the_Protection_of_Personal_Information.pdf (last accessed 20 March 2020).

individual's rights and interests while balancing the utility of personal information. In particular, the APPI seeks to balance the trade-off between protection of the individual's rights, profit interests of companies, and the usefulness of the personal information in general.

We now discuss the major aspects included in the amendment of the APPI. The amended APPI states *several rights of individuals* including transparency, right to be deleted, right to object, right for data transfer, and the right to not be subject to automated decision making. The *territorial scope* of the amended APPI goes beyond Japan and includes personal-information-handling business operators in a foreign country. This applies whenever the business operator acquires personal information from a person in Japan to, eg, offer a service.

The definition of *personal information* has been clarified in the revised APPI to include the so-called *individual identification codes* and *special care-requiring personal information*. *Individual identification codes* refer to the bodily partial features of specific individuals and the codes which are assigned to identify a specific individual. Examples include fingerprint data, voiceprint data, facial recognition data, passport number, driver's licence number, and individual numbers. *Special care-requiring personal information* refers to the information which requires special care in handling personal information to not cause unfair discrimination, prejudice, or other disadvantages to the principal. Examples include race, religious belief, social status, medical history, and criminal record.

A business operator who violates APPI and does not follow the guidelines can be punished. New and tough *sanctions* appear in the revised APPI that addresses the stealthy use of any personal information for illegitimate profit, for example. In severe cases, a punishment by imprisonment is foreseen, which could reach up to two years, or by a fine which could reach up to 1 million yen (currently €8,300 or US$9,000).

The business operator is responsible to exercise necessary and appropriate supervision over the employees to ensure full security control of the personal data processing. The APPI adopts and describes the *data protection principles* in accordance with the GDPR such as data minimisation. In addition, the APPI sets a relatively high bar for *lawful processing*. That is, when acquiring personal information, business operators shall comply with the rules of specifying the purpose of utilising this information as explicitly as possible in the notice. The business operator is obliged to not acquire personal information by deceit or improper means. Altering the utilisation purpose by the business operator requires informing the principal of the new purpose and accordingly obtain consent (if there is a legal obligation to obtain consent for the particular purpose). The APPI gives particular importance to obtaining the principal's consent prior to acquiring 'special care-required' personal information, no matter whether obtained directly from the principal or a third party. Similar to the GDPR, this requirement drops under specific circumstances such as the special need to enhance public health, or when it is physically difficult to obtain the consent.

Transferring data to a third party in Japan requires – in some cases – obtaining the principal's consent in advance. If the transfer is to a third party in a foreign country, then, in addition to the principal consent, the third party should be covered under a data protection regulation that is the equivalent to the amended APPI. In this regard, the APPI considers the EU a territory providing adequate data protection with its GDPR.[27] However, in case of transferring data either nationally or internationally, the business operator shall keep a record for this transfer.

In case of a *data breach*, the business operator shall then consider and enforce countermeasures that include notifying affected principals. However, this is not required if the breach has a minor impact such as, eg, the leaked data is encrypted.

In the APPI, the security control guidelines point out the need for appointing a person in charge of data at each of the lifecycle's phases. However, this person is not a *DPO* per se as the appointment of a DPO is not necessary for the APPI. In the context of the APPI, establishing *security controls* by business operators is required. These controls include organisational, human, physical, and technical security controls. That is, enhancing privacy awareness in addition to technical security controls by preventing unauthorised access to personal data, is required by the APPI. Furthermore, the APPI strongly highlights the necessity of *anonymous* information processing.

ii. APPI Implications on ATS

Following a similar approach of discussing the impact of GDPR and CCPA on ATS, we discuss here the implications of the revised APPI on such a use case. According to the previous discussion on the major changes in the amended APPI, one has to re-design the ATS considering many aspects.

In particular, one should consider the case of collecting *individual iden-tification codes* and *special care-requiring personal information* in a way that is compliant with the APPI. Collection of such information might happen at different phases; for example, when a data subject registers to benefit from the ATS, or when a data subject initiates a ride request and, thus, provides their location information to the business operator.

The collected location information might be used to infer further sensitive information which may be used to enhance the business model at some later point in time. The APPI addresses this issue by advocating the lawful process-ing of personal data. Thus, the processing purpose must be examined to decide whether informed consent for that purpose is to be obtained prior to processing the personal data. This also includes profiling and automated decision making as

---

[27] Haruhi Kumazawa and Vera Jourová, 'Joint Statement by Haruhi Kumazawa, Commissioner of the Personal Information Protection Commission of Japan and Věra Jourová, Commissioner for Justice, Consumers and Gender Equality of the European Commission,' Personal Information Protection Commission, Government of Japan, 2019, www.ppc.go.jp/files/pdf/310123_pressstatement_en.pdf (last accessed 20 March 2020).

the APPI explicitly addresses these aspects. Therefore, business operators have to consider new obligations in this regard.

When transferring personal information to a foreign country, the business operator has to examine many aspects to ensure the transfer is lawful. Among these aspects are whether the principal's consent is necessary or not, and whether the foreign country has an adequate data protection level comparable to the APPI or not. Additionally, if the principal's consent is not required, a clear opt-out option has to be offered to the principal to ensure a lawful transfer.

Documenting and reporting the data lifecycle is addressed in the APPI, therefore, this requires the naming of a person in charge of such reports. Furthermore, the business operator has to advocate privacy through several controls including organisational ones, for example by educating employees handling personal information. Physical controls are also included in the APPI. Therefore, the business operator is required to protect the site at which the personal information is stored (or processed). In the case of ATS, this includes protecting the physical site where information, such as the special-care personal information, of data subjects are stored or processed. In addition, business operators are required to implement the appropriate measures to prevent leakage of personal information. In case of a data breach, the APPI discusses the main action items that need to be conducted which include reporting, investigating, notifying affected principals, and implementing technical countermeasures. Business operators have, therefore, to comply with the APPI regulations throughout the whole business development lifecycle.

IV. Comparison and Synthesis

Our previous discussion on the GDPR, CCPA, and APPI along with their impact on the ATS use case shows that several aspects have to be considered when offering such a service. For some of these aspects, the regulations impose well-aligned requirements. However, for other aspects, they differ substantially. Thus, in many cases, complying with only *one* data protection framework does not imply compliance with another. In the case of a worldwide automotive service like the ATS that is offered by an international company in different markets, complying with several data protection regulations at once becomes a major challenge. This is particularly challenging when it comes to organising the internal processes and the internal relations among the company's branches which may be scattered around the world. To address this issue, we provide a comparison between the three previously discussed regulations while focusing on the system model of the ATS presented in Section II. We classify the comparison aspects into three categories based on how substantial the difference in the comparison aspect is. Particularly, we consider *major differences*, *minor differences*, and *similarities* between the three regulations with respect to their fundamental approaches of protecting personal data and how they achieve their promises. Such (major) differences might create considerable challenges in a worldwide-compliance setting. We provide a summary of the following comparison between the GDPR, the APPI, and the CCPA in Table 1.

A. Major Differences

One of the major differences between the three regulations is where the GDPR mandates the appointment of a *DPO*. Both the CCPA and the APPI do not foresee such an appointment. However, both of them point out the necessity for enhancing privacy awareness within the organisation. In addition, the APPI mandates appointing a person in charge of the data item lifecycle but not an explicit DPO. In the case of an organisation offering a mobility service such as the ATS worldwide, the appointment of a DPO is necessary to comply with the GDPR. This implies that complying with the CCPA and the APPI as one of the duties of the DPO is promoting good data protection principles within the organisation, as well as examining the data item lifecycle.

Aside from the DPO appointment, one of the key differences between the CCPA and the other two acts is the *purpose limitation* principle obliged by both the GDPR and APPI. This plays a big role in the collection of personal information and the utilisation purpose accordingly. The GDPR and APPI seem to be more fundamental, providing higher bars for lawful processing when compared to the CCPA.

One of the major differences between the three regulations lies in the rights granted to individuals, especially the *right to opt-out*. Particularly, the CCPA and the APPI only provide for the right to opt-out of selling and transferring PI, respectively, but not for a general right to opt-out. In the case of GDPR, the right to opt-out is clearly stated which includes the right to opt-out of processing and transferring.

Another difference between the regulations is the explicit consideration of *geolocation data* as personal information. In particular, geolocation data is explicitly stated as personal information in both the CCPA and the GDPR. In the case of a location-based service (LBS) like the ATS, geolocation data is considered the backbone of such a service. Thus, collecting such information, processing, and selling it to third parties should consider complying with the requirements stated in: (1) the GDPR including the purpose limitation and clarify the legal ground of processing, and; (2) the CCPA including a clear option for the consumer to opt-out of selling their personal information, ie, '*do not sell my information*' link. The major difference concerning the geolocation data is that the APPI does not explicitly consider such data personal information and, therefore in some cases, explicit consent may not be necessary to collect, process, or sell such information.

Another major difference between the CCPA, on the one hand, and the GDPR and APPI, on the other, is the consideration of *health data*. In this regard, the

CCPA excludes medical information from its protection because it is protected by other acts in the US, eg, the HIPPA. Therefore, health data is out of the scope of the CCPA. However, health data is not highly relevant for the use case of ATS.

Furthermore, *recording processing activities* is mandatory in the GDPR but neither in the CCPA nor in the APPI. In an ATS scenario, the processing of data might take place with a purpose beyond offering the basic service of the ride-hailing. Processing the data could be to estimate future demand or offer personalised suggestions to consumers. In this case, the processing of data involving any personal data of consumers must be recorded and well-documented according to the GDPR. The APPI, however, mandates keeping *records of data transfer* which is also the case in GDPR but not the CCPA. Therefore, the CCPA differs to a greater extent from both the GDPR and the APPI in this regard by not mandating such records to be kept.

Moreover, both the GDPR and APPI allow *transferring data* to countries with adequate data protection regulations. With this respect, the GDPR considers Japan a country with adequate data protection regulation and, likewise, the amended APPI recognises the EU as a territory with adequate data protection levels. Furthermore, before declaring it invalid by the ECJ, the GDPR recognised the US as a country ensuring an adequate level of protection if the recipient of the data transfer in the US fell under the EU-US privacy shield.[28] Hence, transferring data to a Californian organisation was governed by the privacy shield and not by the CCPA. On the contrary, the CCPA does not regulate transferring data internationally to territorials covered by different privacy acts.

B. Minor Differences

In addition to the previously highlighted major differences between the laws, there exist some aspects where the laws differ only slightly from each other. Concerning the definition of *personal information*, the three regulations have a somewhat similar definition of personal information. The GDPR further considers special categories of personal data that are sensitive. The APPI also defines subcategories of the bodily identifying information and special-care requiring personal information. The CCPA has a broad and wide definition of personal information that requires special care in collecting, processing and sharing, however, without explicitly considering sub-categories of *sensitive* or special care-requiring information. Therefore, an international company offering ATS would, potentially, collect, process, and share its worldwide consumer's information, and thus, must pay particular attention to the definition of personal information in the three regulations as there might be slight differences in their definitions.

---

[28] International Trade Commission, 'Welcome to the privacy shield' (n 15).

Another minor difference is the *terminology* used in the three regulations regarding the responsibility of defining the purpose and the means of processing personal information is different in the three regulations. From a GDPR perspective, the responsibility for such activity falls under the responsibilities of the *data controller*, however, in the CCPA, this responsibility falls to the so-called *business*. Thus, a data controller in the GDPR is equivalent to a business in the CCPA. Furthermore, processing the data on behalf of the controller is a responsibility of a *data processor* in the GDPR, and on behalf of the business is a *service provider*. It is worth noting that activities of the data processor should be governed with a binding contract with the controller under the GDPR, and, analogously under the CCPA.

The APPI takes a slightly different approach as it states that both of the previous activities, ie, the controlling and processing activities, fall under the responsibilities of the *business operator*.

Regarding the *anonymity* of data processing, the APPI refers to the anonymity of processing while the other two regulations refer to the pseudonymity of processing. In this regard, the APPI is slightly superior over the GDPR and CCPA, thus, a worldwide ATS should ensure anonymous processing of data. Here, we note that achieving full anonymity in real-world scenarios is very challenging considering the non-trivial possibility of the risk of de-anonymisation using, eg, publicly available information.[29,30]

C. Similarities

All of the regulations considered in this chapter advocate additional *rights to individuals* for their personal information. Such rights include, among others, the rights for deletion, the right to opt-out from the selling of their information, the right for accessing their information, and the right for data portability. However, data portability is not considered in the APPI, thus we list it under the differences.

One example of the similarities between the three regulations is the explicit consideration of *biometric data* as personal information. The GDPR further considers this data item under the sensitive data items which require special care when dealing with. We note that with the recent and advanced development of AI applications, facial recognition, among others, has high potential to be widely deployed in future autonomous taxicabs for, eg authentication or payment authorisation purposes. Therefore, biometric data is highly relevant in a scenario like the ATS.

An additional similarity between the three regulations is not mandating a specific method for data breach notification. On a side note, one similarity

---

[29] Arvind Narayanan and Vitaly Shmatikov, 'Robust De-anonymization of Large Sparse Datasets' in the proceeding of IEEE Symposium on Security and Privacy 2008, 111–125.
[30] Arvind Narayanan and Vitaly Shmatikov, 'De-anonymizing social networks,' in the proceeding of IEEE Symposium on Security and Privacy 2009, 173–187.

between the APPI and the GDPR is that both of them seek a balance between the data subject's rights and information utility, in the GDPR, this is elucidated in Article 6(1)(f).

We note that other (partial) similarities between any two regulations exist but as they differ from the third one, we consider such a case as a minor difference not as a similarity as exhibited in Table 1.

Table 1 Comparison of data protection regulations between the GDPR, APPI, and CCPA

	Comparison Aspects	Regulations		
		EU-GDPR	**JP-APPI**	**US-CCPA**
Major Differences	*DPO*	Obligatory	Nonobligatory	Nonobligatory
	Geolocation data	Personal	Impersonal	Personal
	Health data	Sensitive	Sensitive	Out-of-scope
	Breach notification deadline	72 hours	Unspecified	72 hours
	Maximum fines	20m EUR or 4% of annual turnover	1m JPY or two-year imprisonment	7.5k USD & 750 USD per consumer per incident
	DPbD	Obligatory	Nonobligatory	Nonobligatory
	DPIA	Obligatory	Nonobligatory	Nonobligatory
	Purpose limitation	Stated	Stated	Unstated
	Right to data portability	Granted	Unstated	Granted
	Right to opt-out	Granted	Opt-out of transfer PI	Opt-out of selling PI
	Right to non-discrimination	Unstated[31]	Implicit[32]	Explicitly granted
	International data transfer	Data protection adequacy		Unregulated
	Process-recording	Obligatory	Nonobligatory	Nonobligatory
	Transfer-recording	Obligatory	Obligatory	Nonobligatory
	Compliance responsibility	Controller & processor	Business operator	Business

(continued)

[31] The right to non-discrimination is regulated and stated in the Charter of Fundamental Rights of the European Union, see www.europarl.europa.eu/charter/pdf/text_en.pdf.
[32] In the definition of special care-requiring personal information.

Table 1 *(Continued)*

	Comparison Aspects	Regulations		
		EU-GDPR	**JP-APPI**	**US-CCPA**
Minor Differences	*Controlling data*	Data controller	Business operator	Business
	Processing data	Data processor	Business operator	Service provider
	Processing	Pseudonymous	Anonymous	Pseudonymous
	Sensitive information category	Stated	Stated	Unstated
Similarities	*Biometric data*	Personal information		
	Right to be forgotten	Granted		
	Right to access	Admissible		
	Breach notification method	Unregulated		

V. Summary and Recommendations

In this chapter, we discussed the challenges when developing a worldwide automotive service such as ATS. The challenges mainly include complying with many data protection regulations at a given point in time as they may differ in many aspects. We focused on three major markets for automotive systems, ie, the EU, the US, and Japan and discussed the corresponding data protection regulations in each territory, ie, the GDPR, the CCPA (as an example of a US regulation), and the APPI, respectively. We discussed the differences and similarities between the three regulations and their implications on a worldwide ATS service. We now provide recommendations on how to approach the design and develop such a worldwide service based on our findings.

First, a team developing such a service should have a legal expert per territorial regulation whose responsibility is to make sure that collecting, processing, and sharing consumer data is applied with compliance to the regulations assigned to that expert. This is important because, in many cases, the legal assessment depends on the specifics and details of the system. Our analysis concerning the use case of ATS showed that the GDPR out performs both the CCPA and APPI in most of the comparison aspects. Thus, we recommend following a paradigm that represents an extended version of the GDPR as the main reference for international mobility-operators such as an ATS provider operating worldwide. The extension of the GDPR is to address the aspects found in the other regulations but not in the GDPR, for example the *don't sell my data* link as stated in the CCPA.

However, there exist some remaining limitations and challenges that none of the previous regulations consider intensively. In particular, the GDPR and

CCPA consider geolocation data as personal information as long as the data is *not* anonymised. As soon as the geolocation data become anonymous, then the regulations do not apply anymore. We note here that geolocation data, in particular, has a huge potential to be de-anonymised easily, which therefore should not be considered anonymous in the first place according to jurisprudence. This is because geolocation data directly represents identifying locations of consumers, eg, home and/or work addresses.[33] Therefore, there is a lack of clarification in all of the regulations regarding the elimination of the anonymised data from their scope because such data items might be identifiable by their nature.

Some remaining challenges include the incompatibility of the terminology used within the three regulations regarding the definition of the data controller and data processor from a GDPR perspective and business and service provider from a CCPA perspective. Another challenge consists of identifying where to host consumers' data in each market.

Figure 2 shows a graphical representation of a simplified ATS system that can be offered in a worldwide setting after the consideration of the GDPR, CCPA, and APPI, altogether. In particular, Figure 2 shows some of the critical components an ATS should have to be offered in a worldwide setting. In the following, we discuss some of these critical components. The consumer of such a service should be able to practice their rights such as consent withdrawing, stored data accessing, data portability and data erasure as the regulations stated. Furthermore, the consumer should be able to request not selling their data through a clear link in, eg, the ATS application's user interface.

Figure 2 An example of a simplified system model of the ATS after the consideration of the three data protection regulations we discussed in this chapter

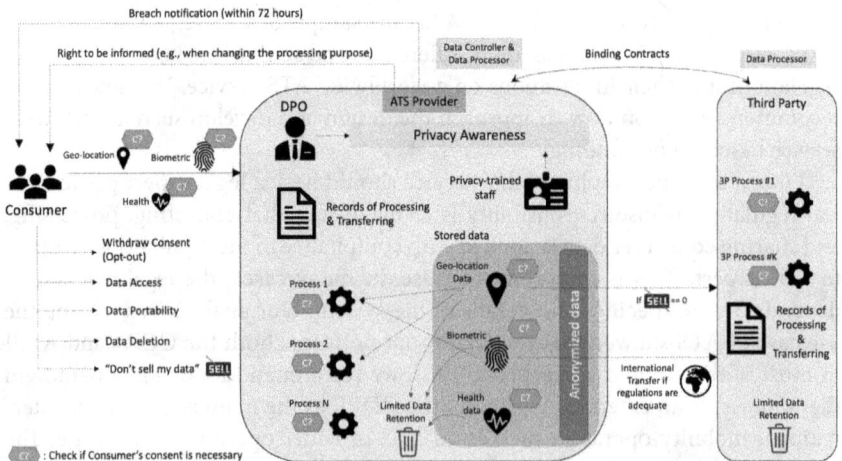

---

[33] Phillippe Golle and Kurt Partridge, 'On the Anonymity of Home/Work Location Pairs,' in the proceedings of the *International Conference on Pervasive Computing* (Springer, 2009), 390–397.

In Figure 2, we consider *collecting* personal information and sensitive data such as geolocation, biometric, and health data. The geolocation data is collected with the purpose of the core functionality of the ATS, ie, dispatching the autonomous taxicab to the requested pick up and drop off location. Biometric data might be collected for consumer identification purposes. Some health data might be monitored and collected during the ride to respond to a sudden health condition of the consumer that would require re-routing to the nearest hospital. Those are just examples of data that might be collected and the reasons for collecting each. A noteworthy remark in this regard is to ascertain a lawful basis to collect each data item whether the lawfulness is due to the data subject's consent or that it lies under the other conditions discussed in GDPR's Article 6 Paragraph (1) and summarised in Section 3.1. This entails *clearly* defining the purpose of collecting each data item to assess the lawfulness of the situation. Furthermore, the ATS provider would *process* the collected data. In this regard, the consumer should be notified with any change of the purpose of processing her data and – accordingly if the case represents a consent-based lawfulness of processing – give their consent to the new purpose of processing or withdraw it. After processing the consumer data, the ATS provider should then implement a limited data retention policy and delete all the data that is no longer needed.

The ATS provider may *store* consumers' data for further processing considering a clear and lawful purpose. The ATS provider, in this case, should inform the consumer about storing their data and for how long the data will be retained. Such information should be provided to the consumer at the time of the collection of that data. In addition, the ATS should store and anonymously process consumers' data as long as the identification of the consumer is not necessary for the service. However, in the case of a data breach, the ATS provider should inform the affected consumers within 72 hours from its discovery, while providing details on the breach as discussed earlier in this chapter. If the ATS provider wishes to *share* consumers' data with a third party, the ATS provider has to, first, make sure that a '*don't sell my data*' option is not selected by the consumer (considering CCPA), and second, the consumer is fully informed about this data transfer (considering GDPR Article 13, Paragraph (1)(f)), and, third, in case of international transfer, the data protection regulation at the receiving end is adequate. The ATS provider should keep records of data processing as the GDPR requests and records for transferring data as both the GDPR and APPI request.

Moreover, the ATS provider should appoint a DPO and train the staff to handle privacy and data protection matters such as handling a request of the consumer for data portability. All of this contributes to enhancing privacy awareness and good data protection practices within the ATS provider organisation.

VI. Further Consideration

Since we discuss data protection through the lens of ATS, it is worth noting that there exist additional regimes that should be considered when designing, generally, an automotive service. An example of these regimes is the self-regulation regime of automakers expressed in the Consumer Privacy Protection Principles (CPPPs) of the Automobile Alliance jointly with the Global Automakers Association.[34] Members of the Alliance not only commit to complying with the CPPPs, but also commit to taking reasonable steps to ensure that third-party service providers adhere to the CPPPs. The CPPPs include: transparency, choice, respect for context, data minimisation (including de-identification and retention), data security, integrity and access, and accountability. Those principles apply to the collection, usage, and sharing of personal information with respect to vehicular technologies available, eg, on leased cars to individuals in the US. Furthermore, the CPPPs give particular attention to, among others, biometrics, identifiable information, geolocation information, and driver behaviour information. Somewhat similar to the previously discussed regulations in this chapter, the CPPPs state the requirement of providing clear, meaningful notice to consumers about the collection of such information and the purposes for the collection. In addition, the CPPPs point out the need for affirmative consent when using geolocation information or biometrics for example, for marketing or sharing with third parties.

While the previous CPPPs is a self-regulatory and non-binding norm, there exist other binding norms automotive service providers should consider. Examples include, but are not limited to, the recently introduced Washington Privacy Act[35] which concerns the management and protection of personal data and the use of facial recognition services. The Act applies to any organisation that processes the personal data of 100,000 consumers or more, whether the organisation is based in Washington or targets Washington consumers. The Act will come into effect by the end of July 2021.

Additionally, New York has introduced a new privacy act, the New York Privacy Act,[36] in May 2019 which gives consumers the rights to have control over their data, such as the right to require companies to disclose their methods of de-identification. Furthermore, the New York Governor has signed the Stop Hacks and Improve Electronic Data Security Act (SHIELD Act)[37] in July 2019. The SHIELD Act applies to entities that conduct business in New York State and collect information from New York residents. The Act places a requirement of implementing reasonable security measures into effect from March 2020. The Act provides a list of measures including a program to identify external and internal risks, to assess, and to control the identified risks.

---

[34] 'Consumer Privacy Protection Principles,' Auto Alliance, 2014, https://autoalliance.org/wp-content/uploads/2017/01/Consumer_Privacy_Principlesfor_VehicleTechnologies_Services-03-21-19.pdf (last accessed 20 March 2020).

[35] Nguyen Carlyle et al, Senate Bill 6281, Washington State Legislature, 2020, lawfilesext.leg.wa.gov/biennium/2019-20/Pdf/Bills/Senate%20Bills/6281.pdf (last accessed 20 March 2020).

[36] Thomas, Carlucci, and Myrie, Senate Bill S5642-New York Privacy Act, The New York State Senate, 2019, www.nysenate.gov/legislation/bills/2019/s5642 (last accessed 22 April 2020).

[37] Thomas, Carlucci and Biaggi, 'Stop Hacks and Improve Electronic Data Security Act (SHIELD Act),' The New York Senate, 2019, https://legislation.nysenate.gov/pdf/bills/2019/S5575B (last accessed 20 March 2020).

Moreover, many countries around the world introduced and adopted data protection regulations whose territorial scopes apply beyond the physical boundaries of their countries. This puts additional challenges for service providers to comply with more regulations at once. Our recommendation here is that automotive service providers should carefully prepare for the rapidly evolving privacy and data protection regimes when developing their services. As we are moving steadily toward more privacy-friendly regulations, taking a step forward that goes beyond merely complying with the current regulations would be beneficial. This step implies designing systems that ethically and truthfully respect consumer's privacy.

In this chapter, we focus on three data protection regulations among the major automotive markets in the world. However, we discuss that such regulations are rapidly evolving worldwide. Therefore, future work should further build on the comparison introduced in this chapter by including additional acts and regulations into consideration while analysing their impact on automotive services, for example. As the impact of such regulations may differ greatly from one scenario to another, future work should consider investigating the impact of the regulations on additional scenarios and services. While we mainly focus on automotive scenarios in this chapter, our work can easily be transferred to other systems and services, that future work should address. We believe that this would ease the deployment and adoption of such regulations by service providers. An interesting venue to investigate in the future is how all these systems of law interact with each other in practice.

VII. Conclusion

In this chapter, we provided a comparison between the data protection regulations in Europe, the US, and Japan. In particular, we investigated the GDPR, the CCPA, and the APPI, respectively. We compared the previous regulations under the consideration of an automotive use case consisting of autonomous taxicab service. We argued that such a service potentially collects, processes, and shares personal and sensitive information of end-users. Therefore, we discussed the implication of each regulation on such a scenario and showed that the design of such a taxi service when considering one regulation differs from when considering another. To this end, we highlighted the challenges that face an international provider operating worldwide in designing a taxicab service that is compliant with the three regulations at once. To address the challenges, we provided recommendations and a design example taking in mind the requirements of each regulation discussed in the chapter.

Acknowledgements

The authors are grateful to Alexander Kiening, Robert Schmidt, Takesi Nakamura, and Junji Otoshi for the insightful discussions. The authors also like to thank the anonymous reviewers for their constructive feedback.

References

Alliance of Automobile Manufacturers, Inc., and Inc. Association of global automakers. 2014. 'Consumer Privacy Protection Principles.' *Auto Alliance.* November 12. Accessed 20 March 2020. https://autoalliance.org/wp-content/uploads/2017/01/Consumer_Privacy_Principlesfor_VehicleTechnologies_Services-03-21-19.pdf.

Carlyle, Nguyen, Rivers, Short, Sheldon, Wellman, Lovelett, et al. 2020. 'SENATE BILL 6281.' *Washington State Legislature.* January 14. Accessed 20 March 2020. lawfilesext.leg.wa.gov/biennium/2019-20/Pdf/Bills/Senate%20Bills/6281.pdf.

Chau, Ed, and Robert Hertzberg. 2018. 'Assembly Bill No. 375 CCPA.' *California Legislative Information.* June 29. Accessed 20 March 2020. https://leginfo.legislature.ca.gov/faces/billTextClient.xhtml?bill_id=201720180AB375.

1981. 'Confidentiality of Medical Information.' *California Legislative Information.* Accessed 21 March 2020. https://leginfo.legislature.ca.gov/faces/codes_displayexpandedbranch.xhtml?tocCode=CIV&division=1.&title=&part=2.6.&chapter=&article=.

European Commission. 2019. 'MYTHBUSTING: General Data Protection Regulation.' *European Commission website.* January. Accessed 20 March 2020. https://ec.europa.eu/commission/sites/beta-political/files/100124_gdpr_factsheet_mythbusting.pdf.

European Parliament, Council of the European Union. 2016. 'General Data Protection Regulation.' *EUR-Lex.* May 04. Accessed 20 March 2020. data.europa.eu/eli/reg/2016/679/oj.

Ghoshal, Abhimanyu. 2018. *Uber CEO: self-driving cabs will hit the streets by mid-2019.* January 24. Accessed 20 March 2020. https://thenextweb.com/insider/2018/01/24/uber-ceos-self-driving-cabs-will-hit-the-streets-by-mid-2019/.

Golle, Philippe, and Kurt Partridge. 2009. 'On the Anonymity of Home/Work Location Pairs.' *International Conference on Pervasive Computing.* (Springer) 390–397.

Gramm, Phil, and Jim Leach. 1999. 'Gramm–Leach–Bliley Act.' *US Government Publishing Office website.* Accessed 21 March 2020. www.govinfo.gov/content/pkg/STATUTE-113/pdf/STATUTE-113-Pg1338.pdf#page=1.

Helling, Brett. 2017. '2017: The Year The Rideshare Industry Crushed The Taxi.' *Rideshare Apps website.* Accessed 20 March 2020. https://rideshareapps.com/2015-rideshare-infographic/.

Hill, Kashmir. 2014. '"God View': Uber Allegedly Stalked Users For Party-Goers' Viewing Pleasure.' *Forbes.* October 3. Accessed 20 March 2020. www.forbes.com/sites/kashmirhill/2014/10/03/god-view-uber-allegedly-stalked-users-for-party-goers-viewing-pleasure/.

Hughes, Owen. 2016. 'Uber employees 'used tracking technology to stalk celebrities, politicians and ex-lovers." *International Business Times.* December 13. Accessed 20 March 2020. www.ibtimes.co.uk/former-uber-employee-reveals-drivers-used-tracking-tec hnology-stalk-celebrities-politicians-1596263.

International Trade Commission. 2016. 'Welcome to the privacy shield.' *Privacy Shield Framework.* July 12. Accessed 20 March 2020. www.privacyshield.gov/.

Kassebaum, Nancy, and Edward Kennedy. 1996. 'Health Insurance Portability and Accountability Act.' *U.S. Government Publishing Office website.* Accessed 20 March 2020. www.govinfo.gov/content/pkg/PLAW-104publ191/pdf/PLAW-104publ191.pdf.

Kumazawa, Haruhi, and Vera Jourova. 2019. 'Joint Statement by Haruhi Kumazawa, Commissioner of the Personal Information Protection Commission of Japan and Věra Jourová, Commissioner for Justice, Consumers and Gender Equality of the European

Commission.' *Personal Information Protection Commission, Government of Japan.* January 23. Accessed 20 March 2020. www.ppc.go.jp/files/pdf/310123_pressstatement_en.pdf.

Moran, Jim. 1994. 'Driver's Privacy Protection Act.' *Cornell Law School website.* Accessed 21 March 2020. www.law.cornell.edu/uscode/text/18/2725.

Murphy, Colum. 2015. 'Uber Orders Drivers in China to Steer Clear of Taxi Protests.' *The Wall Street Journal.* June 13. Accessed March 2020. www.wsj.com/articles/uber-order s-drivers-in-china-to-steer-clear-of-taxi-protests-1434181092.

Narayanan, Arvind, and Vitaly Shmatikov. 2009. 'De-anonymizing social networks.' *2009 30th IEEE symposium on security and privacy.* (Oakland, CA, USA: IEEE) 173–187.

———. 2008. 'Robust De-anonymization of Large Sparse Datasets.' *2008 IEEE Symposium on Security and Privacy (sp 2008).* (Oakland, CA, USA: IEEE) 111–125.

Nissan Co., Ltd., and Dena Co., Ltd. 2017. *Easy Ride.* Accessed March 20, 2020. https://easy-ride.com.

Noordyke, Mitchell. 2019. 'US state comprehensive privacy law comparison.' *International Association of Privacy Professionals.* April 18. Accessed 20 March 2020. https://iapp.org/news/a/us-state-comprehensive-privacy-law-comparison/.

Perry, Douglas. 2014. 'Sex and Uber's 'Rides of Glory': The company tracks your one-night stands and much more.' *Oregon Live.* November 20. Accessed 20 March 2020. www.oregonlive.com/today/index.ssf/2014/11/sex/_the/_single/_girl-/_and/_ubers.html.

Personal Information Protection Commission. 2016. 'Amended Act on the Protection of Personal Information (Tentative Translation).' *Personal Information Protection Commission, Government of Japan.* December. Accessed 20 March 2020. www.ppc.go.jp/files/pdf/Act_on_the_Protection_of_Personal_Information.pdf.

Thomas, Carlucci, and Biaggi. 2019. 'Stop Hacks and Improve Electronic Data Security Act (SHIELD Act).' *The New York Senate.* May 7. Accessed 20 March 2020. https://legislation.nysenate.gov/pdf/bills/2019/S5575B.

Thomas, Carlucci, and Myrie. 2019. 'Senate Bill S5642-New York Privacy Act.' *The New York State Senate.* May 9. Accessed 20 March 2020. https://legislation.nysenate.gov/pdf/bills/2019/S5642.

Waymo LLC. 2019. *Waymo.* Accessed 20 March 2020. https://waymo.com.

4

Misaligned Union laws? A Comparative Analysis of Certification in the Cybersecurity Act and the General Data Protection Regulation

IRENE KAMARA[1]

Abstract

In 2019, the Cybersecurity Act (CSA), the EU law aiming to achieve a high level of cybersecurity in the Union and Member States, entered into force. The CSA belongs to a broader set of Union laws providing a framework of legal protection of individual and collective rights from harmful use of information and communication technologies. Those laws introduce private law instruments for the achievement of legislative goals.[2] Despite the overarching similarities of the regulated fields, the Union legislator adopted seemingly different approaches in introducing private law instruments. This chapter seeks to comparatively present the certification frameworks as introduced in the CSA and the General Protection Regulation, with the aim to provide an understanding on the legislative choices and the normative, implementation and policy reasons underpinning the introduction of private law instruments in Union laws.

Keywords

Accreditation, assurance levels, certification, conformity assessment, cybersecurity, data protection, data security, ex ante transparency, risk-based approach, trust.

---

[1] Tilburg Institute for Law, Technology, and Society (LTMS/Tilburg Law School), Research Group on Law, Science, Technology, and Society, (Law & Criminology – Vrije Universiteit Brussel). i.kamara@tilburguniversity.edu.

[2] Codes of Conduct were already regulated in Art 17 of the Data Protection Directive 95/46/EC, but largely unused in practice. See Irene Kamara, 'Commentary Article 40' in Chrisopher Kuner, Lee Bygrave, and Christopher Docksey (eds) *The European General Data Protection Regulation (GDPR) A Commentary*, (Oxford University Press, 2020).

I. Introduction

CSA entered into force in 2019.[3] The regulation has two main pillars: the update of the mandate of ENISA as the European Union Agency for Cybersecurity, and the introduction of a framework for cybersecurity certification. The two pillars of the CSA aim at addressing the increased cybersecurity challenges, which businesses, organisations, and citizens face in the Union. The urgency for the adoption of legislation and policies in the field of cybersecurity has been spurred by technological developments that enable monitoring and surveillance of individuals, in combination with proven misuse and abuse of such technologies, as demonstrated in several cases brought before national courts, the Court of Human Rights, and the Court of Justice.[4]

In its 2013 Cybersecurity Strategy, the European Commission emphasised the need for the effective protection of citizens' rights, especially those rights enshrined in the Charter of Fundamental Rights of the European Union.[5] The CSA belongs to a series of policy and legislative endeavours of the Union to enhance its cybersecurity capacity and resilience, and arguably provide a framework of legal protection of individual and collective rights from harmful use of information and communication technologies (ICT). The CSA was adopted a few years after the Network and Information Security Directive (NIS),[6] which was a first 'essential step' for the introduction of security requirements as legal obligations.[7] Moreover, in 2018, the General Data Protection Regulation (GDPR) started applying, together with the Law Enforcement Directive (LED), and in 2017 the European Commission set forward a proposal for an ePrivacy Regulation, regulating privacy and confidentiality in electronic communications.[8]

---

[3] Regulation (EU) 2019/881 of the European Parliament and of the Council of 17 April 2019 on ENISA (the European Union Agency for Cybersecurity) and on information and communications technology cybersecurity certification and repealing Regulation (EU) No 526/2013 (Cybersecurity Act) [2019] OJ L151.

[4] Bart Van der Sloot, and Eleni Kosta, 'Big brother watch and others v UK: Lessons from the latest Strasbourg ruling on bulk surveillance' (2015) 5(2) *European Data Protection Law Review* 252–261; Judgment of the Court (Grand Chamber) of 6 October 2015. *Maximillian Schrems v Data Protection Commissioner*. Request for a preliminary ruling Case C-362/14. C:2015:650; Case C-623/17: Reference for a preliminary ruling from the Investigatory Powers Tribunal – London (United Kingdom) made on 31 October 2017 – *Privacy International v Secretary of State for Foreign and Commonwealth Affairs and Others*.

[5] Joint Communication to the European Parliament, the Council, the European Economic and Social Committee and the Committee of the Regions, 'Cybersecurity Strategy of the European Union: An Open, Safe and Secure Cyberspace' 7.2.2013 JOIN (2013) final, 3.

[6] Network and Information Security Directive (2016) Directive (EU) 2016/1148 of the European Parliament and of the Council of 6 July 2016 concerning measures for a high common level of security of network and information systems across the Union [2016] OJ L194.

[7] European Commission, explanatory memorandum CSA.

[8] Regulation (EU) 2016/679 of the European Parliament and of the Council of 27 April 2016 on the protection of natural persons with regard to the processing of personal data and on the free movement of such data, and repealing Directive 95/46/EC (General Data Protection Regulation, [2016] OJ L119;

From a legal design perspective, the new Union laws for the protection of personal data and information, present a relative novelty of introducing inter alia private law instruments for the achievement of their legislative goals. Technical specifications, standards, and certifications, were previously in the shadow of 'information protection laws' in the Union. Certifications in particular were largely developed in areas that were not harmonised under Union law.[9] The choice of the legislator to utilise those instruments emanates from a need to regulate tools that already existed in the market,[10] but also leverage the accumulated experience from using such instruments and direct it to specific legislative goals such as demonstrating compliance with legal obligations or enhancing the harmonised effects of the Union law. Those instruments are in essence voluntary, with the potential to influence whether and how regulatees comply with the corresponding law.

The aim of this chapter is to provide an understanding of the legislative choices and the normative, implementation and policy reasons underpinning the introduction of private law instruments in Union laws. The chapter therefore seeks to analyse certification as introduced in the CSA and the General Protection Regulation. The two laws are selected because of their explicit legal provisions on such instruments, the time proximity with which they were adopted, and their legal classification as Regulations. The underlying assumption of the article is that because of the link between the legislation on cybersecurity and protection of personal data, which can be broadly framed as serving (among other goals) a goal of protecting information,[11] the two laws would follow a similar approach with regard to private law instruments.[12] Even more, if one considers that the entities legally obliged to comply with the cybersecurity and data protection legislation are very often the same. Therefore, an aligned approach towards certification in these laws would allow for common requirements and mutual recognition of certifications. On the other hand, issues may arise from divergent approaches; market 'pollution'[13] and legal uncertainty among the regulatees, potential conflicting

---

Directive (EU) 2016/680 of the European Parliament and of the Council of 27 April 2016 on the protection of natural persons with regard to the processing of personal data by competent authorities for the purposes of the prevention, investigation, detection or prosecution of criminal offences or the execution of criminal penalties, and on the free movement of such data, and repealing Council Framework Decision 2008/977/JHA [2016] OJ L119; Proposal of the European Parliament and of the Council concerning the respect for private life and the protection of personal data in electronic communications and repealing Directive 2002/58/EC (Regulation on Privacy and Electronic Communications) COM/2017/010 final.

[9] Andreas Mitrakas, 'The emerging EU framework on cybersecurity certification' (2018) 42(7) *Datenschutz und Datensicherheit-DuD* 411–414.

[10] Gerrit Hornung, 'A General Data Protection Regulation for Europe: Light and Shade in the Commission's Draft of 25 January 2012' (2012) 9 *SCRIPTed* 9 64.

[11] See s 5.3, 13f.

[12] This shared goal and intersection between the CSA and the GDPR is evident from policy documents such as the Commission Evaluation Report for the two years of GDPR application COM (2020) 264 final, 10.

[13] See Irene Kamara, Ronald Leenes, et al 'Data protection certification mechanisms: Study on Articles 42 and 43 of the Regulation (EU) 2016/679. Annexes' Publications Office of the EU (2019), Annex 6.

requirements following CSA and GDPR certifications on similar subject matters, increased costs, and ultimately undermining of the goal of certification as a transparency, trust, and harmonisation instrument.

The chapter follows an analytical legal comparative method, comparing the rules on certification in the CSA and the GDPR.[14] The development and governance of certifications serves as *tertium comparationis*. The aims of the chapter require not only to target the differences or similarities of the compared rules, but identify both aspects for a comprehensive in-depth understanding of both certification frameworks. Moreover, the chapter does not claim to provide a systematic analysis of the certification frameworks, which means that some procedural or other aspects are not included in the analysis, nor does it assess the strengths and weaknesses of each framework in achieving its intended legislative goals. Last, whereas there is value in general in exploring other private law instruments such as codes of conduct, the chapter's scope is focused on certification and does not extend to such other instruments.

The chapter is structured as follows. First, the certification frameworks in the CSA and following that the GDPR are presented in Sections II and III. Sections IV and V provide the comparative analysis of the certification frameworks in the CSA and GDPR and elements of divergence and convergence respectively. Section VI provides the discussion on the findings and responds to the research questions of the chapter, and Section VII summarises and concludes the article.

II. The European Cybersecurity Certification Framework in the Cybersecurity Act

The CSA establishes a framework for the development and operational life cycle of cybersecurity certification schemes. Besides the identified need for bottom-up governance and dynamic stakeholder regulation,[15] the Cybersecurity certification framework addresses a need for a common approach in the Union and horizontal requirements for European cybersecurity.[16] Common measures ensure that the capabilities of every actor in the chain of, for example, an ICT service are transparent, auditable, and comparable. This aspect is of relevance in particular to cybersecurity, due to the high degree of interdependence of ICT products, processes, and services on third party technologies and components.[17] At the same time, common requirements across the Union would eliminate companies' costs for recertification in each Member State.

---

[14] Mark Van Hoecke, 'Methodology of comparative legal research' [2015] *Law and method* 1–35.

[15] Rolf H Weber and Evelyne Studer, 'Cybersecurity in the Internet of Things: Legal aspects' (2016) 32(5) *Computer Law & Security Review* 715–728.

[16] Recital 69, CSA.

[17] Recital 10, CSA.

The CSA provides an elaborate framework on certification. The drafting of certification schemes,[18] the governance, the supervision of the granted certifications, and other aspects of certification are outlined in the legal provisions in a detailed manner, one that does not leave much room for manoeuvre to certification bodies and Member States. To some extent, this was a necessary step mandated by the nature of cybersecurity and the need for coherent measures across the chain of components and lifecycle of the product, process, or service, since one vulnerability or inconsistency might be enough to undermine the overall level of security. The prescriptive nature of the framework received criticism during the preparatory works in the law-making process.[19] The Commission proposal followed a much more defined/regulated model than the one adopted, in line with the New Legislative Framework and harmonised standards.

As per the framework itself, two phases can be distinguished: the development of the schemes and the implementation (governance) phase, after a certification scheme is adopted. Main actors in the development phase are the Commission and ENISA, with the support of various stakeholders, while in the implementation phase national cybersecurity certification authorities and certification bodies take on the significant roles of granting and supervising certifications.

A. Development of European Cybersecurity Certification Schemes

The procedure for the development and adoption of a cybersecurity scheme is initiated by the European Commission, which requests ENISA to prepare a European cybersecurity certification candidate scheme. The Commission request

---

[18] In the CSA, a European cybersecurity certification scheme is defined as a 'comprehensive set of rules, technical requirements, standards and procedures that are established at Union level and that apply to the certification or conformity assessment of specific ICT products, ICT services or ICT processes' Art 2(9), CSA. More broadly, international standards define a conformity assessment scheme (one type of which are certification schemes) as 'rules, procedures and management for carrying out conformity assessment' 'elated to specified objects of conformity assessment, to which the same specified requirements, specific rules and procedures apply'. See ISO/IEC 17000 Conformity assessment – Vocabulary and general principles.

[19] European Commission, Proposal for a Regulation of the European Parliament and of the Council on ENISA, the 'EU Cybersecurity Agency', and Repealing Regulation (EU) 526/2013, and on Information and Communication Technology Cybersecurity Certification ('Cybersecurity Act'), COM (2017) 477 final; Criticism on the Commission proposal (2017) Kai Peters 'Cybersecurity Act: EU must do better!' VDMA blog, www.vdma.org/en/v2viewer/-/v2article/render/24584915 (last accessed 31 March 2020). Read on the New Legislative Framework: Linda Senden, 'The Constitutional Fit of European Standardization Put to the Test.' (2017) 44(4) *Legal Issues of Economic Integration* 337–352; Carlo Colombo, and Mariolina Eliantonio, 'Harmonized technical standards as part of EU law: Juridification with a number of unresolved legitimacy concerns? Case C-613/14 James Elliot Construction Limited v. Irish Asphalt Limited, EU: C: 2016: 821.' (2017) 24(2) *Maastricht Journal of European and Comparative Law* 323–340.

is in principle based on the Union rolling work programme,[20] which is an annual Commission publication outlining strategic priorities for cybersecurity certification schemes.[21] The Commission or the European Cybersecurity Certification Group (ECCG) may also request ENISA to prepare a candidate scheme that is not based on the Union rolling work programme, but in this case the request should be 'duly justified'.[22] It should be noted that despite what the use of the wording 'request' implies, ENISA is obliged ('shall') to follow the Commission's 'request' and prepare a candidate scheme.[23] This is not the case however for the ECCG request, the acceptance of which lies at the discretion of ENISA.[24] ENISA prepares the candidate schemes, with the assistance of an ad hoc working group and the ECCG, which provides non-binding expert advice. Once the draft candidate scheme is finalised, ENISA submits it to the Commission, which has the power to adopt it with an implementing act.[25]

When preparing the candidate scheme, ENISA is not entirely free to decide on its content. On top of the goals and requirements outlined in the request, the basic yet essential elements of European cybersecurity certification schemes are provided in a non-exhaustive list in the regulation.[26] The legislator aimed at ensuring in this way that all the schemes share a common structure and address the same significant issues. The manner in which they address those issues will inevitably differ depending on the scope, sector and context of the scheme.

Certification schemes provide requirements, on the basis of which the level of cybersecurity of an ICT product, ICT process, or ICT service may be assessed. The schemes to be established under the European cybersecurity certification framework need to be designed to achieve a minimum number of security goals, provided in Article 51, CSA, such as for example security by default[27] and protection of data against accidental or unauthorised storage, processing, access or disclosure.[28] To better determine the level of assurance of the European cybersecurity schemes, the regulation provides for different assurance levels – basic, substantial, high – that correspond to the level of risk associated with the intended

---

[20] Art 48(1), CSA.

[21] Art 47(1), CSA.

[22] The experience so far shows that the legal standard for this justification is not prohibitively high, since two certification schemes are currently being prepared before the adoption of the first Union rolling Work program: See ENISA www.enisa.europa.eu/news/enisa-news/enisa-cybersecurity-certification-preparation-underway (last accessed 31 March 2020).

[23] Art 49(1), CSA.

[24] Art 49(2), CSA '[..]ENISA *may* prepare a candidate scheme [...]' (emphasis added).

[25] Read further on implementing acts: Steve Peers and Marios Costa, 'Accountability for delegated and implementing acts after the Treaty of Lisbon' (2012) 18(3) *European Law Journal* 427–460.

[26] Art 54, CSA. Those include elements such as the subject matter and scope of the scheme, the type or categories of ICT products, systems, services covered, the purpose of the scheme, references to technical standards or specifications, the possibility for conformity self-assessment, additional accreditation requirements for conformity assessment bodies, specific evaluation criteria, the use of marks and labels, rules for monitoring compliance, conditions for the certificates, and others.

[27] Art 51(1)(i), CSA.

[28] Art 51(1)(a), CSA.

use of the ICT product, ICT process, or ICT service. Quite remarkable is the standstill obligation, similar to what exists in European standardisation and harmonised standards: national schemes cease to produce effects, once a European cybersecurity scheme is adopted with the same scope.[29]

B. Governance of European Cybersecurity Certification Schemes

Once a certification scheme is adopted by the European Commission and published in the Official Journal, the competent entities may start working to make it operational, so that manufacturers or providers can apply and have their products, processes, or services certified. Before explaining how the implementation phase works, a remark is in order. While the framework primarily refers to third party conformity assessment (certification), it does allow manufacturers or providers to assess their own ICT product, process, or service following the requirements of the certification scheme and issue an EU statement of conformity.[30] Conformity self-assessment is allowed only for low risk ICT products, processes, and services (basic assurance level). The EU statement of fulfillment is not a certificate, but a self-declaration of conformity, binding for the issuing manufacturer or provider, who 'assumes responsibility for the compliance' and can be held accountable for it.[31] In terms of effects however, a certificate is always more reliable than an EU statement of fulfillment, since it involves an assessment from an independent third party.

Certification is offered in principle by certification bodies, which are private organisations. Certification bodies need to be accredited by the national accreditation body in the Member States of their establishment.[32] Accreditation is a necessary condition for the competence of a certification body to provide services on the European cybersecurity certification scheme. In exceptional cases, the regulation provides that the national competent cybersecurity certification authority may also issue certifications. This power of the national authorities is introduced as a derogation to the general rule that certification bodies issue certificates, but the conditions are not further specified in the regulation.[33] Interestingly, the legislator does not presume the competence of national authorities to issue certificates; like certification bodies, the authorities must be accredited as conformity assessment bodies.[34]

---

[29] Art 57(1), CSA.
[30] Art 53, CSA.
[31] Recital 81, CSA.
[32] Art 7(1), Regulation 765/2008 of the European Parliament and of the Council of 9 July 2008 setting out the requirements for accreditation and market surveillance relating to the marketing of products and repealing Regulation (EEC) No 339/93 OJ L218.
[33] Art 56(5)(a), CSA.
[34] Art 60(2), CSA.

Natural and legal persons that are manufacturers or providers of ICT products, ICT services, or ICT processes qualify as applicants for European cybersecurity certification.[35] The CSA gives the opportunity to both types of entities to apply, recognising an interest for being awarded a cybersecurity certification. Manufacturers and providers may apply for cybersecurity certification to the conformity assessment body of their choice anywhere in the Union.[36] Thus, a legal person is not bound by some territoriality criterion such as the jurisdiction of the main establishment, as long as it is established in the Union. The risk of forum-shopping, ie applicants applying to the conformity assessment body with the most favourable or lenient approach, is expected to be mitigated by the fact that those certification bodies follow the same rules, a common baseline, which is the European cybersecurity certification scheme. This offers some guarantees that differences in the approaches of the certification bodies, will not be detrimental to the quality of the evaluation outcomes, thus achieving a common or comparable quality level. In addition, the obligation for a peer review mechanism, which subjects all the national cybersecurity authorities to evaluations by their 'peers' namely the competent authorities of the other MS, is an additional safeguard against forum-shopping.

Certifications are issued to the applicants after a successful evaluation by the conformity assessment body, based on the requirements and the evaluation methods and standards described in the scheme.[37] The validity of the certifications is different from scheme to scheme. Some certifications need to have a short validity period, as the schemes require regular revisions to keep up with technological developments that might render the requirements and methods prescribed in those schemes obsolete. Others, for example relating to organisational issues and management, might have a longer expiration date.[38] Responsible for the supervision and enforcement are the certification bodies and the national cybersecurity certification authorities,[39] which also handle complaints against issued certificates.[40]

---

[35] Recital 97, CSA.

[36] ibid.

[37] Art 54(1) (b), (c), and (g), CSA.

[38] Common criteria, which are a well-accepted certification in the information security market, provide a distinction between technical validity of the issued certificates and administrative validity. Administrative validity is 'related to administrative tasks such as advertising of certificates on a Certified Products List and archiving of evaluation evidence'; technical validity relates to the resistance of the certified product to attacks. While the administrative validity period of the certificate is 5 years, it is interesting that in relation to the technical validity is stated that: '[...], certificates can only be considered technically valid at their time of issuance. Indeed, because the evolution of the state-of-the-art regarding attack methods cannot be predicted, there can be no time period associated to the technical validity of a certificate.' See SOG-IS Recognition Agreement Management Committee, 'SOG-IS certificate validity v1.0.doc', version 1, (no date) www.sogis.eu/documents/mra/SOG-IS-certificate-validity-v1.0.pdf.

[39] Art 58(7)(a), (b), (e), CSA.

[40] Arts 58(7)(h) and 63(1), CSA.

III. The Data Protection Certification Mechanisms in the General Data Protection Regulation

The GDPR introduces personal data protection certification in Articles 42 and 43. Article 42 provides rules and characteristics of certification, the 'data protection certification mechanisms', while Article 43 is mostly dedicated to the bodies providing certification services. The rationale for introducing certification in the reformed EU data protection law is described in Recital 100:

> In order to enhance transparency and compliance with this Regulation, the establishment of certification mechanisms and data protection seals and marks should be encouraged, allowing data subjects to quickly assess the level of data protection of relevant products and services.[41]

Certification per Article 42(1) has a twofold function. To assist the regulatees, eg data controllers and processors, demonstrate how they comply with the law, and to offer insights into the activities of the controllers and processors to the individuals whose data are processed (data subjects). The help towards regulatees to comply with the law and demonstrate this via certification to supervisory authorities is envisioned to materialise in several manners, for example with certifications that 'translate' legal obligations to tangible controls, measures, and policies for organisations, or adapt requirements to needs and specificities of different sectors.

The legislative history of the provision (former Article 39 in the Commission proposal) reveals a multitude of rationales and approaches, ranging from a stringent certification system with strong oversight in the European Parliament First Reading 2014 version to some looser system where public and private actors intertwine in the Council General Approach (Articles 39 and 39a). The final text of the GDPR is a compromise among different visions of the EU co-legislators.[42] It retains the oversight by the independent data protection authorities (DPAs), which was an element of the Parliament version, but it also allows private entities – that is certification bodies – in parallel to the DPAs, to grant certifications. The Commission and the Member States are obliged to encourage the development of certifications, which are voluntary per Article 42(1).

A. Development of Data Protection Certifications

The GDPR envisages both national and European certifications. The former concern a national jurisdiction of a Member State, whereas the European

---

[41] Recital 100, GDPR.

[42] Irene Kamara and Paul De Hert, 'Data protection certification in the EU: Possibilities, actors and building blocks in a reformed landscape' In Rowena Rodrigues and Vagelis Papakonstantinou (eds) *Privacy and data protection seals* (TMC Asser Press, 2018) 7–34.

certifications (European Data Protection Seals) are pan-European and supervised by the European Data Protection Board. The development of data protection certification is not prescribed in the GDPR. The drafting of a certification scheme, including the criteria to be used for assessing the conformity of the data processing operation, may therefore be performed by any interested entity. Certification bodies, standardisation bodies, industry or industry consortia, consumer associations may draft certification criteria. Supervisory authorities may take on such a role as well. However, this possibility has raised concerns for risks of function creep, competition among DPA-run certifications, and overburden the resources of the authorities.[43]

Since, the GDPR data protection certifications are multi-layered constructs,[44] there are more stages in the development thereof. The competent data protection authority for national certifications or the European Data Protection Board for EU level certifications are tasked to approve the criteria of the candidate schemes. It is questionable whether the supervisory authorities should be restricted by a literal interpretation of their task and limit the assessment and approval to the 'criteria' only, or instead conduct a comprehensive examination of the certification mechanism as a whole. The latter would seem the most reasonable approach towards securing the quality and reliability of data protection certifications. The process and act of approval can be viewed as a balancing factor to the complete lack of limitations in the GDPR on *which actor* drafts the criteria. Since any interested party can draft criteria for certification, the burden of the DPA to assess and approve the criteria is of paramount importance for the quality of the resulting certification. After a certification mechanism is developed and received the approval of the supervisory authority, it is published in a publicly available register, maintained by the EDPB.[45] Additionally, supervisory authorities are tasked to publish certification criteria per Article 42(5) and the accreditation requirements for certification bodies per Article 43(3) and transmit both criteria and requirements to the Board.[46]

B. Governance of Data Protection Certifications

Certifications per Article 42, GDPR are voluntary but do not reduce the responsibility of a data controller or processor to comply with the legal obligations, neither do they offer a presumption of conformity with the law. The supervisory

[43] Rowena Rodrigues, David Barnard-Wills, Paul De Hert, and Vagelis Papakonstantinou. 'The future of privacy certification in Europe: an exploration of options under article 42 of the GDPR' (2016) 30(3) *International Review of Law, Computers & Technology* 248–270.

[44] Ronald Leenes, 'Commentary Article 42' in Chrisopher Kuner, Lee Bygrave, and Christopher Docksey (eds) *The European General Data Protection Regulation (GDPR) A Commentary*, (Oxford University Press, 2020) 739.

[45] Art 42(8), GDPR.

[46] Art 43(6), GDPR.

authorities maintain their regular supervisory powers for compliance with the GDPR, independently of a certification granted to a controller or a processor.[47] Two types of entities/persons qualify to apply for certification: data controllers and processors. The legislator intentionally refers to persons that are involved in the processing of personal data, and thus excludes manufacturers, due to the material scope of the regulation.[48]

The procedure for an entity to apply and be awarded certification follows stages that are familiar to practitioners working in conformity assessment.[49] Depending on the Member State, certification bodies and/or data protection supervisory authorities conduct the evaluation of the application and issue certifications. When the certification process is conducted by a certification body, this body needs to be an accredited one. The GDPR provides three models for the accreditation of certification bodies.[50] Accreditation may be conducted by the competent supervisory authority, the National Accreditation Body (NAB) with the support of the supervisory authority, or both. In practice, most Member States followed one of the models that involves the NAB,[51] presumably due to the accumulated experience of the NAB to conduct assessments on the independence, integrity, competence, and overall suitability of a conformity assessment body to conduct assessments in a given field following standards and certification schemes.

The assessment is conducted against the set of certification criteria approved by the competent supervisory authority or the EDPB. The applicant is obliged to provide the certification body with all relevant information and provide access to its activities, thus to facilitate the assessment.[52] A successful assessment leads to awarding certification, and issuing a certificate (seal and mark) to the applicant. The GDPR places the responsibility for ensuring a proper assessment on certification bodies, when those are issuing the certification.[53] There is no indication in the GDPR, however, on how the assessment should take place, what constitutes a sufficient assessment result and whether some non-conformities should be accepted. Those issues could therefore differ from certification to certification. The European Data Protection Board has stressed the importance of using appropriate evaluation methods (documentation, onsite visits, etc) and adjusting the

---

[47] Art 42(4), GDPR.

[48] Art 2(1), GDPR provides: 'This Regulation applies to the processing of personal data wholly or partly by automated means and to the processing other than by automated means of personal data which form part of a filing system or are intended to form part of a filing system.'

[49] ISO/IEC 17065:2012 Conformity assessment – Requirements for bodies certifying products, processes and services. See Figure 2.

[50] Read further on the accreditation models in the GDPR in Kamara, Leenes, et al 'Data protection certification mechanisms' (n 13) 102f.

[51] See survey among Data Protection Authorities and National Accreditation Bodies, Irene Kamara et al (n 13) Annexes (2019).

[52] Art 42(6), GDPR.

[53] Art 43(4), GDPR.

depth and granularity of the certification procedures to the target of evaluation.[54] Supervisory authorities and certification bodies after informing the authorities, have the power to renew[55] and withdraw certifications.[56] Withdrawal of a certification occurs upon the expiration after a three year period from the issuing of the certificate or prematurely when the criteria for certification are not met or due to changes to the conditions under which the assessment took place, the criteria are no longer met.[57]

IV. Divergence

The description of the CSA and the GDPR frameworks already reveals differences on a number of aspects. This section comparatively presents such aspects with a view to understanding the specific elements of divergence in the models, which are more in depth analysed in Section VI.

A. Centralised Versus Decentralised Approach

The certification frameworks in the CSA and the GDPR follow a different approach in relation to the development and the territorial outreach of the certificates. The CSA cybersecurity certification framework adopts a centralised approach, with the Commission and ENISA playing pivotal roles in the development and publication of candidate schemes. The GDPR certification framework is a largely decentralised system. Any interested entity may draft schemes and submit them for approval to competent authorities at national level. While the intention of the legislator to stir developments at Union level is there – the possibility for a European Data Protection Seal with the involvement of the European Data Protection Board – the GDPR certification framework is primarily designed around national certifications and a multitude of scheme drafters.[58] The CSA framework involves several parties as well, but with a primarily advisory role in the development process. Examples are the European Cybersecurity Certification Group (ECCG), and the

---

[54] European Data Protection Board, 'Guidelines 1/2018 on certification and identifying certification criteria in accordance with Articles 42 and 43 of the Regulation', v.3 2019.

[55] Art 43(1), GDPR.

[56] Arts 43(5) and 58(2)(h), GDPR.

[57] Art 42(7), GDPR.

[58] The legislative intention for a centralised system, was also apparent in the Commission Proposal (2012), according to which (Art 39(2)): 'The Commission shall be empowered to adopt delegated acts in accordance with Article 86 for the purpose of further specifying the criteria and requirements for the data protection certification mechanisms referred to in paragraph 1, including conditions for granting and withdrawal, and requirements for recognition within the Union and in third countries.' However, the Parliament First Reading was in favour of more elaborate provisions, and proposed the limitation of the Commission powers to adopt legislative acts. Read further: Kamara and De Hert (n 42) (2018).

ad hoc working groups, advising and assisting ENISA to develop the candidate schemes. Further, priority is assigned to European cybersecurity certifications over national ones, with an explicit legal provision. The 'standstill' obligation of Article 57 CSA, according to which national certifications cease to produce effects and MS are not allowed to introduce new national cybersecurity certification schemes for ICT products, services, and processes that are already covered by a European cybersecurity certification scheme, demonstrates the centralised approach of the CSA framework. In the GDPR, only the consistency of national certifications with European Data Protection Seals can be assumed.[59] There is no formal prioritisation of the common certification, the European Data Protection Seal, over the national ones, and in principle different certification schemes with the same scope may co-exist at national and Union level.

B. Risk-based Approach and Scalability in Certification

The CSA cybersecurity certification framework is admittedly more granular than the GDPR certification mechanisms. First, it provides for both conformity self-assessments and third party certifications. Second, it provides for assurance levels.[60] As regards self-assessments, the option for manufacturers and service providers to self-assess their conformity to the requirements of the cybersecurity scheme and issue a statement of conformity did not exist in the Commission Proposal,[61] but was introduced in the Parliament First Reading.[62] Two elements stand out; one is that conformity self-assessments are allowed only for low risk ICT products, services and processes, and they need to be explicitly allowed by the scheme itself.[63] The other element is that compliance with the self-assessments is monitored from the national cybersecurity supervisory authorities.[64] The GDPR allows only third party certifications in the scope of Article 42. An intention for scalability of some sort is revealed in Article 42(1), which provides that 'the specific needs of micro, small and medium-sized enterprises shall be taken into

---

[59] Art 63, GDPR.

[60] Assurance levels are defined in Art 2(21), CSA as 'basis for confidence that an ICT product, ICT service or ICT process meets the security requirements of a specific European cybersecurity certification scheme, indicates the level at which an ICT product, ICT service or ICT process has been evaluated but as such does not measure the security of the ICT product, ICT service or ICT process concerned'.

[61] Proposal for a Regulation of the European parliament and of the Council on ENISA, the 'EU Cybersecurity Agency', and repealing Regulation (EU) 526/2013, and on Information and Communication Technology cybersecurity certification ("Cybersecurity Act") COM (2017) 0477 final.

[62] European Parliament legislative resolution of 12 March 2019 on the proposal for a regulation of the European Parliament and of the Council on ENISA, the 'EU Cybersecurity Agency', and repealing Regulation (EU) 526/2013, and on Information and Communication Technology cybersecurity certification ("Cybersecurity Act") (COM (2017) 0477 – C8-0310/2017–2017/0225(COD)).

[63] Art 53(1), CSA.

[64] Art 58(7)(b), CSA.

account'. However, this intention is not further supported in the design of the framework, neither elaborated in the regulation. The EDPB has attempted to flesh out this obligation by explaining that certification criteria should be flexible and scalable for application to different sizes and types of organisations, adopting a risk-based approach.[65] The EDPB provided the example of a local retailer that would probably carry out 'less complex processing operations' than a multinational retailer.[66] Nevertheless, SMEs owning a health tracking or a geolocation app such as the ones being adopted by several governments recently due to the COVID19 pandemic,[67] are likely to conduct as risky data processing as large enterprises. Thus, the size of the organisation does not rule out automatically the high risk of processing factor.

When it comes to assurance levels in the CSA certification framework, those are a good example of a risk-based approach, since the assurance levels are proportionate to 'the level of risk associated with the intended use' of ICT products, services or processes.[68] Interesting here is the weight on the 'intended use'. The product, service, or process is evaluated considering the environment and context in which it is intended to be used, to ensure a more 'reliable and fine-grained description of the security level'.[69] Since manufacturers may apply for certification of their products, the assessment is possible only on an intended use instead of actual use, since the latter is known after the ICT product is purchased. At the same time, this focus on the intention reveals the limitations of certification, which does not offer an image of the risks stemming from the actual use. Developing a certification taking account the *use* and the operational environment, while possible, will not be part of the same evaluation process and certification.[70]

Overall, the establishment of assurance levels in the CSA demonstrates the granular approach in full, as first, the assurance level is related to the level of the risk,[71] and provides the 'rigour and depth of the evaluation',[72] second, depending

---

[65] Recital 77 GDPR. EDPB Guidelines (2019) 20.

[66] ibid.

[67] See examples of Dutch (*NL Times*, 8 April 2020: https://nltimes.nl/2020/04/08/govt-plan-use-apps-track-covid-19-raises-privacy-concerns), UK (*Forbes*, 12 April 2020: www.forbes.com/sites/davidphelan/2020/04/12/covid-19-uk-government-unveils-contact-tracing-phone-app-as-next-step-in-fighting-disease/), and Australian Governments (*The Guardian*, 14 April 2020: www.theguardian.com/australia-news/2020/apr/14/australian-government-plans-to-bring-in-mobile-phone-app-to-track-people-with-coronavirus).

[68] Recital 78, CSA. Those were not introduced without scepticism from the market and standardisation bodies: ETSI, ETSI Position Paper on draft Regulation 2017/0225 "Cybersecurity Act" (2018). www.etsi.org/images/files/ETSI_position_paper-CyberAct_20180206.pdf.

[69] Sara N Matheu, Jose L Hernandez-Ramos, and Antonio F. Skarmeta. 'Toward a cybersecurity certification framework for the Internet of Things' (2019) 17(3) *IEEE Security & Privacy* 70.

[70] ENISA, 'Advancing Software Security in the EU – The role of the EU cybersecurity certification framework' (2019) 11.

[71] Recital 78, CSA.

[72] Recital 86, CSA.

on assurance level, certifications may be issued by public or private authorities,[73] and third, a certification scheme may provide for different assurance levels.[74]

C. Legal Effects and Penalties

A third significant point of divergence between the two frameworks concerns the legal effects of the granted certifications. While in both frameworks, certifications demonstrate compliance with the requirements included in the scheme,[75] and not directly the legislation as such, the CSA leaves the latter open as a possibility. In Article 54, CSA it is provided that a European Cybersecurity certificate or an EU statement of conformity issued under such a scheme 'may be used to demonstrate the presumption of conformity with requirements of that legal act', where a specific Union legal act provides it.[76] This practically entails a reversal of burden of proof, whereby the certification holder is presumed to comply with the law and the counter party needs to prove the opposite. In addition, the CSA cybersecurity schemes may become mandatory in some areas for specific ICT products, services, or processes.[77] On the other hand, as mentioned earlier,[78] the GDPR explicitly provides that certifications are voluntary and do not reduce the responsibility of the regulatees to comply with the legislation.[79] In case of a violation of an obligation, a controller or processor which are certification holders, still have to demonstrate the measures they took to comply with the law. The presence of certification does not reverse the burden of proof and does not offer any benefit of presumed compliance with the law. The ultimate purpose of data protection certifications is in broad terms to offer transparency for data subjects[80] and indirectly in the long term enhance compliance with the law, since the certification criteria are based on the GDPR. Although not provided in the GDPR, the Article 29 Data Protection Working Party had supported the view that 'non-compliance with self-regulatory measures could also reveal the controller's/ processor's negligence or intentional behaviour of non-compliance'.[81]

Moreover, there is a substantial difference between the two certification frameworks when it comes to penalties: the GDPR introduces a (high) upper limit for administrative fines for violation of the obligations of a certification body in

---

[73] Recital 77, CSA.
[74] Recital 87, CSA.
[75] Art 42(1), GDPR, Art 46(2), CSA.
[76] Art 54(3), CSA.
[77] Recital 92 CSA.
[78] See 3.2.
[79] Art 42(3), (4), GDPR.
[80] Recital 100, GDPR.
[81] Art 29, Data Protection Working Party 'Guidelines on the application and setting of administrative fines for the purposes of the Regulation 2016/679' WP 253 (October 2017), 16. Read further Paul Nemitz, 'Fines under the GDPR' in Ronald Leenes et al (eds) *Data Protection and Privacy: The Internet of Bodies*. (Hart Publishing, 2018).

Article 83(4)(b). This provision places a great responsibility on how certification bodies carry out their tasks, living up to requirements such as independence, integrity, and proper expertise.[82] Furthermore, the same goes for controllers and processors that violate their obligations pursuant to certifications per Articles 42 and 43, GDPR. Thus, when those entities have violated in any manner the conditions of the granted certification they are subject to the administrative fines imposed by the data protection authorities. In the case of the CSA, national cybersecurity certification authorities are competent to audit certification bodies, take appropriate measures in case of violations, and also supervise and enforce the rules of certification schemes against manufacturers and service providers,[83] including imposing penalties.[84] However, the amount of those administrative fines is at the discretion of each Member State,[85] leading to potentially a wide range of pecuniary penalties. Despite the overall centralised approach, this 'open clause' in the CSA might pierce the veil of harmonisation and undermine the guarantees to prevent forum-shopping offered by the common baseline rules,[86] which is a substantial difference with the GDPR certification framework.

V. Convergence

The previous section discussed differences of the cybersecurity and the data protection certification frameworks, which point towards a divergent approach in the two regulations, creating a gap between the frameworks that seems difficult to be bridged. This section focuses on the commonalities. One cannot speak of identical or tantamount elements, but it can be said with certainty that the data protection and the cybersecurity frameworks demonstrate aspects of convergence.

A. Ex Ante Transparency

Taking one step back from the specific elements of each framework and reflecting on the rationales for introducing certification in the CSA and the GDPR, there is an underlying concept present in both frameworks: transparency; or rather, ex ante transparency.[87] Certification is traditionally seen as an instrument offering

---

[82] Arts 43(2)(a-e) and 43(1)(b), GDPR.
[83] Art 58(7)(a), CSA.
[84] Art 58(8)(b-c) and (f), CSA.
[85] Art 65, CSA.
[86] See s 2.2, 5f.
[87] Spagnuelo et al, characterised GDPR certifications as an ex ante transparency and awareness tool, helping users being aware of policies and practices, but not providing users with controls over the processing of data. Dayana Spagnuelo, Ana Ferreira, and Gabriele Lenzini, 'Accomplishing transparency within the general data protection regulation.' In *5th International Conference on Information Systems Security and Privacy* (2018) 6.

transparency and increasing trust towards the certified object and organisation, as it may reduce information asymmetry in contracting parties, offer insights for audit purposes, and assure the reliability of the counterpart seller, manufacturer, service provider.[88]

A certification first and foremost provides information to individuals, businesses, or the supervisory authorities about the certified data processing operations or the ICT product/service/process. Information is provided after the evaluation from an independent body, which offers more guarantees for the reliability of the provided information[89] than a self-declaration.[90] The GDPR certification framework, as mentioned earlier, explicitly assigns such a role to data protection certifications, especially helping data subjects assess the processing of controllers and processors.[91] The CSA framework also refers to certification as offering transparency and awareness to citizens, organisations and businesses in relation to cybersecurity issues and practices.[92] The EDPB explained that documentation and communication of the results is important for certification to achieve the transparency goal, and recommended that at least the description of what was certified, the applicable criteria, the evaluation methodology and the duration of the certification should be public information.[93] The prerequisite for a certification to function as a transparency tool is transparency of the certification (scope, evaluation methodology, criteria, complaint mechanisms etc) itself, as hinted in Article 42(3) GDPR.

Interestingly, both frameworks relate certification to embedding cybersecurity and data protection requirements 'by design'. In the CSA framework, security by design and the security requirements being fulfilled 'during the entire lifecycle of the ICT product, ICT service or ICT process' are provided as security objectives of the cybersecurity certifications.[94] The requirement that manufacturers qualify as applicants for certification enables the security by design approach. When a

---

[88] Konrad Stahl and Roland Strausz, 'Certification and market transparency' (2017) 84(4) *The Review of Economic Studies* 1842–1868; Ali Sunyaev and Stephan Schneider, 'Cloud services certification' (2013) 56(2) *Communications of the ACM* 33–36. See slso: Irene Kamara, Thordis Sveinsdottir, and Simone Wurster. 'Raising trust in security products and systems through standardisation and certification: the CRISP approach' [2015] *IEEE ITU Kaleidoscope: Trust in the Information Society* 1–7; Eric Lachaud, 'What could be the contribution of certification to data protection regulation?' Doctoral dissertation (2019).

[89] This is true provided that after certification is granted, the certifiers monitor whether the conditions for granting certification continue to be met, and have mechanisms in place to detect irregularities and non-conformities. See Chris Connolly, Graham Greenleaf, and Nigel Waters, 'Privacy Self-Regulation in Crisis? –TRUSTe's 'Deceptive' Practices' (2014) 132 *Privacy Laws & Business International Report* 13–17; Irene Kamara and Paul De Hert 'Data protection certification in the EU' (n 42) (2018).

[90] Interested parties receive some information also from a mark or a seal. A seal is unique to a certification scheme and provides generic information on the type and scope of certification to which is related, and potentially a unique number connected to the specific processing operation certified.

[91] Recital100, GDPR.

[92] Recital 7, CSA.

[93] EDPB (2019) 19–20.

[94] Art 51, CSA.

certified product is placed in the market, information regarding the security requirements met by the product is already made transparent and verified by an independent third party.[95] The GDPR also refers to certification in relation to data protection by design and by default.[96]

In sum, both frameworks encourage early adoption of measures to comply with requirements, the conformity to which can be put forward via certification, contributing to ex ante transparency and increasing trust.

B. Main Actors in the Implementation of the Certification Schemes: National Authorities and Conformity Assessment Bodies

The analysed certification frameworks follow a similar approach in terms of governance of adopted or approved certifications, despite any differences in the development phase. The main actors are national supervisory authorities, namely the data protection authorities in the GDPR and the national cybersecurity certification authorities in the CSA ('competent public authorities'), and the certification bodies, which are private organisations. A role is also introduced for the National Accreditation Authorities, which are tasked to accredit certification bodies.[97,98] The competent public authorities are granted investigative and corrective powers and tasks which place them in the centre of monitoring and supervision regarding certification. In addition, under both frameworks the competent public authorities have the power to issue certifications themselves.

C. Data Security as a Common Denominator

Certification schemes under the GDPR have an inevitably different scope than the ones under the CSA, since their legal basis differs. In addition, the object

---

[95] See also Art 46(2), CSA referring to certification attesting the availability, authenticity, integrity or confidentiality of data throughout the lifecycle of the ICT products, services, and processes.

[96] Art 25(3), GDPR. However, both the obligation for compliance and the qualification to apply for certification concern controllers, not manufacturers. This issue was raised by the WP29, which pleaded for including manufacturers in the scope of Art 25, GDPR. Article 29 Data Protection Working Party, 'The Future of Privacy.'

Joint contribution to the Consultation of the European Commission on the legal framework for the fundamental right to protection of personal data' (2009) 02356/09/EN, WP168, para 45 (Article 29 Working Party, 'The Future of Privacy'). Read further: Lina Jasmontaite, Irene Kamara, Gabriela Zanfir-Fortuna, and Stefano Leucci, 'Data protection by design and by default: Framing guiding principles into legal obligations in the GDPR' (2018) 4 *European Data Protection Law Review* 168.

[97] This is the case for two out of the three accreditation models of Art 43, GDPR. There is also the option for the data protection authorities to provide accreditation Art 43(1)(a), GDPR, but this is a model not endorsed by many MS in practice.

[98] Additionally, National Accreditation Bodies accredit public authorities which offer certification, as explained in 2.2, 4.

of certification in the data protection certification mechanisms is one or more processing operations, such as the collection, storage and erasure of personal data,[99] while in the CSA cybersecurity certifications, it is ICT products, processes, or services. However, in normative terms, data security is a common denominator of the two certifications. As expected, security of information is at the core of the CSA certifications. Protection against accidental or unauthorised access, disclosure, processing, storage, destruction, loss or lack of availability lie among the core security objectives of the cybersecurity certification schemes.[100]

Furthermore, The GDPR aims at protecting the individual with regard to the processing of his or her personal information. As a means to achieve this goal, the legislator introduces a range of sub-goals/provisions, such as data subjects' rights that empower the individual, but also security of processing that guarantees the protection personal data, and by doing so, contributes to the protection of the individual. It can be asserted therefore, that security of processing is one of the provisions that aim at materialising the sub-goal of protecting information (or more accurately personal data) in the GDPR, and through that, the individual. In parallel, the GDPR assigns weight on (personal) data security by elevating it to a general principle, which did not exist under the Directive 95/46/EC.[101] Article 5(1)(f) introduces a principle of integrity and confidentiality which relates to common information security principles[102] and creates a duty to secure personal data.[103] The principle of Article 5(f), refers to protection against unauthorised or unlawful processing, accidental loss, destruction or damage, and provides that personal data should be processed 'in a manner that ensures appropriate security' using 'appropriate technical or organisational measures'..[104] Unauthorised or unlawful processing includes access or use of personal data, but also the *equipment* used for processing.[105] Following that, security of processing is a legal obligation for controllers and processors, compliance to which may be demonstrated with certification.[106] Although GDPR certifications most likely will (but not necessarily) involve data security requirements, and the CSA certifications focus exclusively on it, data security can be a common ground for both laws, and by extension, certifications.[107]

---

[99] Art 42(1), (6), GDPR.

[100] Recital 51(a), (b), CSA.

[101] The wording of the principle mirrors however Art 17 of the Directive 95/46/EC. Cécile De Terwagne 'Commentary Article 5' in Christopher Kuner, Lee Bygrave, and Christopher Docskey (eds) *The EU General Data Protection Regulation. A commentary* (Oxford University Press, 2020) 318.

[102] Spyridon Samonas and David Coss. 'The CIA strikes back: Redefining confidentiality, integrity and availability in security' (2014) 10(3) *Journal of Information System Security*.

[103] Pieter Wolters, 'The security of personal data under the GDPR: a harmonized duty or a shared responsibility?' (2017) 7(3) *International Data Privacy Law* 165–178.

[104] Art 5(1)(f), GDPR.

[105] Recital 39, GDPR.

[106] Art 32(3), GDPR.

[107] Read further an ENISA study on data security measures under the GDPR and the *bridges* between Art 32, GDPR and information security legislation. ENISA, 'Handbook on security of personal data processing' (ENISA, 2017).

VI. Discussion

Overall, the comparison revealed different certification models at their core, governed and supervised in a similar manner.[108] Several normative and policy reasons both internal, thus attributed to the law and its protected rights, but also external, such as the certification market maturity, explain the divergence.

An internal reason of normative nature relates to the design of the examined Union laws. While the GDPR is a regulation introducing a framework with principles, obligations, and rights for regulatees and individuals, the CSA contains only organisational and procedural provisions such as the provisions around the role of ENISA. This practically means that certification in the case of the GDPR already has a solid normative basis as a starting point for the certification criteria of the scheme. The CSA schemes however need to rely on external sources to the legal framework sources, such as technical standards, which may or may not have been developed with the Union policy and legal framework on cybersecurity and information security in mind.[109] To ensure thus a high degree of harmonisation, the legislator in the case of the CSA needed to centralise the decisions and the development of the schemes.

Another reason relates to the role of certification in the regulations: while in the GDPR certification is a voluntary instrument to demonstrate compliance with legal obligations, the CSA certifications, albeit also in principle voluntary, may become mandatory in Member States with national technical regulations or with a Union law.[110] The importance of harmonised scheme content is heightened, and is better ensured in a centralised than a decentralised certification framework. Furthermore, the maturity in the cybersecurity certification market and the abundance of certifications as opposed to the growing data protection certification market, explains the level of detail in the CSA rules and equal attention to the content of certifications and to the development and governance, as opposed to the primary focus of the GDPR certification framework on the actors, their powers, and supervision.[111] The absence of detail regarding the content of the criteria and certification schemes in the GDPR is compensated with a number of safeguards such as the thorough provisions on accreditation, which ensure the competence of the conformity assessment bodies, the mandatory approval of the criteria by the supervisory authority, and the powers of the Commission

---

[108] Comparative overview in Table 1, 12.

[109] ENISA, 'Standards supporting certification. Analysis of Standards in Areas Relevant to the Potential EU Candidate Cybersecurity Certification Schemes' (ENISA, 2019).

[110] Recitals 91 and 92, Arts 1(1), 56 and 67(3), CSA. See, Dennis-Kenji Kipker, 'EU Cybersecurity Act und Certification Schemes: ein aktueller Fortschrittsbericht' (2020) 44(4) *Datenschutz und Datensicherheit-DuD* 263–265.

[111] The object of certification being the processing operation(s) and potential subject matters are provided in Arts 24, 28, 32, 42, 46, GDPR.

to adopt delegated acts on the criteria and requirements of the data protection certification models.[112]

Another difference is the scalability of the certifications. The CSA endorses clearly granularity in several aspects such as the assurance levels and the first party conformity assessment. On the other hand, the GDPR mentions a risk-based approach and makes a reference to the needs of SMEs when it comes to certification, but does not seem to fully embrace a granular approach. This can be attributed to the fact that a granular approach implies acceptance of some-non-conformities and risks being residual; this possibly contradicts the aim of the GDPR to protect the rights and freedoms of the individuals, which should be balanced, and restricted only under conditions. In addition, first party assessments in the GDPR for conforming to fundamental rights-related requirements would have been a contradiction in itself.

Comparing the certification frameworks in terms of penalties and fines, the GDPR adopts a stricter and more regulated approach than the CSA, which includes an opening clause for MS in that matter. While one would have expected a more streamlined approach in the Cybersecurity Act due to the focus on centralisation and harmonisation, the GDPR approach is fully justified mostly from a policy perspective: certification is relatively novel in data protection, it is introduced for the first time in the Union data protection law, and most importantly the GDPR introduces high fines for the infringements of its provisions, and certification could not be the exception.

Nonetheless, the comparative analysis also revealed convergence. Considering the similarities, those occur where the goals of the CSA and the GDPR converge, but also for organisational efficiency reasons.[113] Data security, as well as data protection and security by design, are fundamental concepts for both data protection and cybersecurity. Thus, where the norms converge, the certification frameworks converge as well and the resulting certifications may be aligned. Alignment does not mean overlap. Taking the example of data security: cybersecurity obviously has broader material scope not limited only to *personal data* security, but of any type of information. And personal data protection is multifaceted, security being only one of the facets in addition to fairness and lawfulness, data minimisation and purpose specification, accountability, and shielding individuals with substantial and procedural rights. Nonetheless, data security is a *topos*, on which certification to be developed in both fields can rely and interlink with one another. In addition, the aim of certification

---

[112] Art 43(8), GDPR. See analysis in Kamara et al (n 13) (2019).

[113] For discussion on points of interaction between the NIS Directive and the GDPR read: Markopoulou et al (n 118) (2019) ibid; for an overview of concepts and values clusters and conflicts in cybersecurity see Ibo van de Poel 'Core Values and Value Conflicts in Cybersecurity: Beyond Privacy Versus Security' n *The Ethics of Cybersecurity*, (Springer, 2020) 45f.

as a transparency mechanism is present in both the cybersecurity certification framework and the data protection certification mechanisms. Certification is presumed to respond to the proclaimed need for transparency through third party audits and publication of information regarding the audited object.[114]

As regards governance, public authorities are strengthened with powers to supervise conformity assessment bodies and act as one, in both frameworks. Accredited certification bodies, conduct the process, and monitor the post-certification phase. The centralised approach of the CSA in the development phase of the schemes, gives its place to a more distributed model, similar to the GDPR certification mechanisms, in the implementation phase. And because in both laws and certification frameworks, consistency and harmonisation is of high importance, the distributed models, whereby national authorities take over pivotal roles, are designed with embedded guarantees such as a consistency mechanism and notification obligations.[115] A closer look, reveals that policy and organisational reasons prompted the legislator to those choices in both frameworks; national authorities have a better control of supervision and enforcement in their jurisdictions than a Union agency or the Commission.

Overall, the adopted models for certification frameworks in the CSA and the GDPR can be explained by the underlying values and goals between data protection and cybersecurity, as expressed in the GDPR and the CSA respectively. As demonstrated by the legal foundations of the CSA and the GDPR, while both laws might qualify at large as 'information protection laws', the CSA is ultimately an internal market legal instrument aiming at approximation of laws for the establishment and functioning of the internal market,[116] while the GDPR protects individuals with regard to the processing of their personal data,[117] thus is concerned primarily with fundamental rights and freedoms.[118]

---

[114] It should be noted that the role of certification as a transparency mechanism has its limitations, as for example only the results of a successful certification process are published.

[115] Art 63, GDPR, and Art 61, CSA (Notification obligation of the national cybersecurity certification authorities towards the European Commission).

[116] CSA Preamble. Art 114 Treaty on the Functioning of the European Union (TFEU). Moreover, the approach of the Union in regulating cybersecurity has been criticised for its blurry role in protecting fundamental rights and freedoms. Gloria González Fuster and Lina Jasmontaite, 'Cybersecurity Regulation in the European Union: The Digital, the Critical and Fundamental Rights' in Markus Christen, Bert Gordijn, Michele Loi (eds) *The Ethics of Cybersecurity*, (Springer, 2020) 113, 97–115.

[117] GDPR Preamble. Art 16, TFEU.

[118] D Markopoulou et al argue that due to the legal foundation of the GDPR on Art 16, TFEU, which establishes a horizontal legal obligation to protect the right to data protection, in a conflict between cybersecurity and data protection, the latter would prevail in a balancing test between the two. Dimitra Markopoulou, Vagelis Papakonstantinou, and Paul de Hert. 'The new EU cybersecurity framework: The NIS Directive, ENISA's role and the General Data Protection Regulation' (2019) 35(6) *Computer Law & Security Review* 105336, 10f.

Table 1 Comparative overview of certification rules under the Cybersecurity Act and the General Data Protection Regulation

Type of component	CSA framework	CSA Article	GDPR mechanisms	GDPR Article
Object of certification	ICT products, ICT process, ICT services or groups thereof	Rec. 73	Data processing operation(s)	Art. 42
Type of conformity assessment	-Third party certification -Conformity self-assessment by manufacturer or provider also possible for low complexity/low risk situations with EU statement of conformity	Rec. 79 Rec. 80 Rec. 82 Art. 53 Art. 56	Third party certification	Art. 43
Voluntary/ mandatory	Voluntary in principle, mandatory also possible in MS	Rec. 91 Rec. 92 Art. 56	Voluntary	Art. 42
Geographical scope	Only Union level, no national certifications under the CSA[119]	Art. 57	Union level (European Data Protection Seal) and national certifications	Art. 42
Minimum scheme content	Yes, provided in the CSA	Rec. 84 Art. 51	Not provided in the GDPR, COM delegated act possible or up to the scheme drafter	Art. 43
Mutual recognition	Yes, throughout the Union (Peer review system across national cybersecurity certification authorities)	Rec. 73 Rec. 99	No	N/A
Granularity	Three assurance levels (basic – substantial – high) for certification. Conformity self-assessment: only basic	Rec. 77 Rec. 86 Rec. 88 Art. 52 Art. 56	Not determined in the GDPR, At the discretion of the scheme drafter	N/A
	Evaluation levels also possible			

(continued)

---

[119] National cybersecurity certification schemes are replaced by a European cybersecurity certification scheme (Recital. 85. CSA).

Table 1 *(Continued)*

Type of component	CSA framework	CSA Article	GDPR mechanisms	GDPR Article
Transparency	Website with schemes maintained by ENISA National authorities notify COM on accredited conformity assessment bodies Penalties in national laws notified to COM	Rec. 85 Art. 50 Art. 61 Art. 65	Registry maintained by the EDPB and supervisory authorities	Rec. 100 Art. 42
Supervision & enforcement	By national cybersecurity certification authorities	Rec. 73 Rec. 102 Art. 58	By certification bodies and national supervisory authorities (DPA)	Art. 43
Consistency	European Cybersecurity Certification Group (ECCG)	Rec. 103	GDPR consistency mechanism	
Revision	Every 5 years, evaluation by ENISA	Art. 49	Not mentioned, in the GDPR. Re-certification every 3 years.	Art. 43

VII. Conclusion

This chapter started with the assumption that the Union cybersecurity and data protection laws both aim, inter alia, at protecting information. Because of this connection, the way some issues are regulated in those laws should be similar. The chapter examined to which extent, a private law voluntary instrument – certification – is introduced and regulated in an aligned or misaligned manner in the GDPR and CSA. The comparative analysis, identifying both similarities and differences, showed that the CSA and the GDPR follow different models in both the development and the governance and implementation phases: a central-ised certification managed by one authority, developed with the consultation of stakeholders in the CSA, national certifications in parallel to Union level ones, developed by any interested party in the GDPR; the possibility of self-assessments in the CSA versus strictly third party assessments in the GDPR; regulated legal effects in the CSA versus implied market benefits in the GDPR; and, mutual recognition of certificates in all Member States in the CSA versus a re-assessment requirement in each Member State in the GDPR, to mention some of the differences in the frameworks for certification in the two Regulations.

The analysis showed that differences are mostly mandated by the nature, goals, and legal basis of the two Union laws. While indeed the CSA and the GDPR both serve to some extent a goal of protecting information, such a classification does not give due account to other important aspects of these laws, which are significant enough to influence their legal design, including their approach to seemingly less impactful provisions, such as those of voluntary private law instruments. Thus, the protected values and the legal bases of the CSA and the GDPR have impacted the legal design of certification frameworks. The common denominators from a normative perspective (eg personal data security, security of equipment, integrity and confidentiality), as well as the decentralised governance approach with embedded harmonisation and consistency mechanisms, offer common grounds for interaction. The form of this interaction in practical terms can manifest itself in various ways: common baseline criteria and requirements, partial mutual recognition, joint certification or accreditation evaluations, combined transparency registries, and others. From the perspective of both the regulated companies and the individuals, the rights of which are affected, the interaction and perhaps channels of collaboration in certification, demonstrable in practice, are necessary, to avoid the negative externalities, as long as the protected values in each law are not undermined. To conclude with, one cannot speak of 'misaligned laws', but justified divergent approaches, that do not exclude interaction when implementing the frameworks.

Acknowledgments

The author would like to thank the two CPDP reviewers and the participants of the Brussels Privacy Hub doctoral seminar for the feedback. This chapter was written while conducting research for the National Cyber Security Centre of the Netherlands on cybersecurity certification. The views expressed here are the author's alone.

References

Article 29 Data Protection Working Party. 'Guidelines on the application and setting of administrative fines for the purposes of the Regulation 2016/679' WP 253 (October 2017).
Colombo, Carlo, and Mariolina Eliantonio. 'Harmonized technical standards as part of EU law: Juridification with a number of unresolved legitimacy concerns? Case C-613/14 James Elliot Construction Limited v. Irish Asphalt Limited, EU: C: 2016: 821.' (2017) 24(2) *Maastricht Journal of European and Comparative Law* 323–340.

Connolly, Chris, Graham Greenleaf, and Nigel Waters, 'Privacy Self-Regulation in Crisis? –TRUSTe's 'Deceptive' Practices' (2014) 132 *Privacy Laws & Business International Report* 13–17.

De Terwagne, Cécile. 'Commentary Article 5' in Christopher Kuner, Lee Bygrave, and Christopher Docskey (eds) *The EU General Data Protection Regulation. A commentary* (Oxford University Press, 2020).

Directive (EU) 2016/680 of the European Parliament and of the Council of 27 April 2016 on the protection of natural persons with regard to the processing of personal data by competent authorities for the purposes of the prevention, investigation, detection or prosecution of criminal offences or the execution of criminal penalties, and on the free movement of such data, and repealing Council Framework Decision 2008/977/JHA [2016] OJ L119.

ENISA. 'Handbook on security of personal data processing', (ENISA, 2017).

ENISA. 'Recommendations on European Data Protection Certification' (ENISA 2017).

ENISA. 'Standards supporting certification. Analysis of Standards in Areas Relevant to the Potential EU Candidate Cybersecurity Certification Schemes' (ENISA, 2019). European Commission. 'Data protection as a pillar of citizens' empowerment and the EU's approach to the digital transition – two years of application of the General Data Protection Regulation' Communication from the Commission to the European Parliament and the Council (2020) COM (2020) 264 final.

European Commission. 'Proposal for a of the European Parliament and of the Council concerning the respect for private life and the protection of personal data in electronic communications and repealing Directive 2002/58/EC (Regulation on Privacy and Electronic Communications)' COM (2017) 010 final.

European Commission. 'Proposal for a Regulation of the European Parliament and of the Council on ENISA, the 'EU Cybersecurity Agency', and Repealing Regulation (EU) 526/2013, and on Information and Communication Technology Cybersecurity Certification ('Cybersecurity Act'), COM (2017) 477 final.

European Data Protection Board. 'Guidelines 1/2018 on certification and identifying certification criteria in accordance with Articles 42 and 43 of the Regulation', v.3 2019.

European Parliament. Legislative resolution of 12 March 2019 on the proposal for a regulation of the European Parliament and of the Council on ENISA, the 'EU Cybersecurity Agency', and repealing Regulation (EU) 526/2013, and on Information and Communication Technology cybersecurity certification ('Cybersecurity Act') (COM (2017) 0477 – C8-0310/2017–2017/0225(COD)).

González Fuster, Gloria, and Lina Jasmontaite. 'Cybersecurity Regulation in the European Union: The Digital, the Critical and Fundamental Rights' in Markus Christen, Bert Gordijn, Michele Loi (eds) *The Ethics of Cybersecurity*, eds. (Springer, 2020) 97–115.

Hornung, Gerrit. 'A General Data Protection Regulation for Europe: Light and Shade in the Commission's Draft of 25 January 2012' (2012) 9 *SCRIPTed* 64.

ISO/IEC 17000 Conformity assessment –Vocabulary and general principles.

ISO/IEC 17065:2012 Conformity assessment – Requirements for bodies certifying products, processes and services.

Jasmontaite, Lina, Irene Kamara, Gabriela Zanfir-Fortuna, and Stefano Leucci. 'Data protection by design and by default: Framing guiding principles into legal obligations in the GDPR' (2018) 4 *European Data Protection Law Review* 168–189.

Kamara, Irene and Paul De Hert. 'Data protection certification in the EU: Possibilities, actors and building blocks in a reformed landscape' in Rowena Rodrigues and

Vagelis Papakonstantinou (eds) *Privacy and data protection seals* (TMC Asser Press, 2018) 7–34.

Kamara, Irene, Ronald Leenes, et al 'Data protection certification mechanisms: Study on Articles 42 and 43 of the Regulation (EU) 2016/679. Final Report' Publications Office of the EU (2019).

Kamara, Irene, Ronald Leenes, et al. 'Data protection certification mechanisms: Study on Articles 42 and 43 of the Regulation (EU) 2016/679. Annexes' Publications Office of the EU (2019).

Kamara, Irene. 'Commentary Article 40' in Christopher Kuner, Lee Bygrave, and Christopher Docksey (eds) *The European General Data Protection Regulation (GDPR) A Commentary* (Oxford University Press, 2020).

Kamara, Irene, Thordis Sveinsdottir, and Simone Wurster. 'Raising trust in security products and systems through standardisation and certification: the CRISP approach' [2015] *IEEE ITU Kaleidoscope: Trust in the Information Society* 1–7.

Kamara, Irene, Ronald Leenes, Kees Stuurman and Jasper van den Boom. 'The cybersecurity certification landscape in the Netherlands after the Union Cybersecurity Act.' National Cyber Security Centre NL (forthcoming).

Kipker, Dennis-Kenji. 'EU Cybersecurity Act und Certification Schemes: ein aktueller Fortschrittsbericht.' (2020) 44(4) *Datenschutz und Datensicherheit-DuD* 263–265.

Lachaud, Eric. 'What could be the contribution of certification to data protection regulation?' Doctoral dissertation (2019).

Leenes, Ronald. 'Commentary Article 42' in Christopher Kuner, Lee Bygrave, and Christopher Docksey (eds) *The European General Data Protection Regulation (GDPR) A Commentary* (Oxford University Press, 2020).

Markopoulou, Dimitra, Vagelis Papakonstantinou, and Paul de Hert. 'The new EU cybersecurity framework: The NIS Directive, ENISA's role and the General Data Protection Regulation.' (2019) 35(6) *Computer Law & Security Review* 105336.

Matheu, Sara N, Jose L Hernandez-Ramos, and Antonio F Skarmeta. 'Toward a cybersecurity certification framework for the Internet of Things' (2019) 17(3) *IEEE Security & Privacy* 66–76.

Mitrakas, Andreas. 'The emerging EU framework on cybersecurity certification' (2018) 47(7) *Datenschutz und Datensicherheit-DuD* 411–414.

Nemitz, Paul. 'Fines under the GDPR' in Ronald Leenes et al (eds) *Data Protection and Privacy: The Internet of Bodies* (Hart Publishing, 2018).

Peers Steve and Marios Costa. 'Accountability for delegated and implementing acts after the Treaty of Lisbon' (2012) 18(3) *European Law Journal* 427–460.

Regulation (EU) 2016/679 of the European Parliament and of the Council of 27 April 2016 on the protection of natural persons with regard to the processing of personal data and on the free movement of such data, and repealing Directive 95/46/EC (General Data Protection Regulation, [2016] OJ L119.

Rodrigues, Rowena, David Barnard-Wills, Paul De Hert, and Vagelis Papakonstantinou. 'The future of privacy certification in Europe: an exploration of options under article 42 of the GDPR' (2016) 30(3) *International Review of Law, Computers & Technology* 248–270.

Samonas, Spyridon, and David Coss. 'The CIA strikes back: Redefining confidentiality, integrity and availability in security' (2014) 10(3) *Journal of Information System Security* 21–45.

Senden, Linda. 'The Constitutional Fit of European Standardization Put to the Test.' (2017) 44(4) *Legal Issues of Economic Integration* 337–352.

Spagnuelo, Dayana, Ana Ferreira, and Gabriele Lenzini. 'Accomplishing transparency within the general data protection regulation' in *5th International Conference on Information Systems Security and Privacy* (2018).

Stahl, Konrad, and Roland Strausz. 'Certification and market transparency' (2017) 84(4) *The Review of Economic Studies* 1842–1868.

Sunyaev Ali and Stephan Schneider. 'Cloud services certification.' (2013) 56(2) *Communications of the ACM* 33–36.

van de Poel, Ibo. 'Core Values and Value Conflicts in Cybersecurity: Beyond Privacy Versus Security' in *The Ethics of Cybersecurity* (Springer, 2020) 45–71.

Van der Sloot, Bart, and Eleni Kosta. 'Big brother watch and others v UK: Lessons from the latest Strasbourg ruling on bulk surveillance' (2015) 5(2) *European Data Protection Law Review* 5 252–261.

Van Hoecke, Mark 'Methodology of comparative legal research' [2015] *Law and Method* 1–35.

Weber Rolf H and Evelyne Studer. 'Cybersecurity in the Internet of Things: Legal aspects.' (2016) 32(5) *Computer Law & Security Review* 715–728.

Wolters, Pieter. 'The security of personal data under the GDPR: a harmonized duty or a shared responsibility?' (2017) 7(3) *International Data Privacy Law* 165–178.

5

Aggregation, Synthesisation and Anonymisation: A Call for a Risk-based Assessment of Anonymisation Approaches

SOPHIE STALLA-BOURDILLON AND ALFRED ROSSI

Abstract

This chapter argues that the de-identification spectrum resulting from the common readings of both the CCPA and the GDPR is oversimplified. This is because in order to assess the output of a data transformation process, including aggregation, one should look beyond the output data and the technique applied on the input data: one should look at the data environment and the combination of both technical and organisational controls implemented to manage access to data. We thus offer a new analysis of anonymisation controls and explain why this analysis is particularly useful in the context of data analytics and machine learning, where models can remember input data. This analysis applies even if decentralised techniques are available such as federated learning. Put simply, a similar approach can be applied to both what are traditionally thought of as a 'dataset' and aggregate data products, such as summary statistics and models, which are key ingredients in producing synthetic data. What is more, we offer guidance for a more nuanced reading of both the CCPA and the GDPR in order to effectively incentivise best data governance practices.

Keywords

Data Protection, Anonymisation, Pseudonymisation, Aggregation, Synthetic Data.

I. Introduction

2018 was the year of the General Data Protection Regulation (GDPR),[1] at least within the European Union (EU). While the GDPR was adopted in 2016 and EU Member States were required from this date to prepare the terrain for its application, its direct effect started on 25 May 2018. From that date both public and private actors within EU Member States have been required to comply with the law.

2020 is the year when the California Consumer Privacy Act (CCPA) comes into effect.[2] Much has been written about both laws, and detailed comparisons[3] have already been released to support the work of compliance teams working for organisations operating in both regions. While the CCPA has certainly been influenced by the GDPR – in fact the language of some of its provisions is very close to the language found in the GDPR[4] – inevitably, differences have emerged. Whether these differences should be seen as merely language differences that should not prevent homogeneity of practices on the ground, or rather as conceptual differences that should lead to divergences of practices, is the big question.

This chapter deals with the way the material scope of this privacy or data protection legislation is defined and raises the question of what process is needed to transform personal information or personal data into non-personal information or non-personal data. We argue that anonymisation warrants a blended approach combining both context and data controls, even when the aggregation route is chosen. This should hold true although modern privacy or data protection legislations developed in different jurisdictions (ie, the US and EU) do not expressly refer to context controls. Context controls should thus be seen as implicit requirements.

To start with the Californian approach, the CCPA distinguishes between two categories of non-personal information, as per section 1798.140 of the California Civil Code:[5] de-identified information and aggregate information.

---

[1] Regulation (EU) 2016/679 of the European Parliament and of the Council of 27 April 2016 on the protection of natural persons with regard to the processing of personal data and on the free movement of such data, and repealing Directive 95/46/EC (General Data Protection Regulation) [2016] OJ L119/ 1–88.

[2] Note that Brazil's General Data Protection Law (GDPL) is also coming into force in August 2020, with Brazil's new data-protection agency to start working in October 2019. The GDPL is very similar to the GDPR both in substance and spirit.

[3] See, eg, OneTrust DataGuidance Staff and Future of Privacy Forum Staff, 'Comparing Privacy Laws: GDPR v. CCPA,' https://fpf.org/2019/12/18/comparing-privacy-laws-gdpr-v-ccpa/ (last accessed 4 March 2020).

[4] Consider for example the definition of pseudonymisation at Cal. Civ. Code §§ 1798.140(r), which borrows from the GDPR definition of pseudonymisation at Art 4(5) or the definition of business at Cal. Civ. Code §§ 1798.140(c)(1), which borrows from the GDPR definition of controller at Art 4(7).

[5] Cal. Civ. Code §§ 1798.140(a) and (h). For other US rules excluding aggregate information from the definition of personally identifiable information, see, eg, rules adopted by the Securities and Exchange Commission, 17 CFR §248.3 (u)(2)(ii)(B) ('Personally identifiable financial information does not include:.. Information that does not identify a consumer, such as aggregate information or blind data that does not contain personal identifiers such as account numbers, names, or addresses.')

The distinction seems to rely upon the assumption that aggregate information is always higher or further right on the de-identification spectrum[6] than de-identified information. Put simply, the distinction seems to rely upon the assumption that aggregate information is (much) safer than de-identified information, in terms of re-identification risks.

A similar assumption could be said to underlie the GDPR, although the GDPR appears more restrictive than the CCPA.[7] While the GDPR does not expressly recognise the concept of de-identified data (it introduces the concept of pseudonymisation), the GDPR excludes from its remit anonymised data in fine. GDPR Recital 26 is usually used as the initial prong of an *a contrario* reasoning in order to derive the test for anonymised data.[8] In addition, GDPR Recital 162, which deals with certain types of processing activities, clearly specifies that '[t]he statistical purpose implies that the result of processing for statistical purposes is not personal data (including pseudonymised data), but aggregate data.'[9] It thus appears that the GDPR also draws a distinction between personal data and aggregates, albeit in its non-binding part.

In this chapter, we argue that the de-identification spectrum commonly used to explain why aggregates are not personal data is oversimplified. This is because in order to assess the output of a data transformation process, including aggregation, one should look beyond the output data and the technique applied on the input data: one should look at the data environment and the combination of both technical and organisational controls implemented to manage access to data. While re-identification scandals such as AOL's release of search terms or Netflix's sharing of movie recommendations because of poor de-identification methods have been heavily discussed,[10] aggregation failures have also been well-documented in the

---

[6] A scale between two extreme points (personal data and anonymised data) is usually used in the literature to explain the concepts of personal data, pseudonymised data, de-identified data, aggregate data and anonymised data. See, eg, Kelsey Finch, 'A Visual Guide to Practical Data De-Identification,' Future of Privacy Forum, https://fpf.org/2016/04/25/a-visual-guide-to-practical-data-de-identification/ (last accessed 4 March 2020).

[7] This is because recital 26 specifies that data that has undergone pseudonymisation should be deemed as personal data. ('Personal data which have undergone pseudonymisation, which could be attributed to a natural person by the use of additional information should be considered to be information on an identifiable natural person.')

[8] GDPR, Recital 26:

'To determine whether a natural person is identifiable, account should be taken of all the means reasonably likely to be used, such as singling out, either by the controller or by another person to identify the natural person directly or indirectly. To ascertain whether means are reasonably likely to be used to identify the natural person, account should be taken of all objective factors, such as the costs of and the amount of time required for identification, taking into consideration the available technology at the time of the processing and technological developments.'

[9] GDPR, Recital 162.

[10] See, eg, Paul Ohm, 'Broken Promises of Privacy: Responding to the Surprising Failure of Anonymization' (2010) 57 *UCLA Law Review* 1701; Article 29, Data Protection Working Party, Opinion 005/2014 on Anonymisation Techniques, adopted on 10 April 2014, WP216 (hereafter Art 29 WP Anonymisation Techniques.)

literature.[11] After all, the US Bureau of the Census would not be looking to employ differential privacy if aggregation was sufficient.[12]

Building upon prior work,[13] we offer a new analysis of anonymisation controls and explain why this analysis is particularly useful in the context of data analytics and machine learning, where models can remember input data.[14] This analysis applies even if decentralised techniques are available such as federated learning.[15] Put simply, a uniform approach can be applied to both traditional datasets and aggregate data products, such as summary statistics and models, which are usually used to produce what is now called synthetic data.

What is more, we suggest that a nuanced reading of both the CCPA and GDPR is preferable in order to effectively incentivise best data governance practices. While the definition of aggregate information under the CCPA does not expressly require a combination of technical and organisational controls, the regulatory goal is that at the end of the aggregation process aggregates are not linked or reasonably linkable to any consumer or household. Yet, this can only be achieved if, on top of the aggregation process itself, a combination of technical and/or organisational measures are implemented with a view to transform the data and control the data environment.

With regard to the GDPR, we suggest that the exclusion of aggregates from the remit of the regulation should not be systematic and at the very least should not be done on the basis of an irrebuttable presumption. Furthermore, data controllers, when producing aggregates, should assess the effectiveness of the combination of technical and organisational measures to properly characterise the output of the aggregation process and determine its legal effect.

Importantly, these suggestions should be followed to assess synthesisation processes and characterise their outputs. This is because, even if synthetic data is

---

[11] In particular in the literature on differential privacy. See, eg, Cynthia Dwork and Aaron Roth. 'The Algorithmic Foundations of Differential Privacy.' Foundations and Trends® in Theoretical Computer Science 9, no. 3–4 (2013): 211–407. https://doi.org/10.1561/0400000042.

[12] John M Abowd, 'Disclosure Avoidance and the 2018 Census Test: Release of the Source Code,' The United States Census Bureau, www.census.gov/newsroom/blogs/research-matters/2019/06/disclosure_avoidance.html (last accessed 4 March 2020).

[13] See, eg, Finch, 'A Visual Guide to Practical Data De-Identification' (n 13). See also Jules Polonetsky, Omer Tene, and Kelsey Finch, 'Shades of Gray: Seeing the Full Spectrum of Practical Data De-Identification' (2016) 56(3) *Santa Clara Law Review* 593.

[14] See, eg, Michael Veale, Reuben Binns, and Lilian Edwards, 'Algorithms That Remember: Model Inversion Attacks and Data Protection Law,' (2018) 376(2133) *Philosophical Transactions of the Royal Society A: Mathematical, Physical and Engineering Sciences* 20180083, https://doi.org/10.1098/rsta.2018.0083.

[15] Federated learning, sometimes called collaborative learning, trains data across multiple decentralised edge devices or servers. Training data is thus kept locally, never exchanged between devices or servers and are not holding local data samples, without exchanging their data samples. In other words, federated learning trains models against data that is separated in silos. The architecture for federated learning can vary widely. See, eg, Brendan McMahan et al, 'Communication-Efficient Learning of Deep Networks from Decentralized Data' [2017] *Artificial Intelligence and Statistics* 1273–82, http://proceedings.mlr.press/v54/mcmahan17a.html.

considered to be a valid alternative to original data,[16] at the end of the day synthetic data is data sampled from a model derived from aggregate data.

This chapter is organised as follows. In Section II, we unpack and refine the inference model that is commonly used to assess re-identification risks, taking into account four types of inference attacks in order to weigh the potential impact of anonymisation processes. The inference model is a general model of a knowledge-based attacker who is seeking to infer personal information that pertains to data subjects. This model is particularly useful for analysing the effectiveness of mitigating technical and organisational measures (ie, controls) in a machine learning context. It is on the basis of this model that we then analyse aggregation and synthesisation methods, highlighting their inherent limits in Section III. In Section IV we explain the concepts of data and context controls with specificity. In Section V, we compare anonymisation controls, and highlight the necessity of context controls. In Section VI, we draw the lessons from previous sections with a view to offer guidance for interpreting de-identification, aggregation or anonymisation provisions found in key privacy or data protection legislations such as the CCPA and GDPR. As the CCPA is representative of the US approach to de-identification since it builds upon the Federal Trade Commission's approach to de-identification,[17] and the US approach to anonymisation is usually opposed to the EU approach, considering both frameworks enable us to explore the potential for convergence.

II. How to Unpack the Inference Model

Our analysis makes use of the attack model used in differential privacy[18] (referred to herein as *the inference model*) as a general framework for analysing data privacy controls. This construct is useful as it is sufficiently general to accommodate a generic knowledge-based attacker in relation to mitigation actions. Also, it can reveal latent assumptions which may lead to inaccurate or misleading comparisons of privacy techniques.

The medical data literature factors privacy (in the sense of confidentiality) risk into the product of two terms: *context risk* and *data risk*.[19] These terms arise

---

[16] Neha Patki, Roy Wedge, and Kalyan Veeramachaneni, 'The Synthetic Data Vault,' in 2016 IEEE International Conference on Data Science and Advanced Analytics (DSAA) (2016 IEEE International Conference on Data Science and Advanced Analytics (DSAA), Montreal, QC, Canada: IEEE, 2016), 399–410, https://doi.org/10.1109/DSAA.2016.49.

[17] Staff, Ftc. 'Protecting Consumer Privacy in an Era of Rapid Change–A Proposed Framework for Businesses and Policymakers' [2011] *Journal of Privacy and Confidentiality*. https://doi.org/10.29012/jpc.v3i1.596; Simson L Garfinkel, 'De-Identification of Personal Information' (National Institute of Standards and Technology, October 2015), https://doi.org/10.6028/NIST.IR.8053.

[18] See, eg, Dwork and Roth, 'The Algorithmic Foundations of Differential Privacy' (n 11) 6.

[19] See, eg, Khaled El Emam and Bradley Malin, 'Appendix B: Concepts and Methods for De-Identifying Clinical Trial Data, Sharing Clinical Trial Data: Maximizing Benefits, Minimizing

naturally from viewing privacy attacks as probabilistic events which occur at some rate but may or may not be successful.

Viewing *attack* and *success* as separate but overlapping events, it follows from Bayes' theorem that the probability of a successful attack is the probability of success once an attack is occurring, scaled by the probability that an attack occurs. From an operational standpoint it is useful to think of attacks as events wherein a party accesses data for unauthorised purposes. A successful attack is then one under which an actor processing under an unauthorised purpose (ie, an attacker) possesses sufficient information to confidently infer the confidential information of a data subject.

Under this lens, controls focusing on limiting access and guarding against unapproved processing lower the odds of unauthorised processing, and there-fore mitigate the attack event. Roughly speaking, attack event mitigations address the access *context*. Perhaps for this reason, the medical data literature refers to the corresponding risk as the *context risk*. In other words, the context risk refers to the likelihood of unauthorised access happening.

In addition, it is also possible to mitigate the success event (ie, relative to the probability that an attack is occurring, what is the likelihood that it is successful?). This risk is referred to in the medical data literature as the *data risk*. Since the data is already understood as being accessed, mitigations of this form focus on how to alter the data such that it proves only marginally valuable in enhancing the attacker's understanding of confidential information of individual data subjects.

It should be noted that we do not necessarily assume sophistication or intent on behalf of the attacker. An actor becomes an attacker when they process infor-mation under an unauthorised purpose. This includes unintentional processing for unapproved purposes, as well as inappropriate reliance on additional informa-tion, including unintentional reliance on prior knowledge resulting in inadvertent recognition. Further, an actor may not be a natural person and should be under-stood to include automated processes.

The inference model (Diagram 1) formalises the thought process of an attacker who utilises a data product to answer a question. To this end, we think of the attacker as having a query, denoted Q. In answering the question, the attacker is

Risk' (National Academies Press (US), 2015), www.ncbi.nlm.nih.gov/books/NBK285994/; Khaled El Emam, *Guide to the De-Identification of Personal Health Information*, 1st edn (Auerbach Publications, 2013), https://doi.org/10.1201/b14764. See, for a generalization of this approach, Information and Privacy Commissioner of Ontario, 'De-identification Guidelines for Structured Data', (2016), www.ipc.on.ca/wp-content/uploads/2016/08/Deidentification-Guidelines-for-Structured-Data.pdf. See also ICO Code of Practice, Anonymisation: 'Managing Data Protection Risk Code of Practice', (2012), https://ico.org.uk/media/1061/anonymisation-code.pdf (last accessed 5 March 2020) [hereafter ICO, Anonymisation Code of Practice]; Elaine Mackey, Mark Elliot, Kieron O'Hara, *The Anonymisation Decision-making Framework*, (UKAN Publications, 2016), https://ukanon.net/wp-content/uploads/2015/05/The-Anonymisation-Decision-making-Framework.pdf.

Diagram 1: A generic query setting aimed at protecting a 'dataset' style data

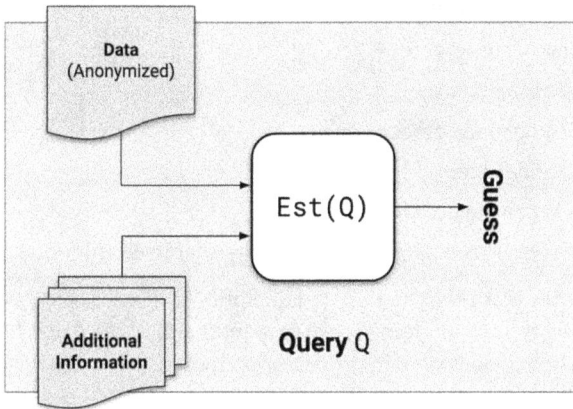

allowed to formulate and execute a plan for guessing (estimating) the answer to Q. This plan, denoted *Est(Q)*, can incorporate both information obtained from the data product (via any modes of access available to the actor), as well as any *additional information* available to the actor.

For clarity, we now elaborate on the components of the model:

(1) The *actor* is a process which aims to process data and formulate queries and their estimations. The actor is not depicted in Diagram 1.
(2) *Data* is the data product being accessed. It can be a dataset, query output from a model trained on private data, a white-box description of a model (eg, a neural network graph and the corresponding weights), etc. Access to data is constrained by the scenario and all data access is subject to any employed data transformation techniques. For instance, the actor may only be permitted authenticated access to data via database software that logs queries for auditing.
(3) The *query* represents the analytic objective of the access, which may be to dump the data, train a model, compute some statistical aggregates, or even access a sensitive item from a patient's treatment history.
(4) *The query estimate, Est(Q)*, denotes the actor's plan for answering the query posed by Q. This plan (and its formulation) may make use of additional information available to the actor.
(5) A *guess* comprises the output of the query estimate. A query may not be answerable with certainty; in this case the actor's plan is allowed to output a guess.
(6) *Additional information* is simply information that the actor knows or has access to. It may, for example, include public or confidential information or data available to the actor, as well as the prior knowledge of the actor including the results of past queries.

The inference model naturally captures a number of common data access patterns. To name a few:

- access to static datasets;
- query access to databases;
- black-box (query) model access;[20]
- white-box model access;[21]
- differentially private access to data;
- interactive scenarios wherein the actor may adaptively query a database.

For the purposes of the discussion, it is helpful to loosely categorise unwanted inferences along types.[22] In doing so we first outline the distinction between direct identifiers, indirectly identifying attributes, attributes, and tokens.

First, recall that an attribute is a piece of information associated with a record or an individual, which can either be unique to one record or common to several records.

Generally speaking, an identifying attribute is any attribute, knowable to an attacker, that can be associated with a natural person. An identifying attribute is a direct identifier when the attribute value is unique to an individual. All other identifying attributes are referred to as indirect identifiers. These are pieces of information (such as height, ethnicity, hair colour, etc) that can be used in combination to single out an individual's records.

A token (ie, the output of a masking process using a tokenisation method) replaces an identifying attribute or a non-identifying (but sensitive) attribute with a mathematically unrelated value through a transformation process that is difficult to reverse. A token replacing an identifier becomes identifying when the attacker possesses (or has access to) additional information that allows them to reverse the transformation.

Notably, even if the token is not reversed, a token that replaces an indirect identifier can still act as an indirectly identifying attribute if tokenisation is not performed by value (and not by record). In other words, a token can still act as an indirectly identifying attribute if the tokenisation method is homogeneously applied to the entire dataset.[23]

---

[20] The actor is not given a complete mathematical description of a model but may present it with test data for classification.

[21] The actor has access to a complete mathematical description of the model.

[22] Of note, Art 29 WP distinguishes between three types of re-identification risks: singling out, linkability and inference. While our terminology overlaps with Art 29 WP's terminology, we offer a more granular approach by distinguishing between participation inference and attribute inference. See Art 29 WP Anonymisation Techniques (n 10) 11–12.

[23] As an example, consider a consistent tokenisation of ethnicity, as this preserves the population statistics of the data, meaning an attacker could use demographic information to re-identify the underlying values.

Crucially, over time it is possible that non-identifying attributes become indirectly identifying attributes due to the progressive enrichment of additional information.[24] Therefore, as explained below, simply removing direct and indirect identifiers will never be enough to mitigate once-and-for-all the four inferences mentioned below.

We now describe the unwanted inference types, and shall sometimes refer to them as *inference attacks* in situations wherein such performances are not permitted:

(1) *Identity inference*: conclusion relating to the identity of an individual reached when considering direct identifiers, indirectly identifying attributes, and/or attribute values alone or in combination with additional information.
(2) *Attribute inference*: conclusion relating to the values of (sensitive) attributes attached to an individual record reached when considering direct identifiers, indirectly identifying attributes, and/or attribute values alone or in combination with additional information.
(3) *Participation inference*: conclusion relating to the participation of an individual to a data source reached when considering direct identifiers, indirectly identifying attributes, and/or attribute values alone or in combination with additional information.
(4) *Relational inference*: conclusion relating to the relationship or link between one or more individual records reached when considering direct identifiers, indirectly identifying attributes, and/or attribute values alone or in combination with additional information.

We now try to understand and mitigate the four kinds of inference attacks in the inference model.[25] Here, the goal becomes prevention of the production of query results that will lead to identity inference, attribute inference, participation inference or relational inference.

In order to assess the strength of the interference mitigation strategy, it is useful to conceptualise a query interaction that will aim at deriving information about the data. A typical query in this context could be 'whose record is it?' (identity disclosure), 'what is John's disease?' (attribute inference), or 'was the model trained on John's credit history?' (participation inference), or 'does this diagnosis relate to the same patient?' (relational inference).

In a generic setting where their actions are not known, an attacker should be prevented from using the data to enhance their ability to confidently make unauthorised inferences concerning the confidential information of data subjects. It should be noted that the attacker may *already* be able to accurately make such inferences based on additional information. It thus follows that if an attack is

---

[24] As explained by Steven M Bellovin et al, 'de-identification suffers from an aging problem'. Steven M Bellovin, Preetam K Dutta, and Nathan Reitinger, 'Privacy and Synthetic Datasets' (2019) 22(1) *Stanford Technology Law Review*.
[25] See Diagram 1.

arbitrary, the focus must be on mitigating the *enhancement* (and not *prevention*) of the attacker's inferential abilities.

Formally, one may think of a generic guessing attack as a Bayesian process wherein prior knowledge is modelled by a probability distribution over guesses, with the probability of each guess reflecting the overall strength of the attacker's belief. The attacker's goal is then to consume query output in order to enrich their prior knowledge.

Note that the only known class of techniques that mitigate an attacker with access performing an arbitrary attack are differentially private.[26] These techniques are specifically designed to control the maximum amount of private information inferable from the data or query results information by an attacker, thereby hampering an actor's ability to significantly enrich their prior knowledge. This means that an attacker's guessing abilities are only marginally enhanced in regard to the content or presence of any single record in the database. As such, their inferential ability remains essentially only as good as their prior knowledge and attackers wishing to learn something new are effectively prevented from doing so for *any* type of inference.

Useful applications of differential privacy work by introducing randomisation into an analysis.[27] The randomisation obscures the contribution of any single record by ensuring that analysis results are essentially equally likely over any pair of databases that differ by the presence of a single record. Such protections come at a cost, however, as any useful analysis must now be robust to noise. The intentional use of randomisation may seem prohibitive, but it turns out that large classes of problems in machine learning remain efficiently learnable, though typically with some reduction in accuracy that can be overcome with additional data.

A crucial secondary goal, then, is to design mitigation measures which maintain utility (ie, allow for good query estimation when the queries pertain to authorised purposes) yet ensure that any misuse of the data access, say by attempting to reverse the anonymisation, gives inconclusive results. This is not hopeless: in terms of the preceding example, a good differentially private analysis gives results with bounded error, yet it follows from the definition of differential privacy that access to the results only marginally increases the attacker's confidence in their attempts to guess confidential information.

The analysis of non-differentially private techniques typically requires a fixed attack scenario. In these analyses, the set of possible attacks executed by an attacker remains limited. The goal becomes to design mitigating measures that mitigate the odds of a successful attack when the full scope of controls is taken into account.

[26] Dwork and Roth, 'The Algorithmic Foundations of Differential Privacy' (n 11) 5. ('"Differential privacy" describes a promise, made by a data holder, or curator, to a data subject: "You will not be affected, adversely or otherwise, by allowing your data to be used in any study or analysis, no matter what other studies, data sets, or information sources, are available."').

[27] It can be shown that deterministic differentially private analyses, ie ones that do not employ randomisation, must always give the same output, and are therefore not useful.

Controls are essentially a means to mitigate risks. As we will explain in Section IV, they can be either data or context related. Competing sets of controls are then meaningfully and directly comparable in terms of their respective probabilities of success.

For fixed attack scenarios, the question thus becomes, 'given a query, how much can one obtain identity, attribute, participation or relational inferences based on their access to query results information?' Using a scale from 0 to 1, it is possible to produce a quantified estimate of the inference risk taking into account all four types of inferences by probability of success.

Note that comparing controls based on the attack success probability does not work for differentially private techniques, since this requires consideration of a specific attack. After all, the attack may be based on extensive prior knowledge. This does not mean that differentially private techniques are inferior to other techniques. In fact, quite the opposite, as they guarantee that an attacker's ability to guess only marginally improves upon additional information. In other words, the attacker is guaranteed to learn little to nothing, and it is preferable to rank differentially private techniques in terms of the maximum amount of per-individual information inferable from the output.

That said, risk-based evaluation remains possible under scenarios where the set of possible attacks is fixed. Roughly speaking, any attack with low probability of success is guaranteed to remain low despite the possible incorporation of the differentially private results information. This works because the amount of usable information present in a differentially private release is bounded, and thus so must be the accompanying reduction in uncertainty of a guessing adversary.

The inference model, as described in Section II, is particularly useful to explain the limits of aggregation and synthesisation methods and compare effective mitigating technical and organisational measures (ie, controls).

III. How to Conceptualise Aggregation and Synthesisation

A. Traditional Aggregation

Aggregated data is summary data. Simply put, aggregated data is metadata that serves to summarise data. Aggregated data is typically produced for statistical purposes (eg, to measure characteristics of population), but the term can be used expansively to encompass other purposes such as processing, compression (eg, to reduce the size of storage), visualisation, or producing a model. In other words, aggregates need not be statistical in nature.

Aggregation operations are common for dataset data. For example, computing maximum (or minimum) value for a particular column within a dataset (eg, what is the *maximum* (*minimum*) salary for the population contained in the data set?), the *average* value for a particular column within a dataset (eg, what is the average salary for the population contained in the dataset?), or the *count* of records with a specified value for a particular column (eg, how many individuals have a salary of X within the population contained in the dataset?) are all processes that will produce aggregated data. The process of producing aggregated data is referred to as data aggregation or, often, aggregation. It should be distinguished from the process of de-identification, which is usually understood as the process of stripping identifiers away, both direct identifiers and indirect identifiers, while keeping the data at the individual or event level.

Aggregation should also be distinguished from the process of generalisation, which consists in replacing a value with a less specific but semantically consistent value (eg, replacing a specific age with an age range within a record).

At present, there appears to be an assumption in privacy and data protection regulations that aggregate information is safe, as efforts to organise anonymisation techniques consistently list aggregation higher (or further right) on the de-identification spectrum than de-identified information. This assumption is known to be incorrect, and solving the problem of rendering aggregate data safe partially motivated the development of differential privacy.[28] For aggregate output to be deemed safe it is necessary to prevent an unauthorised third-party from being able to learn (infer with high confidence) personal information as regards data subjects among the aggregation input.

Mathematically, aggregate functions are functions that output a set of numbers derived from a set of inputs. At first glance this may indeed seem safe: after all, in reducing a database to a single number, a lot of information is thrown away. However, as we shall see, not only is this not necessarily the case, this is also not a sufficient condition to ensure that the data cannot be attributed to an individual.

For example, the *maximum* aggregate must discard a lot of data, as its output only critically depends on rows achieving the maximum value, with all other values in the database remaining irrelevant. Yet when evaluated over company salary data, there may likely be only one row achieving the maximum corresponding to the company chief executive. It follows that an attacker with access to the maximum aggregate may have a good guess as to the executive's salary. One may think that the problem is due to the fact that this aggregate must depend upon more than a single data subject's information. Consider instead an aggregate that *encodes the entire database into a single number* using Gödel numbering.[29]

[28] See Cynthia Dwork et al, 'Calibrating Noise to Sensitivity in Private Data Analysis,' in Shai Halevi and Tal Rabin (eds) *Theory of Cryptography*, vol 3876 (Springer Berlin Heidelberg, 2006), 265–84, https://doi.org/10.1007/11681878_14; Cynthia Dwork et al, 'Calibrating Noise to Sensitivity in Private Data Analysis,' (2017) 7(3) *Journal of Privacy and Confidentiality* 17–51, https://doi.org/10.29012/jpc.v7i3.405.

[29] Eg, through reinterpreting the underlying bits of a record as a number, and then employing Gödel numbering to return a single number whose factorisation reveals the bits of any record. See Kurt Gödel, 'Über formal unentscheidbare Sätze der Principia Mathematica und verwandter Systeme I,' Monatshefte für Mathematik und Physik 38–38, no 1 (December 1931): 173–98, https://doi.org/10.1007/BF01700692.

The aggregate result depends on every record, yet it remains possible to infer the exact contents of any record through repeated division.

As we now outline, it is not necessary to resort to such extreme examples. Consider the following plausible participation inference attack demonstrating that the protections afforded by the *average* aggregate do not guarantee privacy.

Suppose that it is suspected that a local surgeon has a certain rare health condition. It is known that this disease occurs uniformly at random across the population, though a medical study is performed to see if there is a relationship between better outcomes and various socioeconomic attributes. The study publishes its findings, which are irrelevant for our purposes, but reports that all 100 positive local individuals participated, and, the average participant had an income of $58,720, and that one individual making more than $100,000 per year participated. It is well known from census data that individuals in this region have an average salary of $52,175 with a standard deviation of +/- $5,385, with only surgeons making more than $250,000 per year. By Chebyshev's inequality, the odds of observing an average salary that is more than one standard deviation higher due to chance alone is less than 1 per cent for the study size of 100. This suggests to the attacker that the observed shift in the mean is not due to chance. It is likely that the participating outlier is an extreme outlier. Moreover, it gives the attacker an estimate of the outlier's income: as $100*($58,720)–99*($52,175) = $706,675$, and the attacker can even further work out error bounds.

One interesting observation from the example above is that even though the average aggregate, unlike the maximum aggregate, depends on every value, it also tends to favour the privacy of certain individuals over others by responding disproportionately to outlying records.

Indeed, the problem seems to be related to how much an aggregate is influenced by the addition (or removal) of individual records. A goal, then, is to make aggregates safe by rendering them insensitive to the presence or absence of any individual input row. However, if made perfectly safe, the aggregate would be entirely insensitive to its input, and therefore fail to summarise it. This is problematic as safety is at odds with utility, and unconditional safety is, at best, aspirational.

This situation is easily remedied through differential privacy, which serves to guarantee that the resulting data product (eg, a model or query results information) does not carry more than epsilon bits[30] of personal information from any record. This ensures that the data product is of marginal value for enriching inference attacks provided that epsilon remains small.

However, a concern remains that each differentially private response on the same database may leak different information about the same individuals. Situations wherein vast repositories of differentially private results can be referenced or generated should be avoided. Of particular concern are adaptive

---

[30] It should be noted that epsilon may be fractional, for instance epsilon = 0.001, which corresponds to situations wherein one would expect to need about 1,000.

attackers who may issue many differentially private queries with the goal of trying to collect as much information as possible about a group of targets. Put differently, *release context matters*. Controls must be put in place to prevent an adversary from using many aggregate summaries in conjunction to significantly enrich their knowledge of specific participants.

It should be noted that controls are not necessarily mutually exclusive with open data. After all, requiring authenticated access to data and making access to data contingent on access agreements only strengthens protection.

B. Synthesisation

Synthetic data is data drawn from a model which has been trained on real data. The model is generative in the sense it outputs (generates) something it believes to be consistent with the training data. Despite the appeal of using data to which no natural person corresponds, several problems exist. The generative model is trained on real data and thus is derived from the personal, and perhaps sensitive, information of individuals. The question then is to what extent an attacker may be able to make inferences about the participation (or attributes) of these individuals from the behaviour of the model. In the limit of a large number of samples, it is often possible to reconstruct the parameters of the generative model with high fidelity, yielding several precise estimates of aggregate quantities derived from private data.

Synthetic data, without differential privacy, can be a very weak option. To see why, consider the *local surgeon* example of the previous section. A faithful synthetic data model will produce values for the income attribute which statistically agree with the income distribution as seen in the study data: the mean and the standard deviation. Even model parameters are not given directly to the recipient, with enough synthetic data it is possible to estimate both the mean and standard deviation to any desired precision. Given a high-quality estimate of the mean, the attack given in Section III A can be carried out. Namely, an attacker with knowledge of the size of the study (which is public) and an estimate of the mean income can infer the participation of the local surgeon in the training data, and thereby now possess compelling evidence that the local surgeon has a disease, as well as an estimate of the surgeon's income for the year of the study. Note that this is possible *even though all data comes from a synthetic model.*

To mitigate such attacks, it is important to employ controls to limit the amount of personal information that is inferable from such quantities. Again, the natural family of techniques come from the field of differential privacy where such methodology is guaranteed to limit the number of bits of personal information that flow into such aggregates, making aggregate quantities less useful for making inferences.

What Section III shows is that both aggregation and synthesisation are not effective controls per se, despite the belief widely shared within the compliance community that both should automatically put the data outside the scope of privacy and data protection laws.

IV. How to Assess Aggregation Outputs

As hinted above, it is not enough to consider the output of the aggregation process to conclude that the re-identification risk is remote[31] or very small[32] and thereby declare that data usage should not be restricted anymore. Considering the process through which the aggregated output has been obtained is essential, as aggregation processes vary in terms of privacy protections. As outlined in Section II, this should lead us to distinguish two types of controls, *data controls* and *context controls*, which affect either the data itself or its environment.[33]

As aforementioned, controls are essentially a means to mitigate risks. Different types of means can be used: technical means (such as data transformation techniques) or organisational means (such as contracts imposing obligations on data owners and data users, or policies specifying business processes within organisations acting as data owners or data users).

As explained below, in order to be truly effective, controls have to be combined. By effective controls we mean controls that lower the overall risk, both in terms of context and data risk, under at least one attack scenario as explained in Section II. What is more, aggregation should not be seen as an effective control. Mitigation of re-identification risks only happens after several steps are taken and aggregation is only one step in this process. Aggregation will in fact have to involve the implementation of both data and context controls to effectively mitigate re-identification risks.

Data controls are technical measures aimed to strengthen the protection of the confidentiality of the information. The strongest data controls are those that offer data stewards formal mathematical guarantees so that they are able to say to individuals: 'You will not be materially affected, adversely or otherwise, by allowing your data to be used in any study or analysis, no matter what other studies, data sets, or information sources, are available.'[34] Differentially private methods, as

---

[31] ICO Code of Practice, 6 ('The DPA does not require anonymisation to be completely risk free – you must be able to mitigate the risk of identification until it is remote'). Ex-Article 29 WP writes that the 'the "means ... reasonably to be used" test is suggested by the Directive as a criterion to be applied in order to assess whether the anonymisation process is sufficiently robust, i.e. whether identification has become "reasonably" impossible.' Art 29 WP Anonymisation Techniques (n 10) 8. As mentioned, CCPA defines aggregate consumer information as information that is 'is not linked or reasonably linkable to any consumer or household.' Cal. Civ. Code § 1798.140(a).

[32] This is the legal standard found in the US Health Insurance Portability and Accountability Act of 1996 (HIPAA). See 45 CFR § 164.514(b)(1).

[33] For a conceptualisation of the data environment see, eg, Mackey, Elliot, and O'Hara, *The Anonymisation Decision-making Framework* (n 19).

[34] Dwork and Roth, 'The Algorithmic Foundations of Differential Privacy' (n 11) 5.

explained below, are therefore the most obvious type of data control data stewards should be thinking about when wanting to produce aggregates.

Notably, differentially private aggregation can be undertaken through two routes, which are not necessarily equivalent in terms of degree of protection: global differential privacy and local differential privacy, as illustrated in Table 1. It should be noted that when using machine learning techniques to create models, both routes are worth exploring and likely to require fine-tuning over time.[35]

As it has been suggested:

> A good technique for preventing model inversion attacks is simply keeping unnecessary data out of the training set. First, the data scientist should build a version of the model without differential privacy. (She should not release the model to the public at this stage.) She would note its baseline performance and then throw away the model. She would then iteratively build models with more noise until she reaches a minimum acceptable threshold for performance, or a maximum acceptable threshold for privacy loss. Assuming, then, that the privacy loss is acceptable, she could release the model into production.[36]

Table 1 Examples of data controls for producing aggregated data

Data controls	Description
Global differential privacy (GDP)	GDP is a technique employing randomisation in the computation of aggregate statistics. GDP offers a mathematical guarantee against identity, attribute, participation, and relational inferences and is achieved for any desired 'privacy loss'.[37]
Local differential privacy (LDP)	LDP is a data randomisation method that randomises sensitive values. LDP offers a mathematical guarantee against attribute inference and is achieved for any desired 'privacy loss'.[38]

---

[35] While it is known that large classes of efficiently learnable problems in machine learning remain efficiently learnable under differential privacy, significant barriers exist in the adoption of globally differentially private methods due to their reliance on specialised methods.

[36] Sophie Stalla-Bourdillon, Alfred Rossi, and Gabriela Zanfir-Fortuna, 'Data Protection by Process: How to Operationalize Data Protection by Design' (2019), https://fpf.org/2019/12/19/new-white-paper-provides-guidance-on-embedding-data-protection-principles-in-machine-learning/.

[37] Matthew Green, 'What Is Differential Privacy?' A Few Thoughts on Cryptographic Engineering (blog), June 15, 2016, https://blog.cryptographyengineering.com/2016/06/15/what-is-differential-privacy/ (last accessed 5 March 2020).

[38] See, eg, Stanley L Warner, 'Randomized Response: A Survey Technique for Eliminating Evasive Answer Bias' (1965) 60(309) *Journal of the American Statistical Association* 63–69, https://doi.org/10.1080/01621459.1965.10480775. See also Shiva Prasad Kasiviswanathan et al, 'What Can We Learn Privately?' (2011) 40(3) *SIAM Journal on Computing* 793–826, https://doi.org/10.1137/090756090.

While some commentators have argued that differential privacy methods do not leave any room for utility,[39] the trade-off between utility and confidentiality is in fact context dependent. Assuming that the data is well-sampled and that there are no outliers, a satisfactory degree of utility should be reached. By way of example, any problem that is learnable in the probably approximately correct model (or PAC learnable),[40] remains PAC learnable under differential privacy.[41] Further, technologies such as TensorFlow Privacy augment machine learning methods with global differential privacy.[42]

Context controls are technical or organisational measures implemented to strengthen the protection of the confidentiality of the information queried, with no direct impact upon the content of the query results. Instead, external controls can have a direct impact upon who is able to formulate a query (eg, role- or attribute-based access control, data sharing agreement), how many queries a data user will be able to formulate (eg, query monitoring), the purposes for which the query results can be used (eg, purpose-based access control, data sharing agreement), and the mitigation actions the data curator and the data user will have to perform when aware that the re-identification risk is increasing given changes in the data environment. Context controls are illustrated in Table 2.

Table 2 Examples of context controls for producing aggregated data

Context controls	Typology	Description
Access control (RBAC, ABAC)	Technical control	Access rights are granted to data users through either the allocation of roles (function within organisation, department, team) or/and the use of policies which combine attributes. Policies can use any type of attributes (user attributes, data source attributes, column attributes, etc).

(continued)

---

[39] See, eg, Matthew Fredrikson et al, 'Privacy in Pharmacogenetics: An End-to-End Case Study of Personalized Warfarin Dosing,' in Proceedings of the 23rd USENIX Conference on Security Symposium, SEC'14 (San Diego, CA: USENIX Association, 2014), 17–32. (finding utility and privacy mutually exclusive in regard to warfarin dosing studies); id. at 29 ('[F]or ε values that protect genomic privacy, which is the central privacy concern in our application, the risk of negative patient outcomes increases beyond acceptable levels.')

[40] LG Valiant, 'A Theory of the Learnable,' Communications of the ACM 27, no. 11 (November 5, 1984): 1134–42, https://doi.org/10.1145/1968.1972.

[41] Kasiviswanathan et al, 'What Can We Learn Privately?' (n 38).

[42] See H Brendan McMahan et al, 'A General Approach to Adding Differential Privacy to Iterative Training Procedures,' ArXiv:1812.06210 [Cs, Stat], 4 March 2019, http://arxiv.org/abs/1812.06210.

Table 2 *(Continued)*

Context controls	Typology	Description
Purpose-based access control	Combination of technical and organisational controls	Purpose-based access control forces the data user to acknowledge the purpose under which she is requesting access to the data and requires the data user to agree with accessing the data for this purpose only. The purpose for which data is to be accessed can be expressly mentioned within the data sharing agreement concluded between the data curator and the data user or within an internal policy if the data curator and the data user belong to the same organisation.
Prohibition of linking	Combination of technical and organisational controls	In order to reduce the likelihood of all types of inferences, data users are prevented from linking data sources together (through technical means and data sharing agreement and/or internal policy).
Prohibition of re-identification	Organisational control	In order to prevent re-identification from happening, data users can be subject to an obligation not to re-identify individuals to which the information pertains (eg, through a data sharing agreement or an internal policy).
Prohibition of data sharing	Organisational control	The data user (ie, the recipient of the data) is under an obligation not to share the data with other parties.
Query monitoring	Technical or combination of organisational and technical controls	Query monitoring is facilitated by the query interface and is performed in real time by a compliance personnel or auditor. Query monitoring can also be automated through a privacy budget.

(continued)

Table 2 *(Continued)*

Context controls	Typology	Description
Query termination	Technical control or combination of technical and organisational controls	Query termination is facilitated by the query interface and is performed in real time by a compliance personnel or auditor. Query termination can also be enforced automatically when the data user exhausts the privacy budget.
Obligation to monitor additional information	Organisational control	The curator is under an obligation to monitor publicly available information to assess the strength of the anonymisation process.
Obligation to comply with breach mitigation plan	Combination of technical and organisational controls	Each stakeholder (ie, the data curator and the data user) is under an obligation to take immediate mitigation action if they are aware of significant changes within the data environment (eg, the data curator terminates access to the data or the data user reports to the data curator) and could also be under an obligation not to contact re-identified (or likely to be re-identified) individuals. These duties are usually formulated within a data sharing agreement or within an internal policy.

What Section IV suggests is that there exist a variety of controls that are relevant for lowering re-identification risks, be it through both the aggregation or the de-identification route.

This explains why an output-based approach to characterise aggregate data is not enough: a process-based approach is key, which should start by assessing the variety of data and context controls applicable or applied to the data and its environment.

The same holds true for de-identification: only when a process-based approach is adopted should it be possible to characterise the output data.

And the production of synthetic data is no exception to this consideration. After all, synthetic data is just data sampled from a model derived from aggregate data and with enough samples it is possible to reconstruct the model parameters and, therefore, learn everything that is inferable from the aggregate value, possibly including confidential information. This thus leads us to compare anonymisation controls in Section V and suggest that context controls are a must-have.

V. How to Compare Anonymisation Controls

Prior attempts to create representations of de-identification and/or anonymisation solutions have relied upon a two-dimensional spectrum or staircase.[43] Garfinkel, for example, explains that:

> all data exist on an identifiability spectrum. At one end (the left) are data that are not related to individuals (for example, historical weather records) and therefore pose no privacy risk. At the other end (the right) are data that are linked directly to specific individuals. Between these two endpoints are data that can be linked with effort, that can only be linked to groups of people, and that are based on individuals but cannot be linked back. In general, de-identification approaches are designed to push data to the left while retaining some desired utility, lowering the risk of distributing de-identified data to a broader population or the general public.[44]

While this presentation makes sense at a high level, it does not directly enable decision-makers to actually choose among data and context controls.

Omer Tene, Kelsey Finch and Jules Polonetsky go one step further in their attempt to provide effective guidance to both data users and compliance personnel and bridge the gap between technical and legal definitions.[45] They distinguish between pseudonymised, protected pseudonymised, de-identified, protected de-identified and anonymous data and introduce the concept of non-technical safeguards and controls, which are added to data modification techniques to produce either protected pseudonymised or protected de-identified data:

> Non-technical safeguards and controls include two broad categories: 1) internal administrative and physical controls (internal controls); and 2) external contractual and legal protections (external controls). Internal controls encompass security policies, access limits, employee training, data segregation guidelines, and data deletion practices that aim to stop confidential information from being exploited or leaked to the public. External controls involve contractual terms that restrict how partners use and share information, and the corresponding remedies and auditing rights to ensure compliance.[46]

In that model, aggregated data are considered to be safer than de-identified data and are not described as requiring non-technical safeguards and controls. While

---

[43] See, eg, Garfinkel, 'De-Identification of Personal Information' (n 17); Polonetsky, Tene, and Finch, 'Shades of Gray' (n 13).

[44] Garfinkel, 'De-Identification of Personal Information' (n 17) 5.

[45] Polonetsky, Tene, and Finch, 'Shades of Gray' (n 13).

[46] ibid, 606.

this spectrum should certainly be welcome in that it makes it clear that both technical and non-technical safeguards and controls are relevant for assessing the robustness of data modification processes, it relies upon a simplified binary conception of aggregated data for which non-technical safeguards and controls as well as other types of context controls do not seem to be needed. As explained in the introduction, though, such an approach is not surprising, as it seems to underlie several pieces of legislation.

What is more, this spectrum does not specifically locate synthetic data, which is increasingly seen as a valid alternative to aggregation.

Finally, the spectrum is not particularly adapted to an interactive query setting, which should make it possible to compare the robustness of data controls, with a view to select effective data and context controls for the use case at hand.

What Runshan Hu et al show is that, assuming sanitisation techniques are to be combined with contextual controls, in order to effectively mitigate the three re-identification risks identified by ex-Article 29 Data Protection Working Party, a two-dimensional representation of sanitisation techniques through the means of a spectrum is not necessarily helpful, as a different mix of sanitisation techniques and contextual controls could in fact be seen as comparable.[47] While they note that the only sanitisation technique able to mitigate on its own the three re-identification risks studied (ie, singling out, inference, linkability) is differential privacy on the condition that at least additional security controls are implemented, they do not assess the effect of synthesisation.

Bellovin et al only focus upon synthetic data and make it clear that a distinction should be drawn between vanilla synthetic data and differentially private synthetic data. However, they do not offer a comparative diagram for the different types of data controls and do not consider context controls.[48]

The primary difficulty in developing a coherent ranking of privacy techniques is that their effectiveness is highly context dependent. For instance, a medical study may involve exchanging detailed patient data with a partnering hospital in order to develop new treatments or identify subjects for clinical trials. The privacy concerns and controls employed for medical data will undoubtedly differ from those that collect browsing history to build and sell models for marketing purposes. And yet, despite these differences, the toolset in either case is essentially the same. Data risk mitigations include the familiar techniques of tokenisation, k-anonymisation, and local and global differential privacy. Context risk mitigations still include access controls, contracts, training, and auditing.

---

[47] Runshan Hu et al, 'Bridging Policy, Regulation and Practice? A Techno-Legal Analysis of Three Types of Data in the GDPR,' in Ronald Leenes Rosamunde van Brakel, Serge Gutwirth and Paul De Hert (eds) *Data Protection and Privacy: The Age of Intelligent Machines* (Oxford: Hart Publishing, 2017) 115–142.

[48] Bellovin, Dutta, and Reitinger, 'Privacy and Synthetic Datasets' (n 24) 37, 41. ('For synthetic data, this means that without adding privacy-preserving features like differential privacy, there still remains risk of data leakage.')

In both of the preceding examples it remains necessary to ensure that the privacy risk is tolerable. Despite the shared goal and common set of tools, implementations look very different. In the medical data example, it is assumed necessary that sensitive information be exchanged in order to fulfil the purpose. This means that it is not possible to prevent the receiving organisation from making sensitive inferences about the data subjects, after all this is the point. Thus, there is a heavier reliance on more costly context controls, including access and control restrictions, data sharing agreements, training for employees, etc.

The success of knowledge-based attacks is generally limited by two things: the availability of information and processing abilities of the attacker. It follows from this that anonymisation is context dependent. For instance, consider an attacker with intimate medical knowledge of a specific individual. Such knowledge, to the extent that it is not apparent from observation of the individual or their behaviour, would not be considered identifying and would be left in the clear in some approaches to anonymisation. Therefore, such information would not be anonymised to an attacker with access to the subject's medical records.

It is difficult to produce a comparative classification of anonymisation controls without consideration of situational specifics. Attempts to do so fail to acknowledge the role of both technical and non-technical controls and ultimately rely upon a gross oversimplification of the attack scenario that fails to adequately characterise the behaviour of the attacker. Moreover, ignoring situational differences leads to invalid comparisons of the guarantees of formal attack models that may not equally apply.

Let us go back to our generic query setting illustrated by Diagram 1 where we want to protect, through de-identification or aggregation, data to prevent query results from leaking information leading to identity inference, attribute inference, participation inference, or relational inference.

Let us further assume that all direct identifiers are masked in a way that is irreversible to the attacker. This can be achieved through nulling, hashing with salts, or encrypting direct identifiers with state-of-the-art techniques. In other words, let us assume that the first data control applied on the data is pseudonymisation. Pseudonymisation is often the first step towards both de-identification and aggregation and does not as such mitigate against any type of inference, as it leaves indirect identifiers or indirectly identifying attributes as they are, in the clear.[49]

Let us now consider the following five data controls:

- Control 1: a system limits the allowed queries to aggregate queries and returns GDP-protected results.
- Control 2: a system uses LDP on sensitive non-identifying attributes.

[49] See Art 29 WP Anonymisation Techniques (n 10) 20–21.

- Control 3: a system uses k-anonymisation[50] on the indirect identifiers (but not on non-identifying attributes).
- Control 4: a system nulls/tokenises, through hashing with salts[51] or encryption[52] (per record), indirect identifiers.
- Control 5: a system aggregates attribute values.

These five data controls can thus be organised according to their robustness (ie, their formal or mathematical resilience towards the four types of inferences aforementioned).

- Control 1: with a suitable epsilon and limited number of queries, this data control mitigates all four types of inferences. In other words, when control 1 is combined with two context controls (ie, query monitoring and query termination, which can take the form of an automated privacy budget or ad hoc monitoring and query termination), it is superior to controls 2–5.
- Control 2: with a suitable epsilon and limited number of queries, this data control releases data that is safe from attribute inference on sensitive attributes.
- Control 3: with a suitable k, this data control releases data that is safe from identity and relational inference at t=n, but not future proof against future attacks if additional information evolves over time and is enriched. Query monitoring and query termination are not relevant to make control 3 offer a formal guarantee against attribute or participation inference. However, control 3 could then be combined with other techniques, such as control 2, to mitigate against attribute disclosure, for example. The advantage of control 2 over other techniques such as l-diversity[53] and t-closeness[54] is that control 2 guarantees that only a limited amount of private data is transferred.

---

[50] See, eg, Pierangela Samarati and Latanya Sweeney, 'Protecting Privacy When Disclosing Information: K-Anonymity and Its Enforcement through Generalization and Suppression,' 1998, http://citeseerx.ist.psu.edu/viewdoc/summary?doi=10.1.1.37.5829.

[51] Hashing with salts will usually be preferred to nulling in scenarios in which it is possible to effectively segment data users and it is a requirement that at least one segment should be able to link records together.

[52] Of note, homomorphic encryption does not offer any formal guarantee against all four types of inferences (on top of encryption). What it enables the data curator to do is to commission a third party to perform a computation upon the data source, without disclosing the input data or the query results to that third party, who is, per definition, a non-trusted party.

[53] L-diversity is an extension to k-anonymisation designed to mitigate inference attacks by preventing a significant fraction of each k-anonymous cohort from having similar values. This goal is to prevent attacks where, say, every member of the cohort possesses the same sensitive attribute as this would allow an attacker to make a sensitive inference despite being unable to single out an individual's record.

[54] T-closeness is similar to l-diversity except it requires that the distribution of values of a sensitive attribute, when restricted to any cohort, remains close in a certain formal sense to its distribution as observed across the whole dataset.

- Control 4: this control only mitigates identity and relational inference at t=n, but it is not future proof against future attacks if additional information evolves over time and is enriched, and in any case, it does not mitigate against attribute and participation inference. It is thus weaker than GDP, which is future proof against all forms of inferences.
- Control 5: this control does not mitigate against any type of inference without additional controls, such as controls 1-4. Crucially, this is also true for synthetic data. What is obvious, though, is that in several instances aggregating sensitive attributes is a better option than keeping sensitive attributes in the clear.

From this description it becomes clear that both aggregation and synthetic data per se do not offer any means to mitigate against the four types of inferences aforementioned.

What Section V shows is that some forms of context controls are always needed. Ultimately the choice of the data control will depend upon the utility requirements of the use case, but inevitably the weaker the data controls, the stronger and the more diverse the context controls will have to be. The drawback of relying upon a great variety of organisational context controls, however, is that they do not offer by themselves any formal guarantee against inference attacks; further, quantified comparisons require estimations of their effectiveness, which can be difficult to make. This is the reason why we classify them as soft controls, whereas data controls that offer mathematical guarantees when combined with additional context controls can be deemed hard controls. This is not to say that hard controls should always be preferred to soft controls. The selection and combination of controls will depend upon a variety of factors and the specifics of each use case.

VI. How to Inform Legal Interpretation

With this background in mind, it is now possible to reassess anonymisation, de-identification, and aggregation provisions of privacy and data protection legislation and offer interpretative guidance.

The following two premises should now be taken for granted:

(1) Both de-identified and aggregated data require context controls.
(2) Techniques with formal mathematical guarantees should be preferred because they lend well to quantification of control effectiveness.

The legal standards are obviously different from the requirement that a formal guarantee against all four types of inferences should be achieved through the transformation process (ie, anonymisation under EU law or de-identification or aggregation under Californian law). Rather, it is expressed in terms of *'reasonable means likely to be used for re-identification'*[55] or *'reasonably linkable.'*[56] What this implies is that there is no requirement in the law that all four types of inferences should be mitigated through mathematical guarantees.

What has been debated, though, is whether all four types of inferences should be mitigated at all with K El Eman et al, for example, arguing that US healthcare law is only concerned with identity inferences.[57] K El Eman et al have thus been criticising the EU approach as described in ex-Art 29 WP's opinion on anonymisation techniques as being too restrictive.[58]

What seems clear, however, is that modern privacy and data protection laws such as the CCPA or GDPR are as a matter of principle concerned with a wider range of issues than the protection of the confidentiality of the identity of consumers or data subjects.[59] While this is made more explicit in the GDPR, which lists seven data protection principles, including data minimisation and fairness, and regulates profiling more strictly, it is also implicit in the definitions of consumer personal information as well as de-identified information and consumer information in the aggregate that are included in the CCPA.

This consideration should therefore have a direct impact upon the way the scope of these privacy and data protection laws is delineated and should require an initial assessment of all four types of inferences. However, depending upon the use case at stake, some forms of inferences (eg, relational inference and participation inference) could certainly be addressed through context controls only. Importantly, this is not suggesting that anonymised longitudinal studies are not possible anymore because relational inference would have to be mitigated through data controls. It is suggesting, on the contrary, that at a minimum strict attribute-based and role-based access control combined with an obligation not to further share the data should be in place to mitigate against participation, relational, and attribute inferences. For instance, while it may be technically possible to construct effective data controls for certain limited types of longitudinal analysis, doing so is burdensome and rigid in the sense that assumptions about the nature of the final result could hinder exploratory analysis and require vast expertise. Given the rigidity and costs of these data controls, it could make sense

---

[55] GDPR, Recital 26.

[56] Cal. Civ. Code §§ 1798.140(a) and (h).

[57] K El Emam and C Alvarez, 'A Critical Appraisal of the Article 29 Working Party Opinion 05/2014 on Data Anonymization Techniques' (2015 5(1) *International Data Privacy Law* 73–87, https://doi.org/10.1093/idpl/ipu033.

[58] El Emam and Alvarez, 'A Critical Appraisal of the Article 29' (n 57).

[59] Decisions like the ones rendered under older privacy laws such as the 1984 Cable Communications Privacy Act or the 1998 Video Privacy Protection Act in the US should arguably not be of great help to understand key concepts. See, eg, *Pruitt v Comcast Cable Holdings, LLC*, 100 F. App'x 713, 716 (10th Cir. 2004). Compare with *In re Hulu Privacy Litig.*, No C 11-03764 LB, 2014 WL 1724344, at 10-11 (N.D. Cal. Apr. 28, 2014); *Yershov v Gannett Satellite Info. Network, Inc.*, 820 F.3d 482, 485 (1st Cir. 2016); *Eichenberger v ESPN, Inc.*, 876 F.3d 979, 985 (9th Cir. 2017). But see *In re Vizio, Inc.*, 238 F. Supp. 3d 1204, 1212 (C.D. Cal. 2017).

to enforce narrow permitted purposes via context controls and impose legal obligations upon data users.

Studies that require high-fidelity access to sensitive data clearly present an obstacle even for sophisticated data controls. This often includes longitudinal studies where lengthy records tend to leak relatively large amounts of private data. The inability to effectively leverage data controls without hampering utility must be offset by increasing context controls to compensate for increased overall risk.

As a matter of practice, sufficient context controls should be deployed such that the residual risk of accidental or malicious behaviour of individuals is viewed as mitigated. When the fidelity of sensitive data must be kept intact, it may be necessary to exclude all but a few, high trusted individuals in a controlled environment. This, in principle, is a valid approach to reduce the overall risk. By implementing strict access control, low-trust individuals are kept away from the data. Further, by enforcing obligations not to further share the data, the risk due to the accidental or malicious misbehaviour of the data user can be mitigated, as long as monitoring and auditing of data usage are enabled.

What is more, given the start of the art of data and context controls, privacy and data protection regulations should in fact be converging on matters relating to anonymisation, de-identification and aggregation, despite their differences in wording.

As a matter of principle two routes should lead to alleviating restrictions imposed by privacy or data protection laws:

(1) *Local anonymisation*: the process by which the ability to make inferences from event-level data is limited for the release context in which the attacker operates.
(2) *Aggregate anonymisation*: the process by which the ability to make inferences from aggregate data is limited for the release context in which the attacker operates.

Pseudonymisation, understood as the masking of direct identifiers, should be seen as a valuable security and data minimisation measure and constitutes the first step of any anonymisation process. Notably, both the GDPR and CCPA refer to pseudonymisation and distinguish it from de-identification, aggregation or anonymisation.[60]

The two anonymisation routes mentioned above appear compatible with the spirit of the law of modern privacy and data protection,[61] although their letter can appear problematic, which is the case for the CCPA in particular. Older statutes, such as the HIPAA and its Safe Harbor provision would need to be modernised.[62] HIPAA Safe Harbor appears to be particularly problematic, as it only mandates

---

[60] See GDPR, Art 4 and Recital 26; Cal. Civ. Code §1798.140(r).
[61] After all, the CCPA includes within its definition of personal information inferences. See Cal. Civ. Code §1798.140(o)(1)(K).
[62] 45 CFR § 164.514(b)(2).

one data control and no context controls: the removal of 18 identifiers (ie, a partial version of control 4). This has been acknowledged by the US National Committee on Vital and Health Statistics in 2017, which recommends restricting downstream use of data even when complying with the HIPAA Safe Harbor.[63] The HIPAA expert determination provision[64] is, however, more flexible and makes it possible to consider both data and context controls as a means to address the four types of inferences aforementioned.

CCPA section 1798.140(h) governing de-identified data (which should correspond to the local anonymisation route) is interesting in that it lists key context controls and business processes that prohibit re-identification and prevent inadvertent release of personal information on top of technical safeguards. These business processes should however be also relevant for aggregated and synthetic data, which is not something that is expressly acknowledged by section 1798.140 governing aggregate consumer information (ie, what we conceive as aggregate anonymisation).[65] A reasoning by analogy would thus be needed for the interpretation of section 1798.140. What is important to bear in mind is that these business processes should always be assessed in the light of the inference-mitigation goal they seek to achieve. Of note, as synthetic data is a subset of aggregate data, it should be captured by section 1978.140 as it stands.

CCPA section 1798.145(a)(5) is confusing and could lead to unsatisfactory results if interpreted without due consideration of section 1798.140. Section 1798.145(a)(5) seems to suggest that both de-identified data and information in the aggregate can circulate freely, without context controls. Yet, the very definition of de-identified data includes context controls and as explained above, we suggest that the definition of information in the aggregate should implicitly comprise context controls as well.

---

[63] National Committee on Vital and Health Statistics, 'Re: Recommendations on De-Identification of Protected Health Information under HIPAA,' 2017, www.ncvhs.hhs.gov/wp-content/uploads/2013/12/2017-Ltr-Privacy-DeIdentification-Feb-23-Final-w-sig.pdf. The National Committee makes recommendations related to the de-identification of protected health information under HIPAA and suggests controlling downstream use by the recipient of the data through access control. ('For example, covered entities and business associates might consider intended uses or the security and access controls used by recipients of a particular de-identified data set, in addition to considering the attributes of the data set.')

[64] 45 CFR § 164.514(b)(1). De-identifying data through the expert determination route requires the intervention of an expert who will be asked to determine 'that the risk is very small that the information could be used, alone or in combination with other reasonably available information, by an anticipated recipient to identify an individual who is a subject of the information' as per 45 CFR § 164.514(b)(1)(i).

[65] What is more, the first prong ('Has implemented technical safeguards that prohibit reidentification of the consumer to whom the information may pertain') is not properly drafted in that it seems to suggest that technical safeguards alone are sufficient to prevent re-identification. The verb 'prohibit' should therefore be understood in the sense of 'appropriately mitigate.' In addition, the exclusion of publicly available information from the definition of personal information (Cal. Civ. Code § 1798.140(o)(2)) should not prevent the consideration of additional information to determine the re-identification risk level.

GDPR Recital 26 is less specific than the CCPA but is worth pointing to for one reason: the mention that controls should be monitored over time. Both anonymisation routes seem available under the GDPR. The fact that pseudonymised data is considered to be personal data does not mean, as a matter of principle, that local anonymisation is not possible. As aforementioned, local anonymisation implies the treatment of both direct and indirect identifiers, whereas pseudonymisation is usually understood as a technique that masks direct identifiers only.

The GDPR is only one piece of the EU jigsaw and other legislations such as the Clinical Trial Regulation[66] should also be taken into account to make sense of the EU framework. Under Article 43 of the Clinical Trial Regulation, sponsors are required to submit annually 'a report on the safety of each investigational medicinal product used in a clinical trial for which it is the sponsor'.[67,68] What is more, this report 'shall only contain aggregate and anonymised data'.[69] This would thus seem to exclude the local anonymisation route as we defined it above.

This exclusion makes sense in a clinical trial context. This is because it should be clear that longitudinal data can only be transformed into anonymised data within a closed environment. Therefore, public release could only happen if the aggregation route is chosen and if differential privacy is implemented and combined with additional context controls (ie, query monitoring and query termination or privacy budget).

It is true that Art 29 WP Anonymisation Techniques Opinion is not always easy to reconcile with a risk-based approach to anonymisation. While the Opinion has the merit that it is comprehensive, in that it covers a wide range of techniques and goes beyond the concern of identity disclosure or identity inference, it does include statements which are not compatible with a risk-based approach, such as the requirement that raw data should be destroyed to pursue anonymisation.[70] With this said, the Opinion does not suggest that it is not possible to mitigate re-identification risks through a combination of data and context controls. In any case, national regulators are not always aligned with the most contentious part of the Opinion[71] and other sector-specific regulatory authorities at the

---

[66] Regulation (EU) No 536/2014 of the European Parliament and of the Council of 16 April 2014 on clinical trials on medicinal products for human use, and repealing Directive 2001/20/EC Text with EEA relevance [2014] OJ L158/1–76.

[67] The Court of Justice of the European Union (CJEU) actually recognised in Case C-582/14 *Breyer Patrick Breyer v Bundesrepublik Deutschland* 19 October 2016 ECLI:EU:C:2016:779 (*in fine*) the importance of context controls when applying the identifiability test.

[68] Clinical Trial Regulation, Art 43(1).

[69] ibid Art 43(3).

[70] 'Thus, it is critical to understand that when a data controller does not delete the original (identifiable) data at event-level, and the data controller hands over part of this dataset (for example after removal or masking of identifiable data), the resulting dataset is still personal data.' Art 29 WP Anonymisation Techniques (n 10) 9.

[71] See, eg, ICO Anonymisation Code of Practice, 21. While the Code was released in 2012 it was not amended after 2014 ('This does not mean though, that effective anonymisation through pseudonymisation becomes impossible. The Information Commissioner recognises that some forms of research, for example longitudinal studies, can only take place where different pieces of data can be linked reliably to the same individual.'). See also 58–59.

European level have issued guidance suggesting that a risk-based approach to de-identification remains a valid option, even after the Art 29 WP Anonymisation Techniques Opinion. Notably, this is the case of the European Medical Agency.[72]

This chapter does not suggest that because privacy or data protection restrictions are eliminated as a result of the combination of data and context controls, no harm could ever be caused to individuals. It has been demonstrated that in a machine learning context collective harm can be caused to individuals whose data has not been used to generate the models.[73] It is therefore crucial that an ethical impact assessment always be conducted. This essentially boils down to documenting and assessing model assumptions and limitations within the context of use cases illustrating how the model will work once deployed.

Notably, the GDPR framework is superior to the CCPA framework at least in relation to one key process-based requirement: assuming the data analytics process initiates with personal data, which is a sensible assumption to make as training data is likely to be transformed or protected in steps as explained above, an impact assessment of collective harms should always be included in the data protection impact assessment in situations of high risks. This is because data controllers are required to assess the impact of high risks to all 'the rights and freedoms of natural persons'.[74]

With this said, it should not be forgotten that as individual inferences (ie, output data produced when a model is applied upon an individual's data when making an individual decision) are personal data,[75] collective harm eventually leads to individual harm and as such will be captured by the privacy or data protection framework at this later point in time.

---

[72] European Medical Agency, External guidance on the implementation of the European Medicines Agency policy on the publication of clinical data for medicinal products for human use, 15 October 2018, EMA/90915/2016 Version 1.4. ('since in order to achieve a maximum usefulness of the data published, it is unlikely that for clinical reports all three criteria can be fulfilled [Possibility to single out an individual, Possibility to link records relating to an individual, Whether information can be inferred concerning an individual] by any anonymisation solution, it is EMA's view that a thorough evaluation of the risk of re-identification needs to be performed').

[73] See, eg, Ellen W McGinnis et al, 'Giving Voice to Vulnerable Children: Machine Learning Analysis of Speech Detects Anxiety and Depression in Early Childhood' (2019) 23(6) *IEEE Journal of Biomedical and Health Informatics* 2294–2301, https://doi.org/10.1109/JBHI.2019.2913590; Sophie Stalla-Bourdillon et al, 'Warning Signs – The Future of Privacy and Security in the Age of Machine Learning' (Future of Privacy Forum and Immuta Whitepaper, 2019), www.immuta.com/warning-signs-the-future-of-privacy-and-security-in-the-age-of-machine-learning/.

[74] GDPR, Art 40.

[75] CCPA defines inferences as 'the derivation of information, data, assumptions, or conclusions from facts, evidence, or another source of information or data.' Cal. Civ. Code § 1798.140(m) and includes individual inferences within the list of personal data. Cal. Civ. Code § 1798.140(o)(K): 'Inferences drawn from any of the information identified in this subdivision to create a profile about a consumer reflecting the consumer's preferences, characteristics, psychological trends, predispositions, behaviour, attitudes, intelligence, abilities, and aptitudes.' The same should be true with the EU data protection framework, even though the CJCE held in JEU, Joined Cases C-141/12 and C-372/12, *YS v Minister voor Immigratie, Integratie en Asiel and Minister voor Immigratie, Integratie en Asiel v M and S*, 17 July 2014, ECLI:EU:C:2014:2081 that a legal decision is not personal data. The distinction to draw is between the model, ie the reasoning, and the output, ie the inference. See, however, Sandra Wachter and Brent Mittelstadt, 'A Right to Reasonable Inferences: Re-Thinking Data Protection Law

VII. Conclusion

To conclude, refining and implementing the inference model as developed in the literature on differential privacy we have demonstrated that there is no reason to think that aggregated or synthetic data are inherently safe. Both aggregation and synthesisation should not be considered as effective mitigating strategies without the addition of data and context controls. As a consequence, privacy and data protection laws should not carve out exceptions for aggregate or synthetic data without requesting the combination of data and context controls. Data controls are controls that directly transform the data, while context controls affect the data environment and reduce the range of actions available to a data user.

We argue that two routes can lead to anonymisation: local anonymisation and aggregate anonymisation, kept at the event or individual level or aggregated, depending on the characteristics of the use case. In both cases, anonymisation can only be achieved if four types of inferences are taken into account and addressed either through data or context controls with a view to make inferences from data limited for the release context. We show that such an approach does not necessarily mean that it becomes impossible to anonymise longitudinal data.

Finally, we make the case that interpretation of anonymisation, de-identification or aggregation legal provisions should be converging and offer guidance to interpret recent provisions such as the CCPA section 1798.140 and GDPR Recital 26. We suggest that a risk-based assessment provides an objective measure of anonymisation approaches and has the potential to be replicable as long as assumptions related to attack methodologies hold. It should inform future interpretation of both the GDPR and CCPA. Nonetheless, given the confusing language used in provisions dealing with de-identification or anonymisation, in particular in the CCPA, a more detailed specification of the rules would be worth exploring. Guidance on attack methodologies would also prove extremely useful for organisations acting as data controllers.

Ultimately, what should be clear is that the binary dichotomy personal data/anonymised data is misleading for two reasons at least: it is not enough to look at the data to legally characterise the data and it is the potential for inferences which should drive the anonymisation approach, rather than actual inferences.

Acknowledgements

The authors are grateful to Dara Hallinan, Ronald Leenes, Serge Gutwirth, Paul de Hert, as well as the reviewers of this chapter for their insightful comments.

in the Age of Big Data and AI,' 2018, https://doi.org/10.7916/D8-G10S-KA92. This is not to say that models can never remember personal information, in particular when controls have not been put in place during the training phase. See Veale, Binns, and Edwards, 'Algorithms That Remember' (n 14).

References

Abowd, John M 'Disclosure Avoidance and the 2018 Census Test: Release of the Source Code.' The United States Census Bureau. www.census.gov/newsroom/blogs/research-matters/2019/06/disclosure_avoidance.html (last accessed 4 March 2020).

Bellovin, Steven M, Preetam K. Dutta, and Nathan Reitinger. 'Privacy and Synthetic Datasets' (2019) 22(1) *Stanford Technology Law Review*.

Dwork, Cynthia, Frank McSherry, Kobbi Nissim, and Adam Smith. 'Calibrating Noise to Sensitivity in Private Data Analysis' in Shai Halevi and Tal Rabin (eds) *Theory of Cryptography*, 3876:265–84. (Springer Berlin Heidelberg, 2006). https://doi.org/10.1007/11681878_14.

Dwork, Cynthia, Frank McSherry, Kobbi Nissim, and Adam Smith. 'Calibrating Noise to Sensitivity in Private Data Analysis' (2017) 7(3) *Journal of Privacy and Confidentiality* 17–51. https://doi.org/10.29012/jpc.v7i3.405.

Dwork, Cynthia, and Aaron Roth. 'The Algorithmic Foundations of Differential Privacy' (2013) 9(3-4) *Foundations and Trends® in Theoretical Computer Science* 211–407. https://doi.org/10.1561/0400000042.

El Emam, K, and C Alvarez. 'A Critical Appraisal of the Article 29 Working Party Opinion 05/2014 on Data Anonymization Techniques' (2015) 5(1) *International Data Privacy Law* 73–87. https://doi.org/10.1093/idpl/ipu033.

El Emam, Khaled. *Guide to the De-Identification of Personal Health Information* 1st edn. (Auerbach Publications, 2013) https://doi.org/10.1201/b14764.

El Emam, Khaled, and Bradley Malin. *Appendix B: Concepts and Methods for De-Identifying Clinical Trial Data. Sharing Clinical Trial Data: Maximizing Benefits, Minimizing Risk* (National Academies Press (US), 2015) www.ncbi.nlm.nih.gov/books/NBK285994/.

Finch, Kelsey. 'A Visual Guide to Practical Data De-Identification.' Future of Privacy Forum. https://fpf.org/2016/04/25/a-visual-guide-to-practical-data-de-identification/ (last accessed 4 March 2020).

Fredrikson, Matthew, Eric Lantz, Somesh Jha, Simon Lin, David Page, and Thomas Ristenpart. 'Privacy in Pharmacogenetics: An End-to-End Case Study of Personalized Warfarin Dosing.' In Proceedings of the 23rd USENIX Conference on Security Symposium, 17–32. SEC'14. San Diego, CA: USENIX Association, 2014.

Garfinkel, Simson L. 'De-Identification of Personal Information.' National Institute of Standards and Technology, October 2015. https://doi.org/10.6028/NIST.IR.8053.

Gödel, Kurt. 'Über formal unentscheidbare Sätze der Principia Mathematica und verwandter Systeme I.' [1931] 38(1) *Monatshefte für Mathematik und Physik* 173–98. https://doi.org/10.1007/BF01700692.

Green, Matthew. 'What Is Differential Privacy?' A Few Thoughts on Cryptographic Engineering (blog), 15 June 2016. https://blog.cryptographyengineering.com/2016/06/15/what-is-differential-privacy/.

Hu, Runshan, Sophie Stalla-Bourdillon, Mu Yang, Valeria Schiavo, and Vladimiro Sassone. 'Bridging Policy, Regulation and Practice? A Techno-Legal Analysis of Three Types of Data in the GDPR.' In Ronald Leenes Rosamunde van Brakel, Serge Gutwirth and Paul De Hert (eds) *Data Protection and Privacy: The Age of Intelligent Machines* (Oxford: Hart Publishing, 2017) 115–142.

Kasiviswanathan, Shiva Prasad, Homin K Lee, Kobbi Nissim, Sofya Raskhodnikova, and Adam Smith. 'What Can We Learn Privately?' (2011) 40(3) *SIAM Journal on Computing* 40 793–826. https://doi.org/10.1137/090756090.

Mackey, Elaine, Mark Elliot, Kieron O'Hara, *The Anonymisation Decision-making Framework*, (UKAN Publications, 2016), https://ukanon.net/wp-content/uploads/2015/05/The-Anonymisation-Decision-making-Framework.pdf.

McGinnis, Ellen W, Steven P Anderau, Jessica Hruschak, Reed D Gurchiek, Nestor L Lopez-Duran, Kate Fitzgerald, Katherine L Rosenblum, Maria Muzik, and Ryan S McGinnis. 'Giving Voice to Vulnerable Children: Machine Learning Analysis of Speech Detects Anxiety and Depression in Early Childhood' (2019) 23(6) *IEEE Journal of Biomedical and Health Informatics* 2294–2301. https://doi.org/10.1109/JBHI.2019.2913590.

McMahan, Brendan, Eider Moore, Daniel Ramage, Seth Hampson, and Blaise Aguera y Arcas. 'Communication-Efficient Learning of Deep Networks from Decentralized Data.' In Artificial Intelligence and Statistics, 1273–82, 2017. http://proceedings.mlr.press/v54/mcmahan17a.html.

McMahan, H Brendan, Galen Andrew, Ulfar Erlingsson, Steve Chien, Ilya Mironov, Nicolas Papernot, and Peter Kairouz. 'A General Approach to Adding Differential Privacy to Iterative Training Procedures.' ArXiv:1812.06210 [Cs, Stat], March 4, 2019. http://arxiv.org/abs/1812.06210.

National Committee on Vital and Health Statistics. 'Re: Recommendations on De-Identification of Protected Health Information under HIPAA,' 2017. www.ncvhs.hhs.gov/wp-content/uploads/2013/12/2017-Ltr-Privacy-DeIdentification-Feb-23-Final-w-sig.pdf.

Ohm, Paul. 'Broken Promises of Privacy: Responding to the Surprising Failure of Anonymization' (2010) 57 *UCLA Law Review* 1701.

OneTrust DataGuidance Staff, and Future of Privacy Forum Staff. 'Comparing Privacy Laws: GDPR v. CCPA.' Accessed March 4, 2020. https://fpf.org/2019/12/18/comparing-privacy-laws-gdpr-v-ccpa/ (last accessed 4 March 2020).

Patki, Neha, Roy Wedge, and Kalyan Veeramachaneni. 'The Synthetic Data Vault.' In 2016 IEEE International Conference on Data Science and Advanced Analytics (DSAA), 399–410. Montreal, QC, Canada: IEEE, 2016. https://doi.org/10.1109/DSAA.2016.49.

Polonetsky, Jules, Omer Tene, and Kelsey Finch. 'Shades of Gray: Seeing the Full Spectrum of Practical Data De-Identification' (2016) 56(3) *Santa Clara Law Review* 593.

Samarati, Pierangela, and Latanya Sweeney. 'Protecting Privacy When Disclosing Information: K-Anonymity and Its Enforcement through Generalization and Suppression,' 1998, http://citeseerx.ist.psu.edu/viewdoc/summary?doi=10.1.1.37.5829.

Staff, Ftc. 'Protecting Consumer Privacy in an Era of Rapid Change–A Proposed Framework for Businesses and Policymakers' [2011] *Journal of Privacy and Confidentiality*. https://doi.org/10.29012/jpc.v3i1.596.

Stalla-Bourdillon, Sophie, Brenda Long, Patrick Hall, and Andrew Burt. 'Warning Signs – The Future of Privacy and Security in the Age of Machine Learning.' Future of Privacy Forum and Immuta Whitepaper, 2019. www.immuta.com/warning-signs-the-future-of-privacy-and-security-in-the-age-of-machine-learning/.

Stalla-Bourdillon, Sophie, Alfred Rossi, and Gabriela Zanfir-Fortuna. 'Data Protection by Process: How to Operationalize Data Protection by Design,' 2019. https://fpf.org/2019/12/19/new-white-paper-provides-guidance-on-embedding-data-protection-principles-in-machine-learning/.

Valiant, LG 'A Theory of the Learnable.' Communications of the ACM 27, no 11 (November 5, 1984): 1134–42. https://doi.org/10.1145/1968.1972.

Veale, Michael, Reuben Binns, and Lilian Edwards. 'Algorithms That Remember: Model Inversion Attacks and Data Protection Law' (2018) 376(2133) *Philosophical Transactions of the Royal Society A: Mathematical, Physical and Engineering Sciences* 20180083. https://doi.org/10.1098/rsta.2018.0083.

Wachter, Sandra, and Brent Mittelstadt. 'A Right to Reasonable Inferences: Re-Thinking Data Protection Law in the Age of Big Data and AI,' 2018. https://doi.org/10.7916/D8-G10S-KA92.

Warner, Stanley L 'Randomized Response: A Survey Technique for Eliminating Evasive Answer Bias' (1965) 60(309) *Journal of the American Statistical Association* 63–69. https://doi.org/10.1080/01621459.1965.10480775.

6

The Role of the EU Fundamental Right to Data Protection in an Algorithmic and Big Data World

YORDANKA IVANOVA[1,2]

Abstract

To contribute to the ongoing academic and policy debate about the added value of data protection as a distinct fundamental right, this chapter analyses its scope, function, nature, essence and permissible limitations, as interpreted and applied in the latest case law of the Court of Justice of the EU (CJEU). The legal analysis of the case law aims to demonstrate that some of the existing assumptions in the literature may need to be revisited and that the fundamental right to data protection can play rather important functions in the context of the digital environment and the new challenges posed by AI and big data. However, a major identified weakness is the underdeveloped potential of the substance and the core 'essence' of the right to data protection. The second part of the chapter aims to address this shortcoming and proposes to re-conceptualise the substance of data protection understood through a holistic concept of 'control' building on the traditional concept of 'individual control' advanced in the literature, but additionally placing the emphasis on the precautionary, prohibitive and collective oversight mechanisms of data protection and its instrumental role for the protection of broader values and all fundamental rights in the age of big data and AI.

Key words

EU Charter of Fundamental Rights, fundamental rights, data protection, right to informational self-determination, privacy, essence of rights, control over personal data, digital technologies, Artificial Intelligence (AI), Big data.

---

[1] This chapter reflects author's personal opinion as a researcher and is in no way engaging or presenting the position of the EU Institutions.
[2] Law Faculty of Sofia University 'St. Kliment Ohridski', Sofia, Bulgaria Law Faculty of Vrije Universiteit Brussel, Brussels, Belgium d_mintcheva@abv.bg; yoivanov@vub.be.

I. Introduction

Artificial Intelligence (AI)[3] and Big data[4] seem to offer new promises for economic prosperity and solutions to some of the great challenges of our time, but their transformative potential also puts strains on traditional values and poses novel risks to citizens' rights and freedoms and the society at large. With the digital transformation and the mass use of these technologies, data protection was thrown into the spotlight of major policy, legal and technical developments,[5] thus becoming a key legal instrument to regulate the impact of these digital technologies on the fundamental rights. The European Union (EU) has become a global leader in this endeavour with the modernised General Data Protection Regulation (GDPR),[6] characterised by some policy makers and scholars as the global 'golden digital standard'[7] and the first law for AI[8'] expected to change the way internet works. But under the EU legal order, data protection goes well beyond this secondary legislation as it is protected also as a fundamental or quasi 'constitutional' right under the EU Charter of Fundamental Rights.[9] In particular, Articles 7 and 8 of the Charter provide in a unique manner for two distinct rights – the protection of private life (privacy) and the protection of personal data – a novelty in comparison with traditional human rights instruments and remarkably, the first

---

[3] Artificial Intelligence (AI) is a 'catch all' term that generally refers to systems that display intelligent behaviour by analysing their environment and taking actions – with some degree of autonomy – to achieve specific goals. See Communication from the European Commission: Artificial Intelligence for Europe, COM/2018/237 final. In this paper, AI mainly refers to the machine learning technology, including its various forms of deep and reinforced learning that are currently the most commonly used and promising AI techniques for building AI systems.

[4] Big data is usually described by 3 or more Vs, characterised by the large quantity of generated and stored data (volume); diverse type and nature of the data (variety) and the high and real time speed at which the data is generated and processed (velocity). Big data analytics is the automated processing when big datasets are analysed by algorithms in new and unanticipated ways to find patterns and correlations between the datasets, thus producing new knowledge and information about individuals, groups or the society at large.

[5] Orla Lynskey, 'The Europeanisation of Data Protection Law', *Cambridge Yearbook of European Legal Studies* (Cambridge University Press, 2016), 2.

[6] Regulation (EU) 2016/679 of the European Parliament and of the Council of 27 April 2016 on the protection of natural persons with regard to the processing of personal data and on the free movement of such data, and repealing Directive 95/46/EC (General Data Protection Regulation) (Text with EEA relevance) [2016] OJ L119/1–88.

[7] See in this sense Giovanni Buttarelli, 'The EU GDPR as a Clarion Call for a New Global Digital Standard' (2016) 6(2) *International Data Privacy Law* 77–78; Beata Safari, 'Intangible Privacy Rights: How Europe's GDPR Will Set a New Global Standard for Personal Data Protection' (2017) 47 *Seton Hall Law Review* 809–848.

[8] Paul Nemitz, Constitutional Democracy and Technology in the age of Artificial Intelligence, Royal Society Philosophical Transactions, 2018. Available at SSRN: ssrn.com/abstract=3234336 or dx.doi.org/10.2139/ssrn.3234336.

[9] Charter of Fundamental Rights of the European Union, [2012] OJ C/326/391–407. The EU Treaties (and respectively the Charter as primary law after Lisbon) have been consistently treated by the CJEU as a Constitutional Charter, see, eg, C -294/83 *Parti écologiste 'Les Verts' v European Parliament* [1986] ECR -01339, para 23.

time when data protection acquired the status of a fundamental right on its own right under the existing international regulatory instruments.[10]

Defining the purpose, remit, nature and content of this relatively novel fundamental right is of primary importance to properly understand the main object of protection under the GDPR which states in its Article 1(2) that '[t]his Regulation protects fundamental rights and freedoms of natural persons and in particular their *right to the protection of personal data* [emphasis added]', replacing the old reference to the right to privacy under the repealed Directive 98/45 and thus posing some fundamental questions about the relation between these two rights. Importantly, even if the fundamental right to data protection has been to a significant degree derived on the basis of the existing secondary data protection legislation,[11] the CJEU has ruled that the latter is in itself an implementation of the fundamental right, and it must be interpreted and applied in conformity with the Charter.[12] But the importance of data protection as a fundamental right goes well beyond the GDPR as it provides more generally the constitutional benchmark for the legality of any secondary legislation adopted by the EU institutions, as well as any act of the Member States when acting within the scope of EU law,[13] considering the binding force of the Charter and its elevated status into EU primary law.[14] Therefore, the fundamental right to data protection is important not only to properly understand the legal foundations and underlying rules for interpretation of the GDPR when applied to the AI and big data technologies, but also for the constitutional legality test, with which any potential future legislation on AI must comply when complementing the GDPR and filling the gaps in the existing secondary data protection framework, as announced by the Commission in its recent White Paper on AI.[15]

---

[10] Under the European Court of Human Rights' jurisprudence, the right to data protection is a subset of the right to private life under Art 8 of the European Convention on Human Rights (1950). See also European Court of Human Rights, Guide on Article 8 of the European Convention on Human Rights, last updated on 31 December 2018. Convention 108, which is the first international legally binding instrument in the field of data protection, also does not proclaim data protection as a human or fundamental right, but aims generally to protect individual's privacy with regard to the processing of personal data.

[11] See Explanations relating to the Charter of Fundamental Rights, [2017] OJ C/30317–35 that according to Art 52(7) of the Charter shall be given due regard by courts of the Union and of the Member States when interpreting the fundamental rights enshrined in the Charter.

[12] CJEU, C-131/12, *Google Spain SL and Google Inc*, ECLI:EU:C:2014:317, para 69; C-362/14, *Schrems v Data Protection Commissioner*, ECLI:EU:C:2015:650, para 72–73. See also Gloria Gonzalez Fuster and Raphael Gellert, 'The Fundamental Right of Data Protection in the European Union: in Search of an Uncharted Right' (2012) 26 *International Review of Law, Computers & Technology* 73–82.

[13] See Art 51(1) of the Charter and case law of the CJEU ruling that respect of the fundamental rights are a condition of the lawfulness of EU acts, so that measures incompatible with those rights are not acceptable in the EU (see judgments in C-260/89, *ERT*, EU:C:1991:254, para 41; C-112/00, *Schmidberger*, EU:C:2003:333, para 73).

[14] See Art 6(1) of the Treaty on European Union (TEU) [2016] OJ C202/13–388.

[15] European Commission, White Paper On Artificial Intelligence – A European approach to excellence and trust, COM/2020/65 final.

In the academic literature, there have already been extensive discussions and different theories proposed about the scope, purpose and content of the right to data protection and its relation to privacy.[16] Over the years, the CJEU has also accumulated extensive jurisprudence, which has recently indicated a clear tendency towards further interpreting the right to data protection independently as a stand-alone right with a special place within the EU Charter of Fundamental Rights. Still, as noted by González Fuster and Hijmans,[17] even 20 years since its emergence, many unanswered questions remain, and there is a general lack of consensus in the literature about the nature and the content of the two rights and their interactions – questions that are even more pressing with the entering into force of the GDPR and the numerous uncertainties regarding how many of its provisions should be applied in the context of digital technologies.

To contribute to the academic and policy debate with a view to replying to these questions, this chapter aims to make two main contributions. Section II will first analyse the fundamental right to data protection to delimit its scope, function,

---

[16] See, eg, Paul De Hert and Serge Gutwirth, 'Data Protection in the Case Law of Strasbourg and Luxembourg: Constitutionalisation in Action' in Serge Gutwirth et al (eds) *Reinventing Data Protection?*, (Springer, 2009); Antoinette Rouvroy and Yves Poullet, 'The Right to Informational Self-Determination and the Value of Self-Development: Reassessing the Importance of Privacy for Democracy' in Serge Gutwirth et al (eds) *Reinventing Data Protection?* (Springer, 2009) 45; Lee A Bygrave, 'Privacy and Data Protection in an International Perspective', in Peter Wahlgren (ed) *Scandinavian Studies in Law Volume 56: Information and Communication Technology Legal Issues*, (Stockholm Institute for Scandinavian Law, 2010) 172; Marios Koutsias, 'Privacy and Data Protection in an Information Society: How Reconciled are the English with the European Union Privacy Norms?' (2012) 261(18) *Computer and Telecommunications Law Review* 265–266; Gloria Gonzalez Fuster and Serge Gutwirth, 'Opening up Personal Data Protection: a Conceptual Controversy' [2013] *Computer Law & Security Review*; Juliane Kokott and Christoph Sobotta, 'The Distinction between Privacy and Data Protection in the Jurisprudence of the CJEU and the ECtHR' (2013) 3(4) *International Data Privacy Law*; Orla Lynskey, 'Deconstructing Data Protection: the 'Added-value' of a Right to Data Protection in the EU Legal Order' (2014) 63(3) *International and Comparative Law Quarterly* 569–597; Orla Lynskey, *The Foundations of EU Data Protection Law* (Oxford University Press, 2016); Stefano Rodota, 'Data Protection as a Fundamental Right,' Keynote Speech for International Conference 'Reinventing Data Protection,' Bruxelles, 12–13 October 2007; Maria Tzanou, 'Data Protection as a Fundamental Right Next to Privacy? 'Reconstructing' a not so New Right' (2013) 3(2) *International Data Privacy Law*; Herke Kranenborg, 'Article 8,' in Peers et al (eds) *The EU Charter of Fundamental Rights: A commentary* (Hart Publishing, 2014); Van der Sloot, 'Legal Fundamentalism: is Data Protection Really a Fundamental Right?' in Leenes, R., van Brakel, R., Gutwirth, S., De Hert, P. (eds) *Data Protection and Privacy: (In)visibilities and Infrastructures* (Springer, 2017); Maja Brkan, 'The Essence of the Fundamental Rights to Privacy and Data Protection: Finding the Way through the Maze of the CJEU's Constitutional Reasoning,' Paper for conference *The Essence of Fundamental Rights in EU Law* 17–18 May 2018; Leuven; Lorenzo Dalla Corte, 'A Right to a Rule: On the Substance and Essence of the Fundamental Right to Personal Data Protection' in Hallinan, D, Leenes, R, Gutwirth, S & De Hert, P (eds) *Data protection and Privacy: Data Protection and Democracy*, (Hart Publishing, 2020) 27–58.

[17] Gloria Gonzalez Fuster and Hielke Hijmans, 'The EU Rights to Privacy and Personal Data Protection: 20 Years in 10 Questions', Discussion Paper Prepared for the International Workshop 'Exploring the Privacy and Data Protection Connection: International Workshop on the Legal Notions of Privacy and Data Protection in EU Law in a Rapidly Changing World' of 14 May 2019, co-organised by the Brussels Privacy Hub (BPH) and the Law, Science, Technology and Society (LSTS) Research Group at the Vrije Universiteit Brussel (VUB).

nature, essence and permissible limitations, and to clarify its relation to privacy and the other fundamental rights, as interpreted and applied in the latest case law of the CJEU. The legal analysis of the case law will aim to demonstrate that some of the existing assumptions in the literature may need to be revisited and that the fundamental right to data protection can play rather important functions in the context of the digital environment and the new challenges posed by AI and big data. However, a major identified weakness is the underdeveloped potential of the substance and the core 'essence' of the right to data protection, which the CJEU should arguably re-define to employ more effectively its protective function in the data- and technology-driven information society, which not only puts significant strains on the traditional concepts of data protection and privacy, but also poses emerging risks to many other fundamental rights protected by the Charter.

Section III will then provide the main contribution to the existing literature by proposing a holistic reconceptualisation of the content and essence of data protection understood as 'control' which should go beyond the prevailing current understanding of data protection merely as 'individual control' of the data subject over their personal data. The proposed holistic concept of control builds on the traditional concept of 'individual control' advanced (or criticised) in the literature,[18] but it aims to address the shortcomings of its individualist approach by adding new dimensions to it. Data protection understood as 'control' in this chapter additionally places the emphasis on the precautionary, prohibitive and collective oversight mechanisms of data protection that should ensure appropriate protection of the individual and the society with a clear recognition also of its instrumental role for safeguarding other fundamental rights and the broader public values that are seriously impacted by AI and big data. The proposed reconceptualisation could play two important practical functions in legal disputes. First, the different dimensions of the concept of 'control' could be used by the CJEU as the actual substance of the right to data protection when the CJEU assesses the degree of interference with the right to data protection to determine whether the 'essence' of the right under Article 8 is actually violated (in line with the approach followed by the CJEU in construing the 'essence' of other fundamental rights). Second, the fundamental right to data protection understood holistically as 'control' could

---

[18] See, eg, Charles Fried, 'Privacy' (1968) 77 *Yale Law Journal* 475, 482; Jerry Kang, 'Information Privacy in Cyberspace Transactions' (1998) 50 *Stanford Law Review* 1193, 1218; Frederick Schauer, 'Internet Privacy and the Public-Private Distinction', (1998) 38 *Jurimetrics Journal* 555, 556; Richard A Posner, 'Privacy' in Peter Newman (ed) *New Palgrave Dictionary of Economics and the Law* (Palgrave MacMillan, 1998) 103; Paul Schwartz, 'Privacy and Democracy in Cyberspace' (1999) 52 *Vanderbilt Law Review* 1609, 1663; Orla Lynskey, 'Deconstructing Data Protection' (n 16); I van Ooijen and Helena U Vrabec, 'Does the GDPR Enhance Consumers' Control over Personal Data? An Analysis from a Behavioural Perspective' (2019) 42 *Journal of Consumer Policy* 91–10; Daniel Solove, 'Privacy Self-Management and the Consent Dilemma,' (2013) 126 *Harvard Law Review* 1880; GWU Legal Studies Research Paper No 2012-141; Neil Richards and Woodrow Hartzog, 'The Pathologies of Consent for Data Practices' (2019) 96 *Washington University Law Review*; Barry Schwartz, *The Paradox of Choice: Why More is Less* (Harper Collins Publishers, 2005); Woodrow Hartzog, 'The Case Against Idealising Control' (2018) 4 *European Data Protection Law Review* 430.

be also employed as a 'living instrument' to respond to the current societal and technological challenges and serve as an interpretative tool to clarify the existing secondary provisions, solve ambiguities and 'grey areas' and even possibly fill gaps in the protection by deriving novel data subjects' rights or obligations for the controllers, as the CJEU has already done in its past case law.

II. Data Protection as a Distinct Fundamental Right under The EU Legal Order and the CJEU Case Law

Data protection has a special place within the EU legal order, as it does not boil down only to the GDPR, but is enshrined already in primary EU law and protected as a fundamental or 'constitutional' right under the EU Charter of Fundamental Rights, which has the same legal force as the founding EU Treaties. While the traditional right to private life (privacy) under Article 7 of the Charter mirrors (almost) identically the text of Article 8 of the European Convention on Human Rights (ECHR),[19] the novel right to data protection under Article 8 of the Charter consists of very different wording in three separate paragraphs:

1. Everyone has the right to the protection of personal data concerning him or her.
2. Such data must be processed fairly for specified purposes and on the basis of the consent of the person concerned or some other legitimate basis laid down by law. Everyone has the right of access to data which has been collected concerning him or her, and the right to have it rectified.
3. Compliance with these rules shall be subject to control by an independent authority.

The origins of the right to data protection mentioned in the Explanations relating to the EU Charter[20] indicate as sources Article 8 of the ECHR, Convention 108[21] and the Data Protection Directive 95/46/EC, currently replaced by the GDPR. Importantly, the secondary data protection law plays thus a key role not only for informing the fundamental right to data protection, but also for establishing the conditions and the limitations for its application.[22] This makes data protection a *sui generis* fundamental right in the sense that its content is derived from preceding legislation regulating personal data within the EU, while it is also destined

---

[19] Art 7 of the Charter states 'Everyone has the right to respect for his or her private and family life, home and communications' mirroring the text in Art 8 of the ECHR just replacing the word 'correspondence' with the more modern term 'communications'.

[20] Explanations relating to the Charter of Fundamental Rights, [2007] OJ C/30317–35. The preamble of the Charter says that the explanations are binding for the courts of the Union and the Member States when interpreting the Charter.

[21] Council of Europe, Convention 108 for the Protection of Individuals with regard to Automatic Processing of Personal Data (1981) which was recently modernised and served as a basis for the provisions of the Directive 98/45/EC.

[22] Art 52(2) of the Charter.

to serve as a 'constitutional' right for interpretation and legality review of all EU secondary laws and Member States' acts falling within the scope of the EU law. But the relation between the GDPR and the fundamental right to data protection is arguably also reverse, considering that any revision of the secondary legislation should also impact the content of the fundamental right to data protection, which is therefore destined to be constantly in flux and evolution.

While there have been many theories and interpretations advanced in the literature about this innovative distinction,[23] the CJEU remains the solely competent judicial authority to interpret the EU legislation with binding force, including the fundamental rights under the Charter. Thus, the proclamation of the right to data protection has tasked the CJEU with the difficult and pioneering task to define this new right and its relation to the traditional right to privacy. While often conflating the two rights in its pre-Lisbon case law, the CJEU has explicitly defined the scope, nature and essence of the right to data protection in some landmark recent judgments such as *Digital Rights Ireland*, *Schrems*, *PNR Opinion 1/15* and *Google Spain* to be examined in the next subsections.

A. Digital Rights Ireland – The Prohibitive Nature of Data Protection and the Illegality of Mass Surveillance

In *Digital Rights Ireland*[24] and the subsequent *Tele2 Sverije*[25] cases the CJEU reviewed the validity of the Data Retention Directive 2006/24/EC and the national implementing laws in the light of Articles 7 and 8 of the Charter. These cases concern in essence the legality of mass surveillance practices where governments have often been willing to gain bulk and indiscriminate access to the vast amount of the meta-data of the EU citizens' electronic communications held by the private communications services, so as to subsequently analyse this information for law enforcement and intelligence purposes, frequently with the help of new algorithmic profiling technologies.

In these two landmark judgments, the CJEU famously invalidated the Data Retention Directive as incompatible with Articles 7 and 8 of the Charter and prohibited bulk or mass surveillance, which has been subjected to a very strict necessity and proportionality test under Article 52(1) of the Charter. Such restrictive interpretation has been to a great extent justified with the rights and principles derived from 'the protection of personal data resulting from the explicit obligation laid down in Article 8(1) of the Charter' and its 'especially important (role) for the right to respect for private life enshrined in Article 7 of the Charter'.[26] By applying

---

[23] See literature cited in n 15.
[24] CJEU, C-293/12 and C-594/12, *Digital Rights Ireland and Others*, ECLI:EU:C:2014:238, paras 52 and 54.
[25] CJEU, C-203/15 and C-698/15, *Tele2 Sverije AB and Watson* ECLI:EU:C:2016:970, para 104.
[26] *Digital Rights Ireland and Others*, para.53.

the purpose limitation principle in relation to the *ratio personae* of the Data Retention Directive and the national surveillance laws, the CJEU has explicitly prohibited indiscriminate collection of personal data,[27] thus providing a higher level of protection under the Charter to the rights to data protection and privacy as opposed to the ECtHR, which accepts in principle mass surveillance for crime and terrorism prevention purposes.[28] The CJEU has implicitly recognised this higher level of protection within the EU legal order, highlighting in particular the role of the novel right to data protection under Article 8 of the Charter 'which is distinct from that enshrined in Article 7 of the Charter and which has no equivalent in the ECHR'.[29] The fundamental right to data protection has been also clearly conceived as a *prohibitive* right,[30] which shows that Article 8 should protect the personal data even prior to its collection and generation – an understanding that has not been shared by all scholars in the literature who have mainly emphasised the permissible nature of data protection.[31]

On the basis of the proportionality test, the CJEU has also elaborated on other substantive data processing principles not mentioned in Article 8(2) of the Charter, such as storage limitation, security and access restriction, data minimisation, integrity and correctness of the personal data and transparency.[32] Hence, these principles have been 'constitutionalised' into EU primary law as part of the fundamental right to data protection under the Charter, which will require in the future a strict test of judicial review for compliance with them of any legislation that involves data processing operations.

In relation to the proportionality test, the CJEU has also recognised that the need for data protection safeguards is all the greater where personal data is subject to *automated* processing or sensitive data is at stake,[33] construed broadly beyond the restricted categories of Article 9 of the GDPR. In assessing the seriousness of the interference with the rights, emphasis has been placed not only on the characteristics of the *data* (eg, nature, format, quantity, sensitivity and accessibility) and the *processing* (eg, means of processing, scope and systematic nature of processing, storage period, transparency of the processing, security risks etc),[34] but also

---

[27] ibid, para 57–9.

[28] ECtHR, *Big Brother Watch v UK* (nos 58170/13, 62322/14 and 24960/15), § 384.

[29] *Tele2 Sverije AB*, para129.

[30] *Digital Rights Ireland and Others*, para 36. For the two possible readings of Art 8 as permissible or prohibitive right see Fuster and Gutwirth (n 16). Besides *Digital Rights Ireland,* the CJEU has confirmed the prohibitive reading of the right to data protection also in many other judgments such as C-543/09 *Deutsche Telekom AG v Bundesrepublik Deutschland*, ECLI:EU:C:2011:279, para 49; C-291/12, *Schwarz*, para 25, C-131/12, *Google Spain*, para 126.

[31] Eg, Kokott and Sobotta (n 16), De Hert and Gutwirth (n 16), Kranenborg (n 16), Van der Sloot (n 16).

[32] *Digital Rights Ireland*, paras 37, 66–68.

[33] *Digital Rights Ireland*, paras 54 and 55 and *Tele2 Sverije*, paras 109 and 117. See to this effect also C-101/01, *Bodil Linqvist*, ECLI:EU:C:2003:596, para 89 where the CJEU took into account the importance, for the persons concerned, of the protection of the data disclosed.

[34] *Digital Rights Ireland*, paras 54– 66; *Tele2 Sverije AB*, paras 109 and 117 and Opinion of Advocate General Saugmansgaard in cases C-203/15 and C-698/15 *Tele2 Sverije AB*, EU:C:2016:572, para 129.

on the potential results and impacts on the individuals. In particular, the CJEU has considered the potential inferences or 'conclusions' that could be drawn on the basis of the communications' meta-data about the private life of the persons and the detailed profile that could be established revealing their habits of every-day life, permanent or temporary places of residence, daily or other movements, the activities carried out, the social relationships of those persons and the social environments frequented by them.[35] This consideration arguably shows that the fundamental rights to privacy and data protection should protect the individual from the novel impacts of big data analytics and AI, which by analysing highly diverse and large data sources reveal patterns or correlations between data, out of which new information and profiles arise about the behaviours, preferences, personality and private lives of individuals or whole groups of the population.[36] It also confirms that the CJEU considers the AI inferences or outputs from the automated processing as protected personal data, thus putting an end to a much contentious discussion in the literature expressing doubts to the contrary.[37] The emphasis on the impacts and the AI output is also an important conclusion to be borne in mind, as it may address partially the criticism in the academia that data protection ensures at present primarily control over how personal data is collected and processed on the 'input side' of the processing, but protects insufficiently the actual impact of the processing on the data subjects and their rights and freedoms.[38]

It is also noticeable that the CJEU has taken due account of the lack of transparency that characterises many of the current data processing practices and the unspecified threat of being constantly surveilled that could be generated in people's minds.[39] In this way, the 'chilling effect' or the Panopticon effect[40] of surveillance has been legally recognised as making the individuals likely to inhibit their behaviour and to limit their communication, thus interfering also with their freedom of

---

[35] In *Digital Rights Ireland*, para 27. In Opinion 1/15, para 131 when examining the PNR data 'intended to be analysed systematically […] by automated means, based on pre-established models and criteria […] and verified automatically by cross-checking with other databases', the CJEU has also unequivocally stated that 'such processing may provide *additional information on the private lives* of air passengers [emphasis added]'.

[36] Sandra Wachter and Brent Mittelstadt, 'A Right to Reasonable Inferences: Re-Thinking Data Protection Law in the Age of Big Data and AI' (2019) 2 *Columbia Business Law Review* 1. Available at SSRN: https://ssrn.com/abstract=3248829.

[37] For the contentious discussion on whether AI inferences are personal data or not see Wachter and Mittelstadt (n 36).

[38] ibid, 13.

[39] *Digital Rights Ireland and Others*, para 37 referring to Opinion of Advocate General Cruz Villalón delivered on 12 December 2013, para 52.

[40] The panopticon is a type of institutional building and a system of control designed by the English philosopher and social theorist Jeremy Bentham in the 18th century. The concept of the design is to allow all prisoners of an institution to be observed by a single security guard, without the inmates being able to tell whether they are being watched. Crucially, whether or not an individual is actually being monitored is not decisive in these circumstances as the mere feeling and perception of surveillance may be sufficient to inhibit individual behaviour. Bentham Papers 119a/119. UCL Press, 137. See also Michel Foucault, *Discipline and Punish: The Birth of the Prison*, (Penguin, 1991).

expression, and to receive and impart information, guaranteed under Article 11 of the Charter.[41] Consideration of these side effects and dangers clearly shows the instrumental role of the rights to data protection and privacy as a pre-condition for the effective enjoyment of other rights of the individual and more fundamental values such as freedom, democracy and rule of law.

In its effort to draw a distinction between the rights to data protection and privacy, the CJEU has also addressed another key issue, notably what is the 'essence' of these rights that can be restricted under no circumstances, as stated in Article 52(1) of the Charter.[42] How to define the 'essence' of the rights has become one of the most topical questions in both the academic literature and the jurisprudence. For example, Prof. Lenaerts,[43] who is the current President of the CJEU, argues that the 'essence' of a right is compromised when the limitations are so extensive and intrusive so as to call into question the very *existence* of the right or *devoid it of its actual content/substance* – an approach, apparently followed by the CJEU in its recent case law.[44] Consequently, the 'essence' of the right has important implications for conceiving the right to data protection not only in terms of affirmative rights, but also negative liberty claims as data protection should be able not only to regulate, but also to prohibit power.[45]

In relation to the 'essence' of the right to data protection, the interpretation of the CJEU seems to be, however, slightly disappointing. In *Digital Rights Ireland*, the CJEU first adopted an extremely restrictive and technical approach by considering that the essence of this fundamental right is not adversely affected because the contentious Data Retention Directive required the respect of 'certain principles of data protection and data security, in particular appropriate technical and organisational measures against accidental or unlawful destruction, accidental loss or alteration of the data.'[46] This makes the reader wonder why exactly these security measures that are even not mentioned in Article 8(2) and not others could prevent the adverse effect on the essence of this fundamental right. As pointed out by

---

[41] See *Digital Rights Ireland and Others*, para 37 referring to Opinion of Advocate General Cruz Villalón delivered on 12 December 2013, para 52. For the chilling effect of algorithmic profiling and surveillance see also Moritz Büchi, et al, 'The Chilling Effects of Algorithmic Profiling: Mapping the Issues' [2019] *Computer Law & Security Review*; PEN America, 'Chilling Effects: NSA Surveillance Drives U.S. Writers to Self-Censor' (PEN American Center, 2013). Jonathon Penney, 'Chilling Effects: Online Surveillance and Wikipedia Use' [2016] *Berkeley Technology Law Journal*, papers.ssrn.com/sol3/papers.cfm?abstract_id=2769645.

[42] See Art 52(1) of the Charter.

[43] Koen Lenaerts, 'Limits on Limitations: The Essence of Fundamental Rights in the EU' (2019 20 *German Law Journal* 779.

[44] See, eg, CJEU, C-650/13, *Thierry Delvigne v Commune de Lesparre Médoc and Préfet de la Gironde* [GC], 6 October 2015, para 48, CJEU, C-190/16, *Werner Fries v Lufthansa CityLine GmbH*, 5 July 2017, para 38.

[45] As Julie Cohen points out, 'the conventional wisdom is that ... affirmative liberty claims are weaker and less principled than negative liberty claims'. See Julie E Cohen 'Examined Lives: Informational Privacy and the Subject as Object,' (2000) 52 *Stanford Law Review* 1373, 1400; David Currie, 'Positive and Negative Constitutional Rights,' (1986) 53 *University of Chicago Law Review* 864, 887.

[46] *Digital Rights Ireland*, para 40.

Brkan, seeing the essence of a fundamental right as a minimum technical standard deprives this concept of its purpose and misconstrues its role in the fundamental rights' landscape.[47] The CJEU has been also criticised for defining the essence of the right to privacy only in relation to the 'content' of the communications and not the meta-data, which could be used to analyse patterns and create profiles of the persons, and therefore, be as intrusive interference as the access to the content itself, if not even greater. While this has been recognised by both the ECtHR[48] and the CJEU,[49] the CJEU has not changed its position on the 'essence' of the right to privacy, which currently leaves intrusive profiling permitted under EU law subject to the necessity and proportionality test.

B. Schrems – Extra-territorial Scope of Protection of all Charter Rights and an Absolute Requirement for an Independent Supervisory Control

In the subsequent *Schrems* case[50] the CJEU reviewed the validity of the Safe Harbor agreement for transfer of personal data between the EU and US and famously invalidated it as incompatible with Articles 7 and 8 of the Charter. In this judgment, the CJEU set again the benchmark for the essence of the right to privacy on quantitative basis by excluding 'generalised access to content' and introducing similar obligation for differentiating the *ratio personae* and the storage period on the basis of the objective pursued,[51] thus making these data protection principles essential safeguards for the essence of the fundamental right to privacy. However, the CJEU can be criticised for not linking the respect of these principles also to the essence of the right to data protection, which would be a natural conclusion given its reasoning from its past case law. The CJEU also found a violation of the right to effective remedy under Article 47 of the Charter since the EU citizens could not have effective remedy in US courts in relation to their requests for access and rectification,[52] but it did not elaborate on the importance of this finding for Article 8(2) of the Charter, which explicitly enshrines the right to access to one's data and the right to correction.

On a positive note, in *Schrems* the CJEU adjudicated on two other essential criteria linked to the right to data protection. First, it established the novel requirement for 'equivalent level of protection' whenever data controllers transfer

---

[47] Brkan (n 16), 17.

[48] ECtHR, *Big Brother Watch v UK*, §§ 301 and 356.

[49] While in the subsequent *Tele2 Sverije*, the CJEU recognised this fact, it did not change its conclusion that the access to the meta-data does not affect the essence of the right to privacy, para 99.

[50] CJEU, C-362/14 *Maximillian Schrems*, ECLI:EU:C:2015:650.

[51] ibid, para 93. The CJEU concluded that a legislation that 'authorises, on a generalised basis, storage' of such data, 'without any differentiation, limitation or exception being made in the light of the objective pursued', interferes with the essence of privacy.

[52] ibid, para 94.

personal data to third countries outside the EU.[53] In particular, the CJEU ruled that

> the right to the protection of personal data requires, inter alia, that the high level of protection of fundamental rights and freedoms conferred by EU law continues where personal data is transferred from the European Union to a non-member country [...] (with) protection essentially equivalent to that guaranteed within the European Union [emphasis added].[54]

The right to data protection is, therefore, a very special fundamental right as it not only benefits from extra-territorial protection itself, but it also acts as a legal tool to ensure extra-territorially the same high level of protection to all fundamental rights and freedoms conferred by EU law that may be affected by the data transfer and the subsequent data processing. As noted by Kuner,[55] the *Schrems* judgment demands in effect universal adherence to the standards of the Charter, driving international regulatory convergence toward it and effectively setting the global threshold of 'adequate' level of data protection to be respected by all third countries across the globe. The second important criteria set by the CJEU is the absolute character of the requirement for an independent supervisory authority under Article 8(3) of the Charter,[56] which was eventually one of the reasons to repeal the Safe Harbor agreement as a certification scheme enabling the transfer of personal data from EU to US. Its successor – the EU-US Privacy shield – is about to face the same legality scrutiny for compliance with the Charter in a highly anticipated judgment to be delivered on the pending *Schrems II* case,[57] which should review also the validity of the standard contractual clauses as a legal instrument for international data transfers.

C. PNR Opinion 1/15 – New Legal Benchmarks for AI Systems and Explicit Role for Data Protection to Address Algorithmic Discrimination

It the *PNR Opinion 1/15*[58] the CJEU assessed the compatibility of the draft EU-Canada agreement for transfer of passengers name records data (PNR) and

---

[53] ibid, para 73.

[54] ibid, paras 72 to 74.

[55] Christopher Kuner, 'Reality and Illusion in EU Data Transfer Regulation Post Schrems' (2017) 18 *German Law Journal* 881.

[56] In its past case law, the CJEU has also consistently held that the control of the independent authority, carried out on the basis of EU law under Art 8(3) of the Charter, is 'an *essential* component of the protection of individuals with regard to the processing of personal data [emphasis added]' (see, to that effect, Case C-614/10 *Commission v Austria* EU:C:2012:631, para 37, C-293/12 and C-594/12 *Digital Rights Ireland and Others*, para 68.

[57] Opinion of Advocate General Saugmandsgaard Øe delivered on 19 December 2019 on Case C-311/18 *Data Protection Commissioner v Facebook Ireland Limited*, Maximillian Schrems, ECLI:EU:C:2019:1145.

[58] CJEU, Opinion 1/15 on *Draft agreement between Canada and the European Union – Transfer of Passenger Name Record data from the European Union to* Canada, ECLI:EU:C:2017:592.

provided one of its most substantive reasoning on many of the data protection principles and the permissible interference with the rights to data protection and privacy. In this opinion, it is worth noting that the CJEU also interpreted for the first time the automated decision-making in the light of Article 8 of the Charter and set specific requirements for the pre-established AI models and criteria used for the algorithmic analysis and risk profiling of the passengers for terrorism prevention purposes. The CJEU has in particular ruled that the AI models should be specific and reliable and their results accurate, effective and non-discriminatory,[59] which indicates that data protection clearly incorporates non-discrimination concerns and should act as a regulatory instrument for enforcement of algorithmic fairness. Importantly, by setting minimum requirements to which the AI system must adhere in order to comply with Article 8 of the Charter, the CJEU has conceived the right to data protection to be regulating not only the personal data fed into the AI system and the results from the automated processing, but also the AI models themselves. Similarly, the databases from which the data is cross-checked or aggregated must be also reliable, up-to-date and limited to the purpose. The CJEU has also explicitly excluded any solely automated decision-making that 'adversely affect' the individual, which should be obligatory subjected to an individual re-examination by human intervention.[60]

These novel requirements aim to address some of the inherent problematic characteristics of AI recognised in the literature, notably the increasing autonomy of the AI systems and the need for human oversight,[61] the biases imbedded in the algorithms that can reinforce existing discrimination and produce novel forms of emergent discriminatory effects,[62] the de-contextualisation of the personal data and its use in new and unanticipated ways, often violating the purpose limitation principle[63] and the unavoidable risk of certain margins of errors since the AI outputs are derived on the basis of probabilistic statistical correlations on the basis of the training data used for building the model. It is a missed opportunity though that the CJEU has not also set explicit requirements for transparency and explainability of the AI systems, which could address another problematic characteristic of machine learning whose decision-making logic in a particular case remains opaque and incomprehensible not only for the data subjects affected by these systems, but also for the human operators and even developers who have built them.[64] It would be also very beneficial if the CJEU had explicitly clarified

---

[59] ibid, para 172.

[60] ibid, para 173.

[61] Matthew U Scherer, 'Regulating Artificial Intelligence Systems: Risks, Challenges, Competences, and Strategies' (2016) 29 *Harvard Journal of Law & Technology* 2.

[62] See in this sense inter alia Solon Barocas and Andrew Selbst, 'Big Data's Disparate Impact' (2016) 104 *California Law Review* 671–732; Tal Zarsky, 'Understanding Discrimination in the Scored Society', (2014) 89 *Washington Law Review* 4. Available at SSRN: https://ssrn.com/abstract=2550248.

[63] Mireille Hildebrandt, 'Profiling: From Data to Knowledge' (2006) 30 *Datenschutz und Datensicherheit-DuD* 548, 2.

[64] Note that the UK Information Commissioner's Officer has recently paid special attention to this problem and has required explainability of the AI systems and individual explanations for the data subjects, irrespective of whether the decision is taken solely by the AI system or their outputs

that the data subjects have a right to access to their profiles generated by the AI model and a right to correct them,[65] given that it has explicitly confirmed that the automated processing of the PNR data 'intended to be analysed systematically [...] by automated means, [...] may provide additional information on the private lives of air passengers'.[66]

Beyond automated decision-making, this case is also important because the CJEU has further clarified the 'essence' of the two rights to privacy and data protection. Importantly, it switched for first time from a quantitative into a qualitative approach by assessing the interference with the 'essence' of the right to privacy as a degree of how limited or intrusive the nature of the acquired and processed data is.[67] The assessment of the essence aside, the CJEU also took due account of the potential consequences for the individuals, considering that the transferred data and the automated analyses may also give rise to additional checks at borders and possibly to the adoption of individual decisions having binding effects on them.[68] As regards the right to data protection, the CJEU concluded that the envisaged agreement did not adversely affect the essence of the fundamental right to data protection because it, first, limited 'the purposes for which PNR data may be processed' and second, it laid down rules to ensure 'the security, confidentiality and integrity of that data, and to protect it against unlawful access and processing'.[69] Thus, compliance with the purpose limitation principle has also become part of the 'essence' of the fundamental right to data protection. Later in the opinion, the CJEU also raised the standard on this principle as 'too vague or general purpose' was considered insufficient to ensure the necessary 'clarity and precision', required by Article 8 of the Charter.[70] Interestingly enough, the CJEU addressed also the concept of consent as a legal ground for processing, explicitly excluding its use when the data is to be re-used for other secondary purposes, different from the purpose for which it has been initially collected.[71] There has been also a clear prohibition on the transfer of sensitive data, in particular considering the risks of violation of the right to non-discrimination enshrined under Article 21 of the Charter,[72] which again confirms the instrumental role of data protection for the protection of the fundamental rights to non-discrimination and equality.

---

just support human decision-makers. See ICO, ExplAIn guidance. available for public consultation till 24 January 2020, https://ico.org.uk/about-the-ico/ico-and-stakeholder-consultations/ico-and-the-turing-consultation-on-explaining-ai-decisions-guidance/.

[65] Currently, para 221 of Opinion 1/15 confirms that the passengers have a right of access to their PNR data and a right to request the correction of that data, but not to the risk profiles generated by the AI system.

[66] CJEU, Opinion 1/15, para 131.

[67] ibid, para 150. See also Brkan (n 16).

[68] ibid, para 132.

[69] ibid, para 150.

[70] ibid, para 181.

[71] ibid, para 142.

[72] ibid, para 165.

D. Google Spain – Horizontal Direct Effect of the Right to Data Protection Providing a New Legal Basis for Derivation of Novel Data Subjects' Rights

In the line of the landmark judgments regulating the digital environment, we must certainly not miss the *Google Spain*[73] case where the notorious 'right to be forgotten' was forged by the CJEU directly based on Articles 7 and 8 of the Charter. While not addressing here the essence of the rights, the Court emphasised that the search engine is 'liable to affect significantly the fundamental rights to privacy and to the protection of personal data', stressing that the

> processing enables any internet user to obtain through the list of results a structured overview of the information relating to that individual that can be found on the internet – information which potentially concerns a vast number of aspects of his private life and which, without the search engine, could not have been interconnected or could have been only with great difficulty – and thereby to establish a more or less detailed profile of [the data subject].[74]

Furthermore, the effect of the interference with those rights of the data subject was considered 'heightened on account of the important role played by the internet and search engines in modern society, which render the information in such a list of results ubiquitous'.[75] On this basis interpreted in the light of the data processing principles, the CJEU innovatively derived the 'right to be forgotten', which enables any individual to request from the search engine deletion of his/her information when that 'information appears, having regard to all the circumstances of the case, to be inadequate, irrelevant or no longer relevant, or excessive in relation to the purposes of the processing at issue carried out by the operator of the search engine'.[76]

The CJEU also stated that

> '*as a rule* the fundamental rights under Articles 7 and 8 of the Charter override such economic inteest and the interest of the general public in finding that information upon a search relating to the data subject's name. That balance may, however, depend, in specific cases, on the nature of the information in question and its sensitivity for the data subject's private life and on the interest of the public in having that information, an interest which may vary, in particular, according to the role played by the data subject in public life [emphasis added].[77]

As argued by Tzanou,[78] in this way the CJEU has established a general prevalence rule or a rebuttable legal presumption for a priori precedence of the rights to data

---

[73] CJEU, C-131/12, *Google Spain SL and Google Inc*, ECLI:EU:C:2014:317.
[74] ibid, para 37.
[75] ibid, para 80.
[76] ibid, para 94.
[77] ibid, para 81.
[78] Maria Tzanou, 'The Unexpected Consequences of the EU Right to Be Forgotten: Internet Search Engines As Fundamental Rights Adjudicators' in Maria Tzanou (ed) *Personal Data Protection and Legal*

protection and privacy over other interests and the freedom of expression, which may be, however, at odds with the rationale of the balancing exercise that should as a baseline treat as equals the opposing fundamental rights at stake.[79] Although the attention paid by the CJEU on the internet's impact on the fundamental rights to data protection and privacy is indeed highly praised, it seems these rights gain more favourable treatment in the balancing test of the competing interests and the CJEU rather disregards the importance of the freedom of expression and information (mentioned only as a legitimate interest of the public to receive information),[80] which is, however, also a fundamental right of equal importance for the democracy under Article 11 of the Charter, and any restrictions to it must be limited only to what is strictly necessary.[81]

The *Google Spain* judgment is also interesting as it has implicitly answered the question whether the right to data protection under Article 8 of the Charter could produce a horizontal direct effect in disputes between private parties[82] – a rather disputable question in the literature with many scholars rejecting such a possibility.[83] For example, when AG Kokott examined the effect of Article 8, she argued in her article and opinions that the Charter is binding only on Member States when acting within the scope of the EU law and, therefore, individuals should not be able to rely against private parties neither on Article 7, nor on Article 8 of the Charter.[84] It is argued though here that given the CJEU has derived the 'right to be forgotten' notably on the basis of these articles as a right enforceable against a private entity processing personal data (not just states), these provisions are implicitly endowed by the Court with horizontal direct effect, which enables

---

Developments in the European Union (Forthcoming) (IGI Global, 2020), 5. Available at SSRN: https://ssrn.com/abstract=3277348.

[79] See, eg, in C-28/08, *Bavarian Lager*, para 56 the Court had to balance the right to data protection against access to documents, ruling that '[r]egulations Nos 45/2001 and 1049/2001 [..] do not contain any provisions granting one regulation primacy over the other'.

[80] *Google Spain*, para 87. See for criticism, ef, Christopher Kuner, 'The Court of Justice of the EU Judgment on Data Protection and Internet Search Engines,' LSE Law, Society and Economy Working Papers 3/2015, ssrn.com/abstract=2496060; Eleni Frantziou, 'Further Developments in the Right to be Forgotten: The European Court of Justice's Judgment in Case C-131/12, Google Spain, SL, Google Inc v Agencia Espanola de Proteccion de Datos' (2014) 14(4) *Human Rights Law Review* 761–777, doi org/10.1093/hrlr/ngu033.

[81] It is interesting to note that while the CJEU disregards this need, the Article 29 Working Party specifically highlights it in its guidelines on the implementation of the right to be forgotten. See Article 29 Data Protection Working Party, Guidelines on the Implementation of the Court of Justice of the European Union Judgement on 'Google Spain and Inc. v. Agencia Espanola de Proteccion de Datos (AEPD) and Mario Costeja Gonzales' C-131/12, 14/EN WP 225.

[82] In accordance with decades old settled case law starting with the landmark C- 26-62 *Van Gend & Loos* judgment establishing the principle of direct effect of EU law, the direct effect of a provision essentially depends on whether the text of Art 8 of the Charter is sufficiently precise and unconditional to confer rights on individuals that can be invoked in national courts against the state (vertical direct effect) and against private parties in horizontal disputes (horizontal direct effect).

[83] See, eg, Kokott and Sobota (n 16), Damian Clifford and Jef Ausloos, 'Data Protection and the Role of Fairness' (2018) 37(1) *Yearbook of European Law* 130–187, 147 doi:10.1093/yel/yey004.

[84] See Kokott and Sobota (n 16), 224 and AG Kokott's Opinion on Case C-73/07 *Satakunnan Markkinapo¨rssi et Satamedia* [2008] ECR I-9831, paras 102–104.

every individual to rely on these fundamental rights against private parties in legal disputes in front of national courts or out of court. The simple logic is that if the CJEU can forge the horizontally applicable 'right to be forgotten' on the basis of Articles 7 and 8(1) of the Charter, there is no reason why individuals should not be able to rely also on Article 8(2) as it is also sufficiently 'clear, precise and unconditional' to be directly applicable between private parties, if the data processing provision or practice in question cannot be interpreted in harmony with the existing secondary data protection legislation.[85] Such interpretation is also supported by the recent jurisprudence of the CJEU, where it has recognised that some rights in the Charter may be horizontally applicable.[86] Consequently, the direct effect of Article 8(1) and (2) is of key importance for the effective judicial protection of individuals' right to data protection as it could have important implications for possible derogations from the GDPR and sectoral legislations that are not sufficiently harmonised with its requirements or in the context of gaps in the current EU regime for data protection, for example, in the protection of voters' data,[87] the ambiguous existence of a right to an explanation of solely automated decisions[88] and other contentious issues that are not clearly solved by the GDPR.

E. Interim Conclusion on the Right to Data Protection under the CJEU Case Law

The analysis of the case law above has demonstrated that the CJEU has recently significantly clarified the purpose, scope, nature and permitted limitations on the right to data protection, thus enabling it to start its own life in the fundamental rights' landscape. At the same time, while drawing a clearer distinction between data protection and privacy, the Court has also interpreted them as closely interlinked and complementary rights, which this chapter considers as a

---

[85] See to this effect, CJEU, C-414/16, *Egenberger*, para 82 where the CJEU has ruled that 'a national court hearing a dispute between two individuals is obliged, where it is not possible for it to interpret the applicable national law in conformity with Article 4(2) of Directive 2000/78, to ensure within its jurisdiction the judicial protection deriving for individuals from Articles 21 and 47 of the Charter and to guarantee the full effectiveness of those articles by disapplying if need be any contrary provision of national law'.

[86] See in this sense Tzanou (n 78) and Eleni Frantziou, 'Joined Cases C-569/16 and C-570/16 Bauer et al: (Most of) The Charter of Fundamental Rights is Horizontally Applicable', *Europeanlawblog.eu*, November 19, 2018, https://europeanlawblog.eu/2018/11/19/joined-cases-c-569-16-and-c-570-16-bauer-et-al-most-of-the-charter-of-fundamental-rights-is-horizontally-applicable/.

[87] Following the Cambridge Analytica scandal such gap is identified, in particular by the UK Information Commissioner's Office's report to the Parliament. Investigation into the Use of Data Analytics in Political Campaigns, November 6, 2018, https://ico.org.uk/media/2260277/investigation-into-the-use-of-data-analytics-in-political-campaigns-20181107.pdf.

[88] See for this discussion, eg, Sandra Wachter et al, 'Why a Right to Explanation of Automated Decision-Making Does Not Exist in the General Data Protection Regulation' (2017) 7 *International Data Privacy Law* 76, 78.
Andrew Selbst and Julia Powles, 'Meaningful Information and the Right to Explanation', (2017) 7(4) *International Data Privacy Law* 233–245.

positive development that has afforded privacy and data protection a higher level of protection in comparison with the one guaranteed under the ECtHR case law. Recognising data protection as an independent 'constitutional' right has also tremendously elevated its legal status and has allowed it to serve a range of important legal functions, in particular for:

- harmoniously interpreting the provisions of the GDPR conceived as a secondary legislation implementing the fundamental right to data protection, but also informing its content, scope and limits (*Schrems, Google*);
- harmoniously interpreting other EU secondary laws envisaging data processing activities, as well as Member States' acts falling within the scope of EU law (*Promusicae, Huber*);
- reviewing the validity of EU secondary law and other acts of the EU institutions that envisage processing of personal data, including international transfer agreements *(Digital Rights Ireland, PNR Opinion 1/15)*, as well as of acts of the Member States when acting within the scope of EU law (*Tele2 Sverige*);
- acting as coercive regulatory safeguards for the effective protection of the right to privacy and other fundamental rights (*Digital Rights Ireland, PNR Opinion 1/15*);
- enabling horizontal direct application of the protection afforded by the Charter in disputes between private parties *(Google Spain)*;
- providing a legal basis for deriving novel data subjects' rights or filling gaps in the current data protection regime (eg, the 'right to be forgotten' in *Google Spain)*;
- Providing extra-territorial equivalent protection of the EU citizens' rights and freedoms afforded by EU law when personal data is transferred and subsequently processed outside the EU *(Schrems, PNR Opinion 1/15)*.

With all this case law, the CJEU has accomplished a remarkable job in giving purpose and 'teeth' to the novel right to data protection in the digital environment, which was considered by some scholars unnecessary, potentially undermining privacy or generally out-of-place and inadequate to qualify as a fundamental right.[89] Despite all these positive jurisprudential achievements, this chapter still argues the CJEU could have done a better job in delimiting the 'essence' of the right to data protection, which currently boils down to a minimalist technical and procedural standard to serve the essence of the right to privacy without any value of its own.[90] Admittedly, the CJEU failed to explain the logic used to derive the 'essence' of the right to data protection and missed the chance to use a broader and value laden conceptualisation of what is actually its substance and content as a fundamental right. While the data processing principles may be indeed part of the

---

[89] Rouvroy and Poullet (n 16), Van der Sloot (n 16).
[90] Brkan (n 16).

essence of the right to data protection, it is argued that they should be conceived as part of a bigger picture of components and 'means' to protect the inner core of the right to data protection, substantively understood as 'control' in a holistic manner comprising different dimensions and levels, as the next section will argue.

III. Re-conceptualising the Substance and the 'Essence' of the Right to Data Protection as a Power Control and Precautionary Instrumental Right

Before the adoption of the GDPR, many scholars and policymakers have lamented the legal gap that has failed to address the harmful impacts of the digital transformation on the fundamental rights and freedoms. But nowadays too, some scholars have already argued that the GDPR is incompatible and fails to adequately protect the individual and the society against the new risks posed by big data and AI.[91] Indeed, many of the secondary law provisions are too flexible or vague and do not give a clear answer on how to specifically apply the overarching data processing principles in the context of the emerging technologies. Considering this uncertainty and the rapid technological change, this chapter suggests that the proper conceptualisation of the fundamental right to data protection could provide the CJEU with the 'living instrument' to respond to these evolving challenges in line with the proclaimed purpose of the Charter[92] and the settled case of the ECtHR,[93] which has consistently interpreted and applied the human rights enshrined in the Convention in the light of the current societal and technological challenges and developments.

To obtain this effective 'living' instrument, the CJEU should arguably conceive the actual substance and the 'essence' of the right to data protection not only as 'existence of some data processing principles',[94] but additionally in terms of 'control' in line with the concept of informational self-determination and the substance of the right under Article 8(1) of the Charter, which imposes a positive right of every citizen for the protection of his/her personal data. This change in the conceptualisation is arguably not only desirable, but even obligatory because the concept of 'control' is now explicitly introduced in the GDPR,[95] which in accordance with the

---

[91] Eg, Wachter and Mittelstadt (n 36), Tal Zarsky, 'Incompatible: The GDPR in the Age of Big Data' (2017) 47 *Seton Hall Law Review* 995–1020, https://scholarship.shu.edu/cgi/viewcontent.cgi?article=16 06&context=shlr.

[92] The fourth paragraph of the Charter proclaims that it is necessary to 'strengthen the protection of fundamental right in the light of changes in society, social progress and scientific and technological developments'.

[93] Eg, ECtHR, *Tyrer v UK* (App No 5856/72, §31), *Matthews v UK* (App No 24833/94, §39).

[94] *Digital Rights Ireland and Others*, para 40.

[95] Recitals 7, 68, 75 and 85 of the GDPR and the new accountability obligations under Arts 5(2), 24, 25 and 35 of the GDPR.

Explanations of the Charter is binding on the European and national courts and requires interpretation of the fundamental right to data protection in line with the existing EU data protection legislation.[96]

While the concept of control has been traditionally advanced (or criticised) in the literature in terms of 'individual control' of the data subject over their personal data,[97] the next subsections will propose a more holistic and integrated conceptualisation of the right to data protection understood as 'control', which goes well beyond the individual level and places in addition the focus on the collective, precautionary and prohibitive functions of the data protection control mechanisms at all different levels and for many other rights and values than merely the rights to privacy and data protection. In theoretical terms, the added value of the proposed reconceptualisation is that it builds on the majority of the existing academic theories about the role and the content of the right to data protection, which are interpreted in a manner that provides a comprehensive and consistent understanding of the various functions and constitutive elements of data protection as a fundamental right. It is also consistent with the case law of the CJEU and incorporates many of the novel principles and concepts enshrined in the modernised GDPR that should inform now the substance of the fundamental right to data protection.

In practical terms, the proposed reconceptualisation could play two important functions in legal disputes. First, the different dimensions of the concept of 'control' could be used by the CJEU as the actual substance of the right to data protection when the Court assesses the degree of interference with the right to data protection to determine whether the 'essence' of the right under Article 8 is actually violated (in line with the approach followed by the CJEU in construing the 'essence' of other fundamental rights).[98] The analysis below will thus use the terms 'substance/content' and 'essence' as closely interlinked, considering that the assessment whether the 'essence' of the right to data protection is violated will depend to a great extent on the existing safeguards and 'control mechanisms' at every different level for fulfilling the different functions of the right to data protection, as proposed in the chapter. Second, the fundamental right to data protection understood holistically as 'control' could be also employed as a 'living instrument' to respond to the current societal and technological challenges and serve as an interpretative tool to clarify the existing secondary provisions, solve ambiguities and 'grey areas' and even possibly fill gaps in the protection by deriving novel data subjects' rights or obligations for the controllers, as the CJEU has already done in its past case law.[99]

The following subsections will outline the main cornerstones of the right to data protection understood holistically as 'control' aiming to: (1) rectify power and

---

[96] See Art 52(2) and (7) of the Charter and the Explanations in relation to the Charter what constitutes the source of the fundamental right to data protection under Art 8.

[97] See the literature cited in n 17.

[98] See Lenaerts (n 43) and the case law cited in n 41.

[99] Eg, when the CJEU derived the 'right to be forgotten' in *Google Spain* or when it repealed the Data Retention Directive in *Digital Rights Ireland*.

information imbalances between the data subjects and the controllers; (2) establish control mechanisms at different levels (individual-controller-society-supervisory authority); (3) permit interferences with the fundamental rights subject to compliance with procedural checks and balances (eg controllers' obligations and data subjects' rights); (4) prohibit ex ante certain data processing operations adversely affecting collective values and the society at large; (5) act as a precautionary instrument for the protection of privacy, but also all other fundamental rights that could be impacted by the processing.

A.   Control as a Tool to Rectify Power and Information Imbalances

First, it is argued that the substance of data protection should be perceived as an instrument to effectively rectify and mitigate power and information asymmetries between the individual and the powerful states and companies that acquire additional knowledge and power as a result from the processing, irrespective of whether the data subject has agreed to it or not. Understanding data protection through the lens of power relations and control has long-standing traditions in the privacy scholarship, most recently with Lynskey[100] who has argued that the right to data protection is an expression of the right to 'informational self-determination'. Based on the right to dignity and personality, the right to 'informational self-determination' was proclaimed by the German Constitutional Court in the 80s as a novel constitutional right, aiming to ensure

> the power of the individual to determine for himself the disclosure and use of his or her data and preclude a social order in which citizens can no longer know who knows what, when, and on what occasion about them. Otherwise, it would not only impair their chances of development, but it would also impair the common good, because self-determination is an essential functional condition of a free democratic society that builds upon the ability of action and participation of its citizens.[101]

The German Constitutional Court has also specifically highlighted the role of this right to protect the individual in particular against the 'increased danger which is based on the technical possibilities under modern conditions of data processing', resulting in the situation that the 'data are not only, on a second-by-second basis, retrievable at any time and place but can also be, especially in the case of integrated information systems, combined with other data collections leading to multiple possibilities of usage and linking'.[102]

---

[100] Lynskey (n 16).

[101] Judgment of the German Constitutional Court from 15 December 1983, 'Population Census Decision', 1 BvR 209/83, BVerfGE 65, 1.

[102] Judgment of the German Constitutional Court from 4 April 2006, BVerfG, 1 BvR 518/02 (Dragnet Investigation), para 65.

Data protection understood as informational self-determination is also closely related to the Kafkaesque interpretation, advanced by the legal scholar Daniel Solove who has underscored the powerless and vulnerable position of the individual against those taking decisions in an increasingly arbitrary way, based on secretly accumulated and aggregated comprehensive digital dossiers.[103] Nowadays, both the academia and the policy-makers have recognised that the deployment of AI surveillance and profiling technologies and the delegation of important decisions to algorithms in key sectors provides states and private companies with novel and much more powerful tools for exercising political, economic and social control over the individuals, thus reinforcing and redistributing authority and resources in the society.[104] The most daunting example how citizens' personal data can be used in the algorithmic society in terms of control is China, which is creating a system for total online and offline surveillance, algorithmic classification and scoring of its population.[105] But such new technologies are also extensively used by the states in the western world with the objective to combat crime and terrorism[106] or by dominant global players who hold the vital digital infrastructure with profitable business models built on the users' data, providing the same cutting-edge services to other companies and actors. The existing traditional asymmetries of power and information between state and private structures (acting often in collaboration) and citizens have thus further widened, creating a new form of governance by algorithms or 'algocracy', as argued by Aneesh.[107] Neil Richards and Jonathan King frame this also as the power paradox of big data and AI, which admittedly 'will create winners and losers, ultimately benefiting the institutions and the companies who wield their tools over the individuals being mined, analyzed, and sorted out'.[108] It has been also recognised in the literature that this shift in the interests and power relations at play in the 'datafied' society enables also novel forms of exclusion, subordination and discrimination that should find appropriate legal response and remedies.[109] It is beyond doubt today that personal data is not just a commodity or an asset with a significant monetary value in the

[103] Daniel J Solove, *The Digital Person: Technology and Privacy in the Information Age* (NYU Press. 2004); GWU Law School Public Law Research Paper 2017-5; GWU Legal Studies Research Paper 2017-5. Available at SSRN: https://ssrn.com/abstract=2899131.

[104] Council of Europe, Algorithms and Human rights, Study on the human rights dimensions of automated data processing techniques and possible regulatory implications, DGI (2017) 12, 41.

[105] See, eg, Yongxi Chen and Anne Cheung, 'The Transparent Self Under Big Data Profiling: Privacy and Chinese Legislation on the Social Credit System' (2017) 12(2) *The Journal of Comparative Law* 356–378; *University of Hong Kong Faculty of Law Research Paper* No 2017/011.

[106] Eg Asaf Lubin, 'A New Era of Mass Surveillance is Emerging Across Europe', *Medium*, January 17, 2017.

[107] Aneesh Aneesh, 'Technologically Coded Authority: The Post-Industrial Decline in Bureaucratic Hierarchies' (2002) Stanford University, web.stanford.edu/class/sts175/NewFiles/Algocratic Governance.pdf.

[108] Neil Richards and Jonathan King, 'Three Paradoxes of Big Data' (2013) 66 *Stanford Law Review online* 41, 45.

[109] See in this sense Dencik L, Hintz A, and Cable J, 'Towards Data Justice? The Ambiguity of Anti-surveillance Resistance in Political Activism' (2016) 3(2) *Big Data and Society* 1–12.

digital age,[110] but it also means power and control, and it is notably as such that it should be protected and regulated by the fundamental right to data protection, as argued in this chapter.

In the context of this sweeping technological and societal transformation, informational self-determination, understood traditionally as individual control over one's personal data and respect of personal autonomy, is an essential element to mitigate these growing power imbalances, but it may be ineffective and insufficient to effectively solve this problem. Under certain circumstances, research has shown that individual control may be even counterproductive, if other limitations and safeguards are not imposed on the controllers ex ante to prevent any potential arbitrariness and abuses of this growing power. As Schwartz has argued:

> thinking of privacy in terms of control either leads people to think they are acting more autonomously than they really are, or collapses completely in the face of the weighty reasons in support of revealing personal information. The danger is one that a belief in the virtue of self-reliant data control cannot acknowledge: information processing itself can undermine an individual's ability to participate in social and political life.[111]

Hartzog has also pointed out that '[i]ndividual control over one data flow won't change the fact that the data ecosystem is vast [...] and mind-bogglingly complex, with many different kinds of information collected in many different ways, stored in many different places, processed for many different functions, and shared with many other parties.'[112] Furthermore, 'networked online disclosures make individualistic conceptions of control outdated and require deeper thoughts about networked privacy – the idea that a great deal of personal information can be revealed by other people in ways that no individual can possibly control.'[113] These conclusions have been also backed up with recent research that has demonstrated that the collective result of atomised individual decisions of data subjects who are uncertain, contextually dependent, malleable or possibly irrational may not be always best for privacy and the common good.[114] People need fewer and better personal data choices driven by moral values[115] such as privacy, trust, dignity, justice, but as highlighted by Richards and Hartzog, they should also have a baseline, fundamental level of protection regardless of what they choose.[116] It has been

---

[110] See OECD, 'Exploring the Economics of Personal Data: A Survey of Methodologies for Measuring Monetary Value', OECD Digital Economy Papers, No 220, (2013) dx.doi.org/10.1787/5k486qtxldmq-en.

[111] Paul Schwartz, 'Privacy and Democracy in Cyberspace', (n 18).

[112] Hartzog, 'The Case Against Idealising Control' (n 18).

[113] Evan Selinger and Woodrow Hartzog, 'Facebook's Emotional Contagion Study and the Ethical Problem of Co-opted Identity in Mediated Environments where Users Lack Control' (2015) 12(1) *Research Ethics* 35–43. https://doi.org/10.1177/1747016115579531. See also Scott R Peppet, 'Unraveling Privacy: The Personal Prospectus and the Threat of a Full-Disclosure Future', (2015) 105 *Northwestern University Law Review* 1153.

[114] Alessandro Acquisti, Laura Brandimarte and George Loewenstein, 'Privacy and Human Behavior in the Age of Information' 347 Science (2015): 509-514.

[115] Schwartz, *The Paradox of Choice: Why More is Less* (n 18).

[116] Richards and Hartzog, 'The Pathologies of Consent for Data Practices' (n 18).

thus widely recognised in the academia that what is actually required are further safeguards and tools to regulate and take into account the landscapes of power and social (in)justice in this new mode of 'surveillance capitalism' and algorithmic governance.[117]

The understanding of control as a combination of personal autonomy and precautionary limitations of power seems to be already integrated in the GDPR with the notion of 'freely given' consent of the data subject, which is excluded in relations of power imbalances, for example, between employee-employer and citizen-public authorities, or when there would be no real choice for the individual, or the latter would suffer harmful consequences.[118] With the introduction of the novel risk-based approach, the GDPR also puts the focus on the specific impacts of the processing on the rights and freedoms of the natural subjects, thereby imposing a backstop on certain high risk processing activities unless sufficient safeguards are envisaged to minimise those risks and the growing power and information imbalances.[119] Accordingly, it is argued that interpreting the data subject-controller relation as a power relation through the lens of a novel no domination principle[120] and consideration of the vulnerability of the data subject[121] and the impact of the processing on data subject should also become an additional criterion for the CJEU to determine the degree of interference with the right to data protection and whether its 'essence' is violated with a view to substantially mitigating these growing power and information imbalances and reducing the negative impacts. Control should not be perceived, therefore, literally only in

---

[117] Zuboff, Shoshana, 'Big Other: Surveillance Capitalism and the Prospects of an Information Civilization' (2015) 30 *Journal of Information Technology* 75–89. doi:10.1057/jit.2015.5. Available at SSRN: https://ssrn.com/abstract=2594754.

[118] Recital 43, GDPR.

[119] Arts 24 and 35, GDPR.

[120] Derived on the basis of the imbalance considerations between data controllers and data subjects as recognised in Recital 43. This principle is in particular advocated by the republican theory which sees citizens' freedom not in terms of interference with rights, but in terms of power relations and potential of abuse. https://plato.stanford.edu/entries/republicanism/. See in this sense also Bart van der Sloot, 'A New Approach to the Right to Privacy, or How the European Court of Human Rights Embraced the Non-domination Principle' (2018) 34 *Computer Law & Security Review* 539–549, 540.

[121] The vulnerability of the data subject is referred to in Recital 75 of the GDPR and considered as a criterion by the ECtHR in some cases when assessing the existence and the degree of interference with the right to privacy under Article 8 ECHR. See, eg, *S. and Marper v the United Kingdom* (App Nos 30562/04 and 30566/04) where the young age of the applicant was one of the factors taken into account or *Chapman v The United Kingdom*, (App No 27238/95 (18 January 2001)), §95 where the ethnic origin of the applicants was considered inherent vulnerability. See in this sense also Article 29 Working Party (2014). Guidelines on the implementation of the Court of Justice of the European Union judgment on 'Google Spain SL, Google Inc v Agencia Española de Protección de Datos and Mario Costeja González' C-131/12, WP 225, 26 November 2014, 41. See also Article 29 Data Protection Working Party: Guidelines on Data Protection Impact Assessment (DPIA) and determining whether processing is 'likely to result in a high risk' for the purposes of Regulation 2016/679, 4 October 2017, 17/EN WP 248 (revised on 4 October 2017), 10. Some scholars particularly advocate for consideration of the data subjects' vulnerability in the data protection law such as Ryan Calo, 'Privacy, Vulnerability, and Affordance' (2017) 66 *DePaul Law Review* 66 592–593; Gianclaudio Malgieri, and Jędrzej Niklas, 'Vulnerable Data Subjects' [2020] *Computer Law and Security Review*, Special Issue on Data Protection and Research, Forthcoming. Available at SSRN: https://ssrn.com/abstract=3569808.

terms of the data subject's individual choices and available individual remedies, but it should be also conceived as a system of precautionary safeguards over the processing and an oversight architecture of control at different levels, as it will be argued in the next subsection.

B. Control at Different Levels (Individual-Controller-Society-Supervisory Authority)

As argued above, the concept of 'control' must be interpreted broadly not simply as individual control over one's personal data,[122] but in terms of a robust architecture of control implemented at all different levels (individual-controller-society-supervisory authority) as the structure of Article 8 of the Charter also suggests. Starting with the data subject's level, individual control should move beyond the initial phase of collection and traditional concepts such as consent (which has proven to provide rather ineffective protection in practice)[123] to address instead the increasing power and information asymmetries and re-balance the individual-controller relationship with novel remedies and rights already enshrined in the GDPR (eg, data portability, right to be forgotten, due process rights in solely automated decision-making) or rights yet to be explicitly proclaimed (eg, right to an explanation of individual automated decisions, right to have access to one's profile and correct it, right not to be subject to unjustified discriminatory decisions, right to know when interacting with an AI system, etc).

The individual should be also 'de-responsabilised' with greater proactive obligations placed at the level of the controller, in particular with the novel accountability principle,[124] the new requirements for meaningful human control over automated systems,[125] the concept of joint controllership,[126] strict and joint liability,[127] the risk-based and by design approaches[128] already introduced in the GDPR as key cornerstones of the overall control architecture. As Lazaro and Le Me'tayer point out, the accountability principle and the risk-based approach

---

[122] As it could be perceived if reading literally Recital 7 of the GDPR.

[123] Daniel Solove, 'Privacy Self-Management and the Consent Dilemma' (n 18); GWU Legal Studies Research Paper No 2012-141; GWU Law School Public Law Research Paper No 2012-141. Available at SSRN: https://ssrn.com/abstract=2171018.

[124] Art 5(2) of the GDPR which requires from the controllers to demonstrate compliance with all data processing principles under Art 5(1) of the GDPR.

[125] Art 22, GDPR.

[126] Art 26 of the GDPR provides that where two or more controllers jointly determine the purposes and means of processing, they shall be joint controllers. The CJEU has largely extended this concept in its recent case-law on C-210/16 *Facebook fan page* (*Wirtschaftsakademie Schleswig Holstein*), C-25/17, *Jehovah Witnesses* or C-40/17, *Fashion ID GmbH & Co. KG v Verbraucherzentrale NRW eV.*

[127] Art 87(1) of the GDPR envisages that any person who has suffered material or non-material damage as a result of an infringement of this Regulation shall have the right to receive compensation from the controller or processor for the damage suffered.

[128] Art 25, GDPR.

are indicative of a more collective view of control, which aims to guarantee the protection of the data subjects collectively and the society as a whole.[129] Such new control mechanisms could also better advance some ideas that groups also need proper protection, especially in the age of big data analytics, which drives decisions and actions at group rather than individual level, as demonstrated in the literature.[130] Conceiving the substance of data protection as control could also possibly help the CJEU to further strengthen the responsibility of the controller by imposing new obligations of fiduciary nature and non-delegable duties of loyalty, honesty and care about the best interest for the data subjects and the society that should in principle take precedence over the controller's own interests.[131] In any case, the new obligations already imposed by the GDPR considerably redistribute legal and social powers and re-balance the overall control architecture – they place additional proactive obligations and increase the liability of the controllers, while inevitably enhancing also the responsibilities of the national data protection authorities to supervise any (non-) compliance, to enforce effectively the GDPR and to chase after the flagrant personal data misuses and those reported by data subjects. As already demonstrated in the *Schrems* judgment, the effective and independent public control exercised by the supervisory bodies forms part and parcel of the 'essence' of the right to data protection as one of the different levels of control under Article 8 of the Charter (individual – controller – supervisory body). It is argued that while there may be permissible justified limitations and restrictions at the level of individual control (justified limitations on the data subjects' rights and consent as a legal basis), lack of control at the levels of the controller and the supervisory authorities should be unacceptable and considered impairing the very 'essence' of the right to data protection. The admitted failure of some data protection authorities to exercise effective control over the large corporations[132] may thus indicate impairment of the very essence of the fundamental right to data protection, if its public oversight mechanism is not properly functioning and fails to safeguard the rights of the individuals.

With the novel collective representation rights introduced in the GDPR,[133] it is also suggested that a fourth intermediary actor has been added to this triangle control architecture, notably 'the society', whose interests can be represented by specialised civil society organisations even in the absence of explicit empowerment

---

[129] Christophe Lazaro and Daniel Le Me'tayer, 'Control over Personal Data: True Remedy or Fairytale?' (2015) 12 SCRIPTed script-ed.org/?p=1927.

[130] Luciano Floridi, 'Open Data, Data Protection, and Group Privacy, Philosophy & Technology', March 2014, DOI: 10.1007/s13347-014-0157-8; Linnet Taylor et al (eds) *Group Privacy: the Challenges of New Data Technologies* (Springer, 2017).

[131] Jack M Balkin, 'Information Fiduciaries and the First Amendment Lecture' (2015) 49 *University of California Davis Law Review* 1183–1234. Hartzog, 'The Case Against Idealising Control' (n 18) 423–433.

[132] For the overwhelming criticism in this sense see, eg, Nicholas Vinocur, 'We have a huge problem': European regulator despairs over lack of enforcement,' Politico.eu, 27 December 2019, www.politico.eu/article/we-have-a-huge-problem-european-regulator-despairs-over-lack-of-enforcement/.

[133] Art 80, GDPR.

by the data subjects. Arguably, the more controllers affect significantly the data subjects' rights and use novel technologies that pose collective and societal risks, the more the supervisory authority's and the 'societal' oversight should be strengthened, possibly with new control mechanisms such as obligatory participation and consultation of data subjects and external stakeholders in carrying out the Data Protection Impact Assessment[134] and its publicity with a right to contestation in front of the supervisory authority and the court, class actions for damages, etc. In this context, the *Digital Rights Ireland* case already exposed the importance of grassroots civil society organisations and citizens' movements for the private enforcement of the data protection legislation, which can act as public watchdogs and play a key role as external non-governmental structures exercising oversight over the controllers' processing in strategic cases of major public interest,[135] especially when some national supervisory authorities seem to be rather passive for various reasons, including lack of sufficient human resources.

C. Control as A Permissive Instrument and a System of Procedural Checks and Balances to Reconcile Data Protection with Opposing Interests and Rights

Third, it is important to highlight that data subjects do not have absolute control over their data because personal information plays an important role in the society and the fundamental right to data protection should be applied in the light of its function in the social, political and economic life.[136] Control should be, therefore, perceived also in terms of the *checks and balances*[137] and the oversight control mechanisms[138] for justified impairment of one's privacy and individual control, thus highlighting also the permissive nature of data protection that requires a 'fair' balance to be struck between the data subjects' rights against other legitimate public interests and competing rights. In the end, such balancing requires a context-specific assessment to be made for each restriction to assess whether it is indeed necessary and proportionate and the processing can be eventually considered 'fair' and in compliance with the proportionality principle and the requirements under Article 52(1) of the Charter. In the secondary data protection law and the CJEU case law, these *checks and balances* are embodied in the data subjects' rights (to access, correction, deletion, objection, etc) and the data processing principles of lawfulness, transparency, fairness, purpose limitation, data minimisation, accuracy, storage limitation, security and accountability, which

---

[134] Art 35, GDPR.

[135] The preliminary references were initiated by the small non-governmental organisation (NGO) of Digital Rights Ireland and some 12,000 Austrian residents.

[136] C-112/00, *Schmidberger*, EU:C:2003:333, para 80; C-92/09 and C-93/09 *Volker und Markus Schecke and Eifert*, para 48; C-291/12 *Schwarz*, para 33.

[137] See in this sense Kranenborg (n 16), 176.

[138] Clifford and Ausloos (n 83), 147.

have been 'constitutionalised' by the Court as part of the fundamental right to data protection (see Section II A above).

Compliance with the purpose limitation principle and security have been even proclaimed by the CJEU to constitute the very 'essence' of the right to data protection,[139] thus highlighting their coercive force and recognising their importance as absolute constitutive elements of the right to data protection. While the absolute absence of the above mentioned rights and principles may lead to a violation of the 'essence' of the right to data protection, it is also argued that they should be applied in a flexible and systemic manner, taking into account the inherent interdependencies between these principles, but also the potential trade-offs between them,[140] as well as the specific purposes and context of application. Such interpretation of the data subjects' rights and the data processing principles as part of an overarching system of control with interdependent checks and balances is increasingly important in the big data world, which puts strains on the traditional principles such as purpose limitation and minimisation, and challenges in principle the concept of individual control. As suggested by Tene and Polonetsky,[141] the principles should be, therefore, flexible enough to guarantee the overarching concept of control and oversight by relaxing some principles, where necessary, depending on the context, while reinforcing others (eg accuracy, transparency, accountability, fairness) and guaranteeing as a compensation the effective enjoyment of the data subjects' rights, for example, by allowing data subjects to have full access to their personal data and profiles, as well as the rights to object, correct and challenge these profiles, to know the reasons for a particular individual decision, to delete their data, etc.

D. Control as a Prohibitive Instrument for Collective Protection of the Society and Wider Values

Next, it is argued that the concept of 'control' should actively pursue individual autonomy and freedom of every citizen,[142] while effectively protecting privacy

---

[139] *Digital Rights Ireland*, para 40 and Opinion 1/15, para 150.

[140] Eg, data minimisation may enter into conflict with the principle of security, or the principle of accuracy may be inconsistent with the principle of transparency or fairness in terms of non-discriminatory impact. See Reuben Binns, 'Trade-offs', 25 July 2019, https://ico.org.uk/about-the-ico/news-and-events/ai-blog-trade-offs/.

[141] Omer Tene and Jules Polonetsky, 'Big Data for All: Privacy and User Control in the Age of Analytics' (2011) 11(5) *Northwestern Journal of Technology and Intellectual Property* 242 suggests that the data processing principles should be viewed as a set of levers that must be adjusted to adapt to varying business and technological conditions. They highlight in particular their flexibility how some principles retract while others expand depending on the circumstances. In the context of big data, this means relaxing data minimisation and consent requirements while emphasising transparency, access and accuracy. The shift is from empowering individuals at the point of information collection, which traditionally revolved around opting into or out of seldom read, much less understood corporate privacy policies; to allowing them to engage with and benefit from information already collected, thereby harnessing big data for their own personal usage.

[142] Lynskey (n 16) 268.

and other collective values[143] such as dignity, freedom, democracy, pluralism, rule of law, equality and justice.[144] While data protection is generally framed as an individual right, the case law of the CJEU above has demonstrated that it plays a key role to prevent our societies from turning into societies of control, surveillance, social subordination and arbitrariness.[145] Beyond the protection afforded to the single individual, data protection with its control mechanisms at the upper system and oversight levels (the controller, the societal oversight and the supervisory authority) should consequently also safeguard collectively the values, rights and freedoms of whole groups of individuals and the society at large. Therefore, it should act not only as a permissive instrument (as it is generally perceived in the scholarship), but also as a *prohibitive tool*, which prohibits certain data processing ex ante, especially in circumstances where the data processing creates adverse harms for large groups or affects other persons, different from the data subjects or the society at large.[146]

This prohibitive collective function of data protection is all the more important in the age of the digitalisation and big data analytics, where data is constantly generated and analysed and practically all individuals are turned into an object under constant surveillance, datification, profiling and nudging in a manner, often incompatible with the underlying values of freedom, dignity and autonomy and the very essence of the rights to data protection and privacy.[147] Furthermore, big data and AI may often produce only minor or imperceptible effects at individual level, but at macro societal level they often create external 'pollution' and public harms, causing much more serious social, economic, cultural and political consequences and even threatening underlying values such as the rule of law, democracy and equality.[148] One salient example to this effect is the Cambridge Analytica scandal, where the access granted by Facebook to the personal data of its 80 million users allowed third parties to try to distort voting decisions with the negative effects, captured not only by the private injuries to the specific individuals who were intrusively profiled and micro-targeted with political ads and whose voting decisions may have been influenced, but far broader inflicting also serious damage to the entire political environment and electoral process, and posing a serious threat to the functioning of the democracy itself.[149] Other examples of

---

[143] For privacy as a collective value see Poullet (n 16), PM Regan, *Legislating Privacy, Technology, Social Values and Public Policy*, (New York, 1995), 321.

[144] Art 2, TEU.

[145] Rodota (n 16), 4.

[146] See Omri Ben-Shahar, 'Data Pollution.' University of Chicago Coase-Sandor Institute for Law & Economics Research Paper No 854; U of Chicago, Public Law Working Paper No 679 (2017).

[147] Rodota (n 16), 4.

[148] See in this sense Ben-Shahar (n 146).

[149] See UK Information Commissioner's Office, Report to the Parliament. Investigation into the Use of Data Analytics in Political Campaigns, November 6, 2018, https://ico.org.uk/media/2260277/investigation-into-the-use-of-data-analytics-in-political-campaigns-20181107.pdf; European Commission, Guidance on the application of Union data protection law in the electoral context, 12 September 2018 COM (2018) 638 final, 2.

harmful external consequences of data processing include also the mass person-
alisation and 'filter bubbles,' which fragmentise and polarise the society, disrupting
democratic deliberation and degrading the 'social glue',[150] or the negative impacts
on equality and justice, whereby AI systems have been found not only to reinforce existing structural discrimination, but also to produce novel subtle forms of
emergent and intersectional discrimination, and to make invisible many victims of
social injustice who often do not fall under the scope of existing protections under
anti-discrimination law.[151]

The prohibitive potential of data protection has been already recognised
in the mass surveillance case law of both the ECtHR[152] and the CJEU,[153] which
shows that privacy and data protection are public interests and collective goods
and essential pre-conditions for the flourishment of any democratic society. But
beyond these high-stake, mass surveillance cases, the CJEU has arguably played
a key role in conceptualising data protection in principle as a prohibitive rather
than a permissive fundamental right, which protects the personal data even before
its generation and collection.[154] Further examples of this prohibitive function can
also be found with the coercive application of the data processing principles of
purpose and storage limitation, data minimisation, etc, or with the new stringent requirements for the validity of consent as a legal ground for processing,[155]
the limitations on the processing of sensitive data,[156] the new focus on impacts
and risks and the obligatory prior consultation with the supervisory authority in
case of highly risky processing,[157] the qualified prohibition of solely automated
decision-making, including profiling, with legal and similarly significant effects.[158]
The prohibitive function of data protection could be also further strengthened if
as part of the necessity and proportionality assessment under Article 52(1) of
the Charter and Article 35(7)(b) of the GDPR, the Court explicitly clarifies that
collective group and wider societal impacts of the data processing should also be
assessed and taken into account, including any risks to more fundamental values
such as dignity, democracy, rule of law, justice, etc.[159] Any positive externalities

---

[150] Cass Sunstein, *#Republic: Divided Democracy in the Age of Social Media* (Princeton University Press, 2017).

[151] Torin Monahan, 'Regulating Belonging: Surveillance, Inequality, and the Cultural Production of Abjection' (2017 10(2) *Journal of Cultural Economy* 191–206, 202; Monique Mann and Tobias Matzner, 'Challenging Algorithmic Profiling: The Limits of Data Protection and Anti-discrimination in Responding to Emergent Discrimination, Brussels privacy Hub', Working Paper Vol 6, No 18, 12 January 2020.

[152] ECtHR, *Leander v Sweden* (App No 9248/81) and *Malone v the United Kingdom* (App No 8691/79).

[153] *Digital Rights Ireland and Others* and *Tele2 Sverije* and Opinion of AG Saugmandsgaard Øe in Joined Cases C-203/15 and C-698/15, *Tele2 Sverije*, ECLI:EU:C:2016:572, para 248.

[154] See to this effect *Digital Rights Ireland*, para 36 and the case law cited in n 30.

[155] Recital 43 and Art 4(11) and 7(4), GDPR.

[156] Art 9 and 10, GDPR.

[157] Art 36, GDPR.

[158] Art 22, GDPR.

[159] See in this sense also Alessandro Mantelero, 'AI and Big Data: A Blueprint for a Human Rights, Social and Ethical Impact Assessment' (2018) 34(4) *Computer Law & Security Review* 754–772.

and 'data rewards' from the processing should also be considered as part of this assessment, because as some scholars rightly point out, the data processing and AI in particular can also help to solve some endemic problems with human rights violations and be designed in a way that actually contributes to enhanced protection of some fundamental rights and public interests, while minimising to the extent possible the negative impacts on the individual's privacy and the societal values.[160] In assessing these impacts in line with the changes introduced in the GDPR,[161] the fundamental right to data protection should also be explicitly recognised as a precautionary instrument for the protection of the right to privacy, but also for all other individuals' fundamental rights and freedoms protected by the Charter, as the next section will argue.

E. Control as a Precautionary Instrument for both Procedural and Substantive Protection of all Fundamental Rights

Finally, it is argued that data protection understood as control should play an instrumental function and safeguard from current and future risks, not only privacy, but all other fundamental rights protected by the Charter. This proposition builds on the theory of Rouvroy and Poullet[162] who argue that privacy and data protection are 'tools' through which more fundamental values, or more 'basic' rights are protected – namely human dignity and individual personality rights, which are necessary for sustaining a lively democracy. While these two authors negate data protection as a 'stand-alone' right based notably on its instrumentalist role, this chapter suggests on the contrary that its main added value understood as control resides in its new precautionary and risk-based approach that should substantively protect both the individual and the society against unjustified interferences or future risks and safeguard all individuals' fundamental rights – certainly privacy, but also the right to human dignity, freedom of expression, freedom of thought, association and assembly, equality and non-discrimination, integrity and security, effective remedy and fair trail, good administration, the right to free and fair elections, free movement, the presumption of innocence, etc.

To illustrate this precautionary instrumental function of data protection, it is argued that always when a data processing activity risks to unjustifiably affect a

Available at SSRN: https://ssrn.com/abstract=3225749; Yves Poullet, 'Is the General Data Protection Regulation the Solution?' (2018) 34(4) *Computer Law & Security Review* 773–778.

[160] Ben-Shahar (n 146); Gabe Maldoff, and Omer Tene, 'Putting Data Benefits in Context: A Response to Kift and Nissenbaum,' (2017) 13 *I/S: A Journal of Law and Policy* 2, 3. Available at SSRN: https://ssrn.com/abstract=3081548.

[161] See Art 35(7)(c) of the GDPR, which states that the data protection impact assessment should obligatorily contain an assessment of the risks to the 'rights and freedoms of data subjects'.

[162] Rouvroy and Poullet (n 16) 53. See also Manon Oostveen and Kristina Irion, 'The Golden Age of Personal Data: How to Regulate an Enabling Fundamental Right?' in Bakhoum and others (eds) *Personal Data in Competition, Consumer Protection and IP Law – Towards a Holistic Approach?* (Springer, 2017).

certain fundamental right, the CJEU should simultaneously identify a failure of the procedural checks and balances over the control mechanism how personal data has been processed. For example, when a discriminatory or arbitrary decision has been taken, based on certain personal data or a data processing activity has led to unjustified interference with the right to privacy, or one's electoral decision compromised, this should automatically mean that not only the said substantive right has been violated, but also the right to data protection under Article 8 of the Charter, given that its 'gateway' function has been compromised as a control mechanism to prevent such a violation in the first place. Contrary to Dalla Corte, who perceives the role of data protection only as a *procedural* right or a 'right to a rule',[163] this chapter argues that data protection as a procedural instrument should ultimately also result in *substantive* protection of all fundamental rights that may be put at risk as a result of the processing. Such interpretation resembles the two-step approach, proposed by the German scholar Albers[164] who suggests that the 'right to informational self-determination' should be interpreted through a combination of an objective and a subjective regulatory approach. On a first *objective* level, data protection should provide the necessary procedural guarantees or objective requirements, for example that the data shall be only collected and processed in a lawful, fair and transparent manner for a specific purpose etc and that data subjects should participate in the informational process by means of their rights to access, correction, etc. On a second *substantive* level, privacy and all other fundamental rights should provide additionally the scale, context and level for informational protection and inform which processing should be considered permitted or prohibited.

At present, it can be reasonably argued that the CJEU has recognised the *objective* procedural aspects of the right to data protection (in terms of security and other data processing principles and rights) and the *substantive* protection that these data protection rules should afford to the right to privacy[165] and to a certain extent the right to non-discrimination (Article 21 of the Charter),[166] freedom of expression (Article 11),[167] the presumption of innocence (Article 48(1))[168] and

---

[163] Dalla Corte (n 16).

[164] Marion Albers, 'Umgang mit personenbezogenen Informationen und Daten' in Wolfgang Hoffmann-Riem, Eberhard Schmidt-Aßmann, Andreas Voßkuhle (eds) *Grundlagen des Verwaltungsrechts* Vol II, 2nd edn (Beck, 2012), 11.

[165] *Digital Rights Ireland and Others*, and *Tele2 Sverige and Watson and Others*.

[166] See analysis above in Section II C and Opinion 1/15 above and paras 165 and 172.

[167] See analysis of analysis above in Section II A and *Digital Rights Ireland and Others*, para 28 and *Tele2 Sverije*, para 101.

[168] In *Puskar*, the CJEU specifically highlighted the potential negative effect of the data processing on the presumption of innocence, ruling that the inclusion of a natural person in lists/databases of potential suspects interferes with both the right to data protection and the presumption of innocence which can be proportionate 'only if there are sufficient grounds to suspect the person concerned of purportedly' undermining the public interest, in that case in the collection of taxes and combating tax fraud. CJEU, C-73/16, *Peter Puskar*, ECLI:EU:C:2017:725, para 114.

the right to an effective remedy (Article 47).[169] The horizontal protective function of data protection has been also explicitly proclaimed in the *Schrems* judgment, in relation to the international data transfers,[170] and it should accordingly also apply internally, because otherwise the EU would lack legitimacy and legal authority to impose stricter rules on third countries, when not adhering to the equivalent standard internally.[171] While the instrumental role of data protection has been explicitly recognised in the cited case law, it is unfortunate that in the *YS* judgment[172] the CJEU has neglected its importance in the decision-making context by ruling that the data protection law is not intended to ensure accuracy of the decisions and the decision-making processes involving personal data, or to make these processes fully transparent by filling gaps in sectoral legislations. As argued by Wachter and Mittelstadt,[173] this judgment would limit the remit of data protection law alarmingly, especially when applicable decision-making legal standards are often missing in the private sector, while big data analytics and AI technologies allow controllers to increasingly infer information about the private lives of individuals, to modify and solidify their identity and take decisions that affect their lives and rights. Arguably, such restrictive interpretation comes into conflict with the other case law of the CJEU above and the independent status of the fundamental right to data protection, which is distinct and complementary to other rights, and which should, therefore, afford protection always when the data processing enters into its scope, thus acting as a 'safety net' for the protection of the other fundamental rights impacted by the processing, including if necessary by filling gaps in sectoral laws and making more transparent the decision-making process.[174]

While the CJEU has been partially inconsistent in its case law, the proposed horizontal protective function of data protection is arguably fully in line with the provisions of the GDPR. In particular, it flows from the overarching purpose of

---

[169] The crucial role played by the data processing principle of transparency as a pre-condition for the exercise of the right to an effective remedy has also been highlighted in *Digital Rights Ireland*, paras 66 to 68 where notification of the data subjects providing them with relevant information was found, in fact, necessary to enable the persons affected to exercise, inter alia, their right to a legal remedy where their rights have been infringed. In addition to the right to know, the right to access to one's data has also been proclaimed by the CJEU as closely related to the right to an effective remedy, because gaining access to one's personal data can provide the necessary evidence in court to prove any alleged violation of the applicable legislation. See CJEU, C-73/16, *Peter Puskar*, ECLI:EU:C:2017:725, para 97.

[170] *Schrems*, paras 72 to 74.

[171] Christopher Kuner, 'The Internet and the Global Reach of EU Law', LSE Law, Society and Economy Working Papers 4/2017 London School of Economics and Political Science Law Department, 33.

[172] CJEU, Joined Cases C-141/12 and C-372/12, *YS, M and S v Minister voor Immigratie, Integratie en Asiel*, paras 45–47.

[173] Wachter and Mittelstadt (n 36), 26.

[174] See for similar interpretation of the interaction between consumer protection law and other EU sectoral laws, Recital 10 and Art 3(4) of the Unfair Commercial Practice Directive 2005/29/EC. Such interpretation is advanced also by Commission Staff Working Document Guidance on the Implementation/Application of Directive 2005/29/EC on Unfair Commercial Practices Accompanying the document Communication from the Commission, A comprehensive approach to stimulating cross-border e-Commerce for Europe's citizens and businesses SWD/2016/0163 final.

the GDPR,[175] the provision on solely automated decision-making[176] and the new enforcement tools, including the new risk-based approach and the data protection impact assessment (DPIA)[177] as well as the principles of accountability[178] and data protection by design and by default,[179] which aim to protect all data subjects' fundamental rights and freedoms. These novel tools also highlight the precautionary function of the concept of 'control' that should protect as a rule one's 'future life' and prevent and minimise ex ante the risks to the data subjects' rights, insofar as the data processing may not cause any harm at the time of its collection, but the potential that this data can be processed at a later date to profile or make assessments or take adverse decisions about the person or group of persons.[180]

Therefore, it is suggested that in view of the concept of 'control' introduced in the GDPR,[181] the overarching purpose of the data protection rules and the new enforcement tools,[182] the CJEU should re-define the role of data protection as a fully-fledged power control and precautionary instrument to provide both *procedural* and *substantive* protection to all individuals' fundamental rights against current and future risks and harms. This would be not only consistent with the instrumental function of data protection already recognised by the CJEU,[183] but also with the principle of 'effective and complete protection' of the data subject and their rights, applied by the CJEU in some recent judgments,[184] and consistently reiterated by the ECtHR to guarantee that the human rights are 'practical and effective' and not just an 'empty confession'.[185]

Beyond the legal arguments, such re-conceptualisation is also indispensable from a practical point of view, given that all these rights are indivisible and interlinked,[186] and they increasingly depend on how personal data is processed in the digital world, thus making data protection a pre-condition for the effective enjoyment of many other rights that used to be independent in the past

---

[175] Art 1, GDPR.

[176] Art 22, GDPR.

[177] Art 35, GDPR.

[178] Art 24, GDPR.

[179] Art 25, GDPR.

[180] See in this sense Wachter and Mittelstadt (n 36).

[181] Recitals 7, 68, 75, 85, GDPR.

[182] Art 1(2) of the GDPR states that 'This Regulation protects fundamental rights and freedoms of natural persons and in particular their right to the protection of personal data.' See also Arts 22, 25 and 35, GDPR.

[183] See case law cited in nn 152–157.

[184] Eg, CJEU, C-362/14 *Maximillian Schrems* [GC], ECLI:EU:C:2015:650, para 39, C-210/16 *Facebook Fanpage*, ECLI:EU:C:2018:388, para 30.

[185] See, eg, ECtHR, *Sabanchiyeva and Others v Russia* (App No 38450/05), para 132.

[186] See to this effect United Nations, Vienna Declaration and Programme of Action. Geneva: United Nations, 1993 which states that 'All human rights are universal, interdependent and interrelated. The international community must treat human rights globally in a fair and equitable manner, on equal terms, and with the same emphasis.' In its case law the ECtHR has also consistently ruled that the Convention must be read as a whole. Consequently, a matter specifically dealt with by one of its provisions may also, in some of its aspects, be regulated by other provisions of the Convention.

analogous world.[187] Without a general EU competence to adopt legislation on the fundamental rights and data protection being one of the few rights where the EU can in fact adopt harmonised rules,[188] it is argued that such an interpretation of the remit and function of the data protection law could be one way to address the existing gaps and ensure effective protection of these rights, increasingly endangered by the new technologies. As noted by von Grafenstein, this substantive protection function of data protection serving all fundamental rights would also rationalise the broad scope of application of the GDPR by providing the practical means to reduce the vagueness of its principles, resolve conflicts between conflicting interests and rights, and apply flexibly the data processing principles and data subjects' rights in particular cases.[189] Framing data protection and GDPR as a legal instrument for fundamental rights protection would also confirm that 'personal data' has a relational value, and as Poullet points out, data protection does not aim to protect the data just for the sake of it, but rather what through the personal data deserves protection – notably the people and their rights and interests.[190]

IV. Conclusion

The technological revolution has always acted as the main driving force for the evolution of the fundamental rights' landscape, thus giving birth to new rights – from the emergence of privacy at the end of the nineteenth century to the increasing importance today of its offspring – the fundamental right to data protection. The analysis of the recent judgments of the CJEU has highlighted the importance of this relatively novel and distinct right within the EU legal order and its essential role for the protection of privacy, but also other fundamental rights, which face increasing challenges in the era of big data and artificial intelligence. Still, to better explore its potential, it has been suggested that the right to data protection should be re-defined in terms of 'control' understood in a holistic sense as a robust control architecture at different levels, which should aim to address power and information imbalances, and act as a collective, prohibitive and precautionary

---

[187] Maximilian von Grafenstein, *The Principle of Purpose Limitation in Data Protection Laws*, (Nomos Verlagsgesellschaft mbH, 2018), 119 who has argued that 'Before digitization, different areas of social life were covered by the diversity of all fundamental rights. [..] Instead, in a digital world, the more digitization penetrates all these different areas of social life, the more comprehensively the rights to private life and to data protection apply, substituting the other fundamental rights.'

[188] See, eg, Art 6(2) of the TEU and Art 51(2) of the Charter which provides that the Charter does not extend the field of application of Union law beyond the powers of the Union or establish any new power or task for the Union, or modify powers and tasks as defined in the Treaties, while the Lisbon Treaty now provides in Art 15(1), TFEU a specific legal basis for adoption of legislation in the field of data protection.

[189] Von Grafenstein (n 187), 122.

[190] Wachter and Mittelstadt (n 36), Reasonable inferences 53; Hildebrandt, 'Profiling: From Data to Knowledge' (n 63).

instrument to avoid harms and risks to wider values and all citizens' fundamental rights protected by the Charter. Arguably, such re-conceptualisation could help the CJEU to substantiate in a more value laden way the actual content of the fundamental right to data protection and delimit what constitutes its core 'essence' in addition to the current reductionist approach, whereby the essence of the right boils down only to 'certain data processing principles and security'. Importantly, this would also allow the fundamental right to data protection to be the 'living instrument' in the hands of the CJEU to effectively protect the fundamental rights, enshrined in the EU Charter, while the emerging technologies will inevitably outpace again even the most advanced for its time data protection legislation – the General Data Protection Regulation (GDPR). As a matter of fact, the GDPR's provisions are already fraught with a great deal of uncertainties and ambiguities as to how they should be applied in the context of these emerging technologies, and the CJEU's answers to these questions will be of decisive importance for the effectiveness of the protection of the individual and our societies in today's algorithmic and big data world.

Acknowledgements

The author is grateful to Prof Dr Gloria González Fuster for her insightful comments on this chapter.

References

Acquisti, Alessandro, Laura Brandimarte and George Loewenstein. 'Privacy and Human Behavior in the Age of Information' (2015) 347 Science 509–514.

Albers, Marion. 'Umgang mit personenbezogenen Informationen und Daten' in Wolfgang Hoffmann-Riem, Eberhard Schmidt-Aßmann, Andreas Voßkuhle (eds) *Grundlagen des Verwaltungsrechts* Vol II, 2nd edn (Beck, 2012).

Aneesh, Aneesh. 'Technologically Coded Authority: The Post-Industrial Decline in Bureaucratic Hierarchies' (Stanford University, 2002) web.stanford.edu/class/sts175/NewFiles/Algocratic Governance.pdf.

Article 29 Data Protection Working Party. 'Guidelines on the Implementation of the Court of Justice of the European Union Judgement on "Google Spain and Inc. v. Agencia Espanola de Proteccion de Datos (AEPD) and Mario Costeja Gonzales"' C-131/12, 14/EN WP 225.

Article 29 Data Protection Working Party. 'Guidelines on Data Protection Impact Assessment (DPIA) and determining whether processing is "likely to result in a high risk" for the purposes of Regulation 2016/679.' 4 October 2017, 17/EN WP 248 (revised on 4 October 2017).

Balkin, Jack M. 'Information Fiduciaries and the First Amendment Lecture' (2015) 49 University of California Davis Law Review 1183–1234.

Barocas, Solon and Selbst, Andrew. 'Big Data's Disparate Impact' (2016) 104 *California Law Review* 671–732.

Ben-Shahar, Omri. 'Data Pollution.' University of Chicago Coase-Sandor Institute for Law & Economics Research Paper No 854; U of Chicago, Public Law Working Paper No 679 (2017). Available at SSRN: https://ssrn.com/abstract=3191231 or dx.doi.org/10.2139/ssrn.3191231.

Binns, Reuben, 'Trade-offs', 25 July 2019, https://ico.org.uk/about-the-ico/news-and-events/ai-blog-trade-offs/.

Brkan, Maja. 'The Essence of the Fundamental Rights to Privacy and Data Protection: Finding the Way through the Maze of the CJEU's Constitutional Reasoning.' Paper for conference The Essence of Fundamental Rights in EU Law 17–18 May 2018, Leuven.

Büchi, Moritz et al. 'The Chilling Effects of Algorithmic Profiling: Mapping the Issues' [2019] *Computer Law & Security Review*.

Buttarelli, Giovanni. 'The EU GDPR as a Clarion Call for a New Global Digital Standard.' (2016) 6(2) *International Data Privacy Law* 77–78.

Bygrave, Lee A. 'Privacy and Data Protection in an International Perspective' in Peter Wahlgren (ed) *Scandinavian Studies in Law Volume 56. Information and Communication Technology Legal Issues* (Stockholm Institute for Scandinavian Law, 2010).

Calo, Ryan. 'Privacy, Vulnerability, and Affordance.' (2017) 66 *DePaul Law Review* 592–593.

Council of Europe. Algorithms and Human Rights, Study on the Human Rights Dimensions of Automated Data Processing Techniques and Possible Regulatory Implications. DGI (2017) 12.

Council of Europe. Convention 108 for the Protection of Individuals with regard to Automatic Processing of Personal Data (1981).

Council of Europe. European Convention on Human Rights (1950).

Charter of Fundamental Rights of the European Union, [2012] OJ C326/ 391–407.

Chen, Yongxi and Cheung, Anne. 'The Transparent Self Under Big Data Profiling: Privacy and Chinese Legislation on the Social Credit System.' (2017) 12(2) *The Journal of Comparative Law* 356–378; *University of Hong Kong Faculty of Law Research Paper* No 2017/011.

CJEU, C-26/62, *Van Gend en Loos*, ECLI:EU:C:1963:1.

CJEU, C-294/83, *Parti écologiste "Les Verts" v European Parliament*, ECLI:EU:C:1986:166.

CJEU, C-260/89, *ERT*, EU:C:1991:254.

CJEU, C-112/00, *Schmidberger*, ECLI:EU:C:2003:333.

CJEU, C-101/01, *Bodil Linqvist*, ECLI:EU:C:2003:596.

CJEU, AG Kokott's Opinion on Case C-73/07 *Satakunnan Markkinapörssi et Satamedia*, ECLI:EU:C:2008:266.

CJEU, C-28/08, *European Commission v Bavarian Lager*, ECLI:EU:C:2010:378.

CJEU, Joined Cases C-92/09 and C-93/09, *Volker und Markus Schecke and Eifert*, ECLI:EU:C:2010:662.

CJEU, C-163/10, *Patriciello*, ECLI:EU:C:2011:543.

CJEU, C-614/10, *Commission v Austria* ECLI:EU:C:2012:631.

CJEU, C-291/12, *Schwarz*, ECLI:EU:C:2013:670.

CJEU, Joined Cases C-141/12 and C-372/12, *YS, M and S v Minister voor Immigratie, Integratie en Asiel*, ECLI:EU:C:2014:2081.

CJEU, C-131/12, *Google Spain SL and Google Inc*, ECLI:EU:C:2014:317.

CJEU, Joined Cases C-293/12 and C-594/12, *Digital Rights Ireland and Others*, ECLI:EU:C:2014:238.

CJEU, Opinion of Advocate General Cruz Villalón on Joined Cases C-293/12 and C-594/12 *Digital Rights Ireland and Others*, ECLI:EU:C:2013:845.

CJEU, C-362/14, *Maximilian Schrems v. Data Protection Commissioner*, ECLI:EU:C:2015:650.

CJEU, Joined Cases C-203/15 and C-698/15, *Tele2 Sverije AB and Watson*, ECLI:EU:C:2016:970.

CJEU, Opinion of AG Saugmandsgaard Øe in Joined Cases C-203/15 and C-698/15, Tele2 Sverije, ECLI:EU:C:2016:572.

CJEU, Opinion 1/15 on *Draft agreement between Canada and the European Union – Transfer of Passenger Name Record data from the European Union to Canada*, ECLI:EU:C:2017:592.

CJEU, C-650/13, *Thierry Delvigne v. Commune de Lesparre Médoc and Préfet de la Gironde*, ECLI:EU:C:2015:648.

CJEU, C 73/16, *Peter Puskar*, ECLI:EU:C:2017:725.

CJEU, C-190/16, *Werner Fries v. Lufthansa CityLine GmbH*, ECLI:EU:T:2017:201.

CJEU, C-210/16, *Wirtschaftsakademie Schleswig-Holstein (Facebook fan page)*, ECLI:EU:C:2018:388.

CJEU, C-414/16, *Egenberger*, ECLI:EU:C:2018:257.

CJEU, C-25/17, *Tietosuojavaltuutettu (Jehovah Witnesses)*, ECLI:EU:C:2018:551.

CJEU, C-40/17, *Fashion ID GmbH & Co. KG*, ECLI:EU:C:2019:629.

Clifford, Damian and Ausloos, Jef. 'Data Protection and the Role of Fairness.' (2018) 37(1) *Yearbook of European Law* 130–187, doi:10.1093/yel/yey004.

Cohen, Julie. 'Examined Lives: Informational Privacy and the Subject as Object.' (2000) 52 *Stanford Law Review* 1373, 1400.

Currie, David. 'Positive and Negative Constitutional Rights.' (1986) 53 *University of Chicago Law Review* 864.

Dalla Corte, Lorenzo. 'A Right to a Rule: On the Substance and Essence of the Fundamental Right to Personal Data Protection' in Hallinan, D., edited by Leenes, R., Gutwirth, S. & De Hert, P. (eds) *Data protection and Privacy: Data Protection and Democracy* (Hart Publishing, 2020) 27–58.

De Hert, Paul and Gutwirth, Serge. 'Data Protection in the Case Law of Strasbourg and Luxembourg: Constitutionalisation in Action' in Serge Gutwirth et al (eds) *Reinventing Data Protection?* (Springer, 2009).

Dencik L, Hintz A, and Cable J. 'Towards Data Justice? The Ambiguity of Anti-surveillance Resistance in Political Activism' (2016) 3(2) *Big Data and Society* 1–12.

European Commission. Communication on Artificial Intelligence for Europe, COM/2018/237 final.

European Commission. Guidance on the application of Union data protection law in the electoral context Brussels, 12 September 2018 COM (2018) 638 final.

European Commission. Staff Working Document Guidance on the Implementation/ Application of Directive 2005/29/EC on Unfair Commercial Practices Accompanying the document Communication from the Commission, A comprehensive approach to stimulating cross-border e-Commerce for Europe's citizens and businesses. SWD/2016/0163 final.

European Commission. 'White Paper On Artificial Intelligence – A European approach to excellence and trust.' COM/2020/65 final.

ECtHR, *Tyrer v UK* (App No 5856/72).

ECtHR, *Malone/the United Kingdom* (App No 8691/79).

ECtHR, *Big Brother Watch v The United Kingdom*, (App Nos 58170/13, 62322/14 и 24960/15).

ECtHR, *Chapman v The United Kingdom*, (App No 27238/95).

ECtHR, Guide on Article 8 of the European Convention on Human Rights, 31 December 2018.

ECtHR, *Leander/Sweden* (App No 9248/81).

ECtHR, *Matthews v The United Kingdom* (App No 24833/94).

ECtHR, *S and Marper v the United Kingdom* (App Nos 30562/04 and 30566/04).

ECtHR, *Sabanchiyeva and Others v Russia* (App No 38450/05).

Explanations relating to the Charter of Fundamental Rights, [2007] OJ C303/17–35. which according to Article 52(7) of the Charter shall be given due regard by courts of the Union and of the Member States when interpreting the fundamental rights enshrined in the Charter.

Floridi, Luciano. 'Open Data, Data Protection, and Group Privacy.' Philosophy & Technology (2014). DOI: 10.1007/s13347-014-0157-8.

Foucault, Michel. *Discipline and Punish: The Birth of the Prison.* (Penguin, 1991).

Frantziou, Eleni. 'Further Developments in the Right to be Forgotten: The European Court of Justice's Judgment in Case C-131/12, Google Spain, SL, Google Inc v Agencia Espanola de Proteccion de Datos' (2014) 14(4) *Human Rights Law Review* 761–777, https://doi.org/10.1093/hrlr/ngu033.

Frantziou, Eleni. 'Joined Cases C-569/16 and C-570/16 Bauer et al: (Most of) The Charter of Fundamental Rights is Horizontally Applicable.' *Europeanlawblog.eu*, November 19, 2018, https://europeanlawblog.eu/2018/11/19/joined-cases-c-569-16-and-c-570-16-bauer-et-al-most-of-the-charter-of-the-charter-of-fundamental-rights-is-horizontally-applicable/.

Fried, Charles. 'Privacy.' (1968) 77 *Yale Law Journal* 475, 482.

German Constitutional Court, Judgment from 15 December 1983, 'Population Census Decision', 1 BvR 209/83.

German Constitutional Court, Judgment from 4 April 2006, 'Dragnet Investigation', BVerfG, 1 BvR 518/02.

Gonzalez Fuster, Gloria and Gellert, Raphael. 'The Fundamental Right of Data Protection in the European Union: in Search of an Uncharted Right' (2012) 26 *International Review of Law, Computers & Technology* 73–82.

Gonzalez Fuster, Gloria and Gutwirth, Serge. 'Opening up Personal Data Protection: a Conceptual Controversy' [2013] *Computer Law and Security Review*.

Hartzog, Woodrow. 'The Case Against Idealising Control' (2018) 4 *European Data Protection Law Review* 430.

Hildebrandt, Mireille. 'Profiling: From Data to Knowledge' (2006) 30 *Datenschutz und Datensicherheit-DuD* 548, 2.

Kang, Jerry. 'Information Privacy in Cyberspace Transactions.' (1998) 50 *Stanford Law Review* 1193, 1218.

Kranenborg, Herke. 'Article 8' in Peers et al (eds) *The EU Charter of Fundamental Rights: A commentary* (Hart Publishing 2014).

Kokott, Juliane and Sobotta, Christoph. 'The Distinction between Privacy and Data Protection in the Jurisprudence of the CJEU and the ECtHR' (2013) 3(4) *International Data Privacy Law*.

Koutsias, Marios. 'Privacy and Data Protection in an Information Society: How Reconciled are the English with the European Union Privacy Norms?' (2012) 261(18) *Computer and Telecommunications Law Review* 265–266.

Kuner, Christopher. 'Reality and Illusion in EU Data Transfer Regulation Post Schrems' (2017) 18 *German Law Journal* 881.

Kuner, Christopher. 'The Court of Justice of the EU Judgment on Data Protection and Internet Search Engines.' LSE Law, Society and Economy Working Papers 3/2015, ssrn.com/abstract=2496060.

Kuner, Christopher. 'The Internet and the Global Reach of EU Law.' LSE Law, Society and Economy Working Papers 4/2017 London School of Economics and Political Science Law Department.

Lazaro, Christophe and Le Me'tayer, Daniel. 'Control over Personal Data: True Remedy or Fairytale?' 12 SCRIPTed (2015) script-ed.org/?p=1927.

Lenaerts, Koen. 'Limits on Limitations: The Essence of Fundamental Rights in the EU' (2019) 20 *German Law Journal* 779.

Lynskey, Orla. 'Deconstructing Data Protection: the 'Added-value' of a Right to Data Protection in the EU Legal Order' (2014) 63(3) *International and Comparative Law Quarterly* 569–597.

Lynskey, Orla. 'The Europeanisation of Data Protection Law.' *Cambridge Yearbook of European Legal Studies* (Cambridge University Press, 2016).

Lynskey, Orla. *The Foundations of EU Data Protection Law.* (Oxford University Press, 2016).

Lubin, Asaf. 'A New Era of Mass Surveillance is Emerging Across Europe.' *Medium*, January 17, 2017.

Malgieri, Gianclaudio and Niklas, Jędrzej. 'Vulnerable Data Subjects.' [2020] *Computer Law and Security Review*, Special Issue on Data Protection and Research (Forthcoming). Available at SSRN: https://ssrn.com/abstract=3569808.

Maldoff, Gabe and Tene, Omer. 'Putting Data Benefits in Context: A Response to Kift and Nissenbaum,' (2017) 13 *I/S: A Journal of Law and Policy* 2, 3. Available at SSRN: https://ssrn.com/abstract=3081548.

Mann, Monique and Matzner, Tobias. 'Challenging Algorithmic Profiling: The Limits of Data Protection and Anti-discrimination in Responding to Emergent Discrimination. Brussels Privacy Hub, Working Paper Vol 6, No 18 January 2020.

Mantelero, Alessandro. 'AI and Big Data: A Blueprint for a Human Rights, Social and Ethical Impact Assessment.' (2018) 34(4) *Computer Law & Security Review* 754–772. Available at SSRN: https://ssrn.com/abstract=3225749.

Monahan, Torin. 'Regulating Belonging: Surveillance, Inequality, and the Cultural Production of Abjection' (2017) 10(2) *Journal of Cultural Economy* 191–206.

Nemitz, Paul. 'Constitutional Democracy and Technology in the Age of Artificial Intelligence.' Royal Society Philosophical Transactions A, 2018. Available at SSRN: https://ssrn.com/abstract=3234336 or dx.doi.org/10.2139/ssrn.3234336.

Oostveen, Manon and Irion, Kristina. 'The Golden Age of Personal Data: How to Regulate an Enabling Fundamental Right?' in Bakhoum et al *Personal Data in Competition, Consumer Protection and IP Law – Towards a Holistic Approach?* (Springer, 2017).

Organisation for Economic Cooperation and Development. 'Exploring the Economics of Personal Data: A Survey of Methodologies for Measuring Monetary Value.' OECD Digital Economy Papers, No 220, (2013) dx.doi.org/10.1787/5k486qtxldmq-en.

PEN America. 'Chilling Effects: NSA Surveillance Drives U.S. Writers to Self-Censor.' New York: PEN American Center, 2013.

Penney, Jonathon. 'Chilling Effects: Online Surveillance and Wikipedia Use' [2016] *Berkeley Technology Law Journal*, papers.ssrn.com/sol3/papers.cfm?abstract_id=2769645.

Peppet, Scott R. 'Unraveling Privacy: The Personal Prospectus and the Threat of a Full-Disclosure Future' (2015) 105 Nortwestern University Law Review 1153.

Posner, Richard A. 'Privacy' in Peter Newan (ed) *New Palgrave Dictionary of Economics and the Law* (Palgrave MacMillan, 1998) 103.

Poullet, Yves. 'Is the General Data Protection Regulation the Solution?' (2018) 34(4) *Computer Law & Security Review* 773–778.

Regan, Priscilla M. *Legislating Privacy, Technology, Social Values and Public Policy*. (Palgrave MacMillan, 1995).

Regulation (EU) 2016/679 of the European Parliament and of the Council of 27 April 2016 on the protection of natural persons with regard to the processing of personal data and on the free movement of such data, and repealing Directive 95/46/EC (General Data Protection Regulation) (Text with EEA relevance) [2016] OJ L119/1–88.

Richards, Neil and King, Jonathan. 'Three Paradoxes of Big Data' (2013) 66 *Stanford Law Review online* 41, 45.

Richards, Neil and Hartzog, Woodrow. 'The Pathologies of Consent for Data Practices' (2019) 96 *Washington University Law Review*.

Rodota, Stefano. 'Data Protection as a Fundamental Right.' Keynote Speech for International Conference 'Reinventing Data Protection,' Bruxelles, 12–13 October 2007.

Rouvroy, Antoinette and Poullet, Yves. 'The Right to Informational Self- Determination and the Value of Self-Development: Reassessing the Importance of Privacy for Democracy' in Serge Gutwirth et al (eds), *Reinventing Data Protection?* (Springer, 2009).

Safari, Beata. 'Intangible Privacy Rights: How Europe's GDPR Will Set a New Global Standard for Personal Data Protection' (2017) 47 *Seton Hall Law Review* 809–848.

Schauer, Frederick. 'Internet Privacy and the Public-Private Distinction.' (1998) 38 *Jurimetrics Journal* 555, 556.

Scherer, Matthew U. 'Regulating Artificial Intelligence Systems: Risks, Challenges, Competences, and Strategies' (2016) 29 *Harvard Journal of Law & Technology* 2.

Schwartz, Paul. 'Privacy and Democracy in Cyberspace' (1999) 52 *Vanderbilt Law Review* 1609, 1663.

Schwartz, Barry. *The Paradox of Choice: Why More is Less* (HarperCollins Publishers, 2005).

Selbst, Andrew and Powles, Julia. 'Meaningful Information and the Right to Explanation' (2017) 7(4) *International Data Privacy Law* 233–245.

Selinger, Evan and Hartzog, Woodrow. 'Facebook's Emotional Contagion Study and the Ethical Problem of Co-opted Identity in Mediated Environments where Users Lack Control.' (2015) 12(1) *Research Ethics* 35–43.

Solove, Daniel J. *The Digital Person: Technology and Privacy in the Information Age* (NYU Press 2004); GWU Law School Public Law Research Paper (2017) 5. Available at SSRN: https://ssrn.com/abstract=2899131.

Solove, Daniel J. 'Privacy Self-Management and the Consent Dilemma,' (2013) 126 *Harvard Law Review* 1880.

Sunstein, Cass. *#Republic: Divided Democracy in the Age of Social Media* (Princeton University Press, 2017).

Taylor, Linnet, van der Sloot, Bart., Floridi, Luciano. *Group Privacy: the Challenges of New Data Technologies* (Springer, 2017).

Tene, Omer and Polonetsky, Jules. 'Big Data for All: Privacy and User Control in the Age of Analytics' (2013) 11(5) *Northwestern Journal of Technology and Intellectual Property*.

Treaty on European Union (TEU) [2016] OJ C202/13–388.

Tzanou, Maria. 'Data Protection as a Fundamental Right Next to Privacy? 'Reconstructing' a not so New Right' (2013) 3(2) *International Data Privacy Law*.

Tzanou, Maria. 'The Unexpected Consequences of the EU Right to Be Forgotten: Internet Search Engines As Fundamental Rights Adjudicators' in Maria Tzanou (ed) *Personal Data Protection and Legal Developments in the European Union* (Forthcoming) (IGI Global, 2020). Available at SSRN: https://ssrn.com/abstract=3277348/.

United Nations. Vienna Declaration and Programme of Action. Geneva: United Nations, 1993.

UK Information Commissioner's Office. ExplAIn guidance available for public consultation until 24 January 2020, https://ico.org.uk/about-the-ico/ico-and-stakeholder-consultations/ico-and-the-turing-consultation-on-explaining-ai-decisions-guidance/.

UK Information Commissioner's Office. Report to the Parliament. Investigation into the Use of Data Analytics in Political Campaigns, November 6, 2018, https://ico.org.uk/media/2260277/investigation-into-the-use-of-data-analytics-in-political-campaigns-20181107.pdf.

Van der Sloot, Bart. 'Legal Fundamentalism: is Data Protection Really a Fundamental Right?' in Leenes, R., van Brakel, R., Gutwirth, S., De Hert, P. (eds) *Data Protection and Privacy: (In)visibilities and Infrastructures* (Springer, 2017).

Van der Sloot, Bart. 'A New Approach to the Right to Privacy, or How the European Court of Human Rights Embraced the Non-domination Principle.' (2018) 34 *Computer Law & Security Review* 34 539–549.

Van Ooijen. I. and Vrabec, Helena. 'Does the GDPR Enhance Consumers' Control over Personal Data? An Analysis from a Behavioural Perspective' (2019) 42 *Journal of Consumer Policy* 91–10.

Vinocur, Nicholas. 'We Have a Huge Problem: European Regulator Despairs over Lack of Enforcement.' Politico.eu, 27 December 2019, www.politico.eu/article/we-have-a-huge-problem-european-regulator-despairs-over-lack-of-enforcement/.

Von Grafenstein, Maximilian. *The Principle of Purpose Limitation in Data Protection Laws.* (Nomos Verlagsgesellschaft mbH., 2018).

Wachter, Sandra and Mittelstadt, Brent, 'A Right to Reasonable Inferences: Re-Thinking Data Protection Law in the Age of Big Data and AI' (2019) 2 *Columbia Business Law Review*. Available at SSRN: https://ssrn.com/abstract=3248829.

Wachter, Sandra, Mittelstadt, Brent and Floridi, Luciano. 'Why a Right to Explanation of Automated Decision-Making Does Not Exist in the General Data Protection Regulation' (2017) 7 *International Data Privacy Law* 76, 78.

Zarsky, Tal. 'Incompatible: The GDPR in the Age of Big Data' (2017) 47 *Seton Hall Law Review* 995-1020, https://scholarship.shu.edu/cgi/viewcontent.cgi?article=1606&context=shlr.

Zarsky, Tal. 'Understanding Discrimination in the Scored Society' (2014) 89 *Washington Law Review* 4. Available at SSRN: https://ssrn.com/abstract=2550248.

7

Implementing AI in Healthcare: An Ethical and Legal Analysis Based on Case Studies

EDUARD FOSCH-VILLARONGA,[1] DAVIT CHOKOSHVILI,[2]
VIBEKE BINZ VALLEVIK,[3] MARCELLO IENCA[4] AND ROBIN L PIERCE[5]

Abstract

The integration of artificial intelligence (AI) technologies in healthcare promises safer, more efficient, and more personalised care. Typical applications of such systems include personalised diagnosis, early disease detection, hospitalisation risk prediction, and drug discovery. These technologies process vast amounts of data, can learn from experience, and are capable of autonomously improving their performance. This also challenges the applicability of existing regulations that were not designed for progressive and adaptive aspects of AI. The automated processing of data that will evaluate, analyse, and predict health-related outcomes may also affect not only data protection regulations but also safety and other aspects of the individual's environment. This chapter explores the challenges to existing legal frameworks brought about by the potential uptake and integration of several AI-based technologies in healthcare. Specifically, we look at AI-driven analytic tools for precision medicine, assistive technologies that adapt and facilitate rehabilitation and recovery, and various types of decision aids that may assist in critical processes such as diagnosis and screening. Although, in reality, the use of these technologies may not be limited to a single context, this approach allows

[1] Marie Skłodowska-Curie Postdoctoral Researcher at the eLaw Center for Law and Digital Technologies, Leiden University, the Netherlands.
[2] Regulatory Affairs and Bioethics Manager at Megeno.
[3] Project Manager BIGMED Project, DNV GL Precision Medicine research, OUS Intervention Center.
[4] Senior Researcher at Health Ethics & Policy Lab, Department of Health Sciences and Technology at ETH Zurich, Switzerland.
[5] Associate Professor at the Tilburg Institute of Law, Technology, and Society (TILT), Tilburg Law School, Tilburg Universit, the Netherlands.

us to focus the legal and ethical analysis on particular types of issues that may be based on function, usage, and implications. This analysis then examines both the practical and theoretical challenges and their possible impact on the use of AI in healthcare. The chapter concludes with a forward look at how these issues could be addressed proactively.

Keywords

Artificial Intelligence, AI, Healthcare, Medical chatbots, Virtual Conversational Agents, Neuroengineering, AI-powered assistive technologies, Personalised medicine, Privacy, Safety, Data Protection, General Data Protection Regulation, Responsibility.

I. Introduction

Computers may not quite think like humans, but they can process vast amounts of data extremely fast, learn from experience, and self-improve their performance over time. Researchers use these powerful capabilities of artificial intelligence (AI) to improve our lives by, among other efforts, developing convenient personal assistants, facilitating language translation, and enabling various AI-powered applications for improving customer services.[6]

A growing area of AI application is healthcare. AI is expanding the frontiers of medical practice.[7] Various medical domains previously reserved for human experts are increasingly augmented or changed thanks to the implementation of AI, including clinical practice (eg, disease diagnosis, automated surgery, patient monitoring), translational medical research (such as improvements in drug discovery, drug repurposing, genetic variant annotation), and tasks related to basic biomedical research (eg, automated data collection, gene function annotation, literature mining).[8] However, beyond potential benefits such as resource efficiency, increased productivity, or augmented care, these technologies come in different forms and raise several concerns of different nature, such as safety, responsibility, and data protection. For instance, these technologies may have the potential to predict healthcare-related outcomes, including genetic disorders or

---

[6] Jelena Stajic, Richard Stone, Gilbert Chin, and Brad Wible. 'Rise of the Machines' (2015) 349(62450 *Science* 248–249; Yonghui Wu, Mike Schuster, Zhifeng Chen, Quoc V Le, Mohammad Norouzi, Wolfgang Macherey, Maxim Krikun et al 'Google's neural machine translation system: Bridging the gap between human and machine translation.' *arXiv preprint: arXiv:1609.08144* (2016); see also www.cogitocorp.com/.

[7] Abhimanyu S Ahuja 'The impact of artificial intelligence in medicine on the future role of the physician' (2019) 7 *PeerJ* e7702.

[8] Kun-Hsing Yu, Andrew L Beam, and Isaac S Kohane. 'Artificial intelligence in healthcare' (2018) 2(10) *Nature biomedical engineering* 719–731.

suicide risk.[9] This could lead to an earlier intervention, and potentially save more lives. However, owing to the highly sensitive nature of the medical data processed by such a system, there are significant privacy risks for patients should their data be mishandled or compromised.

Built on an expert panel discussion held at the conference CPDP 2020[10] and a literature review, our chapter provides an overview of three expanding areas of AI application in healthcare: (a) AI-driven data analytical tools for personalised medicine; (b) virtual conversational agents; and (c) AI-powered assistive robots and neuroengineering. We have chosen to conduct the analysis using these groupings because they each involve different functionalities designed to be applied in different contexts. Furthermore, due to their differing direct and indirect impacts on patients and their social environment, these applications each raise ethical, legal, and social (ELS) issues that arise in that context. In this chapter, we describe four main concerns: (1) the link between privacy and safety; (2) health data-related concerns; (3) data accuracy and privacy; and (4) responsibility in highly automated health environments. In doing so, this chapter contributes to the growing body of literature on ELS issues in AI for healthcare – a field only in its early stages – and sets the scene for more careful consideration of ELS issues of AI for healthcare.

In addition to contributing to the academic debate on ELS issues in AI technologies for healthcare,[11] this chapter can also guide the integration of ELS considerations in the design process, alerting developers, users, and stakeholders to potential concerns. An overview of some of these ELS challenges is also valuable for policy-making, as it highlights areas of concern that require further exploration. The chapter concludes with a forward look at how these issues are likely to impede or facilitate integration and a final reflection on whether machine-powered care is desirable or may have repercussions for human dignity.[12]

II. Emerging AI Technologies in Healthcare

Activities such as managing electronic health records, analysing tests, X-rays or CT scans, healthcare monitoring, and healthcare system analysis, which are highly

---

[9] Raquel Dias and Ali Torkamani. 'Artificial intelligence in clinical and genomic diagnostics' (2019) 11(1) *Genome medicine* 1–12; Mason Marks 'Artificial Intelligence Based Suicide Prediction' (2019) 21 *Yale Journal of Health Policy, Law, and Ethics* 98. Available at SSRN: https://ssrn.com/abstract=3324874 (last accessed 25 April 2020).

[10] 'CPDP 2020: AI, Healthcare and the Law,' filmed January 2020 at Computers, Privacy, & Data Protection (CPDP) 2020, www.youtube.com/watch?v=8nkXIicIoLQ.

[11] Zrinjka Dolic, Castro, Rosa, and Moarcas, Andrei, 'Robots in healthcare: a solution or a problem?,' *Study for the Committee on Environment, Public Health, and Food Safety, Policy Department for Economic, Scientific and Quality of Life Policies*, European Parliament, Luxembourg (2019). www.europarl. europa.eu/RegData/etudes/IDAN/2019/638391/IPOL_IDA(2019)638391_EN.pdf (last accessed 24 April 2020.

[12] Dolic et al (n 11).

repetitive, cumbersome, and take much time from specialists, will be increasingly performed with the help of AI-driven technologies.[13] One successful application of AI is in the field of radiology. Radiologists use multiple imaging modalities, including X-ray radiography, computed tomography (CT), magnetic resonance imaging (MRI), and positron emission tomography (PET), for disease screening and diagnosis, to determine the cause of illness and to monitor the patient trajectory during the course of a disease, all of which are ideal tasks for automation and delegation to AI.[14]

Since the integration of AI in medicine breathes into existence a multifaceted change to the entire medical landscape, including how care is delivered and how it impacts practitioners and caregivers, in this section, we restrict our focus on exploring three expanding areas of application that have not received proper scrutiny: (a) AI-driven data analytical tools for personalised medicine; (b) virtual conversational agents; and (c) AI-powered assistive robots and neuroengineering. These applications are of particular interest for their predictive capabilities (a), the focus on psychological/cognitive/emotional interaction (b), and their behaviour when they are confined and embodied (c).

A. AI-Driven Data Analytic Tools for Personalised Medicine

Technological advances in informatics, biomolecular science, gene sequencing, and medical imaging allow us to move towards greater precision in the delivery of healthcare, making better predictions and tailoring treatment to the individual patient, that is, enabling *personalised medicine*.[15] The term *personalised medicine* has been used to describe 'treatment[s] focusing on patients based on their individual clinical characterisation, considering the diversity of symptoms, severity, and genetic traits.'[16]

One application of personalised medicine that has attracted considerable attention over the past few years is pharmacogenomics. Pharmacogenomics refers to the use of a patient's genetic information to select individualised pharmacotherapies to reduce the likelihood of adverse drug reactions and optimise therapeutic efficacy. As such, pharmacogenomics has been described as one of the core elements of personalised medicine.[17] According to recent estimates, in the general population, approximately 90 per cent of individuals carry at least one

[13] ibid.

[14] Saurabh Jha, and Eric J Topol. 'Adapting to artificial intelligence: radiologists and pathologists as information specialists' (2016) 316(22) *Jama* 2353–2354.

[15] Gary R Cutter, and Yuliang Liu 'Personalized medicine: The return of the house call?' (2012) 2(4) *Neurology: Clinical Practice* 343–351.

[16] Fernando AL Marson, Carmen S Bertuzzo, and José D Ribeiro 'Personalized or precision medicine? The example of cystic fibrosis' (2017) 8 *Frontiers in pharmacology* 390.

[17] Dragan Primorac, Lidija Bach-Rojecky, Dalia Vađunec, Alen Juginović, Katarina Žunić, Vid Matišić, Andrea Skelin et al 'Pharmacogenomics at the center of precision medicine: challenges and perspective in an era of Big Data' (2020) 21(2) *Pharmacogenomics* 141–156.

pharmacologically relevant genetic variant that could potentially influence drug selection and/or dosing recommendations for a given individual.[18]

The disease risk prediction and early diagnosis domain offer several other examples where the personalised approach improves medical outcomes. This improvement is particularly significant for medical conditions with a strong genetic component, such as hereditary breast and ovarian cancer (HBOC). In HBOC, it is well-established that the accuracy of disease risk prediction for an individual patient can be significantly improved by accounting for multiple types of information specific to the individual, including the individual's genomic data, ethnic background, family history for HBOC, and lifestyle information.[19] The use of machine learning algorithms has increased accuracy in HBOC prediction, therefore enabling the stratification of prevention strategies and individualised clinical management.

With the growing availability of highly accurate biomedical analytical methods, it can be expected that soon, additional types of personal biomedical data will be explored to improve further the accuracy of predictive, screening, and diagnostic tools in healthcare.[20] The sources of biomedical data that show promise in personalised medicine are genomics, epigenomics, transcriptomics, proteomics, and the microbiome.[21] However, each of these areas constitutes a highly complex domain within biomedical sciences and an emerging discipline of research in its own right. Therefore, the pursuit of eliciting clinically actionable insights by synthesising patient data across a growing number of biomedical domains is associated with significant challenges that can only be overcome using advanced AI and data analytics methods.

The increased amount and growing complexity of clinical information necessitate the adoption of AI-powered clinical decision support to process and integrate many different types of data efficiently. Using medically relevant information unique to the patient, including personal and family medical history, genetic data, imaging data, information relating to lifestyle and environmental factors, robust AI-driven systems may second personalised medicine, including predictions on how well a particular drug may work on a specific individual. This information can support decision making also for disease risk determination or diagnosis.

[18] Paul CD Bank, Jesse J Swen, Rowena D Schaap, Daniëlle B Klootwijk, Renée Baak–Pablo, and Henk-Jan Guchelaar 'A pilot study of the implementation of pharmacogenomic pharmacist initiated pre-emptive testing in primary care' (2019) 27(10) *European Journal of Human Genetics* 1532–1541.

[19] Chang Ming, Valeria Viassolo, Nicole Probst-Hensch, Pierre O Chappuis, Ivo D Dinov, and Maria C Katapodi 'Machine learning techniques for personalized breast cancer risk prediction: comparison with the BCRAT and BOADICEA models' (2019) 21(1) *Breast Cancer Research* 75.

[20] Stephen A Williams, Mika Kivimaki, Claudia Langenberg, Aroon D Hingorani, JP Casas, Claude Bouchard, Christian Jonasson et al 'Plasma protein patterns as comprehensive indicators of health' (2019) 25(12) *Nature Medicine* 1851–1857.

[21] Wayne G Shreffler. 'Promise of personalized medicine' (2019) 123(6) *Annals of Allergy, Asthma & Immunology* 534.

However, the clinical uptake of AI-driven aids for personalised medicine appears to be moving slowly. Many unanswered challenges require attention before implementing clinical decision support, such as how to ensure safe use or how data protection and privacy should be balanced with the need to deliver adequate healthcare.[22] Other questions refer to how suitable healthcare data are for secondary use and to what extent systems need to be explicable or opaque in their functioning and decision-making process.[23]

B. Virtual Conversational Agents as Medical Counselors

Among the most promising applications of AI in healthcare are virtual conversational agents (VCAs) such as chatbots or virtual assistants, whose popularity has been growing steadily over the past several years. Chatbots are computer programs that use natural language as the medium to interact with users. While chatbots have been in existence since the early 1960s,[24] their ability to mimic complex human conversations had remained severely limited for several decades, which has hindered their widespread adoption. However, following recent developments in natural language processing, the conversational performance of chatbots has improved measurably, making the use of chatbots more practical as well as more specific and sensitive to context, allowing for humanised computer interactions.[25] As a consequence, these improved systems are being increasingly utilised as virtual assistants and decision-making aids in various domains, including customer service, where AI-driven agents detect human signals from customers and provide real-time behavioural guidance to human agents.[26]

In healthcare, chatbots have the potential to assist both patients and healthcare professionals. For example, chatbots hold considerable promise in the context of patient education, where they can provide, in an interactive manner, information tailored to the patient's personal informational needs and knowledge level.[27]

---

[22] BigMed. 'Big data management for the precise treatment of three patient groups.' Available at: https://bigmed.no/assets/Reports/Big_data_management_for_the_precise_treatment_of_three_patient_groups.pdf (last accessed 24 June 2020).

[23] Heike Felzmann, Eduard Fosch-Villaronga, Christoph Lutz, and Aurelia Tamò-Larrieux 'Transparency you can trust: Transparency requirements for artificial intelligence between legal norms and contextual concerns' (2019) 6(1) *Big Data & Society* 2053951719860542.

[24] Joseph Weizenbaum 'ELIZA – a computer program for the study of natural language communication between man and machine' (1966) 9(1) *Communications of the ACM* 36–45.

[25] Daniel Adiwardana, and Thang Luong 'Towards a Conversational Agent that Can Chat About … Anything', *Google Research*, Brain Team, (2020). Available at: https://ai.googleblog.com/2020/01/towards-conversational-agent-that-can.html (last accessed 25 April 2020).

[26] Ana Paula Chaves, and Marco Aurelio Gerosa 'How should my chatbot interact? A survey on human-chatbot interaction design.' *arXiv preprint arXiv:1904.02743* (2019). This technology was first applied to health and care management programmes at premier health and insurance companies. See, for instance, www.cogitocorp.com/company/ (last accessed 25 April 2020).

[27] Kyungyong Chung, and Roy C Park 'Chatbot-based healthcare service with a knowledge base for cloud computing' (2019) 22(1) *Cluster Computing* 1925–1937.

At the same time, chatbots can be designed to ask patients medical questions and elicit essential insights that will help the treating medical professional select an appropriate medical intervention. In another instance, BabylonHealth, a type of health information clearinghouse, helps people access information to assist in the treatment of common medical conditions from chronic kidney disease, glandular fever, or gastroenteritis.[28]

Current applications of medical chatbots can be grouped into two (not mutually exclusive) broad categories: (1) applications serving informational needs; and (2) applications for intervention in the form of counselling and psychological support. While both avenues of chatbot development are actively pursued, the latter raises more ELS issues due to its significant potential implications for the psychological wellbeing of particularly vulnerable patients. Furthermore, VCAs for counselling purposes are more challenging to develop than purely informational VCAs, given that in addition to natural language processing capabilities, they should also demonstrate the necessary social skills for engaging patients in a meaningful way. Therefore, it is probable that, in the short-term, VCAs such as chatbots may bring the most significant benefits to medical domains where information provision plays a more pronounced role.

One profession where addressing the informational needs of patients is increasingly becoming a challenge is genetic counselling. Genetic counselling has been defined as 'the process of helping people understand and adapt to the medical, psychological, and familial implications of genetic contributions to disease'.[29] As such, genetic counsellors are recognised as serving the dual purpose of patient education and psychological support. Traditionally, these two roles of genetic counselling had been complementary, owing to the limited scope of most genetic tests. Genetic testing has been typically performed for a specific reason, such as confirming the genetic mutation associated with a particular disease to facilitate diagnosis. As a consequence, educating the patient by providing information on the nature of a genetic test was a feasible task. However, ongoing progress in molecular genetics has led to the emergence of much more comprehensive forms of genetic testing, such as whole-genome sequencing (WGS), which can reveal a plethora of additional information about the tested individual. For example, through WGS, the patient can learn even more about their predisposition to various diseases, their reproductive risks of having a child with a genetic disorder, and numerous non-medical traits. With the rapidly diminishing costs and improving accuracy, WGS is poised to become a mainstream procedure, with the number of whole genome-sequenced individuals worldwide expected to surpass 60 million by the mid-2020s.[30]

---

[28] See BabylonHealth available at www.babylonhealth.com/ai (last accessed 25 April 2020).

[29] Robert Resta, Barbara Bowles Biesecker, Robin L Bennett, Sandra Blum, Susan Estabrooks Hahn, Michelle N Strecker, and Janet L Williams 'A new definition of genetic counseling: National Society of Genetic Counselors' task force report' (2006) 15(2) *Journal of genetic counseling* 77–83.

[30] Jessica Vamathevan, Rolf Apweiler, and Ewan Birney 'Biomolecular data resources: Bioinformatics infrastructure for biomedical data science' (2019) 2 *Annual Review of Biomedical Data Science* 199–222.

Owing to the multitude of information that can be obtained through WGS, patient education and information-provision are a necessary component of modern genetic counselling practice. This means that genetic counsellors are devoting an increasingly smaller proportion of their time and resources to aspects such as providing psychosocial support. In particular, it has been estimated that *pre-test* genetic counselling and education of a patient before undergoing WGS may require as much as one hour of the counsellor's time, while this extensive patient education does not always result in an improved knowledge level.[31] In the *post-test* context, genetic counselling services are frequently required to interpret genetic test results. However, of the vast amounts of genetic information generated through WGS, only a small proportion of the results may be of clinical significance, which has traditionally been the primary basis for recommending genetic counselling. Regardless, in practice, many genetic counsellors tend to spend a considerable amount of time educating patients on the aspects of WGS test results that are not of immediate clinical relevance.[32] As a consequence, the profession of genetic counselling has been experiencing a systemic issue of understaffing, with not enough genetic counsellors available to meet the growing demand for genetic testing.

The use of VCAs, particularly chatbots, to address the informational needs of patients in the context of genetic counselling is a relatively new but highly promising area of research. In 2019, Schmidlen and colleagues reported positive outcomes of a user experience study that focused on a genetic counselling chatbot. Overall, the chatbot was well-received and was found helpful by the users of genetic counselling services who were asked to test the chatbot for three different cases: pre-test education and consenting; post-test test explanation of results and follow-up; facilitation of sharing genetic risk information with family members where cascade testing of immediate blood relatives may be beneficial.[33] Similarly, in another recent study, a different research group reported high efficacy of and positive user experiences with a VCA designed to assist patients with the process of inputting their family medical history for genetic diseases.[34] Given this initial success with chatbots in genetic counselling, they are currently pilot-tested in more extensive clinical trials to establish their utility for scalable delivery of genetic counselling services.

---

[31] Sabrina A Suckiel, Michael D Linderman, Saskia C Sanderson, George A Diaz, Melissa Wasserstein, Andrew Kasarskis, Eric E Schadt, and Randi E Zinberg 'Impact of genomic counseling on informed decision-making among ostensibly healthy individuals seeking personal genome sequencing: the HealthSeq project' (2016) 25(5) *Journal of genetic counseling* 1044–1053.

[32] Frances L Lynch, Patricia Himes, Marian J Gilmore, Elissa M Morris, Jennifer L Schneider, Tia L Kauffman, Elizabeth Shuster et al 'Time costs for genetic counseling in preconception carrier screening with genome sequencing' (2018) 27(4) *Journal of genetic counseling* 823–833.

[33] Tara Schmidlen, Marci Schwartz, Kristy DiLoreto, H Lester Kirchner, and Amy C Sturm 'Patient assessment of chatbots for the scalable delivery of genetic counseling' (2019) 28(6) *Journal of genetic counseling* 1166–1177.

[34] Amal Ponathil, Firat Ozkan, Brandon Welch, Jeffrey Bertrand, and Kapil Chalil Madathil 'Family health history collected by virtual conversational agents: An empirical study to investigate the efficacy of this approach' [2020] *Journal of Genetic Counseling*.

C. AI-Powered Assistive Technologies and Neuro-Engineering

Over the past two decades, assistive and rehabilitation technologies have increased in number and variety due to concurrent advances in both hardware and software technology as well as human-machine interaction. These technologies can be grouped into five major functional families: devices for robot-assisted training, functional electrical stimulation (FES) techniques, prosthetics, brain-computer interfaces (BCIs), and powered mobility aids. Many of these technologies were listed as competing disciplines in the CYBATHLON, an international competition in which people with physical disabilities compete against each other to complete everyday tasks using state-of-the-art technical assistance systems.[35] AI played an essential role in leveraging assistive and neuro-engineering technologies to help people with vision, hearing, mobility, cognition, and learning disabilities – whether temporary or permanent – and to improve their quality of life. AI-powered assistive technologies have proven to offer significant benefits for people with disabilities, especially in terms of human connection, social interaction, activities of daily living, and other everyday life aspects in the physical or virtual world.[36] AI has the power to enhance assistive products through robust and adaptive features.

For example, randomised controlled trials performed on robotic devices for post-stroke therapy and rehabilitation showed that neuroengineering, assistive and rehabilitation technologies could enable significant improvements in the therapeutic outcomes compared to usual care, especially for motor function and quality of life.[37] A concrete example is the lower-limb exoskeletons. Until now, advancements in lower-limb exoskeletons allowed patients to complete movements with an assist-as-needed model. Still, these training techniques often required a predetermined trajectory for periodic movements, but for complex, real-life scenarios that usually do not have periodic movements, it was not possible to define the ideal path in advance. Some researchers took advantage of the developments of AI and integrated AI capabilities into the robotic device to allow the exoskeleton to explore and make decisions similar to human beings, making the

[35] Robert Riener 'The Cybathlon promotes the development of assistive technology for people with physical disabilities.' (2016) 13(1) *Journal of neuroengineering and rehabilitation* 49.

[36] Marcello Ienca, Jotterand Fabrice, Bernice Elger, Maurizio Caon, Alessandro Scoccia Pappagallo, Reto W Kressig, and Tenzin Wangmo 'Intelligent assistive technology for Alzheimer's disease and other dementias: a systematic review' (2017) 56(4) *Journal of Alzheimer's Disease* 1301–1340; E Fosch-Villaronga, *Robots, healthcare, and the law: Regulating automation in personal care* (Routledge, 2019).

[37] Verena Klamroth-Marganska, Javier Blanco, Katrin Campen, Armin Curt, Volker Dietz, Thierry Ettlin, Morena Felder et al 'Three-dimensional, task-specific robot therapy of the arm after stroke: a multicentre, parallel-group randomised trial' (2014) 13(2) *The Lancet Neurology* 159–166; Albert C Lo, Peter D Guarino, Lorie G Richards, Jodie K Haselkorn, George F Wittenberg, Daniel G Federman, Robert J Ringer et al 'Robot-assisted therapy for long-term upper-limb impairment after stroke' (2010) 362(19) *New England Journal of Medicine* 1772–1783.

'assistance-as-needed' more intelligent and, ultimately, improving the gait of patients.[38]

Microsoft has developed the 'Emma Watch,' a wearable assistive device that helps to compensate for the tremors caused by Parkinson's Disease. Like a wrist-watch, the device is fitted with tablet-controlled vibrating mechanisms similar to the ones found in phones that cause a brain's attention shift and counteracts the patient's tremors. The integration of AI and sensors into the device could allow for the detection and monitoring of complex symptoms associated with the disorder, including body rigidity, gait slowness, and falling and tremors.[39]

Advances in AI are increasingly expanding the computational resources of neuro-devices, such as neuroprosthetics.[40] Neuroprosthetics stimulate a person's nervous system through electrical stimulation to compensate for the deficiencies that impede motor skills, including cognition, hearing, vision, communication, or sensory abilities. They are often employed in conjunction with robotic limb replacements in amputees to achieve improved motor skills and performance. By combining neural engineering, robotics, and AI, some researchers were able to semi-automate a part of the motor command for 'shared control', thereby improving myoelectric prostheses, which are intuitive but provide little dexter-ity, are complex, and costly.[41]

All of the devices described above utilise machine learning algorithms to analyse neural patterns of a user and predict the desired movement of the robotic limb the user intends to use. While the accuracy of these predictive tools is not yet perfect,[42] this technology is showing considerable promise and will likely continue to attract research interest in the future. These applications of AI-driven technologies are not only illustrative, but also demonstrate how addressing the regulatory issues and challenges discussed below are funda-mental to the successful functioning of these technologies in the healthcare context.[43]

---

[38] Mingxing Lyu, Wei-Hai Chen, Xilun Ding, and Jianhua Wang 'Knee exoskeleton enhanced with artificial intelligence to provide assistance-as-needed' (2019) 90(9) *Review of Scientific Instruments* 094101.

[39] Bill Briggs. '"My God, it's better": Emma can write again thanks to a prototype watch, raising hope for Parkinson's disease,' *Microsoft Transform*, https://news.microsoft.com/transform/emma-can-write-again-thanks-to-prototype-watch-raising-hope-for-parkinsons-disease/ (last accessed 26 April 2020).

[40] Marcello Ienca. 'Brain Machine Interfaces, Artificial Intelligence and Neurorights' (2017) 3 https://brain.ieee.org/newsletter/2017-issue-3/brain-machine-interfaces-artificial-intelligence-neurorights/ (last accessed 26 April 2020).

[41] Katie Z Zhuang, Nicolas Sommer, Vincent Mendez, Saurav Aryan, Emanuele Formento, Edoardo D'Anna, Fiorenzo Artoni et al 'Shared human–robot proportional control of a dexterous myoelectric prosthesis' (2019) 1(9) *Nature Machine Intelligence* 400–411.

[42] Thomas C Noel, and Brian R Snider 'Utilizing Deep Neural Networks for Brain–Computer Interface-Based Prosthesis Control' [2019] *The Journal of Computing Sciences in Colleges* 93.

[43] Robin Pierce 'Machine learning for diagnosis and treatment: Gymnastics for the GDPR' (2018) 4 *European Data Protection. Law Review* 333.

III. Ethical, Legal, and Societal Issues

AI-driven technologies in healthcare may help perform mental therapy, support impaired patients, enable personalised treatments, and help in the neurorehabilitation of patients. Despite several clear benefits, the robotisation of healthcare raises questions concerning quality and safety, as systems that exert direct control over the world interacting with vulnerable users may cause harm in ways humans cannot necessarily correct or oversee, primarily if users interact with these systems socially. Moreover, predictive analytics for diagnosis raises questions about predictions' accuracy and who is responsible in case something goes wrong. Although healthcare is a highly sensitive domain of application and robots may cause harm to patients in many different ways, it is still unclear how current regulatory frameworks frame these developments.[44]

In this chapter, we contribute to the increasing body of literature on ELS issues of AI by turning our attention to four main concerns arising from emerging AI-driven systems in healthcare: (1) the link between privacy and safety; (2) health data-related concerns; (3) data accuracy and privacy; and (4) responsibility in highly automated health environments. We focus on these four concerns because we regard them as fundamental to the eventual success of AI-driven systems in healthcare. Although not exhaustive, our chapter highlights areas of concern that require further exploration, setting the scene for more careful consideration of AI ELS issues for healthcare.

A. The Missing Link between Data Protection and Safety

The processing of personal data in clinical applications may be used towards healthcare-related outcomes, which could subsequently have a direct or indirect impact on patients and could potentially compromise patients' safety. This presents a foundational issue for assistive and prosthetic robotics, and applies generally to AI-powered assistive technologies and neuro-engineering, as these cyber-physical systems have an immediate physical effect on their environment, making security concerns particularly salient.[45] In this respect, the US Food and Drug Administration (FDA) stresses that cybersecurity is of paramount importance, and that 'vulnerabilities could allow unauthorized users to remotely access, control, and issue commands to compromised devices, potentially leading to patient harm.'[46] Thus, an appropriate regulatory approach to cybersecurity with regard to the particular characteristics of each of these devices is paramount.

---

[44] Eduard Fosch-Villaronga. *Robots, healthcare, and the law: Regulating automation in personal care* (Routledge, 2019).

[45] Santiago Morante, Juan G Victores, and Carlos Balaguer 'Cryptobotics: Why robots need cyber safety' (2015) 2 *Frontiers in Robotics and AI* 23.

[46] Food and Drug Administration, FDA, 'Cybersecurity.' (2019), www.fda.gov/medical-devices/digital-health/cybersecurity (last accessed 24 April 2020).

Of course, safety, by itself, is insufficient to recommend the use of a particular device or intervention given the importance of such considerations as efficacy, access, and need at the policy level, and privacy, acceptance, and autonomy at the user level. Nevertheless, it stands among all considerations as non-negotiable and essential. As the EU Medical Device Regulation (MDR) mentions in its recitals 'medical devices should be introduced, to improve health and safety'. Therefore, any system that improves the way care is delivered should ensure the highest safety standards available.

In a joint report based on the outcomes of a workshop between the US National Science Foundation and the German Research Foundation on 'New Perspectives in Neuroengineering and Neurotechnology,'[47] a group of international experts in neuroengineering identified critical technological, social and ethical challenges to the adoption of assistive and neuroengineering technologies in the clinical setting. They concluded that the envisaged progress in neuroengineering requires a careful reflection on the ethical and social implications, in particular concerning the following ethical issues: safety, security, privacy, public acceptance, and respect for autonomy.

Since AI-powered assistive technologies are data-driven technologies, a cyberattack may compromise the safety of the robot's operation and its users. The rules focusing on safety, however, often imply that cybersecurity plays second fiddle. Robots can inflict bodily harm either because of a technical malfunction, or due to a cyberattack, but this insight is only partly accounted for in the EU safety legislation. For example, the EU medical device regulation focuses in detail on safety, while it addresses cybersecurity only briefly. According to the EU MDR, medical devices must be safe and effective and 'shall not compromise the clinical condition or the safety of patients, or the safety and health of users or, where applicable, other persons(…)' (MDR Annex I No 1). These requirements refer to the manufacturer of the medical device. However, other actors involved in the use of a robot, such as hospitals and other care providers, as well as patients, are not directly addressed in the medical device regulation while they play a significant role in managing risks related to the actual use of the device, for example, by installing regular software updates. Furthermore, cybersecurity threats are by no means static; new threats always arise, and any vulnerability may endanger the consistency and reliability of the entire system.

Moreover, algorithms can learn very complex behavioural skills, but they do not operate in a vacuum. Translating those methods in the physical world involves much training, learning, and experience. In the course of learning, a system may try to perform a task, gradually introduced to selected scenarios to support learning (aka reinforcement learning).[48] Bad policies may bring the system to an

---

[47] Chet T Moritz, Patrick Ruther, Sara Goering, Alfred Stett, Tonio Ball, Wolfram Burgard, Eric H Chudler, and Rajesh PN Rao 'New perspectives on neuroengineering and neurotechnologies: NSF-DFG workshop report' (2016) 63(7) *IEEE Transactions on Biomedical Engineering* 1354–1367.

[48] Annelies Raes, Tammy Schellens, Bram De Wever, and Ellen Vanderhoven 'Scaffolding information problem solving in web-based collaborative inquiry learning' (2012) 59(1) *Computers & Education*: 82–94.

unrecoverable state from which learning is no longer possible.[49] After each attempt, the environment is reset to start the process again and improve. However, not all tasks are easily or automatically reversible: if an AI-powered assisted technology breaks a window or falls down the stairs, the environment requires human intervention to reset it between learning attempts.[50] In a real-life healthcare setting, attempts to reverse an action may no longer be possible or ineffective if the system has already caused patient harm.

Although concerns related to physical safety of AI-powered medical devices are of utmost importance, safety considerations should not be limited to possible physical harms arising from AI in healthcare. In particular, ensuring psychological safety of such tools should be pursued with equal rigor. Arguably, this is especially true for VCAs which, as discussed earlier, are being increasingly integrated into healthcare practice. For example, healthcare organisations actively pursue VCAs as AI-based solutions for the delivery of medical consultation services. However, from the psychological safety point of view, an important drawback to the use of VCAs as medical counsellors is VCAs' current inability to communicate psychologically impactful information in a sensitive manner. As an illustrative example, one user experience study with counsellor VCAs has reported cases where a VCA avatar delivered information about patients' elevated risk for cancer with a smile, which was deemed insensitive and incongruous with the content of the message.[51] Psychological safety concerns are even more salient with respect to VCAs designed to provide psychological support in mental health therapy – an emerging, but highly controversial area of VCA use.[52] Due to the intensely personal and emotionally sensitive nature of mental health counselling sessions, concerns arise regarding whether the VCA technology is sufficiently mature to be routinely utilised in this context. In this regard, some authors caution that rigorous studies evaluating long-term patient safety and clinical utility should precede the widespread deployment of medical counsellor VCAs.[53]

Another growing concern is addressing the changing functionality of AI systems. Devices that rely on machine learning with continuously learning models will adapt over time and modify the functioning of tools – both prediction tools and hardware devices – during their lifecycle. Although the FDA has issued a

[49] Benjamin Eysenbach, Shixiang Gu, Julian Ibarz, and Sergey Levine 'Leave no trace: Learning to reset for safe and autonomous reinforcement learning' *arXiv preprint arXiv:1711.06782* (2017).

[50] Eysenbach et al (n 49); Yevgen Chebotar, Karol Hausman, Marvin Zhang, Gaurav Sukhatme, Stefan Schaal, and Sergey Levine 'Combining model-based and model-free updates for trajectory-centric reinforcement learning.' In *Proceedings of the 34th International Conference on Machine Learning-Volume 70*, 703–711. JMLR. org, 2017.

[51] Schmidlen (n 33).

[52] See for instance the Cognitive Behaviour Therapy (CBT)-based AI agent at https://woebot.io/about (last accessed 25 April 2020).

[53] Kira Kretzschmar, Holly Tyroll, Gabriela Pavarini, Arianna Manzini, Ilina Singh, and NeurOx Young People's Advisory Group 'Can your phone be your therapist? Young people's ethical perspectives on the use of fully automated conversational agents (chatbots) in mental health support' (2019) 11 *Biomedical informatics insights* 1178222619829083.

discussion paper to seek solutions for overcoming this, existing legislation focuses on ensuring safety risks that are present when the device entered the market, but largely ignores that the progressive and adaptive AI outcomes may be utterly different after market entry.[54]

B. Privacy and Data Protection Concerns Arising from AI in Healthcare

Privacy and data protection regulations aiming at ensuring data subjects' rights often limit the development and uptake of AI-driven healthcare. However, to work adequately, AI needs a great deal of data, including personal data. The privacy risks of AI-based technologies relate to how data is collected, stored, and used to train the models and determine health-related outcomes, also if these technologies are embodied.[55] Risks stem from the leak of sensitive information through data breaches, personal data transfer, or sale to third parties, and the accuracy of predictions made. Should these risks materialise, the impact on patients and their trust in the system could be such that refrain from seeking healthcare even when needed.[56]

The need to handle sensitive data regularly increases the risk of data breaches. The types of information utilised by these algorithms for personalised medicine may cover personal medical history, lifestyle data, genomic data, and, in some cases, medical histories of family members. Many scholars point to this as a red flag for the development of AI solutions in healthcare, suggesting that it implies that 'the machine' will read through our personal information.[57] Most countries have laws that regulate access to health data, but it is uncertain how well-adapted governance is regarding parameters and requirements for machine access to

---

[54] FDA. 'Proposed Regulatory Framework for Modifications to Artificial Intelligence/Machine Learning (AI/ML)-Based Software as a Medical Device (SaMD) – Discussion Paper and Request for Feedback.' Available at: www.fda.gov/media/122535/download (last accessed 24 June 2020). See also White Paper on Artificial Intelligence, 'A European approach to excellence and trust,' European Commission, (2020) https://ec.europa.eu/info/sites/info/files/commission-white-paper-artificial-intelligence-feb2020_en.pdf (last accessed 26 April 2020).

[55] Suzanne Martin, Johan E Bengtsson, and Rose-Marie Dröes 'Assistive technologies and issues relating to privacy, ethics and security' in Maurice D Mulvenna and Chris D Nugent (eds) *Supporting people with dementia using pervasive health technologies* (Springer, 2010) 63–76; Marcello Ienca, and Eduard Fosch Villaronga 'Privacy and security issues in assistive technologies for dementia' in Jotterand, Fabrice, Marcello Ienca, Bernice Elger, and Tenzin Wangmo (eds) *Intelligent Assistive Technologies for Dementia: Clinical, Ethical, Social, and Regulatory Implications* (Oxford University Press, 2019) 221–239; Wiktoria Wilkowska, and Martina Ziefle 'Privacy and data security in E-health: Requirements from the user's perspective' (2012) 18(3) *Health informatics journal* 191–201.

[56] Robin Pierce 'Medical Privacy: Where Deontology and Consequentialism Meet' in de Groot and van der Sloot (eds) *Handbook of Privacy Studies* (Amsterdam University Press, 2018) 327–332.

[57] Ivana Bartoletti 'AI in healthcare: Ethical and privacy challenges.' In Conference on Artificial Intelligence in Medicine in Europe, (Springer, 2019) 7–10.

health data. Moreover, in Europe, the General Data Protection Regulation (GDPR) has provisions on automated individual decision-making, ie, making a decision solely by automated means without any human involvement; and profiling, ie, automated processing of personal data to evaluate certain things about an individual (Article 22, GDPR), which, in the healthcare setting, can be particularly problematic.

The purpose of big data analytics for personalised medicine is to find patterns in big data, not to identify single persons and influence them. So in principle, the potential societal benefit should be weighed against the potential privacy risk of confidentiality breaches of sensitive information. In the national lighthouse project BigMed (Big Data Medical Solutions) at Oslo University Hospital,[58] many examples allude to the GDPR as an argument against AI development projects in healthcare, stressing the inevitable strict data minimisation or constraining consent requirements. Often distributed data sources are not permitted to be shared with external servers or other companies. This presents immense challenges to the possibility of training AI-models in healthcare settings, which require patients' data to boost accuracy, allow real-time decision-making, and ensure tailored safety to patients. In this respect, AI researchers are advancing novel methods to train machine-learning models while preserving personal data confidentiality.[59] The idea is to enable one person to start training a deep-learning model and another person to finish it.[60] Thus, hospitals could train their models with patients' data locally and share their half-trained model to a centralised location to finalise the training. In this way, the second company would never see raw patient data, only the model itself and the partial-model.

In this sense, it is important to note that the GDPR opens up the possibilities for research and healthcare, based, in part, on the protection that patient confidentiality laws already give, but also on Articles 6(1) e, and 9(2) g-j of the GDPR. Furthermore, the provisions made through Article 89 can be used to open access to data for artificial intelligence (although Article 89 is limited to the purpose of research and not direct clinical use). A more harmonised understanding needs to be developed through a careful dialogue between all relevant stakeholders to balance the patient's needs for both access to healthcare and patient privacy.

Rapidly evolving clinical disciplines and the use of genetic information challenge this segregation and will force a different organisation of diagnostic processes. Future developments in healthcare services and research must take place within a formal framework where testing, diagnostics, and research converge. However, when the integration of research into clinical care challenges how data subjects consent to the processing of personal data, existing governance

---

[58] See https://bigmed.no/.

[59] Praneeth Vepakomma, Tristan Swedish, Ramesh Raskar, Otkrist Gupta, and Abhimanyu Dubey 'No Peek: A Survey of private distributed deep learning' arXiv preprint arXiv:1812.03288 (2018).

[60] Praneeth Vepakomma, Otkrist Gupta, Tristan Swedish, and Ramesh Raskar 'Split learning for health: Distributed deep learning without sharing raw patient data' *arXiv preprint arXiv:1812.00564* (2018).

structures, which typically do not address these dual practices in a single space, can lead to inadequate protections or counterproductive results. This concern stems from the different regulations of clinical practice and research activities in many countries. In cases where standardised care pathways are not established, the diagnostic process must be organised as clinical research even if it is part of the healthcare delivery. While consenting to data processing for research is widely accepted and adopted, permitting the processing of personal data to contribute to a machine learning model to treat the next patient is largely ungoverned and may come as a surprise, even if regarded as a responsibility.

It is important to note that some AI technologies are more likely than others to raise privacy and data protection concerns. Among the high-risk AI-driven technologies are VCAs such as chatbots, whose utility in the healthcare context is largely determined by the extent to which they can replicate human-like conversational patterns. VCAs that excel at this task will incentivise the human user to enter in a sustained conversation with the VCA, providing potentially useful information for healthcare professionals to analyse. However, as reported in a recent study, some users of VCAs may be inclined to voluntarily share more personal information than what is requested by the VCA.[61] Not only does this create challenges from GDPR's data minimisation point of view, but it also exacerbates potential harms for the patient should their data be accessed by malicious third parties.

C. Data Accuracy and Biases

Health data often differs from other industrial data because it is created in an unstructured way, often partially accurate, and collected from a wide variety of healthcare settings, often lacking integration across datasets. Moreover, much of the data available is gathered for documentation purposes, not for secondary use, and may lack rigorous quality controls and adequate data access.[62] In this sense, natural language processing (NLP) could be of much help to analyse and structure such text. However, the clinical text has several characteristics, such as imperfect structure, abounding shorthand, or domain-specific jargon, that make the application of NLP challenging.[63]

---

[61] Carolin Ischen, Theo Araujo, Hilde Voorveld, Guda van Noort, and Edith Smit 'Privacy concerns in chatbot interactions' in Asbjorn Folstad et al (eds) *International Workshop on Chatbot Research and Design* (Springer, 2019) 34-48.

[62] Richard E Gliklich, Nancy A Dreyer, and Michelle B Leavy 'Chapter 11: Data Collection and Quality Assurance' in *Registries for evaluating patient outcomes: a user's guide.* (Government Printing Office, 2014). Available from: www.ncbi.nlm.nih.gov/books/NBK208601/ (last accessed 25 April 2020).

[63] Kory Kreimeyer, Matthew Foster, Abhishek Pandey, Nina Arya, Gwendolyn Halford, Sandra F Jones, Richard Forshee, Mark Walderhaug, and Taxiarchis Botsis 'Natural language processing systems for capturing and standardizing unstructured clinical information: a systematic review' (2017) 73 *Journal of biomedical informatics* 14–29.

Data accuracy for the full-scale use of clinical AI is essential, despite the scattered nature of a large part of the information. However, even in well-established registries, large amounts of the data may be inaccurate, not fit-for-purpose, or biased. For instance, available medical datasets on heritable disorders used by machine learning algorithms in the screening and diagnostic contexts are known to under-represent ethnic minorities.[64] Given the relevance of ethnicity for accurately predicting the risk of various heritable diseases, this systemic bias significantly limits the accuracy of predictive screening and diagnostic algorithms for the general population. This limitation extends to underrepresented communities, including the LGBTQ+ community, who may also suffer from inherent bias and discrimination of AI systems and have primarily been deprived historically from equal access to healthcare.[65] In assistive and neurorehabilitation technology, biases and other inaccuracies in the datasets are of particular concern as they could lead to discrimination based on neurocognitive features (eg, signatures of cognitive decline or neuroprogressive disorder). This neuro-specific risk of algorithmic discrimination has been labelled 'neurodiscrimination'.[66]

Predictive algorithms utilised in medical data analytics may exhibit various statistical biases stemming from systemic errors in the data and measurement errors in predictor variables. Statistical bias refers to algorithms that produce a result that differs from the actual underlying estimate.[67] For example, in the case of suicide prediction, not only can a flaw in data processing pose a threat to the physical well-being of high-risk psychiatric patients, but it can also stigmatise individuals by over-estimating the risk of suicidal behaviour. In this scenario, an AI algorithm designed to support suicide prevention may trigger unnecessary interventions or exacerbate other illnesses.[68]

Statistical biases may reinforce or even exacerbate social biases in healthcare ie, inequity in care delivery may result in suboptimal outcomes for a particular socio-economically disadvantaged group. For example, as discussed by Parikh and colleagues, 'clinicians may incorrectly discount the diagnosis of myocardial infarction in older women because these patients are more likely to present with

---

[64] Poppy Noor. 'Can we trust AI not to further embed racial bias and prejudice?' (2020) 368 *BMJ*; Milena A Gianfrancesco, Suzanne Tamang, Jinoos Yazdany, and Gabriela Schmajuk 'Potential biases in machine learning algorithms using electronic health record data' (2018) 178(11) *JAMA internal medicine* 1544–1547; Ayal A Aizer, Tyler J Wilhite, Ming-Hui Chen, Powell L Graham, Toni K Choueiri, Karen E Hoffman, Neil E Martin, Quoc-Dien Trinh, Jim C Hu, and Paul L Nguyen 'Lack of reduction in racial disparities in cancer-specific mortality over a 20-year period' (2014) 120(10) *Cancer* 1532–1539.

[65] Adam Poulsen, Eduard Fosch-Villaronga, and Roger Andre Søraa 'Queering machines' (2020) 2(3) *Nature Machine Intelligence* 152–152; Human Rights Watch, 'US: LGBT People Face Healthcare Barriers,' www.hrw.org/news/2018/07/23/us-lgbt-people-face-healthcare-barriers (last accessed 26 April 2020); Francesca Robinson. 'Caring for LGBT patients in the NHS' (2019) 266 *BMJ* 366 l5374.

[66] Marcello Ienca, and Karolina Ignatiadis 'Artificial Intelligence in Clinical Neuroscience: Methodological and Ethical Challenges' (2020) 11(2) *AJOB neuroscience* 77–87.

[67] Ravi B Paikh, Stephanie Teeple, and Amol S Navathe 'Addressing Bias in Artificial Intelligence in Health Care' (2019) 322(24) *Jama* 2377–2378.

[68] Marks (n 9).

atypical symptoms'.[69] In this sense, the authors warn that an algorithm learn-ing from 'historical electronic health records (EHR) data and existing practice patterns may not recommend testing for cardiac ischemia for an older woman, thus delaying potentially life-saving treatment'.

More worryingly, clinicians may be inclined to accept the suggestions of AI, thus reinforcing problematic current practices and perpetuating implicit social biases. Known as 'confirmation bias', clinicians may overly rely on data that support their diagnosis and largely ignore those data that refute it, or that change an established pattern. In some instances, clinicians may rely on the guidance of an automated system and desist from searching for corroborative evidence, giving life to the 'automation bias'.[70]

The presence of systematic biases in data and clinical practice poses signifi-cant challenges to the development and implementation of reliable AI medical tools. In a controlled setting, there are inherent limitations to training medical AI algorithms that do not fully capture the complexity of the real-world environment in which the algorithm is intended to work. Moreover, given subtle, unforeseen differences between hospital environments, researchers should be aware that idio-syncrasies specific to a particular medical institution may arise and potentially challenge core assumptions about the data of a model.

D. Opacity and Responsibility in Highly Automated Environments

The growing use of AI brings about uncertainties concerning the attribution of responsibilities among different stakeholders involved in the production of an AI solution if something goes wrong. Some years ago, Ash and colleagues showed that clinical decision support systems (CDSS) shift roles, make it challenging to keep the content current, or show inappropriate content, which may have unintended consequences.[71] Some CDSS are designed to remove the verification performed by clerical staff, nurses, and pharmacists, but under-valuing this gatekeeper function can result in medication being incorrectly ordered or X-ray orders being unques-tioned after a certain amount of time.

Some of these unintended consequences may result in harmful outcomes, which may occur when, despite having a well-defined function, a system behaves in a way that deviates from the designer's intent. An AI system may behave strangely because the designer did not include some environmental variables, the evaluation method used was not correct, the system used limited samples as training data,

---

[69] Parikh et al (n 67).

[70] Robert Challen, Joshua Denny, Martin Pitt, Luke Gompels, Tom Edwards, and Krasimira Tsaneva-Atanasova 'Artificial intelligence, bias and clinical safety' (2019) 28(3) *BMJ Qual Saf* 231–237.

[71] Joan S Ash, Dean F Sittig, Emily M Campbell, Kenneth P Guappone, and Richard H Dykstra 'Some unintended consequences of clinical decision support systems.' In *AMIA Annual Symposium Proceedings*, vol 2007, 26. American Medical Informatics Association, 2007.

or wrong extrapolations negatively impacted the learning model of the system.[72] In this respect, the medical device regulation in Europe states in Article 19.3 that 'by drawing up the EU declaration of conformity, the manufacturer shall assume responsibility for compliance with the requirements of this Regulation and all other Union legislation applicable to the device'. Importantly, this EU declaration of conformity states that the MDR requirements have been fulfilled concerning the covered device (Article 19.1, EU MDR).

However, a medical doctor might not be able to identify whether the basis of a treatment decision is an erroneous prediction from an AI system because these systems are often opaque. AI opacity in healthcare can be extremely dangerous. Generally speaking, decisions in autonomous driving are directly transparent to the driver, who can intervene immediately. If the decision-making process of the AI-driving system is opaque to the driver, it may matter little. The driver is mostly concerned with the result. As Lynn explains, in medical care, however, the effectiveness of a decision for a patient's condition is not immediately apparent until days later when recovery or complications occur.[73] In this sense, the transparency of the decision-making process of an AI-driven system for diagnosis may be of paramount importance to understand the complexities and implications of comorbidities and other features for a patient.

Ensuring accountability in highly automated environments is of paramount importance. Some researchers supported the idea that if a system learns from experience, and in the course of its operation can autonomously change its governing rules; then there is no apparent reason why humans should be held responsible for the autonomous behaviours of the system.[74] However, AI technologies operate as a part of a complex system involving various elements, comprising multiple processes over which different persons, natural or legal, exercise some control and, therefore, might be responsible.[75] In this sense, the High-Level Expert Group on AI established by the European Commission in 2019, stress that AI technologies need mechanisms 'to ensure responsibility and accountability for AI systems and their outcomes, both before and after their development, deployment, and use'.[76]

---

[72] Dario Amodei, Chris Olah, Jacob Steinhardt, Paul Christiano, John Schulman, and Dan Mané 'Concrete problems in AI safety' *arXiv preprint arXiv:1606.06565* (2016); Eduard Fosch-Villaronga, and Christopher Millard 'Cloud robotics law and regulation: Challenges in the governance of complex and dynamic cyber–physical ecosystems' (2019) 119 *Robotics and Autonomous Systems* 77–91.

[73] Lawrence A Lynn 'Artificial intelligence systems for complex decision-making in acute care medicine: a review' (2019) 13(1) *Patient safety in surgery* 6.

[74] Andreas Matthias. 'The responsibility gap: Ascribing responsibility for the actions of learning automata' (2004) 6(3) *Ethics and information technology* 175–183; Johnson, Deborah G Johnson 'Technology with no human responsibility?' (2015) 127(4) *Journal of Business Ethics* 707–715.

[75] Jatinder Singh, Christopher Millard, Chris Reed, Jennifer Cobbe, and Jon Crowcroft 'Accountability in the IoT: Systems, law, and ways forward' (2018) 51(7) *Computer* 54–65; Jatinder Singh, Ian Walden, Jon Crowcroft, and Jean Bacon 'Responsibility & machine learning: Part of a process' *SSRN 2860048* (2016), https://papers.ssrn.com/sol3/papers.cfm?abstract_id=2860048, (last accessed 26 April 2020).

[76] High-Level Expert Group on AI (HLEG AI) 'Ethics Guidelines for Trustworthy AI,' (2019), European Commission, https://ec.europa.eu/digital-single-market/en/news/ethics-guidelines-trustworthy-ai (last accessed 26 April 2020).

The standard practice of using tools 'off label', ie, using tools labelled 'for research use only' in a clinical application, will shift the responsibility from the producer to the clinic applying the tool.

These aspects breathe into existence the need to develop a new educational strategy geared towards empowering health practitioners and potentially policy-makers to maintain oversight of AI while stressing the responsibility that designers and manufacturers bear in the design and production process. AI researchers and developers should not see this complex ecosystem as an opportunity to avoid and redirect responsibilities, but rather a coherent regulatory approach guiding the standards, use, and parameters for the acceptability of opaque systems, when and for what opaque systems may be permitted and under which circumstances. Addressing this foundational issue will reduce the risk of multiple types of harm, as set forth above, arising from the use of AI-driven systems such as CDSS in healthcare.

IV. A Proactive Forward Look

As described above, many ethical, legal, and societal issues arise from the use and integration of AI in medicine. Medical device regulations are becoming more stringent in the interest of improving patient safety, and as a response to rapid technology innovation and the globalisation of medical device manufacturing processes. In this direction, the European Commission released new regulations in the medical sphere, the Medical Device Regulation (MDR)[77] and the In Vitro Diagnostic medical devices Regulation[78] that replace the former Council Directives 93/42/EEC on medical devices (MDD), 90/385/EEC on active implantable medical devices, and 98/78/EC on in vitro diagnostic medical devices.

The increased impact of software on medical decisions led software to be included in these regulations in Europe and the US. Among the most relevant updates for the qualification of Clinical Decision Support (CDS) software in the EU are the inclusion of the words 'prediction' and 'prognosis' of disease into the definition of a medical device, which extends the range of devices covered by MDR compared to the former MDD definition.[79] Moreover, the software is generally re-qualified to higher risk devices in the new regulations. Any software intended

---

[77] Regulation (EU) 2017/745 of the European Parliament and of the Council of 5 April 2017 on medical devices, amending Directive 2001/83/EC, Regulation (EC) No 178/2002 and Regulation (EC) No 1223/2009 and repealing Council Directives 90/385/EEC and 93/42/EEC (Text with EEA relevance.)

[78] Regulation (EU) 2017/746 of the European Parliament and of the Council of 5 April 2017 on in vitro diagnostic medical devices and repealing Directive 98/79/EC and Commission Decision 2010/227/EU (Text with EEA relevance.)

[79] Food and Drug Administration, 'Clinical Decision Support Software,' (2020), www.fda.gov/regulatory-information/search-fda-guidance-documents/clinical-decision-support-software (last accessed 26 April 2020).

by the manufacturer to be used, alone or in combination for human beings for certain specific medical purposes is a medical device in Europe and regulated under the new MDR or IVDR.[80]

These regulations, however, are not prepared for the automated processing of data that will evaluate, analyse, and predict health-related outcomes, and that may well also affect data protection rights and the safety of the individual. Most software products for clinical settings with an intended medical purpose are medical devices, which are static products that cannot be substantially modified without seeking new regulatory approval. As is the case with the EU framework, these devices for concrete applications and purposes have an approval process taking approximately two months. Similarly, the medical AI software applications approved by the FDA so far are models trained on a specific set of data and then locked, preventing substantial changes to the software without seeking new regulatory approval. These regulatory constraints make it challenging to design adaptive medical AI software systems that can be continuously updated to reflect the latest scientific developments and improvements in data analytical methods.

On the contrary, the regulatory frameworks prescribe that the medical device requiring a substantial update undergoes a separate regulatory approval process, which may result in long delays and prevent timely modification of the outdated software. Consequently, many open questions remain regarding how best to regulate AI- and machine learning-based software as medical devices. Acknowledging the need to reconsider the current regulatory landscape, the FDA issued a discussion paper in 2019 on how to approve adaptive AI algorithms and proposed continuous monitoring of AI systems.[81]

The FDA aims at regulating AI and machine learning in medical-device software from their premarket development to their postmarket performance. In this direction, their intended regulatory framework for adaptive AI would force developers to anticipate modifications and record methodology used to implement such changes in a controlled environment that manages the risks to patients (named 'algorithm change protocol'). According to the FDA, 'this potential framework allows for the FDA's regulatory oversight to address the iterative improvement power of artificial intelligence and machine learning-based software as a medical device while assuring patient safety'.[82] Nevertheless, this approach's adequacy remains to be seen given the range of possible adaptations over time. Consequently, it will be essential to maintain empirical data on the regulatory impacts on adaptive outcomes.[83]

---

[80] Regulation (EU) 2017/746 of the European Parliament and of the Council of 5 April 2017 on in vitro diagnostic medical devices and repealing Directive 98/79/EC and Commission Decision 2010/227/EU (Text with EEA relevance.)

[81] Food and Drug Administration, 'AI and Software as a medical device' (2019) www.fda.gov/medical-devices/software-medical-device-samd/artificial-intelligence-and-machine-learning-software-medical-device (accessed 26 April 2020).

[82] ibid.

[83] Eduard Fosch-Villaronga, and Michiel Heldeweg '"Regulation, I presume?" said the robot–Towards an iterative regulatory process for robot governance' (2018) 34(6) *Computer law & security review* 1258–1277.

From the above, one can derive that the current framework is incomplete and evolving to frame and address advances in AI adequately. The lack of a complete, updated regulatory framework should not impede AI researchers in developing AI solutions that serve society. In the absence of clearly defined regulatory requirements, in the short term, the AI community itself may be well-positioned to help develop a responsible and ethically sound governance framework around AI in medicine by devising technical contributions to solutions for complex normative problems.

In the context of innovation, particularly medical innovation, ethics should be operationalised only reactively and proactively. Reactive ethics focuses on retrospectively assessing the critical ethical implications of novel technologies and their compatibility with existing normative ethical principles, usually only at the end of the development process when the complete system is being implemented. In contrast, proactive ethics is characterised by anticipating ethically-aligned strategies and solutions before a new technology becomes a source of potential ethical confrontation or conflict, usually involving bottom-up and user-driven approaches to the design of novel medical technologies user-centred and value-sensitive design.[84]

Researchers have developed a proactive framework for ethically-aligned technology development specific to AI-powered neuroengineering and rehabilitation technology. This framework is called 'proactive ethical design'.[85] This framework is characterised by the convergence of user-centred and value-sensitive approaches to technology design and a proactive mode of ethical evaluation based on four basic normative-procedural requirements: minimisation of power imbalances between developers and end-users, compliance with biomedical ethics, translationality, and social awareness. Power imbalances decrease if end users (eg, neurological patients) are involved on an equal footing in the design process and incentivised to inform developers about their needs and wishes regarding technology usage. Novel neuroengineering technologies should align with, at least, four common ground moral principles to ensure compliance with the principles of biomedical ethics: beneficence, non-maleficence, autonomy and justice.[86]

The translationality principle acknowledges that the ethical goal of maximising well-being for neurological patients or other users of neuroengineering and assistive technologies is highly dependent on the successful translation of research from the designing lab to the clinics/rehabilitation centre. This results

---

[84] Carol Pavlish, Katherine Brown-Saltzman, Alyssa Fine, and Patricia Jakel 'Making the call: a proactive ethics framework' in *HEC forum*, vol 25, no 3, (Springer, 2013) 269–283; Batya Friedman, Peter Kahn, and Alan Borning 'Value sensitive design: Theory and methods' *University of Washington technical report* 2–12 (2002).

[85] Marcello Ienca, Reto W Kressig, Fabrice Jotterand, and Bernice Elger 'Proactive ethical Design for Neuroengineering, assistive and rehabilitation technologies: the Cybathlon lesson' (2017) 14(1) *Journal of neuroengineering and rehabilitation* 115.

[86] Tom L Beauchamp, and James F Childress *Principles of biomedical ethics* (Oxford University Press, 2001) 618.

in a moral obligation to ensure that new technologies reach the patients or population for whom they are intended and are implemented correctly as slow or unsuccessful translation across the bench, bedside, and community is likely to reduce the beneficial impact of neuroengineering and assistive technology on the global healthcare system. Finally, the framework postulates a moral obligation to raising social awareness and favouring knowledge dissemination across stakeholders and society.

Such proactive ethical design has been further expanded, most notably within the framework of the IEEE's Ethically aligned design, ie a framework for AI systems focused on the preservation and promotion of human wellbeing. While they hold promise for preventing and promptly reacting to ethical lapses as well as for promoting a patient-centred (or, more broadly, user-centred or even human-centred) approach to technology development, proactive approaches are subject to some limitations. The main limitation, as well captured in the famous Collingridge dilemma, is that ethical and social impacts cannot be easily predicted until a technology is extensively developed and widely used due to the limited availability of relevant information prior to its deployment.[87] Therefore, proactive ethical design inevitably entails some degree of dealing with uncertainty. However, as the flipside of the Collingridge quandary makes explicit, control or change is difficult when a technology has become entrenched. Therefore, proactively intervening before a technology is entrenched and pervasive is necessary to shape it in an ethical and human-centred manner. These two considerations highlight that proactive ethical design is well-suited to complement and integrate but not to replace conventional reactive ethics. Furthermore, they illustrate the inevitability of crafting adaptive governance mechanisms that can adequately deal with risk and uncertainty in an evidence-based manner.[88]

V. Conclusion

While AI solutions can improve medicine and healthcare, including making products and processes safer, it could also lead to patient harm. As the European Commission highlights, the use, and development of AI technologies may harm users, materially (safety and health of individuals, including loss of life) and immaterially (loss of privacy, discrimination, or human dignity).[89]

---

[87] Jenifer A Buckley, Paul B Thompson, and Kyle Powys Whyte 'Collingridge's dilemma and the early ethical assessment of emerging technology: The case of nanotechnology enabled biosensors' (2017) 48 *Technology in Society* 54–63.

[88] Andreas Klinke, and Ortwin Renn. 'Adaptive and integrative governance on risk and uncertainty' (2012) 15(3) *Journal of Risk Research* 273–292.

[89] European Commission, White paper (n 54).

In this chapter, we looked at AI-driven analytic tools for precision medicine, assistive technologies that adapt and facilitate rehabilitation and recovery, and various decision aids that may assist in critical processes such as diagnosis and screening. Although these technologies may transcend categories, this approach allowed us to highlight pressing legal and ethical issues that challenge the effective implementation of AI in healthcare. This analysis then examined both the practical and theoretical challenges and their possible impact on the use of AI in healthcare. We concluded that the development and integration of AI in healthcare are complex and multidimensional and require the involvement of multiple actors at multiple levels. Here, we have given particular attention to bringing AI-powered products to market, an endeavour that brings together policy-makers, legislators, designers, developers, and end-users at both the institutional and individual levels. The successful integration of AI into healthcare requires careful attention to a broad range of interests, rights, and goals. This chapter brings the range of considerations into view within the broader context of the multiple dimensions of healthcare.

Acknowledgements

This project comes as a result of the Panel AI, Healthcare, and the Law organized by eLaw Center for Law and Digital Technologies at the Conference on Privacy and Data Protection, during 22–23 January 2020. Part of this project is also funded by the LEaDing Fellows Marie Curie COFUND fellowship, a project that has received funding from the European Union's Horizon 2020 research and innovation programme under the Marie Skłodowska-Curie Grant Agreement No 707404.

References

Ahuja, Abhimanyu S. 'The impact of artificial intelligence in medicine on the future role of the physician' (2019) 7 *PeerJ* e7702.

Aizer, Ayal A, Tyler J Wilhite, Ming-Hui Chen, Powell L Graham, Toni K. Choueiri, Karen E Hoffman, Neil E Martin, Quoc-Dien Trinh, Jim C Hu, and Paul L Nguyen. 'Lack of reduction in racial disparities in cancer-specific mortality over a 20-year period' (2014) 120(10) *Cancer* 1532–1539.

Adiwardana, Daniel, and Luong, Thang. 'Towards a Conversational Agent that Can Chat About … Anything', *Google Research*, Brain Team, (2020). Available at: https://ai.googleblog.com/2020/01/towards-conversational-agent-that-can.html (last accessed 25 April 2020).

Amodei, Dario, Chris Olah, Jacob Steinhardt, Paul Christiano, John Schulman, and Dan Mané. 'Concrete problems in AI safety.' *arXiv preprint arXiv:1606.06565* (2016).

Ash, Joan S, Dean F Sittig, Emily M Campbell, Kenneth P Guappone, and Richard H Dykstra. 'Some unintended consequences of clinical decision support systems.' In *AMIA*

Annual Symposium Proceedings, vol 2007 (American Medical Informatics Association, 2007) 26.

Bank, Paul CD, Jesse J Swen, Rowena D Schaap, Daniëlle B Klootwijk, Renée Baak–Pablo, and Henk-Jan Guchelaar. 'A pilot study of the implementation of pharmacogenomic pharmacist initiated pre-emptive testing in primary care' (2019) 27(10) *European Journal of Human Genetics* 27 1532–1541.

Beauchamp, Tom L, and James F. Childress. *Principles of biomedical ethics* (Oxford University Press, 2001), 618.

Briggs, Bill. '"My God, it's better": Emma can write again thanks to a prototype watch, raising hope for Parkinson's disease,' *Microsoft Transform*, https://news.microsoft.com/transform/emma-can-write-again-thanks-to-prototype-watch-raising-hope-for-parkinsons-disease/ (last accessed 26 April 2020).

Buckley, Jenifer A, Paul B. Thompson, and Kyle Powys Whyte. 'Collingridge's dilemma and the early ethical assessment of emerging technology: The case of nanotechnology enabled biosensors' (2017) 48 *Technology in Society* 54–63.

Challen, Robert, Joshua Denny, Martin Pitt, Luke Gompels, Tom Edwards, and Krasimira Tsaneva-Atanasova. 'Artificial intelligence, bias and clinical safety' (2019) 28(3) *BMJ Qual Saf* 231–237.

Chaves, Ana Paula, and Marco Aurelio Gerosa. 'How should my chatbot interact? A survey on human-chatbot interaction design.' *arXiv preprint arXiv:1904.02743* (2019). This technology was first applied to health and care management programs at premier health and insurance companies, see, for instance, www.cogitocorp.com/company/ (accessed 25 April 2020).

Chebotar, Yevgen, Karol Hausman, Marvin Zhang, Gaurav Sukhatme, Stefan Schaal, and Sergey Levine. 'Combining model-based and model-free updates for trajectory-centric reinforcement learning.' In *Proceedings of the 34th International Conference on Machine Learning-Volume 70*, 703–711. JMLR. org, 2017.

Chung, Kyungyong, and Roy C. Park. 'Chatbot-based healthcare service with a knowledge base for cloud computing' (2019) 22(1) *Cluster Computing* 1925–1937.

Cutter, Gary R, and Yuliang Liu. 'Personalized medicine: The return of the house call?' (2012) 2(4) *Neurology: Clinical Practice* 343–351. Dias, Raquel, and Ali Torkamani. 'Artificial intelligence in clinical and genomic diagnostics' (2019) 11(1) *Genome medicine* 1–12.

Dolic, Z, Castro, R, Moarcas, A, 'Robots in healthcare: a solution or a problem?,' *Study for the Committee on Environment, Public Health, and Food Safety, Policy Department for Economic, Scientific and Quality of Life Policies*, European Parliament, Luxembourg (2019), www.europarl.europa.eu/RegData/etudes/IDAN/2019/638391/IPOL_IDA(2019)638391_EN.pdf (last accessed 24 April 2020).

Eysenbach, Benjamin, Shixiang Gu, Julian Ibarz, and Sergey Levine. 'Leave no trace: Learning to reset for safe and autonomous reinforcement learning.' *arXiv preprint arXiv:1711.06782* (2017).

Felzmann, Heike, Eduard Fosch-Villaronga, Christoph Lutz, and Aurelia Tamò-Larrieux. 'Transparency you can trust: Transparency requirements for artificial intelligence between legal norms and contextual concerns' (2019) 6(1) *Big Data & Society* 2053951719860542.

Fosch-Villaronga, Eduard. *Robots, healthcare, and the law: Regulating automation in personal care* (Routledge, 2019).

Fosch-Villaronga, Eduard, and Michiel Heldeweg. "'Regulation, I presume?" said the robot–Towards an iterative regulatory process for robot governance' (2018) 34(6) *Computer law & security review* 1258–1277.

Food and Drug Administration, 'AI and Software as a medical device' (2019) www.fda.gov/medical-devices/software-medical-device-samd/artificial-intelligence-and-machine-learning-software-medical-device (last accessed 26 April 2020).

Food and Drug Administration, 'Clinical Decision Support Software,' (2020), www.fda.gov/regulatory-information/search-fda-guidance-documents/clinical-decision-support-software (last accessed 26 April 2020).

Food and Drug Administration, FDA, 'Cybersecurity.' (2019), www.fda.gov/medical-devices/digital-health/cybersecurity (last accessed 24 April 2020).

Fosch-Villaronga, Eduard. *Robots, healthcare, and the law: Regulating automation in personal care* (Routledge, 2019).

Fosch-Villaronga, Eduard, and Christopher Millard. 'Cloud robotics law and regulation: Challenges in the governance of complex and dynamic cyber–physical ecosystems' (2019) 119 *Robotics and Autonomous Systems* 77–91.

Friedman, Batya, Peter Kahn, and Alan Borning. 'Value sensitive design: Theory and methods.' *University of Washington technical report* 2–12 (2002).

Gianfrancesco, Milena A, Suzanne Tamang, Jinoos Yazdany, and Gabriela Schmajuk. 'Potential biases in machine learning algorithms using electronic health record data' (2018) 178(11) *JAMA internal medicine* 1544–1547.

Gliklich, Richard E, Nancy A Dreyer, and Michelle B Leavy. 'Chapter 11: Data Collection and Quality Assurance' in *Registries for evaluating patient outcomes: a user's guide.* (Government Printing Office 2014). Available from: www.ncbi.nlm.nih.gov/books/NBK208601/ (last accessed 25 April 2020).

High-Level Expert Group on AI (HLEG AI) 'Ethics Guidelines for Trustworthy AI,' (2019), European Commission, https://ec.europa.eu/digital-single-market/en/news/ethics-guidelines-trustworthy-ai (last accessed 26 April 2020).

Human Rights Watch, 'US: LGBT People Face Healthcare Barriers,' www.hrw.org/news/2018/07/23/us-lgbt-people-face-healthcare-barriers, (last accessed 26 April 2020).

Ienca, Marcello, and Karolina Ignatiadis. 'Artificial Intelligence in Clinical Neuroscience: Methodological and Ethical Challenges' (2020) 11(2) *AJOB neuroscience* 77–87.

Ienca, Marcello. 'Brain Machine Interfaces, Artificial Intelligence and Neurorights' (2017) 3, https://brain.ieee.org/newsletter/2017-issue-3/brain-machine-interfaces-artificial-intelligence-neurorights/ (last accessed 26 April 2020).

Ienca, Marcello, Jotterand Fabrice, Bernice Elger, Maurizio Caon, Alessandro Scoccia Pappagallo, Reto W. Kressig, and Tenzin Wangmo. 'Intelligent assistive technology for Alzheimer's disease and other dementias: a systematic review' (2017) 56(4) *Journal of Alzheimer's Disease* 1301–1340. Ienca, Marcello, and Eduard Fosch Villaronga. 'Privacy and security issues in assistive technologies for dementia' in Jotterand, Fabrice, Marcello Ienca, Bernice Elger, and Tenzin Wangmo, (eds) *Intelligent Assistive Technologies for Dementia: Clinical, Ethical, Social, and Regulatory Implications* (Oxford University Press, 2019) 221–239.

Ienca, Marcello, Reto W Kressig, Fabrice Jotterand, and Bernice Elger. 'Proactive ethical Design for Neuroengineering, assistive and rehabilitation technologies: the Cybathlon lesson' (2017) 14(1) *Journal of neuroengineering and rehabilitation* 115.

Ischen, Caroline, Theo Araujo, Hilde Voorveld, Guda van Noort, and Edith Smit. 'Privacy concerns in chatbot interactions' in Asbjorn Folstad et al (eds) *International Workshop on Chatbot Research and Design* (Springer, 2019) 34–48.

Jha, Saurabh, and Eric J Topol. 'Adapting to artificial intelligence: radiologists and pathologists as information specialists' (2016) 316(22) *Jama* 2353–2354.

Johnson, Deborah G. 'Technology with no human responsibility?' (2015) 127(4) *Journal of Business Ethics* 707–715.

Klamroth-Marganska, Verena, Javier Blanco, Katrin Campen, Armin Curt, Volker Dietz, Thierry Ettlin, Morena Felder et al. 'Three-dimensional, task-specific robot therapy of the arm after stroke: a multicentre, parallel-group randomised trial' (2014) 13(2) *The Lancet Neurology* 159–166.

Klinke, Andreas, and Ortwin Renn. 'Adaptive and integrative governance on risk and uncertainty' (2012) 15(3) *Journal of Risk Research* 273–292.

Kreimeyer, Kory, Matthew Foster, Abhishek Pandey, Nina Arya, Gwendolyn Halford, Sandra F. Jones, Richard Forshee, Mark Walderhaug, and Taxiarchis Botsis. 'Natural language processing systems for capturing and standardizing unstructured clinical information: a systematic review' (2017) 73 *Journal of biomedical informatics* 14–29.

Kretzschmar, Kira, Holly Tyroll, Gabriela Pavarini, Arianna Manzini, Ilina Singh, and NeurOx Young People's Advisory Group. 'Can your phone be your therapist? Young people's ethical perspectives on the use of fully automated conversational agents (chatbots) in mental health support' (2019) 11 *Biomedical informatics insights* 1178222619829083.

Lo, Albert C, Peter D Guarino, Lorie G. Richards, Jodie K Haselkorn, George F Wittenberg, Daniel G Federman, Robert J Ringer et al. 'Robot-assisted therapy for long-term upper-limb impairment after stroke' (2010) 362(19) *New England Journal of Medicine* 1772–1783.

Lynn, Lawrence A. 'Artificial intelligence systems for complex decision-making in acute care medicine: a review' (2019) 13(1) *Patient safety in surgery* 6.

Lynch, Frances L, Patricia Himes, Marian J Gilmore, Elissa M Morris, Jennifer L Schneider, Tia L Kauffman, Elizabeth Shuster et al. 'Time costs for genetic counseling in preconception carrier screening with genome sequencing' (2018) 27(4) *Journal of genetic counseling* 823–833.

Lyu, Mingxing, Wei-Hai Chen, Xilun Ding, and Jianhua Wang. 'Knee exoskeleton enhanced with artificial intelligence to provide assistance-as-needed' (2019) 90(9) *Review of Scientific Instruments* 094101.

Marks, Mason. 'Artificial Intelligence Based Suicide Prediction.' (2019) 18 *Yale Journal of Health Policy, Law, and Ethics* 98. Available at SSRN: https://ssrn.com/abstract=3324874 (accessed 25 April 2020).

Marson, Fernando AL, Carmen S Bertuzzo, and José D. Ribeiro. 'Personalized or precision medicine? The example of cystic fibrosis' (2017) 8 *Frontiers in pharmacology* 390.

Martin, Suzanne, Johan E Bengtsson, and Rose-Marie Dröes. 'Assistive technologies and issues relating to privacy, ethics and security' in Maurice D Mulvenna and Chris D Nugent (eds) *Supporting people with dementia using pervasive health technologies* (Springer, 2010) 63–76.

Matthias, Andreas. 'The responsibility gap: Ascribing responsibility for the actions of learning automata' (2004) 6(3) *Ethics and information technology* 175–183.

Ming, Chang, Valeria Viassolo, Nicole Probst-Hensch, Pierre O Chappuis, Ivo D Dinov, and Maria C Katapodi. 'Machine learning techniques for personalized breast cancer risk prediction: comparison with the BCRAT and BOADICEA models' (2019) 21(1) *Breast Cancer Research* 75.

Morante, Santiago, Juan G Victores, and Carlos Balaguer. 'Cryptobotics: Why robots need cyber safety' (2015) 2 *Frontiers in Robotics and AI* 23.

Moritz, Chet T, Patrick Ruther, Sara Goering, Alfred Stett, Tonio Ball, Wolfram Burgard, Eric H. Chudler, and Rajesh PN Rao. 'New perspectives on neuroengineering and neurotechnologies: NSF-DFG workshop report' (2016) 63(7) *IEEE Transactions on Biomedical Engineering* 1354–1367.

Noel, Thomas C, and Brian R Snider. 'Utilizing Deep Neural Networks for Brain–Computer Interface-Based Prosthesis Control' [2019] *The Journal of Computing Sciences in Colleges* 93.

Noor, Poppy. 'Can we trust AI not to further embed racial bias and prejudice?' (2020) 368 *BMJ*.

Palanica, Adam, Peter Flaschner, Anirudh Thommandram, Michael Li, and Yan Fossat. 'Physicians' perceptions of chatbots in health care: cross-sectional web-based survey.' *Journal of medical Internet research* 21, no. 4 (2019):e12887.

Parikh, Ravi B, Stephanie Teeple, and Amol S Navathe. 'Addressing Bias in Artificial Intelligence in Health Care' (2019) 322(24) *Jama* 2377–2378.

Pavlish, Carol, Katherine Brown-Saltzman, Alyssa Fine, and Patricia Jakel. 'Making the call: a proactive ethics framework.' In *HEC forum*, vol 25, no 3, (Springer, 2013) 269–283.

Pierce, Robin. 'Machine learning for diagnosis and treatment: Gymnastics for the GDPR' (2018) 4 *European Data Protection. Law Review* 333.

Pierce, Robin. 'Medical Privacy: Where Deontology and Consequentialism Meet' in de Groot and van der Sloot (eds) *Handbook of Privacy Studies* (Amsterdam University Press, 2018) 327–332.

Primorac, Dragan, Lidija Bach-Rojecky, Dalia Vađunec, Alen Juginović, Katarina Žunić, Vid Matišić, Andrea Skelin et al. 'Pharmacogenomics at the center of precision medicine: challenges and perspective in an era of Big Data' (2020) 21(2) *Pharmacogenomics* 141–156.

Ponathil, Amal, Firat Ozkan, Brandon Welch, Jeffrey Bertrand, and Kapil Chalil Madathil. 'Family health history collected by virtual conversational agents: An empirical study to investigate the efficacy of this approach' [2020] *Journal of Genetic Counseling*.

Poulsen, Adam, Eduard Fosch-Villaronga, and Roger Andre Søraa. 'Queering machines' (2020) 2(3) *Nature Machine Intelligence* 152–152.

Raes, Annelies, Tammy Schellens, Bram De Wever, and Ellen Vanderhoven. 'Scaffolding information problem solving in web-based collaborative inquiry learning' (2012) 59(1) *Computers & Education* 82–94.

Regulation (EU) 2017/746 of the European Parliament and of the Council of 5 April 2017 on in vitro diagnostic medical devices and repealing Directive 98/79/EC and Commission Decision 2010/227/EU (Text with EEA relevance).

Regulation (EU) 2017/745 of the European Parliament and of the Council of 5 April 2017 on medical devices, amending Directive 2001/83/EC, Regulation (EC) No 178/2002 and Regulation (EC) No 1223/2009 and repealing Council Directives 90/385/EEC and 93/42/EEC (Text with EEA relevance).

Resta, Robert, Barbara Bowles Biesecker, Robin L Bennett, Sandra Blum, Susan Estabrooks Hahn, Michelle N Strecker, and Janet L Williams. 'A new definition of genetic counseling: National Society of Genetic Counselors' task force report' (2006) 15(2) *Journal of genetic counseling* 77–83.

Riener, Robert. 'The Cybathlon promotes the development of assistive technology for people with physical disabilities' (2016) 13(1) *Journal of neuroengineering and rehabilitation* 49.

Robinson, Francesca. 'Caring for LGBT patients in the NHS' (2019) 366 *BMJ* l5374.

Schmidlen, Tara, Marci Schwartz, Kristy DiLoreto, H. Lester Kirchner, and Amy C. Sturm. 'Patient assessment of chatbots for the scalable delivery of genetic counseling' (2019) 28(6) *Journal of genetic counseling* 1166–1177.

Shreffler, Wayne G. 'Promise of personalized medicine' (2019) 123(6) *Annals of Allergy, Asthma & Immunology* 534.

Singh, Jatinder, Christopher Millard, Chris Reed, Jennifer Cobbe, and Jon Crowcroft. 'Accountability in the IoT: Systems, law, and ways forward' (2018) 51(7) *Computer* 54–65.

Singh, Jatinder, Ian Walden, Jon Crowcroft, and Jean Bacon. 'Responsibility & machine learning: Part of a process.' *SSRN 2860048* (2016), https://papers.ssrn.com/sol3/papers.cfm?abstract_id=2860048, (last accessed 26 April 2020).

Stajic, Jelena, Richard Stone, Gilbert Chin, and Brad Wible. 'Rise of the Machines' (2015) 349(6245) *Science* 248–249.

Suckiel, Sabrina A, Michael D Linderman, Saskia C Sanderson, George A Diaz, Melissa Wasserstein, Andrew Kasarskis, Eric E Schadt, and Randi E Zinberg. 'Impact of genomic counseling on informed decision-making among ostensibly healthy individuals seeking personal genome sequencing: the HealthSeq project' (2016) 25(5) *Journal of genetic counseling* 1044–1053.

Vamathevan, Jessica, Rolf Apweiler, and Ewan Birney. 'Biomolecular data resources: Bioinformatics infrastructure for biomedical data science' (2019) 2 *Annual Review of Biomedical Data Science* 199–222.

Vepakomma, Praneeth, Otkrist Gupta, Tristan Swedish, and Ramesh Raskar. 'Split learning for health: Distributed deep learning without sharing raw patient data.' *arXiv preprint arXiv:1812.00564* (2018).

Vepakomma, Praneeth, Tristan Swedish, Ramesh Raskar, Otkrist Gupta, and Abhimanyu Dubey. 'No Peek: A Survey of private distributed deep learning.' arXiv preprint arXiv:1812.03288 (2018).

Weizenbaum, Joseph. 'ELIZA – a computer program for the study of natural language communication between man and machine' (1966) 9(1) *Communications of the ACM* 36–45.

White Paper on Artificial Intelligence, 'A European approach to excellence and trust,' European Commission, (2020) https://ec.europa.eu/info/sites/info/files/commission-white-paper-artificial-intelligence-feb2020_en.pdf (last accessed 26 April 2020).

Williams, Stephen A, Mika Kivimaki, Claudia Langenberg, Aroon D Hingorani, J P Casas, Claude Bouchard, Christian Jonasson et al. 'Plasma protein patterns as comprehensive indicators of health' (2019) 25(12) *Nature Medicine* 1851–1857.

Wilkowska, Wiktoria, and Martina Ziefle. 'Privacy and data security in E-health: Requirements from the user's perspective' (2012) 18(3) *Health informatics journal* 191–201.

Wu, Yonghui, Mike Schuster, Zhifeng Chen, Quoc V Le, Mohammad Norouzi, Wolfgang Macherey, Maxim Krikun et al. 'Google's neural machine translation system: Bridging the gap between human and machine translation.' *arXiv preprint: arXiv:1609.08144* (2016); see also www.cogitocorp.com/.

Yu, Kun-Hsing, Andrew L Beam, and Isaac S Kohane. 'Artificial intelligence in healthcare' (2018) 2(10) *Nature biomedical engineering* 719–731.

Zhuang, Katie Z., Nicolas Sommer, Vincent Mendez, Saurav Aryan, Emanuele Formento, Edoardo D'Anna, Fiorenzo Artoni et al. 'Shared human–robot proportional control of a dexterous myoelectric prosthesis' (2019) 1(9) *Nature Machine Intelligence* 400–411.

8

Technological Experimentation Without Adequate Safeguards? Interoperable EU Databases and Access to the Multiple Identity Detector by SIRENE Bureaux

DIANA DIMITROVA[1] AND TERESA QUINTEL[2]

Abstract

The Interoperability Regulations that were adopted in May 2019 are expected to connect all large-scale EU databases and shall establish three new centralised components to store personal data of all third country nationals coming or seeking to come to the European Union (EU). One of the interoperability components is the Multiple Identity Detector (MID), which is supposed to link personal data that exist in more than one of the underlying databases in order to alert competent authorities where there is a suspicion of identity fraud. The authorities that are granted access to the MID, and therewith to data held in the underlying databases, include the national SIRENE Bureaux, specialised police units responsible for exchanging information with their counterparts, which are currently set up to manage alerts in the Schengen Information System (SIS) as their primary task.

This chapter questions both the legal basis and the purposes allowing SIRENE Bureaux to access the MID and critically assesses necessity and proportionality of such access in the light of Article 52(1) of the Charter of Fundamental Rights of the European Union (CFREU). In addition, the chapter will take into consideration the risks for data subjects regarding the right to be informed and the right to

[1] Diana Dimitrova is a Research Assistant at FIZ Karlsruhe – Leibniz Institute for Information Infrastructures, Germany and a PhD student at VUB/LSTS, Brussels, Belgium. For correspondence: Diana.dimitrova@fiz-Karlsruhe.de.

[2] Teresa Quintel, LL.M. is an FNR-funded Ph.D. student at the University of Luxembourg and Uppsala University under co-supervision of Prof. Mark D Cole and Assistant Prof. Maria Bergström. For correspondence: teresa.quintel@uni.lu. The authors are listed in a purely alphabetical order, both authors contributed equally to this work.

an effective remedy when data exchanges take place between multiple authorities and on different levels. The chapter concludes that the interoperable system might open a backdoor for law enforcement authorities to obtain access to personal data stored in systems that they were previously not authorised to consult.

Key words

Interoperability, EU databases, Multiple Identity Detector, SIRENE Bureaux, Data Protection, Access to Personal Data.

I. Introduction

Since the aftermath of the so-called migration crisis in September 2015, when the crossing of the external Schengen borders by over a million asylum seekers and migrants dominated the news, a lot has been done in terms of technological experimentation in order to prevent more people from entering the EU. Such experimentation included the proliferation of EU databases[3] used to monitor and control people who move or seek to move across the EU's external borders. This proliferation ultimately culminated with the proposal to connect these databases, making them interoperable.

In order to close the (alleged) information gap between EU databases, the European Commission (EU Commission) proposed, in December 2017,[4] the Interoperability of EU large-scale IT-systems, which was adopted in May 2019.[5] The interoperability framework is supposed to connect six EU databases, half of which are currently operational,[6] the other half foreseen to be established by 2023.[7]

---

[3] Large-scale IT systems that were set up in the Area of Freedom Security and Justice (AFSJ).

[4] European Commission, 'Proposal for a Regulation of the European Parliament and of the Council on establishing a framework for interoperability between EU information systems (borders and visa) and amending Council Decision 2004/512/EC, Regulation (EC) No 767/2008, Council Decision 2008/633/JHA, Regulation (EU) 2016/399 and Regulation (EU) 2017/2226' COM (2017) 793 final and European Commission, 'Proposal for a Regulation of the European Parliament and of the Council on establishing a framework for interoperability between EU information systems (police and judicial cooperation, asylum and migration)' COM (2017) 794 final, hereafter 'COM (2017) 793 and 794 final.'

[5] Regulation (EU) 2019/817 of the European Parliament and of the Council of 20 May 2019 on establishing a framework for interoperability between EU information systems in the field of borders and visa and amending Regulations (EC) No 767/2008, (EU) 2016/399, (EU) 2017/2226, (EU) 2018/1240, (EU) 2018/1726 and (EU) 2018/1861 of the European Parliament and of the Council and Council Decisions 2004/512/EC and 2008/633/JHA [2019] OJ L135/27 and Regulation (EU) 2019/818 of the European Parliament and of the Council of 20 May 2019 on establishing a framework for interoperability between EU information systems in the field of police and judicial cooperation, asylum and migration and amending Regulations (EU) 2018/1726, (EU) 2018/1862 and (EU) 2019/816 [2019] OJ L135/85 (hereafter 'Interoperability Regulations').

[6] The founding acts of two of the currently operational databases – Eurodac and VIS – are under revision.

[7] As stated in the proposals, the Commission aims to achieve interoperability by the end of 2023. See: Katrien Luyten and Sofija Voronova, 'Interoperability between EU border and security information systems', EPRS (June 2019), 2.

The establishment of EU-wide databases should be regarded as compensation measure for the abolition of the internal borders within the Schengen Area. A majority of these databases serve border control, visa and asylum objectives, and, as ancillary purpose, pursue law enforcement functions. For the time being, the SIS[8] is the only EU database that serves primarily law enforcement purposes.

As of today, the three operational EU databases are the Visa Information System (VIS),[9] Eurodac[10] and the SIS, which are used to store the personal data of visa applicants, individuals who applied for international protection, and, within the scope of the SIS, also personal data of criminals, missing people and persons subject to alerts.

Over time, the founding acts of those databases, initially established for specific purposes and with strict access requirements, were revised in order to serve more purposes, retain additional categories of personal data and to provide broader access possibilities to more authorities, in particular to law enforcement authorities. In addition to the VIS, the SIS and Eurodac, three new databases, the Entry Exit System (EES),[11] the European Travel Information and Authorization

---

[8] Regulation (EU) 2018/1860 of the European Parliament and of the Council of 28 November 2018 on the use of the Schengen Information System for the return of illegally staying third-country nationals [2018] OJ L312/1; Regulation (EU) 2018/1861 of the European Parliament and of the Council of 28 November 2018 on the establishment, operation and use of the Schengen Information System (SIS) in the field of border checks, and amending the Convention implementing the Schengen Agreement, and amending and repealing Regulation (EC) No 1987/2006 [2018] OJ L312/14 and Regulation (EU) 2018/1862 of the European Parliament and of the Council of 28 November 2018 on the establishment, operation and use of the Schengen Information System (SIS) in the field of police cooperation and judicial cooperation in criminal matters, amending and repealing Council Decision 2007/533/JHA, and repealing Regulation (EC) No 1986/2006 of the European Parliament and of the Council and Commission Decision 2010/261/EU [2018] OJ L312/56, hereafter 'SIS Regulation on the use of the Schengen Information System for the return of illegally staying third-country nationals', 'SIS Regulation in the field of border checks' and 'SIS Regulation in the field of police and judicial cooperation'.

[9] Regulation (EC) No 767/2008 of the European Parliament and of the Council of 9 July 2008 concerning the Visa Information System (VIS) and the exchange of data between MS on short-stay visas (VIS Regulation) [2008] OJ L218/60, hereafter 'VIS Regulation'. In May 2018, the Commission issued a proposal for the revision of the VIS, see: European Commission, 'Proposal for a Regulation of the European Parliament and of the Council amending Regulation (EC) No 767/2008, Regulation (EC) No 810/2009, Regulation (EU) 2017/2226, Regulation (EU) 2016/399, Regulation XX/2018 [Interoperability Regulation], and Decision 2004/512/EC and repealing Council Decision 2008/633/JHA' COM (2018) 302 final.

[10] Regulation (EU) No 603/2013 of the European Parliament and of the Council of 26 June 2013 on the establishment of 'Eurodac' for the comparison of fingerprints for the effective application of Regulation (EU) No 604/2013 establishing the criteria and mechanisms for determining the MS responsible for examining an application for international protection lodged in one of the Member States by a third-country national or a stateless person and on requests for the comparison with Eurodac data by Member State law enforcement authorities and Europol for law enforcement purposes, and amending Regulation (EU) No 1077/2011 establishing a European Agency for the operational management of large-scale IT systems in the area of freedom, security and justice (recast) [2013] OJ L180/1, hereafter 'Eurodac Regulation'.

[11] Regulation (EU) 2017/2226 of the European Parliament and of the Council of 30 November 2017 establishing an Entry/Exit System (EES) to register entry and exit data and refusal of entry data of third-country nationals crossing the external borders of the MS and determining the conditions for access to the EES for law enforcement purposes, and amending the Convention implementing the Schengen Agreement and Regulations (EC) No 767/2008 and (EU) No 1077/2011 [2017] OJ L327/20, hereafter 'EES Regulation'.

System (ETIAS)[12] and the European Criminal Record Information System for TCNs and stateless persons (ECRIS-TCN)[13] were recently adopted and are soon to be operational.

Just like the debate on the need to protect the external Schengen borders against illegal or irregular migration and to establish mechanisms in order to prevent the entry of too many unwanted individuals, suggestions on *improving* the EU databases by connecting them with each other are not entirely new.[14] However, while 15 years ago the technology to establish such an interconnected system of databases was not sufficiently advanced, those technological considerations are at most subject to legal constraints nowadays.

The interoperability framework includes four different components: a European Search Portal (ESP),[15] a shared Biometric Matching Service (sBMS),[16] a Common Identity Repository (CIR)[17] and the MID. The latter component facilitates identity checks and combats identity fraud by detecting multiple identities that are either legitimately or unlawfully used by the same Third Country Nationals (TCNs). Moreover, the MID shall support the objectives of the underlying databases, which are, inter alia, enhancing the efficiency of

---

[12] Regulation (EU) 2018/1240 of the European Parliament and of the Council of 12 September 2018 establishing a European Travel Information and Authorisation System (ETIAS) and amending Regulations (EU) No 1077/2011, (EU) No 515/2014, (EU) 2016/399, (EU) 2016/1624 and (EU) 2017/2226 [2018] OJ L236/1, hereafter 'ETIAS Regulation'.

[13] Regulation (EU) 2019/816 of the European Parliament and of the Council of 17 April 2019 establishing a centralised system for the identification of Member States holding conviction information on third-country nationals and stateless persons (ECRIS-TCN) to supplement the European Criminal Records Information System and amending Regulation (EU) 2018/1726 [2019] OJ L135/1, hereafter 'ECRIS-TCN Regulation'.

[14] See for instance: Communication from the Commission to the Council and the European Parliament, 'on improved effectiveness, enhanced interoperability and synergies among European databases in the area of Justice and Home Affairs', COM (2005) 597 final, Brussels, 24 November 2005.

[15] As a central infrastructure, the ESP shall enable competent authorities the simultaneous querying of the underlying systems. Instead of queries being carried out in eight different databases separately, searches via the ESP will be systematically conducted within all systems in parallel using both biographical and biometric data, and the combined results will be displayed on one single screen. The results shown shall solely contain the data to which the end-user has access according to his or her access rights under the provisions of the underlying databases.

[16] The BMS will create a common platform that uses data from the Central-SIS, Eurodac, the EES, VIS and the proposed ECRIS-TCN to generate and store biometric templates. The BMS seeks to make the identification of TCNs more reliable by automatically comparing biometric data in all connected systems with the biometric templates, thereby substituting the checking of each underlying database in five separate searches.

[17] According to Art 17 of the Interoperability Regulations, the CIR is supposed to facilitate and assist in the correct identification of persons registered in the EES, VIS, ETIAS, Eurodac and ECRIS-TCN in accordance with Art 20. Connected to the ESP, the BMS and the MID, as well as to the central systems of the EES, Eurodac, the VIS, the upcoming ETIAS, and the upcoming ECRIS-TCN, the CIR will create an individual file for each person registered in the five databases and store their data in a central repository. The individual files shall contain both biometric and biographical data as well as a reference indicating the system from which the data were retrieved. The main purposes of the CIR are to facilitate the correct identification of TCNs and supporting the detection of false identities. Moreover, the CIR shall contribute to simplifying and streamlining law enforcement-access to non-law enforcement databases for the prevention, investigation, detection or prosecution of serious crime.

border checks,[18] facilitating the administration of visa and asylum applications as well as the processing of alerts and return decisions,[19] improving the detection and identification of overstayers,[20] identifying those TCNs who do not or no longer fulfil the conditions for entry to the EU,[21] combating identity fraud and the misuse of travel documents,[22] as well as contributing to the prevention of illegal immigration,[23] to a high level of security within the Union[24] and the protection of public health[25] more generally.

For those purposes, the MID is supposed to create links between sets of personal data stored in the underlying databases in order to signal any suspicious correlations between the data in connection with document fraud or identity theft to the competent authorities. Those links shall specify the level of likelihood of such suspicion in different colours, ranging from white to green, yellow and red links. Whereas white and green links generally indicate that a TCN is a bona fide traveller,[26] yellow and red links require action to be taken by the designated authority.[27] While a yellow link needs to be manually verified, a red link requires follow-up action to be taken in accordance with Union and national law concerning identity or document fraud.[28]

The processing of personal data of TCNs which are stored in the MID, as well as the MID's purposes, access conditions to the MID and the verification procedures regarding suspected identity fraud, will be the focal point of this chapter. The chapter will examine whether the Interoperability Regulations provide authorities, more specifically the SIRENE Bureaux that were set up within the framework of the SIS,[29] with broader access possibilities to the data stored in the MID, the CIR or the SIS and whether this widened access is legitimate and proportionate.

In that vein, Section II will briefly illustrate the MID in terms of its rationale, the different types of links to be stored and the conditions applicable when those links are accessed by competent authorities. Moreover, that section will particularly focus on the access that SIRENE Bureaux are expected to obtain in the context of red MID links. Thereafter, Section III will examine the necessity and proportionality of access by SIRENE Bureaux to the so-called MID identity confirmation

---

[18] VIS Regulation, Art 2(d) and EES Regulation, Art (1)(a).
[19] VIS Regulation, Art 2(a), Eurodac Regulation, Art 1(1) and Art 1, SIS Regulation on the use of the Schengen Information System for the return of illegally staying third-country nationals, art 1.
[20] VIS Regulation, Art 2(e) and EES Regulation, Art 1(c).
[21] EES Regulation, Art 1(b).
[22] VIS Regulation, Art 2(c) and EES Regulation, Art 1(i).
[23] ETIAS Regulation, Art 4(b).
[24] SIS Regulation in the field of police cooperation and judicial cooperation in criminal matters and the SIS Regulation in the field of border checks, Art 1, VIS Regulation, Art 2(g) and ETIAS Regulation, Art 4(a).
[25] ETIAS Regulation, Art 4(c).
[26] Thus, not leading to additional inquiries or repercussions in terms of processing of personal data except for the unjustified storage of those links in so-called identity confirmation files.
[27] Interoperability Regulations, Arts 26 and 29.
[28] Interoperability Regulations, Art 32(2).
[29] List of N.SIS II Offices and the national Sirene Bureaux [2018] OJ C226/02.

files and point out the risks that are involved when the SIRENE Bureaux manually verify yellow links[30] or follow up on red links. Section IV will briefly summarise the main points of the debate.

II. The MID in a Nutshell: Rationale, Types of Links and Access Conditions

Accommodating a broad range of purposes, the MID shall be interconnected with the CIR, the ESP, the sBMS and the SIS in order to check whether any newly added data concerning a person already exist in one of the systems connected to it.[31] This process of multiple identity detection shall be launched whenever a data entry is created or updated in one or more of the underlying systems.[32] Hence, where an authorised user such as a visa, immigration or other designated authority, and, in the case of the SIS, the SIRENE staff, would add or update data in the underlying databases, this would enable the detection of multiple identities by matching the newly added data against sets of stored biometric and biographical data across the systems.[33]

The links would be distinguished in different colours, indicating whether there is a low or a high likelihood of identity fraud, ranging from white links to red ones. With a yellow link, the authority which added the data would be notified that the verification of different identities did not yet take place and would need to be manually carried out due to a suspicion of identity fraud. Theoretically, whenever personal data of an individual would be stored in more than one of the underlying databases and would report some kind of a match,[34] the MID should indicate either a white or a yellow link. The latter yellow links would have to be manually verified and subsequently turned into either a green, white or a red link.[35] Where more than one link would be created, the authority responsible for the manual verification of different identities would have to assess each link separately.[36]

In a nutshell, the case handling authority that added or updated the data in the respective database, where this led to the creation of a yellow link,

---

[30] In the framework of Art 29, Interoperability Regulations.

[31] COM (2017) 793 and 794 final, (n 4), 7.

[32] It is not quite clear why the Eurodac is not included in this process, but the authors of this chapter assume that it will be added once there has been agreement on the Asylum Package (Reform of the Common European Asylum System). Interoperability Regulation on borders and visa, Art 27(1)(a), (b), (c), (d) and Interoperability Regulation on police and judicial cooperation, asylum and migration, Art 27(1)(a) and (b).

[33] COM (2017) 793 and 794 final, (n 4), 7.

[34] Interoperability Regulations, Art 28(1).

[35] In accordance with Art 28(1), Interoperability Regulations, where the queries do not report any match, the procedures shall continue in accordance with the legal instruments governing them.

[36] Interoperability Regulation on police and judicial cooperation, asylum and migration, Art 29(4) and Interoperability Regulation on borders and visa, Art 29(5).

would then have to classify the link into white, green or red categories: white and green links would indicate that the authority responsible for the manual verification concluded that the linked identities lawfully belong to the same person, or refer to two different persons in a legitimate manner,[37] respectively, and that there is no risk of identity fraud, either from the results of automatic checks or after manual verification. In the case of red links, the authority responsible for the manual verification concluded that identity fraud occurred.[38] However, the mere existence of a red link shall not lead to legal consequences for the individual but requires follow-up action in accordance with national or EU law.[39]

The automated matching of datasets in the MID would verify whether data about an individual is already stored in one of the underlying databases and generate a yellow link by way of cross-checking the data with those in the other interoperability components, namely the ESP, sBMS, the CIR and the SIS.[40] When a Member State authority or Union agency launches a query in the ESP, all underlying databases, the CIR, the MID, as well as the Europol[41] and Interpol databases[42] shall provide the data that they hold in response to the query.[43] It needs to be noted that the ESP will be configured in a way that only the underlying databases to which the querying authority has access under the founding acts of those databases will show results.[44] Both the authorities having access to the MID as well as the data to be stored in the MID are only vaguely determined under the Interoperability Regulations.

The ESP will enable both alphanumeric and biometric searches. The latter would be carried out through the sBMS, which will store templates of biometric data obtained from the underlying databases,[45] which it shall compare to any new biometric data added to the system or the SIS. In this way, the sBMS shall verify whether data on a person are already stored in the CIR or in the Central SIS.[46] As the CIR and the sBMS will replace great parts of the central systems of the underlying databases, all of the latter will therefore be included when the multiple identity detection is carried out.

---

[37] See Interoperability Regulations respectively, Arts 31 and 33.

[38] See Interoperability Regulations, Art 32.

[39] Interoperability Regulations, Art 32(2).

[40] The CIR would not contain data from the SIS II system, as the architecture of the SIS is too complex and not technically feasible to be included within the CIR, COM (2017) 793 and 794 final, (n 4) 7.

[41] In accordance with Art 4(16), Interoperability Regulation, 'Europol data' means personal data processed by Europol for the purpose referred to in Art 18(2)(a), (b) and (c) of Regulation (EU) 2016/794.

[42] In accordance with Art 4(17), Interoperability Regulations, 'Interpol databases' means the Interpol Stolen and Lost Travel Document database (SLTD database) and the Interpol Travel Documents Associated with Notices database (TDAWN database).

[43] Interoperability Regulations, Art 9(4).

[44] ibid.

[45] Biometric data from the VIS, Eurodac, ECRIS-TCN, the EES and the SIS. Data from the ETIAS will not be included in the sBMS, as the ETIAS will not store biometric data.

[46] Interoperability Regulations, Art 27(2).

A. Data to be Stored in the MID

Pursuant to the Interoperability Regulations, the MID shall be composed of a central infrastructure storing the different links, the references to the underlying databases and the so-called identity confirmation files.[47]

An MID identity confirmation file shall denote the authority responsible for the manual verification of different identities,[48] the date of creation of the link or of any update to it[49] and a single identification number allowing for the retrieval of the linked data from the corresponding EU databases.[50] Red and white MID links would not only be contained in the identity confirmation files, but also be added to an individual file that would be stored in the CIR and which is supposed to hold the data of each person whose data are present in the underlying databases.[51] National police authorities that may access the CIR under Article 20 of the Interoperability Regulations for the purposes of identifying individuals[52] could thus not only get access to identity data stored in the CIR, but would also be notified about the existence of red and white MID links.[53] Hence, while access under Article 20 of the Interoperability Regulations is supposed to serve the sole purpose of identifying an individual, the querying police officer would concurrently be informed whether a person committed identity fraud or is a bona fide traveller.

Different conditions apply to accessing those links when they are retained in the MID. In order to be granted access to green[54] or white links[55] stored in the

---

[47] ibid, Art 25(1) and (2)(a).

[48] ibid, Art 34(d).

[49] ibid, Art 34(e).

[50] ibid, Art 34(c).

[51] ibid, Art 19(2).

[52] For an in-depth analysis of law enforcement access to the CIR under Art 20 of the Interoperability Regulations see: Teresa Quintel, 'Interoperability of EU Databases and Access to Personal Data by National Police Authorities under Article 20 of the Commission Proposals' (2018) 4 *European Data Protection Law Review* 470.

[53] See Interoperability Regulations, Arts 20(3) j, 18 (1) and 17(1).

[54] It is not certain what data are included in the term 'green links', but in accordance with Art 31 of the Interoperability Regulations, those could include all personal data stored in the different underlying systems that created the link when matched against each other. This would be: (1) linked data have different biometric data but share the same identity data and the authority responsible for the manual verification of different identities has concluded that the linked data refer to two different persons; (2) linked data have different biometric data, have similar or different identity data, share the same travel document data and the authority responsible for the manual verification of different identities has concluded that the linked data refer to two different persons; or (3) linked data have different identity data but share the same travel document data, at least one of the EU information systems does not contain biometric data on the person concerned and the authority responsible for the manual verification of different identities has concluded that the linked data refer to two different persons.

[55] It is not certain what data are included in the term 'white links', but in accordance with Art 33 of the Interoperability Regulations, those could include all personal data stored in the different underlying systems that created the link when matched against each other. This would be: (1) linked data that share the same biometric data and the same or similar identity data; (2) linked data that share the same or similar identity data and the same travel document data where at least one of the EU information systems does not have biometric data on the person concerned; (3) linked data that share the same biometric data, the same travel document data and similar identity data; or (4) linked data share the same biometric data but have similar or different identity data.

MID identity confirmation files, Member State authorities or Union agencies must be authorised to access at least two of the underlying databases in accordance with the access conditions laid down in the acts establishing the SIS, the VIS, Eurodac, the EES, the ETIAS, or the ECRIS-TCN. Yet, other requirements are to be applied in order to access red or yellow MID links: In order to be granted access to information stored in the identity confirmation files regarding red links,[56] Member State authorities and Union agencies only need to be authorised to access one of the underlying databases.[57] The conditions for accessing yellow links will be discussed below.

B. Access to the MID for the Manual Verification of Yellow Links

By default, the authority creating or modifying the information in the respective underlying database shall be the authority responsible for the manual verification of different identities.[58] Hence, a simple search in the ESP would not allow the querying authority to manually verify a link, as no data would be created or updated.[59] The verifying authority shall not only have access to the linked data contained in the MID identity confirmation file, but also to the identity data linked in the CIR and in the SIS.[60] As mentioned above, the MID identity confirmation files not only include the different links and a reference to the underlying databases in which the linked data are held, but also a single identification number that allows for the retrieval of the linked data from the corresponding databases.[61] This might signify that an authority, which would normally not be authorised to access the systems that contain those data that generated a link, could nevertheless be granted access for the manual verification of different identities.

In the case of the SIS, the authority responsible for the manual verification whenever the creation or updating of an entry in one of the underlying databases led to the generation of a yellow MID link, is supposed to be the SIRENE Bureau of the Member State that created the SIS alert, which generated a match.[62] Hence, this

---

[56] Data under Art 34(a) and (b), which includes the respective links and a reference to the EU information systems in which the linked data are held.

[57] Interoperability Regulations, Art 29(2).

[58] Art 29 of the Interoperability Regulations lays down the procedure on the verification of yellow MID links.

[59] It is unclear what will happen if an ESP query shows a red link, but the querying authority is not competent to manually verify the link. This could happen in cases where the verifying authority concluded that a person should receive a re-entry ban after a red link was followed up. However, the person could seek to re-enter the EU with the same travel document. Until the red link would be verified and follow-up action could be taken, the person suspected of having committed identity fraud might be held in custody at the border.

[60] Interoperability Regulations, Art 29(3).

[61] ibid, Art 34(c).

[62] ibid, Art 29(2). This concerns SIS alerts in relation to persons sought for surrender or extradition purposes, missing or vulnerable persons, witnesses, or persons subject to discreet, inquiry or specific checks.

SIRENE Bureau would be granted access not only to the links and a reference to the underlying database(s) in which the linked data are held. In addition, it would be allowed to retrieve all the linked data from the corresponding EU information systems with an identification number in order to check the sources of the yellow link. Consequently, SIRENE Bureaux would not only have access to alerts stored in the SIS, but also to data held in immigration databases, which law enforcement authorities may generally only access for the purpose of fighting *serious* crime, on a need-to-know basis, following a strict procedure, and after prior verification by an independent body.[63] For SIRENE Bureaux, such access is even more restricted, as their functions are primarily linked to the SIS.[64] However, neither the use of fraudulent identity or travel documents are listed as serious criminal offence in relevant EU legislation,[65] nor do the Interoperability Regulations foresee any prior verification of SIRENE Bureaux access to the underlying databases.

SIRENE Bureaux were initially established within the framework of the SIS for the purposes of enabling the exchange of supplementary information between the different Member State law enforcement authorities concerning SIS alerts. Nevertheless, further tasks related to police cooperation may be assigned to SIRENE Bureaux.[66] However, the authors have not come across a piece of EU legislation which grants SIRENE Bureaux unconditional access to other EU-wide immigration databases. Hence, the provisions in the Interoperability Regulations which grant SIRENE Bureaux access to the MID files for verification purposes seem to be a departure from the existing legal provisions and go beyond the access by SIRENE Bureaux to information in the SIS. For this reason, an analysis of the legality and proportionality of such an access needs to be performed.

Thus, both the legality and proportionality of such retrieval from the underlying databases, which normally do not grant access to SIRENE Bureaux, shall be

---

[63] Eg, Council Decision 2008/633/JHA of 23 June 2008 concerning access for consultation of the Visa Information System (VIS) by designated authorities of Member States and by Europol for the purposes of the prevention, detection and investigation of terrorist offences and of other serious criminal offences [2008] OJ L218/129; Chapter VI Eurodac Regulation; Chapter IV EES Regulation; Chapter X ETIAS Regulation. Note that in emergency situations the prior verification may be dispensed with. In these cases, only an ex post verification takes place.

[64] The SIRENE manual and other implementing measures for the second generation Schengen Information System (SIS II), Annex to Commission Implementing Decision (EU) 2017/1528 of 31 August 2017 replacing the Annex to Implementing Decision 2013/115/EU on the SIRENE Manual and other implementing measures for the second generation Schengen Information System (SIS II) (notified under document [C 2017] OJ L231/6 (SIRENE Manual 2017).

[65] European Arrest Warrant Framework Decision, Art 2(2) only includes forgery of administrative documents and trafficking therein in the list of offences that give rise to surrender pursuant to a European arrest warrant. In addition, those offences must be punishable in the issuing Member State by a custodial sentence or a detention order for a maximum period of at least three years and as they are defined by the law of the issuing Member State. See: Council Framework Decision 2002/584/JHA of 13 June 2002 on the European arrest warrant and the surrender procedures between Member States – Statements made by certain Member States on the adoption of the Framework Decision [2002] OJ L190/1.

[66] SIRENE Manual 2017, 16 and fn 14 therein.

discussed in Section III of this chapter. The subsequent sections will address the unclear purposes as well as the opaque role of EU agencies accessing the MID.

C. Access to Red MID Links

While access to green and white MID links requires the accessing authority to have access to both underlying databases that hold the data which led to those links,[67] Member State authorities and EU agencies only need to be granted access to one of the underlying databases when accessing data concerning red MID links.[68] Hence, the threshold for access is much lower regarding red links and therefore, includes more authorities.

Authorities having access to the individual underlying systems are to be designated under Member State law. Depending on the system, these may include, inter alia, the ministry of interior, border guards, immigration authorities, central visa authorities, embassies and other authorities responsible for issuing visas, asylum offices, as well as the national police and SIRENE Bureaux.[69]

While the Interoperability Regulations make reference to the access conditions stipulated in the underlying databases with regard to queries in the ESP, these conditions do not seem to apply for access to the MID. It could therefore be argued that the degree of intrusion when access is granted to personal data stored in the MID and in the CIR regarding red links is lower than when it comes to access to the underlying databases. At the same time, the limitations and safeguards for access to links, especially by SIRENE Bureaux, are comparatively low, as shall be demonstrated in the following sections. In addition, the Interoperability Regulations facilitate access by SIRENE offices, as they commonly only have access to one single system, namely the SIS.

It might be argued that access under Article 26(2) to data regarding red links is allegedly limited by three provisions of the Interoperability Regulations.[70]

First, with regards to the purposes, it is clarified that the combating of identity fraud is the sole purpose for which access may be granted to the data relating

---

[67] Interoperability Regulations, Art 26(3) concerning white links and Interoperability Regulations, Art26(4) concerning green links.

[68] Interoperability Regulations, Art 26(2).

[69] See, for instance, with regard to access to Eurodac, Notices from the Member States, List of designated authorities which have access to data recorded in the Central System of Eurodac pursuant to Article 27(2) of Regulation (EU) No 603/2013, for the purpose laid down in Article 1(1) of the same Regulation [2015] OJ C237/1. SIRENE Bureaux may be designated authorities under SIS, see Notices from Member States List of competent authorities which are authorised to search directly the data contained in the second generation Schengen Information System pursuant to Article31(8) of Regulation (EC) No 1987/2006 of the European Parliament and of the Council and Article 46(8) of Council Decision 2007/533/JHA on the establishment, operation and use of the second generation Schengen Information System [2019] OJ C222/01.

[70] Interoperability Regulations, Arts 21(2), 32(2), 36 and in addition also 34(c) as discussed above.

to MID links that are stored in the individual files in the CIR.[71] These data are information that is normally stored on passports, such as names, data of birth, fingerprint data and facial image as well as information concerning the document itself.[72] In addition, the individual files in the CIR store a reference to the underlying databases to which the data belong[73] as well as red and white MID links.[74] Hence, that provision allows access for the detection of identity fraud in order to be able to combat the latter. Yet, whether the combating of identity fraud may qualify as a legitimate purpose to access and subsequently process personal data is questionable, as will be discussed in Section III B of this chapter.

Second, the mere existence of a red link should not lead to legal consequences for the individual concerned and where follow-up action would lead to such consequences, this should take place in accordance with national and EU law and should only be based on relevant personal data concerning the individual.[75] The provision neither makes references to concrete national or EU legislation, nor explains how to assess which relevant data would be included in follow-up measures. It solely refers to Article 34, which lists the content of MID identity confirmation files.[76]

Finally, there is an obligation to keep logs of all processing operations in the MID carried out by Member State authorities or EU agencies.[77] The logging of processing activities is a very specific obligation and an important tool to monitor whether databases are used and accessed lawfully. For instance, within the SIS central system, every access and all exchanges of personal data have to be logged and these logs should be kept between one and three years in order to verify whether searches in the database have been carried out lawfully, by persons authorised to access the SIS, and whether the reasons for access were justified. If properly kept and monitored, logs may be used as a powerful tool to investigate personal data breaches.[78] However, the obligation to create logs does not automatically prevent unauthorised access to the systems or the misuse of personal data.

While the authorities accessing the MID for the verification of yellow links and in order to take follow-up measures of red links will not be granted

---

[71] Interoperability Regulations, Art 21(2).

[72] ibid Art 18(1): fingerprint data and facial images from all systems, surname, first name or names, former surname(s) and name(s), other names (alias(es), artistic name(s), usual name(s)), date of birth and country/place of birth, nationality or nationalities, sex, the date of issue of the travel document(s), first name(s) of the parents of the applicant and reference to the information system to which the data belong.

[73] Interoperability Regulations, Art 18(2).

[74] ibid, Art 19(2).

[75] ibid, Art 32(2).

[76] The MID identity confirmation file shall include: (a) the red, white and green links; (b) a reference to the EU information systems in which the linked data are held; (c) a single identification number allowing retrieval of the linked data from the corresponding EU information systems; (d) the authority responsible for the manual verification of different identities; (e) the date of creation of the link or of any update to it.

[77] Interoperability Regulations, Art 36.

[78] Juraj Sajfert and Teresa Quintel, 'Data Protection Directive (EU) 2016/680 for Police and Criminal Justice Authorities' in Mark Cole and Franziska Boehm (eds) *GDPR Commentary* (Edward Elgar Publishing, forthcoming).

access to all data held in the underlying databases, and are subject to certain limitations laid down in the abovementioned provisions, MID accesses are highly problematic. Concerns arise not only with regard to the legal basis of such access. The purpose, necessity and proportionality of MID access under both Articles 26 and 29 of the Interoperability Regulations is highly controversial. In addition, adequate safeguards to prevent unauthorised access and misuse of the MID data are either too weak, not in place at all, or inconsistent with the access requirements set out in the underlying databases. Finally, access logs do not as such prevent unauthorised access, but are rather a means to investigate data breaches.

Overall, the access conditions regarding the MID indicate serious gaps with regard to key data protection principles and may cause high risks for data subjects, as will be shown in Section III. This is particularly true where the SIRENE Bureaux of the Member States may access the different links either for verification purposes or with regard to follow-up action of red links. Hence, the unclear formulation of the relevant provisions on SIRENE access to the MID seemingly expands the tasks of these national authorities and risks to facilitate abuses and unauthorised processing of personal data.

D. Concerns Arising with EU Agencies Having Access to the MID

Besides the national authorities having broader access to the interoperable system, EU agencies will also obtain widened access possibilities to the underlying databases as well as to the MID, the CIR and the ESP. In that vein, two EU agencies, Europol and the European Border and Coast Guard Agency (EBCGA) should be mentioned as being particularly pertinent regarding the processing of personal data in the context of migration, asylum and border control.

The EBCGA, initially established as supranational agency tasked to assist with migration management and border control, developed into a powerful coordination hub between Member States and other EU agencies as well as third countries, progressively gaining operational competences in further areas related to migration. Under its new Regulation, which was proposed in September 2018[79] and agreed on 15 April 2019,[80] the EBCGA obtained even more competences to cooperate with relevant actors, such as Europol, and to exchange information in the fight against organised cross-border crime and

---

[79] Proposal for a Regulation of the European Parliament and of the Council on the European Border and Coast Guard and repealing Council Joint Action 98/700/JHA, Regulation (EU)1052/2013 of the European Parliament and of the Council and Regulation (EU) 2016/1624 of the European Parliament and of the Council, COM (2018) 631 final.

[80] Regulation (EU) 2019/1896 of the European Parliament and of the Council of 13 November 2019 on the European Border and Coast Guard and repealing Regulations (EU) No 1052/2013 and (EU) 2016/1624 [2019] OJ L295/1.

terrorism. At the same time, Europol, an EU agency originally responsible for supporting national law enforcement authorities in the fight against organised crime and terrorism, became increasingly involved in migration related investigations such as migrant smuggling or document fraud. Both agencies will play a central role with regard to the development and operation of EU large-scale databases and interoperability.[81]

Against that background, discrepancies may arise in the context of interoperability where systematic data exchanges take place between actors that apply different data protection regimes. While national authorities such as immigration offices or the SIRENE Bureaux apply the General Data Protection Regulation (GDPR)[82] and the Law Enforcement Directive[83] to their processing activities, Europol and the EBCGA process personal data within the scope of the Europol Regulation[84] and Regulation (EU) 2018/1725[85] respectively. Such fragmented data protection rules may not only lead to problems where personal data are being exchanged between authorities and agencies on different levels. In addition, concerns arise with regard to the supervision of processing operations, as Member State authorities are supervised by national Data Protection Authorities (DPAs), while the supervision of EU agencies falls within the remit of the European Data Protection Supervisor (EDPS).

III. Access to the MID by SIRENE Bureaux: Necessity and Proportionality Aspects

Access by SIRENE Bureaux to personal data stored in the MID poses concerns with regard to the adherence to established data protection standards, which will

---

[81] Teresa Quintel, 'Interoperable Data Exchanges Within Different Data Protection Regimes: The Case of Europol and the European Border and Coast Guard Agency', (2020) 26 *European Public Law* Issue 1, 205–26.

[82] Regulation (EU) 2016/679 of the European Parliament and of the Council of 27 April 2016 on the protection of natural persons with regard to the processing of personal data and on the free movement of such data, and repealing Directive 95/46/EC (General Data Protection Regulation) [2016] OJ L119/1. (GDPR)

[83] Directive (EU) 2016/680 of the European Parliament and of the Council of 27 April 2016 on the protection of natural persons with regard to the processing of personal data by competent authorities for the purposes of the prevention, investigation, detection or prosecution of criminal offences or the execution of criminal penalties, and on the free movement of such data, and repealing Council Framework Decision 2008/977/JHA [2016] OJ L119/89. (Law Enforcement Directive)

[84] Regulation (EU) 2016/794 of the European Parliament and of the Council of 11 May 2016 on the European Union Agency for Law Enforcement Cooperation (Europol) and replacing and repealing Council Decisions 2009/371/JHA, 2009/934/JHA, 2009/935/JHA, 2009/936/JHA and 2009/968/JHA [2016] OJ L135/53.

[85] Regulation (EU) 2018/1725 of the European Parliament and of the Council of 23 October 2018 on the protection of natural persons with regard to the processing of personal data by the Union institutions, bodies, offices and agencies and on the free movement of such data, and repealing Regulation (EC) No 45/2001 and Decision No 1247/2002/EC [2018] OJ L295/39.

be examined in the following paragraphs. A legitimate question is whether the widened access which the interoperability framework[86] would grant SIRENE Bureaux to information stored in the underlying databases fulfils the requirements that are enshrined in Articles 8[87] and 52(1) of the CFREU.[88]

To that end, the following paragraphs will assess whether the interference with the fundamental right to data protection is justified. Two main reasons give rise to concerns regarding such justification. First, where SIRENE Bureaux process personal data of individuals who are not even suspected of being involved in criminal activities, this could lead to misleading inferences and negatively affect those data subjects.[89] Second, under EU secondary data protection law, the level of protection granted where processing is carried out in a law enforcement context is weaker than the one provided under the GDPR. This is particularly true with regard to data subject rights and their restriction.[90] Processing carried out for law enforcement purposes allows controllers to restrict data subject rights more flexibly. As a result, exercising those rights against law enforcement authorities proves more challenging than in a non-law enforcement context. Therefore, the question whether there are sufficient safeguards and remedies against arbitrary interference in place is essential.

As the Court of Justice of the European Union (CJEU) has established in its case law, access to the personal data of identified or identifiable individuals, including by law enforcement authorities, constitutes an interference within Articles 7 and 8 of the Charter.[91] For this interference to be justified, it must satisfy

---

[86] In particular Arts 26(2) and 29, Interoperability Regulations.

[87] Art 8, CFREU: Protection of personal data:

 1. Everyone has the right to the protection of personal data concerning him or her.
 2. Such data must be processed fairly for specified purposes and on the basis of the consent of the person concerned or some other legitimate basis laid down by law. Everyone has the right of access to data which has been collected concerning him or her, and the right to have it rectified.
 3. Compliance with these rules shall be subject to control by an independent authority.

    Art 7, CFREU on the fundamental right to privacy might also be relevant. However, it will not be examined separately, although it is admitted that a strict delineation between the impact on the rights to privacy and data protection due to SIRENE Bureaux access to the MID data is difficult to make.

[88] European Union, Charter of Fundamental Rights of the European Union [2012] OJ C326.

[89] Eg, once the data is in the hands of law enforcement authorities, it might be processed (by mistake) for incompatible law-enforcement purposes. It might also lead the affected individuals to believe that they are under suspicion and be stigmatised, even if the red link is not correct.

[90] Diana Dimitrova and Paul De Hert, 'The Right of Access under the Policy Directive: Small Steps forward' in Manel Medina; Andreas Mitrakas; Kai Rannenberg; Erich Schweighofer; Nikolaos Tsouroulas (eds) *Privacy Technologies and Policy: 6th Annual Privacy Forum, APF 2018, Barcelona* (Springer, 2018).

[91] Case C-293/12 *Digital Rights Ireland* and 594/12 *Seitlinger and Others* [2014] ECLI:EU:C:2014:238, para 35; Case C-362/14 *Maximillian Schrems v Data Protection Commissioner* [2015] ECLI:EU:C:2015:650; *Opinion 1/15* (EU-Canada PNR Agreement) [2017] EU:C:2017:592, para 124 and 126; Case C-207/16 *Ministerio Fiscal* [2018] ECLI:EU:C:2018:788, para 51. Another interesting case is Case C-70/18 *Staatssecretaris van Justitie en Veiligheid v A, B, P* [2019] ECLI:EU:C:2019:823. It concerns the storage of biometric data of Turkish people living in the Netherlands. The CJEU ruled that the storage served

all the requirements laid down in Article 52(1), CFREU. In accordance with those requirements, any interference with Charter rights must be provided for by law, respect the essence of the concerned right, be necessary and proportionate, and meet objectives of general interest recognised by the Union or the need to protect the rights and freedoms of others.[92] In the following, the widened SIRENE Bureaux access granted under Articles 26(2) and 29 of the Interoperability Regulations will be tested against Article 52(1) of the CFREU, focussing in particular on the legal basis for such access, the legitimate purpose it pursues and its necessity and proportionality.

When carrying out this test, the analysis will rely on criteria and data protection requirements derived from CJEU case law and from EU secondary law on data protection, namely Directive (EU) 2016/680 (Law Enforcement Directive, LED) and where relevant – the GDPR. In particular the LED, covering processing of personal data in the context of police and criminal justice, is relevant as being applicable to the processing of personal data by SIRENE Bureaux in the framework of SIS alerts. While the current SIS II legal framework provides for many stand-alone data protection provisions, under the new SIS III legal framework, the applicability of both GDPR and LED is regulated in a more straightforward manner. With the *de-pillarisation*, all SIS III Regulations primarily refer to the GDPR and the LED as applicable data protection instruments, although some of the specific data protection rules in the SIS III framework remained as *leftovers* from the old regime. Once data are being accessed and further or subsequently processed by competent authorities in the Member States, the GDPR or the Directive apply, depending on the purpose of the processing.

The scope of the LED covers processing that is carried out by a competent law enforcement authority for the prevention, investigation, detection and prosecution of crime or the execution of criminal penalties.[93] In all other cases, the GDPR applies to the processing of personal data.[94] Hence, the Directive only applies where both its material and personal scope are satisfied. Yet, particularly with regard to the material scope, the wording of the LED leaves a wide margin for interpretation. For instance, the *prevention* of crime is not clearly defined under the Directive,

---

purposes of general interest of the Union. However, in that case law enforcement access to the said database was not discussed. Thus, the conclusions from this case do not automatically translate to the topic discussed in the present chapter, ie on law enforcement access to data. See also FRA Opinion on the interoperability proposals, April 2018, 29.

[92] See case law above. See also European Data Protection Supervisor, 'EDPS Guidelines on assessing the proportionality of measures that limit the fundamental rights to privacy and to the protection of personal data,' 19 December 2019, 6–7.

[93] Including the safeguarding against and the prevention of threats to public security, see Law Enforcement Directive, Art 1(1).

[94] Except cases where personal data is processed in the framework of the Common Foreign and Security Policy (CFSP), activities which fall outside the scope of Union law, or where processing falls within the scope of Regulation (EU)2018/1725, see Art 2, GDPR.

which allows competent authorities to include more processing activities within its scope than might have been anticipated or foreseeable for data subjects.

The SIS III Regulations in the field of police cooperation and on border checks set out that the LED only applies when the processing is carried out for law enforcement purposes.[95] However, the distinction between the purposes of the processing is not always clear-cut. For example, it is unclear whether the verification of a yellow link concerning a SIS alert in relation to a suspect could fall within such a purpose.[96] Such a clarification about the data protection law applicable to SIRENE Bureaux is missing in the Interoperability Regulations, which could create legal uncertainty. Yet, the existing ambiguity under the data protection framework should not have to be clarified in other legislation, as this would provide a considerable amount of leeway to the legislator. Ultimately, such a decision taken by the legislator could lead to a political decision on whether the GDPR or the LED should apply, whereas it would be necessary to apply the scope of those two instruments in a coherent manner, based on objective and legally justified criteria, in order to avoid such an interpretative discretion. The clarification on the applicable data protection instruments could, for instance, be provided in the recitals of those instruments that envisage the processing of personal data. This is because interoperability, and especially the links in the MID, will render the delineation between the GDPR and the LED even more difficult. For those situations, it would have been advisable to inform, via the recitals, which data protection law should apply to different types of processing.[97]

A. Provided for by Law: Access is not Foreseeable

The European Court of Human Rights (ECtHR) has ruled on several occasions that a legal provision needs to fulfil several criteria in order to satisfy the quality of law requirement, namely a law should be clear, foreseeable and adequately accessible.[98] Hence, it must be sufficiently foreseeable to enable individuals to act in accordance with the law.[99] The CJEU has endorsed this line of interpretation in

---

[95] SIS III Regulation in the field of police and judicial cooperation, Art 66; SIS III in the field of border checks, Art 51(2).

[96] Eg, it is not immediately clear whether the processing of personal data for the purposes of verifying a yellow link is always subject to LED, bearing in mind that one of the purposes of the MID is facilitating identity checks. This latter purpose cannot be argued to be exclusively a law enforcement purpose. The reason is that the facilitation of identity checks could be related also to non-law enforcement situations, eg for identity check purposes in assessing visa applications. Interoperability Regulations, Art 25(1).

[97] Currently, the recitals only repeat that processing for law enforcement purposes is subject to the LED, see Interoperability Regulations, recital 54.

[98] See for instance: *Del Río Prada v Spain*, App No 42750/09 (ECHR, 21 October 2013), para 91; *S.W. v the United Kingdom*, App No 20166/92 (ECHR, 22 November 1995), para 35.

[99] *Lebois v Bulgaria*, App No 67482/14 (ECHR, 19 October 2017), paras 66–67.

its case law.[100] Whereas it could be argued that the Interoperability Regulations are accessible in the sense that access is provided for in publicly accessible legal instruments, in particular access to the MID[101] is neither clear nor necessarily foreseeable.

This may be illustrated by a comparison of Articles 26(2) and 29 of the Interoperability Regulations, which lay down the procedure for accessing the MID. According to the latter provision, the purpose of access to the MID by SIRENE Bureaux is restricted to the purpose of verifying whether a yellow MID link should be re-classified into a white, green or red link, or whether the match is false and the linked data should be corrected. By contrast, as explained in Section II, access pursuant to Article 26(2) is considerably less restricted, as it is not clear which processing operations the purpose of fighting identity fraud would entail. Thus, situations in which SIRENE Bureaux would have access to the MID 'regarding any red link' are not foreseeable as the purpose for such access is not strictly specified. Even if one would assume that the purpose of the access pursuant to Article 26(2) of the Interoperability Regulations would be to follow up on a link in accordance with Union or Member State law, presumably to investigate and prosecute identity fraud, it remains unclear how SIRENE Bureaux would participate in such an investigation and why they should have access to red links.

As SIRENE Bureaux are currently not directly involved in investigations and are not competent to prosecute, the abovementioned provisions could be interpreted by SIRENE Bureaux as a carte blanche for extending their tasks. The scope of the authorisation under Article 26(2) for SIRENE Bureaux to process the personal data in question is not sufficiently restricted by the Interoperability Regulations. This could thus lead to a function creep, which is 'pre-arranged' by law.[102] Whereas it remains to be seen whether such a function creep would indeed occur in practice or would be restricted by national law, it cannot be denied that Article 26(2) of the Interoperability Regulations is not sufficiently precise to preclude such a situation. This is problematic for complying with Article 52(1) CFREU, because as the CJEU has held, 'the EU legislation in question must lay down clear and precise rules governing the scope and application of the measure in question'.[103]

This is a problem not only for the foreseeability requirement under ECtHR case law. In addition, the provisions granting SIRENE Bureaux access to MID links and thus, the data in the underlying databases, are in conflict with the provisions on access in the underlying databases and risk weakening the access provisions in the SIS instruments, which foresee security measures against unauthorised access and misuse of data. Besides the SIS, SIRENE Bureaux are

---

[100] *Opinion 1/15* (EU-Canada PNR Agreement), 26 July 2017, EU:C:2017:592, para 146.

[101] Interoperability Regulations, Art 26(2).

[102] Franziska Boehm and Mark Cole, 'Data Retention after the Judgement of the Court of Justice of the European Union,' June 30, 2014, funded by the Greens/EFA Group in the European Parliament, www.cr-online.de/Boehm-Cole-Studie_zum_EuGH-Urteil_v._30.06.2014.pdf, 83.

[103] *Digital Rights Ireland*, para 54.

currently not authorised to access directly any of the underlying databases included in the Interoperability framework.[104] Hence, both Article 26(2) and 29 of the Interoperability Regulations present a backdoor for SIRENE Bureaux to be granted access to all of the underlying databases. In a nutshell, SIRENE Bureaux might not only receive new tasks and therefore competences to process personal data. They will be allowed to access immigration databases for unspecified and extremely wide purposes, although the founding acts of those databases do not foresee SIRENE Bureaux access.

B. Concerns Arising with Regard to the Objective of Accessing the MID

Second, according to Article 52(1) CFREU, an interference must genuinely meet objectives of general interest recognised by the Union or the need to protect the rights and freedoms of others.[105] Article 2(1) of the Interoperability Regulations lists seven objectives that interoperability shall fulfil, amongst which are improving the effectiveness and efficiency of border checks, combatting illegal immigration, and ensuring a high level of security in the Union and its Member States. These objectives are broadly phrased, which creates a risk of misuse to justify any type of access. For example, Article 2(2)(a) and (b) of the Interoperability Regulations broadly states that in order to achieve these general objectives, the authorities shall take *measures* to combat identity fraud and ensure the correct identification of individuals. Hence, combatting identity fraud should solely be seen as a measure to achieve the objective to prevent illegal immigration.[106] However, the Interoperability Regulations do not clarify how these measures are related to the objectives, ie whether combating identity fraud is automatically deemed to pursue the overall objective of fighting illegal immigration.

The specific objectives of access to the MID by SIRENE Bureaux are not stated in the Interoperability Regulations. Yet, the MID provides for the detection of multiple identities in order to serve the dual purpose of facilitating identity checks and combating identity fraud.[107]

In previous judgments, the CJEU established that preventing the falsification of passports and the fraudulent use of passports pursues an objective of

---

[104] Besides the SIS, SIRENE Bureaux are allowed to access the Europol SIENA system and Interpol databases. Moreover, the individual SIRENE Bureaux have access to the respective national databases.

[105] European Data Protection Supervisor, 'Assessing the necessity of measures that limit the fundamental right to the protection of personal data: A Toolkit' (April 2017), 14.

[106] See a similar argument by the FRA in Fundamental Rights Agency, 'Interoperability and fundamental rights implications. Opinion 1/2018 of the European Union Agency for Fundamental Rights,' Vienna, April 11, 2018, 31.

[107] Interoperability Regulations, Art 25(2).

public interest recognised by the EU, namely prevention of illegal entry into its territory.[108] It is regrettable that in its most recent case law the CJEU unexpectedly established that the objective of preventing and combating identity and document fraud may in itself constitute an overriding reason in the public interest.[109]

The CJEU's reference to the Interoperability Regulations in *A, B and P v Staatssecretaris van Justitie en Veiligheid* is problematic, as the Court superficially accepts the objectives under Article 2(2) of the Interoperability Regulations without further definition or in-depth analysis. Therefore, it remains unclear how the CJEU draws the line between an objective of general interest as recognised by the Union under Article 52(1) CFREU, a legitimate purpose for the processing, or a means for achieving these. The Court's deviation from previous case law creates a certain level of uncertainty about one of the most fundamental requirements in the CFREU. This is regrettable because it does not allow for a consistent interpretation of the provision on an objective of general interest. Moreover, it opens the door for potentially fitting any purpose or means to qualify as an objective of general interest. This could lead to arbitrary interferences with fundamental Charter rights.

Yet, the declared MID purpose of fighting identity fraud and ensuring better identification of persons could at most serve as a *means* to achieve the overall objective of fighting illegal immigration and not as a self-standing purpose/objective in itself. Hence, at present, pursuant to the wording of the Interoperability Regulations, no objective of general interest recognised by the Union is stated as concerns access to red MID links by SIRENE Bureaux.

In addition, because the tasks of SIRENE Bureaux are not specified under the Interoperability Regulations and the purposes and circumstances of access provided for by Article 26(2) are not precise, it is not clear how SIRENE access to any red MID link would contribute to objectives of general interest recognised by the Union. Arguing that the purpose of SIRENE access to the MID is combatting identity fraud could at most be recognised as a means to pursue an objective of general interest as argued above.

Moreover, the right to access red links under Article 22(2) of the Interoperability Regulations means that SIRENE Bureaux could possibly obtain access to red MID links between data from other databases which currently do not authorise SIRENE access. Where such access would be granted for follow-up purposes of red MID links, it is not clear whether SIRENE Bureaux could actually engage in such a measure, as this is not part of their tasks at the moment. Without regulating the

---

[108] C-291/12 *Schwarz v Stadt Bochum* [2013] ECLI:EU:C:2013:670, paras 36–38 and C-225/12 *Demir* [2013] EU:C:2013:725, para 41.

[109] C-70/18 *Staatssecretaris van Justitie en Veiligheid v A, B, P* [2019], paras 46–49. See: Niovi Vavoula, 'Is Processing Biometric Data of Turkish Nationals in a National Database Lawful under the EEC-Turkey Agreement? Reflections on the Judgment in A, B and P (C-70/18),' Blogpost for EU Immigration and Asylum Law and Policy (December 2019); eumigrationlawblog.eu/is-processing-biometric-data-of-turkish-nationals-in-a-national-database-lawful-under-the-eec-turkey-agreement-reflections-on-the-judgment-in-a-b-and-p-c-70-18/.

tasks and competences of SIRENE Bureaux in that respect, or explicitly stating that SIRENE Bureaux may have access only to the red links which concern SIS alerts, such broad access rights could very well be misused by SIRENE Bureaux. This arbitrariness poses risks for data subjects concerned, as will be discussed below.

C. Access to the MID is not Necessary and is Disproportionate

Third, to test the necessity and proportionality of an interference, one needs to look at whether the interference is: (1) appropriate for achieving the specified legitimate objective; and (2) whether it is the least intrusive measure to attain the said objective.[110] In addition, the CJEU has introduced the concept of 'strict necessity' when examining interferences with Articles 7 and 8 CFREU, in particular when such interference is performed by law enforcement authorities.[111] Furthermore, when examining interferences with these two fundamental rights, the CJEU has also examined whether adequate safeguards against misuse of the concerned data have been put in place.[112]

With regards to the appropriateness of the measure, it could be argued that for the purposes of verification, the verifying authorities, *in casu* the SIRENE Bureaux, would need to have access to the data concerning yellow links in order to examine whether a link is false or how it should be re-classified. Since the purpose of access in the framework of red links is neither precise nor conclusive,[113] it is impossible to ascertain whether the personal data to which the SIRENE Bureaux would have access[114] complies with the requirement of appropriateness. It could be presumed that where a SIRENE Bureau would be competent to participate in the verification of a red MID link, then the access to that link might be appropriate. However, the same cannot be argued where

---

[110] *Digital Rights Ireland*, para 46. EDPS, 'EDPS Guidelines on assessing the proportionality of measures that limit the fundamental rights to privacy and to the protection of personal data,' 19 December 2019. Jonida Milaj, 'Privacy, surveillance, and the proportionality principle: The need for a method of assessing privacy implications of technologies used for surveillance,' (2016) 30(3) *International Review of Law, Computers & Technology* 115 –130, www.tandfonline.com/doi/full/10.1080/13600869.2015.10 76993?scroll=top&needAccess=true. Damian Clifford and Jef Ausloos, 'Data Protection and the Role of Fairness' (2018) 37(1) *Yearbook of European Law*; Catherine Jasserand-Breeman, 'Reprocessing of biometric data for law enforcement purposes: Individuals' safeguards caught at the Interface between the GDPR and the 'Police' directive?' (PhD diss., University of Groningen, 2019) 122–123. Article 29 Working Party, 'Opinion 01/2014 on the application of necessity and proportionality concepts and data protection within the law enforcement sector,' 27 February 2014; Boehm and Cole, 'Data Retention' (n 104) 35–40.

[111] Boehm and Cole, 'Data Retention' (n 104) 36.

[112] *Digital Rights Ireland*, 54–55; Jasserand-Breeman, 'Reprocessing of biometric data' (n 112) 123. Boehm and Cole, 'Data Retention' (n 104) 36 and 38, who argue that safeguards were added in addition to the necessity requirement.

[113] Interoperability Regulations, Art 26(2).

[114] For instance, under (future) national law provisions.

a certain SIRENE Bureau of a Member State is not involved in the verification related to a red link, but nevertheless is granted access. It remains a fact that the Interoperability Regulations neither sufficiently restrict the purposes of SIRENE access nor provide for adequate safeguards in relation such access, as will be demonstrated below.

As to the proportionality *strictu sensu* and the necessary safeguards, the following aspects stand out: the amount of data to which SIRENE Bureaux would have access and number of affected individuals, the duration of the access, and the safeguards regarding access. In addition, transparency towards the data subject regarding red links and the possibility to exercise data subject rights as well as the role of independent supervision is relevant in that respect.

As to the amount of data to which SIRENE Bureaux would have access and the number of affected individuals, SIRENE Bureaux would gain access to additional information.[115] Thus, SIRENE Bureaux would be informed whether someone is a visa or ETIAS applicant, if that person applied for international protection, or whether there is an entry in the ECRIS-TCN. Under the current legal framework on EU databases, law enforcement access is only granted on a case-by-case basis and after prior approval by an independent verification authority. The change regarding law enforcement access to data in EU databases that interoperability will create is problematic with regard to access to data of individuals who are not even suspected of having committed a crime.[116]

On the one hand, SIRENE Bureaux might have access to data concerning individuals who are not stored in a law enforcement database and hence, no valid ground for law enforcement authorities to access these data exists. On the other hand, SIRENE Bureaux are, in any event, not competent to prosecute individuals against whom there are justified suspicions of identity fraud.[117] Such a problem of competence could emerge in practice when the whole of SIRENE Bureaux have access to all red MID links, even when certain parts of SIRENE Bureaux are not involved in the follow-up action concerning a red MID link. This would be the case when the SIS alert which led to a match was not entered by the Member State(s) of the SIRENE Bureaux that access the red link and where these SIRENE Bureaux are not involved in the exchange of supplementary information for the purpose of following-up on that link.[118] This is highly problematic, as compliance with the proportionality requirement in the law enforcement sector foresees

---

[115] For instance, to a reference indicating the databases in which the linked information is stored.

[116] SIRENE Bureaux might end up processing data of such individuals, eg when the yellow link concerns two different individuals who share common identity data and in relation to one of whom there is an SIS alert in cases of examining yellow links, or where the yellow link was false and neither of the two individuals are actually of law enforcement interest, or where SIRENE Bureaux have access to any red link, even when it does not concern an SIS alert which is entered by the Member State authority of the concerned SIRENE Bureau.

[117] Access to the data of innocent people by law enforcement authorities was considered to be a problem from a necessity and proportionality point of view in *Digital Rights Ireland*.

[118] Interoperability Regulations, Art 26(2).

that only the minimum amount of people are subject to a certain data processing operation.[119]

Furthermore, SIRENE staff would obtain access to the linked identity data, which presumably includes all information stored in a CIR individual file. While identity information might be necessary for SIRENE Bureaux to examine a yellow link concerning SIS alerts, it is not clear why SIRENE Bureaux would receive access to the underlying databases where this information is stored. Hence, access to the underlying databases by SIRENE Bureaux is neither appropriate nor necessary.[120]

In addition, SIRENE Bureaux currently do not have the power to investigate or prosecute cases of identity fraud, and it is unclear why and under which legal provisions SIRENE Bureaux should have access to red MID links for that purpose. As the Interoperability Regulations seem unable to confer such a new task, one could wonder whether this is because they are responsible for the exchange of supplementary information with law enforcement authorities in other Member States, such as in the framework of the SIS. Should this be the case, this could imply that in cases of investigating and prosecuting identity fraud, SIRENE Bureaux may only have access to data which the law enforcement authorities in the respective Member State have entered or where cooperation is requested by other Member States, and transfer the necessary information to the competent authorities under national law. The role of the SIRENE Bureaux in this respect could have been clarified for the purposes of legal certainty and also for the purposes of restricting the powers of SIRENE Bureaux in light of strict necessity and proportionality. Without those additional national laws, the proportionality of SIRENE access to the abovementioned data may not be evaluated appropriately at this stage. Pursuant to the CJEU case law, in order to comply with the requirement of strict necessity of a measure, the applicable national laws may not be simply limited to requiring that access should be necessary for attaining a legitimate objective. Rather, a law should regulate the procedural and substantive rules on access to personal data stored in the MID.[121] Whether this would be the case in all the Member States needs to be examined in the future.

In that respect it should be noted that the Interoperability Regulations would effectively allow SIRENE Bureaux to go around the existing safeguards concerning access to the underlying databases which form part of the CIR. As mentioned above, SIRENE Bureaux do not currently have access to those databases and

---

[119] Article 29 Working Party, 'Opinion 01/2014 on the application of necessity and proportionality concepts and data protection within the law enforcement sector,' 27 February 2014, 20, https://ec.europa.eu/justice/article-29/documentation/opinion-recommendation/files/2014/wp211_en.pdf.

[120] For proportionality concerns with regards to law-enforcement access to immigration databases in the framework of interoperability, see M Gutheil, et al, 'Interoperability of Justice and Home Affairs Information Systems,' Study for the LIBE Committee, April 2018 68.

[121] Cases C-203/15 and C-698/15, *Tele2 Sverige AB v Post och telestyrelsen and Secretary of State for the Home Department v Watson, Brice, Lewis* [2016] ECLI:EU:C:2016:970, para 118.

access by other law enforcement authorities to migration databases is subject to strict safeguards. The latter are being abolished with regard to the widened access possibilities under the Interoperability Regulations. Neither is the abolition of those safeguards sufficiently motivated and strictly necessary or proportionate, nor is the logging obligation under Article 36 of the Interoperability Regulations a veritable means to prevent unauthorised SIRENE access.

As to the duration and frequency of accesses to verify MID links, for those to be proportionate, SIRENE Bureaux should ideally have access to the data until the link is verified. However, this restriction is not specified in the Interoperability Regulations. Only with regard to the duration of access for the purposes of Article 26(2) it may be presumed that such access is granted for as long as the red link exists.[122] However, it is questionable in how far the possibility of SIRENE Bureaux to access red links and the associated data during the whole storage period of the red link in the MID/identity confirmation file is proportionate, bearing in mind that the purpose of the access is not clarified. This is especially problematic where red links do not concern alerts entered by the Member State authorities of the concerned SIRENE Bureau or where no international coopera-tion is needed. As the CJEU has noted, the fact that a legal act does not specify the duration of the interference and require that it be based on objective criteria is problematic, because it does not ensure that the interference is limited to what is strictly necessary.[123] Whereas one could argue that currently such a proportional-ity requirement applies in relation to data storage via the applicability of the LED to SIRENE Bureaux, it does not seem fit to regulate the duration of the access to personal data such as red links and that this access has to be on a need-to-know basis. It would be disproportionate if a SIRENE Bureau would have access to the red links in the MID after it has verified the colour of the link and where no further role in the investigation or prosecution of the red link is envisaged for it in the specific case.

An essential element of safeguards against abuse concerns the data subject's right to information about and access to his or her data as a type of remedial action, especially for those individuals in relation to whom red links have been created. Those rights may be restricted by the controller, as long as the restriction is necessary, for instance, to prevent the obstruction of ongoing investigations.[124] However, the data subject should be informed that processing took place as soon as such notification may no longer jeopardise ongoing investigations.[125] In addi-tion, data protection law requires oversight by an independent authority and the right to seek judicial remedy. Whereas the ECtHR has examined the issue of notification and remedies in relation to the necessity of an interference and the

---

[122] Interoperability Regulations, Art 35.
[123] See, eg, *Digital Rights Ireland.*
[124] See, for instance, Law Enforcement Directive, Art 15.
[125] ibid, Art 15(1).

quality of the law on which such interference is based[126] the CJEU has, at least for the time being, addressed the right of access and the requirement of independent control under Article 8(2) and (3) CFREU.[127] Since subjective rights should be considered a safeguard,[128] it is logical that they be examined also in the necessity and proportionality test, similar to the examination of safeguards in several CJEU landmark judgments on data protection.[129]

With regards to data subject rights, under the LED individuals enjoy the right to information, the right of access, the right to rectification,[130] erasure, restriction of processing and the right to have their rights exercised by a supervisory authority on their behalf.[131] The level of rights under the LED is lower than the one under the GDPR, as rights may be restricted in a more flexible manner.[132] This is logical, as in the law enforcement context, competent authorities must be able to restrict rights in order to protect ongoing investigations. However, where SIRENE Bureaux process personal data for non-law enforcement purposes, problems may arise with regard to the delineation between the GDPR and the LED, which ultimately could affect data subject rights.[133]

Under the Interoperability Regulations, a web portal is supposed to facilitate the exercise of data subject rights of access, rectification, erasure or restriction.[134] Via this web portal, a data subject would be informed of a red MID link and would receive the contact details of the authority responsible for the manual verification of different identities.[135] In addition, the web portal would contain information on the exercise of the rights of the individuals who have been informed that a red link concerning their data has been created.[136] For that purpose, the portal would contain a user interface enabling the exercise of data subject rights by providing a template e-mail to facilitate communication between the data subject and the

---

[126] *Zakharov v Russia* App No 47143/06 (ECtHR, 4 December 2015), *Máté Szabó and Beatrix Vissy v Hungary* App No 37138/14 (ECtHR, 12 January 2016).

[127] See Canada PNR Opinion (GC) para 65 218 228 ff; *Tele 2 Svergie* para 123, *Digital Rights Ireland* para 68.

[128] Council of Europe, 'Explanatory Report to the Convention for the Protection of Individuals with regard to Automatic Processing of Personal Data,' Strasbourg, 28 January 1981 10.

[129] See, eg, *Digital Rights Ireland.*

[130] The right to access and rectification are also explicitly mentioned under CFREU, Art 8(2). See also Yordanka Ivanova, 'The role of the EU fundamental right to data protection in an algorithmic and big data world,' International Workshop on the Legal Notions of Privacy and Data Protection in EU Law in a Rapidly Changing World of 14 May 2019, co-organised by the Brussels Privacy Hub (BPH) and the Law, Science, Technology and Society (LSTS) Research Group at the Vrije Universiteit Brussel (VUB).

[131] See Arts 13, 14, 16 and 17, Directive (EU) 2016/680. For an overview of the different rights under the GDPR and the LED, see: Sajfert and Quintel (n 78).

[132] Dimitrova and De Hert, 'The Right of Access under the Policy Directive' (n 90).

[133] Art 48, Interoperability Regulations on the rights of access, rectification, erasure and restriction of processing in relation to the MID does not clarify this either.

[134] Interoperability Regulations, Art 49.

[135] ibid, Art 49(2).

[136] ibid, Art 49(3).

verifying authority.[137] However, this transparency obligation may be restricted if the provision of information concerning a red MID link would jeopardise ongoing investigations relating to SIS alerts.[138] This is likely to be the case when a SIRENE Bureau acts as the verifying authority. Whereas the Interoperability Regulations do not place any temporary restrictions on the limitation and allow for further restrictions of data subject rights, this balancing exercise is laid down under the LED.

According to the LED, data subject rights may be limited only for as long as such a restriction constitutes a necessary and proportionate measure in a democratic society and to the extent that there is a real risk for the investigation of criminal offences or the protection of public and national security.[139] Hence, as soon as the notification no longer jeopardises ongoing investigations, the concerned individual must be notified.[140]

Nevertheless, it remains rather unclear in how far individuals could challenge red links in cases where SIRENE Bureaux consider that informing the concerned individuals of red links would jeopardise criminal investigations. This is because the individuals might not immediately learn about the existence of red links and evoke their rights. In addition, it has been reported that the notification requirement under the LED has been insufficiently transposed in many Member States[141] and the right to indirect access by a national supervisory authority is rarely evoked.[142] Consequently, this affects individuals from exercising their data subject rights and impedes independent review by the supervisory authority of a red MID link on behalf of the person.

Verifying the legality of processing, whether by an independent supervisory authority or by the data subject him- or herself is crucial to allow individuals to detect and challenge false matches, which could lead to (incorrect) red links and suspicion of identity fraud being cast on him or her. This problem is not purely theoretical. False matches have already been reported, both with regards to biometric and alphanumeric data in the framework of the operational EU databases.[143]

---

[137] ibid.

[138] ibid, Art 32(4).

[139] Law Enforcement Directive, Art 13(3).

[140] ibid, art 13(3), art 15(1), art 16(4).

[141] Many national transposition acts do not provide for a legislative measure that would allow for the restriction of data subject rights as stipulated by the LED. Instead, many Member States simply adopted the horizontal wording of the LED, which allows competent authorities to restrict data subject rights more easily.

[142] Speech by Marit Hansen at CPDP 2020: DPAs, Policing and Law Enforcement; www.youtube.com/watch?v=0tJ0WV3sdU0. Indirect exercise of the rights of the data subjects is provided for under Art 17, Directive 2016/680. It is to be evoked when one of the subjective rights has been restricted by the controller and works as follows: if the data subject has become aware of a restriction, then he may request from the responsible data protection supervisory authority that it carries out all the necessary checks about the legality of the legality of the processing of the data.

[143] Fundamental Rights Agency, in its 'Interoperability and fundamental rights implications. Opinion 1/2018 of the European Union Agency for Fundamental Rights,' Vienna, 11 April 2018, 49.

These false matches could be due to the low quality of the stored data. If these quality problems are not fully solved with interoperability,[144] it would be essential that there are effective means to verify the accuracy of the matches by data subjects and have wrong links deleted. However, data subjects seldomly exercise their rights[145] and therefore, a wrong MID link might not be corrected in a timely manner. In addition, where the verification of red links in relation to SIS alerts would be carried out by SIRENE Bureaux, data subject rights could be limited in a more flexible manner. This is particularly the case in those Member States that do not provide for a separate legislative measure on the restriction of rights, as required by the LED, but simply use the horizontal wording of the Directive.

It is also unclear in how far individuals could technically challenge a red MID link where that link is based on a false match. The data subject might have to bear the burden of proof that the data a certain authority processes is wrong or of insufficient quality. This might make it more difficult for the data subject to exercise his or her right to rectification or erasure. Particularly the increased use of biometric data under the Interoperability Regulations bears risks for individuals.[146] Due to their particularly sensitive nature, biometric data are defined as special categories of personal data[147] and require additional safeguards and quality checks.[148] Yet, despite the fact that controllers are under the obligation to ensure the accuracy of the data they process,[149] it is troubling that in the past there were reports where the data subjects had to prove that the biometric match was wrong.[150] Moreover, it could be technically more challenging to demonstrate the accuracy of biometric data, in particular, where the data subject is banned from travelling to the EU. Regarding the possibility to

---

[144] ibid. As the FRA notes in its opinion, interoperability might lead to discovery and correction of mistakes. However, whether it will eliminate them fully is not certain.

[145] Eurodac Supervisory Coordination Group, 'Report on the exercise of the data subjects' rights in relation to Eurodac,' November 2019 9, 11 and 12; VIS Supervisory Coordination Group, 'Activity Report 2015-2016.'

[146] See: European Data Protection Supervisor, 'Opinion 4/2018 on the Proposals for Two Regulations Establishing a Framework for Interoperability between EU Large-Scale Information Systems' (2018) https://edps.europa.eu/sites/edp/files/publication/2018-04-16_interoperability_opinion_en.pdf (last accessed 8 May 2020).

[147] See, for instance, GDPR, Art 9 or Law Enforcement Directive, Art 10, Convention 108+ also defines biometric data as special categories of personal data.

[148] Niovi Vavoula, 'Is Processing Biometric Data of Turkish Nationals in a National Database Lawful under the EEC-Turkey Agreement? Reflections on the Judgment in A, B and P (C-70/18) – EU Immigration and Asylum Law and Policy' eumigrationlawblog.eu/is-processing-biometric-data-of-turkish-nationals-in-a-national-database-lawful-under-the-eec-turkey-agreement-reflections-on-the-judgment-in-a-b-and-p-c-70-18/ (last accessed 18 May 2020).

[149] Pursuant to the accuracy principle in Art 4(1)(d) and the accountability principle in Art 4(4), Directive 2016/680.

[150] See on instances where Member States assumed that a match is automatically correct: European Union Agency for Fundamental Rights, 'Under watchful eyes: biometrics, EU IT systems and fundamental rights,' (2018) 82. The quoted case concerns a Eurodac transfer pursuant to a biometric match. Although the processing of data by the national asylum authorities is subject to the GDPR and previously to Directive 95/46 (see Eurodac Regulation, recital 38), which also required the data controller to ensure the accuracy of the data, this appears not to always have functioned well in practice.

challenge both red MID links and the underlying data which generated the link, it should be noted that the LED provides for the possibility to restrict processing where the accuracy of data is contested by the data subject.[151] In cases where the accuracy of the data in question cannot be ascertained, the stored data should be marked in order to limit their processing in the future.[152] Whereas this is an adequate safeguard, it is regrettable that the Interoperability Regulations do not specify how this right should be applied in cases of (red) links in the MID.[153] Hence, where the disagreement on the accuracy of certain data persists for a long time, it is unclear whether the restriction of the processing would imply that the authorities are not allowed to further process the red link and take follow-up actions in relation to it or whether it would lead to the effective prolongation of the link, since the data generating the link would be blocked. In the latter case, the data subject could be banned from entering the EU because the verification of the link was not solved. For the sake of legal certainty both on the side of data subjects and the SIRENE Bureaux and in order to ensure the coherent interpretation and application of the right to restriction of processing, it should be clarified what the consequences of such a restriction for the data subject would be.

Whereas application issues in relation to the right to the restriction of processing under the LED are not unique to the MID, the complex content and structure of red links poses its own challenges to the applicability of the right. As previously illustrated, where a MID link was generated by data from the underlying databases that were inserted by different authorities, the verification of links might prove challenging and lengthy. For data subjects, it might be difficult to exercise their rights against Member State authorities in the EU via their embassies or consulates when they have been denied entry to the EU due to erroneous data in the databases.

As illustrated previously, the effectiveness of the supervision of the processing operations in the interoperable system by national supervisory authorities and the EDPS, which follows from the widened access by both Member State authorities and EU Agencies, might be impeded due to the fragmented data protection framework. Such effectiveness could be prejudiced where national supervisory authorities in different Member States need to cooperate, for instance, if data leading to a match inserted by different Member State authorities is being challenged. As reported by academics and regulators, cooperation between supervisory authorities has not always been smooth,[154] albeit

---

[151] Law Enforcement Directive, Art 16(3)(a).

[152] In accordance with Law Enforcement Directive, Art 3(3); also see Law Enforcement Directive, recital 47.

[153] See Interoperability Regulations, Art 48, where the clarification is missing.

[154] Evelien Brouwer, *Digital Borders and Real Rights. Effective Remedies for Third-Country Nationals in the Schengen Information System* (Martinus Nijhoff Publishers, 2008). Also, European Commission, 'Communication from the Commission to the European Parliament and the Council. Data protection as a pillar of citizens' empowerment and the EU's approach to the digital transition -two years of application of the General Data Protection Regulation,' COM (2020) 264 final, Brussels, 24 June 2020.

Regulation (EU) 2018/1725 seeks to remedy such gaps to a certain extent via the coordinated supervisory mechanism in the framework of the EU large-scale information systems.[155] Yet, cooperation between national supervisory authorities as provided for under the GDPR, or between national supervisory authorities and the EDPS as stipulated under Regulation (EU) 2018/1725, is not foreseen in a similar extent under the LED. This might remain an unsolved problem, which will ultimately hinder the right to an effective remedy against unlawful processing.[156]

IV. Conclusion

This chapter set out to examine whether the widened access, which SIRENE Bureaux would obtain to personal data under the Interoperability Regulations is necessary and proportionate. The chapter concludes that the provisions of the Interoperability Regulations, including on the legal basis, purposes, data protection aspects and the whole functionality of the MID, are ambiguous and thus risk leading to an arbitrary interference with the rights of the concerned individuals.

The purposes of the MID are intertwined, broad, and difficult to grasp, ranging from the facilitation of identity checks and combating identity fraud, to supporting both the functioning of the CIR[157] and the objectives of all six underlying databases. Apart from the fact that the facilitation of identity checks is anything but a clearly predefined and conclusive purpose, the MID's ancillary purposes to support the functioning of the CIR and the objectives of the underlying databases could have hardly been formulated in a broader manner.

Surprisingly, it seems as if the CJEU, in its recent judgment, accepts the use of such purposes in order to allow for retention of biometric data, despite a different approach in earlier case law. The Interoperability Regulations use the fight against identity fraud as a purpose, although combating identity fraud could only serve as a means to prevent illegal entry, which is the real objective. Backed up by the CJEU itself, the Interoperability Regulations open up the door to use extremely undefined purposes for legal instruments that should, due to their potential to seriously impact huge numbers of individuals in the case of misuse of personal data, be clearly defined and limited.

---

[155] Regulation (EU) 2018/1725, Art 62.

[156] As recognised by Art 47 CFREU. See: Simona Demková and Teresa Quintel, 'Allocation of Responsibilities in Interoperable Information Exchanges: Effective Review Compromised?' [2020] *Cahiers Jean Monnet.*

[157] According to the Interoperability Regulations, Art 17, the CIR is supposed to facilitate and assist in the correct identification of persons registered in the EES, VIS, ETIAS, Eurodac and ECRIS-TCN in accordance with Art 20. Moreover, the CIR shall support the functioning of the MID and facilitate and streamline access by designated authorities and Europol to the EES, VIS, ETIAS and Eurodac for the prevention, detection or investigation of terrorist offences or other serious criminal offences.

The broadly defined purposes for which MID links may be accessed by SIRENE Bureaux provide possibilities for them to access personal data stored in the underlying databases to which they would normally not be granted access. Hence, national authorities could circumvent the conditions laid down in the legal instruments establishing the underlying databases in order to access links that are stored in the MID identity confirmation files. In that regard, SIRENE Bureaux that would be responsible for the manual verification of yellow MID links relating to SIS alerts would be able to retrieve data from all connected systems to which they are currently not granted access. The provisions laying down the procedure on the manual verification of different identities by SIRENE staff are highly worrying and in conflict with the provisions of the underlying databases.

These provisions could have a serious impact on the EU fundamental rights to privacy and data protection. This could be due to the fact that, first, the interference with these rights as discussed in this chapter, would not always be foreseeable. This is a problem from the quality of the law point of view. Second, it is doubtful whether the access provisions pursue an objective of legitimate interest. Third, the analysis has shown that the access provisions are neither necessary nor proportionate because the MID provisions deprive data subjects of safeguards regarding the discussed SIRENE access. This is because the new modalities of access dispense with independent prior authorisation which is currently in place even *before* a law enforcement authority obtains knowledge that the data concerning a certain individual are stored on an immigration database. In addition, the Interoperability Regulations create new tasks for SIRENE Bureaux through the backdoor of verifying MID links. Although SIRENE Bureaux are currently not authorised to investigate or prosecute identity fraud, they would obtain access to personal data in the underlying databases for those purposes, which could eventually lead to a function creep. It is also to be seen whether the exercise of data subject rights in relation to red links would be effective enough in practice. This is unlikely in relation to red MID links due to the flexibility that law enforcement authorities enjoy with regard to the restriction of these rights and because the Interoperability Regulations create novel processing operations for which it is unclear how the existing data protection rights apply.

Under the Interoperability Regulations, numerous provisions aim at fostering exchanges between competent (law enforcement) authorities in the future. Although each EU agency and national authority must implement procedures to monitor and log processing activities, this might not be sufficient. Supervisory authorities should be able to cooperate effectively in order to follow data flows across the different networks, instead of looking at each specific controller separately.[158] This would not only help supervisory authorities to monitor the compliance with data protection requirements but would also help data subjects

---

[158] Demková and Quintel, 'Allocation of Responsibilities' (n 157).

exercise their rights more effectively. However, cooperation between national authorities regarding the operational databases has not always been smooth and it is to be seen whether it will improve under the Interoperability Regulations.

Finally, interoperability calls into question the validity of the fundamental rights system in the EU. While it is true that all fundamental rights, including the right to the protection of personal data, apply to everyone in the Union, in reality this is not the case. The interoperable system of EU databases is supposed to only hold personal data of TCNs whereas personal data of EU citizens shall be excluded from storage. Hence, not only were the underlying databases revised to broaden law enforcement access and to store more categories of personal data. Interoperability de facto turns these databases from immigration – into law enforcement databases and from search – into investigatory tools. This criminalisation of migrants, asylum seekers and other TCNs may eventually lead to a weakening of data protection standards. Although the same data protection rules apply to everyone whatever nationality or residence, in reality, those rules are circumvented. The unclear delineation between the GDPR and the LED allows competent law enforcement authorities to interpret the scope of application of the LED widely and thus, restrict data subject rights more flexibly.

Article 5 of the Interoperability Regulations as non-discrimination clause applies horizontally and prohibits the processing of personal data that results in discrimination. That provision makes specific reference to persons in need of international protection. However, whether vulnerable groups such as asylum seekers and other TCNs are actually aware of their rights under EU law is doubtful, as may be observed in the low number of access requests submitted with regard to EU databases.

While understanding the interoperable system is already challenging for experts working in the field of EU databases, one can only imagine the difficulties that TCNs would experience trying to understand the interconnected regime of databases, how to exercise their rights, or what negative consequences they might face when submitting incorrect information. This might lead to a situation where the increased connectivity of EU databases will allow more authorities to have access to the system, while those whose data are stored in the databases might be less and less capable of understanding and exercising their data subject rights.[159]

Hence, the already existing gap between the promise to protect everyone in the EU with the same standards of fundamental rights and the actual practice intensifies with Interoperability. Whether this is justifiable or not, it is argued that such a differentiation is not supported by the current spirit of the CFREU. On the other hand, this gap might change in the future. Eventually, once interoperability is operational, it will not require much of an effort to expand the interoperable system and connect it with further databases that hold, for instance, financial data, PNR data or data from social media accounts.

---

[159] Teresa Quintel, 'Why Should We Care about the Privacy of Asylum Seekers?' – Migration Policy Centre – MPC' www.migrationpolicycentre.eu/privacy-of-asylum-seekers/ (last accessed 9 May 2020).

Acknowledgements

The authors are grateful to Dara Hallinan, Ronald Leenes, Serge Gutwirth, Paul de Hert, Mark D Cole and Franziska Boehm, as well as Juraj Sajfert (VUB) for his useful input.

References

Annex to Commission Implementing Decision (EU) 2017/1528 of 31 August 2017 replacing the Annex to Implementing Decision 2013/115/EU on the SIRENE Manual and other implementing measures for the second-generation Schengen Information System (SIS II) (notified under document [2017] OJ L231/6.

Article 29 Working Party, 'Opinion 01/2014 on the application of necessity and proportionality concepts and data protection within the law enforcement sector', 27 February 2014.

Boehm, Franziska and Cole, Mark. 'Data Retention after the Judgement of the Court of Justice of the European Union', June 30, 2014, funded by the Greens/EFA Group in the European Parliament.

Brouwer, Evelien. *Digital Borders and Real Rights. Effective Remedies for Third-Country Nationals in the Schengen Information System* (Martinus Nijhoff Publishers, 2008).

Case C-291/12 *Schwarz v Stadt Bochum* [2013] ECLI:EU:C:2013:670.

Case C-225/12 *Demir* [2013] EU:C:2013:725.

Case C-293/12 *Digital Rights Ireland* and C-594/12 *Seitlinger and Others* [2014] ECLI:EU:C:2014:238.

Case C-362/14 *Maximillian Schrems v Data Protection Commissioner* [2015] ECLI:EU:C:2015:650.

Cases C-203/15 and C-698/15, *Tele2 Sverige AB v Postoch telestyrelsen and Secretary of State for the Home Department v Watson, Brice, Lewis* [2016] ECLI:EU:C:2016:970.

Case C 207/16 *Ministerio Fiscal* [2018] ECLI:EU:C:2018:788.

Case C-70/18 *Staatssecretaris van Justitie en Veiligheid v A, B, P* [2019] ECLI:EU:C:2019:823

Clifford, Damian and Ausloos, Jef. 'Data Protection and the Role of Fairness' (2018) 37(1) Yearbook of European Law.

Communication from the Commission to the Council and the European Parliament, 'on improved effectiveness, enhanced interoperability and synergies among European databases in the area of Justice and Home Affairs', COM (2005) 597 final.

Council Framework Decision 2002/584/JHA of 13 June 2002 on the European arrest warrant and the surrender procedures between Member States – Statements made by certain Member States on the adoption of the Framework Decision [2002] OJ L 190/1.

Council Decision 2007/533/JHA on the establishment, operation and use of the second generation Schengen Information System (SIS II) (2007) OJ L205/63.

Council Decision 2008/633/JHA of 23 June 2008 concerning access for consultation of the Visa Information System (VIS) by designated authorities of Member States and by Europol for the purposes of the prevention, detection and investigation of terrorist offences and of other serious criminal offences (2008) OJ L 218/129.

Council of Europe, 'Explanatory Report to the Convention for the Protection of Individuals with regard to Automatic Processing of Personal Data', Strasbourg, January 28th, 1981.

Del Río Prada v. Spain, App. No. 42750/09 (ECHR, 21 October 2013).

Demková, Simona and Quintel, Teresa. 'Allocation of Responsibilities in Interoperable Information Exchanges: Effective Review Compromised?' [2020] *Cahiers Jean Monnet*.

Dimitrova, Diana and De Hert, Paul. 'The Right of Access under the Policy Directive: Small Steps forward' in Manel Medina, Andreas Mitrakas, Kai Rannenberg, Erich Schweighofer and Nikolaos Tsouroulas (eds) *Privacy Technologies and Policy: 6th Annual Privacy Forum, APF 2018, Barcelona* (Springer, 2018).

Directive (EU) 2016/680 of the European Parliament and of the Council of 27 April 2016 on the protection of natural persons with regard to the processing of personal data by competent authorities for the purposes of the prevention, investigation, detection or prosecution of criminal offences or the execution of criminal penalties, and on the free movement of such data, and repealing Council Framework Decision 2008/977/JHA [2016] OJ L119/89.

Eurodac Supervisory Coordination Group, 'Report on the exercise of the data subjects' rights in relation to Eurodac,' November 2019. European Commission, 'Proposal for a Regulation of the European Parliament and of the Council on establishing a framework for interoperability between EU information systems (borders and visa) and amending Council Decision 2004/512/EC, Regulation (EC) No 767/2008, Council Decision 2008/633/JHA, Regulation (EU) 2016/399 and Regulation (EU) 2017/2226' COM (2017) 793 final.

European Commission, 'Proposal for a Regulation of the European Parliament and of the Council on establishing a framework for interoperability between EU information systems (police and judicial cooperation, asylum and migration)' COM (2017) 794 final.

European Commission, 'Proposal for a Regulation of the European Parliament and of the Council amending Regulation (EC) No 767/2008, Regulation (EC) No 810/2009, Regulation (EU) 2017/2226, Regulation (EU) 2016/399, Regulation XX/2018 [Interoperability Regulation], and Decision 2004/512/EC and repealing Council Decision 2008/633/JHA' COM (2018) 302 final.

European Commission, 'Communication from the Commission to the European Parliament and the Council. Data protection as a pillar of citizens' empowerment and the EU's approach to the digital transition -two years of application of the General Data Protection Regulation,' COM (2020) 264 final, Brussels, 24 June 2020.

European Data Protection Supervisor, 'Assessing the necessity of measures that limit the fundamental right to the protection of personal data: A Toolkit,' 11 April 2017: 1-27.

European Data Protection Supervisor, 'Opinion 4/2018 on the Proposals for Two Regulations Establishing a Framework for Interoperability between EU Large-Scale Information Systems,' 16 April 2018.

European Data Protection Supervisor, 'EDPS Guidelines on assessing the proportionality of measures that limit the fundamental rights to privacy and to the protection of personal data,' 19 December 2019: 1-35.

European Union Agency for Fundamental Rights, 'Interoperability and fundamental rights implications. Opinion 1/2018 of the European Union Agency for Fundamental Rights.' Vienna, April 11, 2018.

European Union Agency for Fundamental Rights, 'Under watchful eyes: biometrics, EU IT systems and fundamental rights,' (2018).

Gutheil, M, et al 'Interoperability of Justice and Home Affairs Information Systems,' Study for the LIBE Committee, April 2018.

Ivanova, Yordanka. 'The role of the EU fundamental right to data protection in an algorithmic and big data world.' International Workshop on the Legal Notions of Privacy and Data

Protection in EU Law in a Rapidly Changing World' of 14 May 2019, co-organised by the Brussels Privacy Hub (BPH) and the Law, Science, Technology and Society (LSTS) Research Group at the Vrije Universiteit Brussel (VUB).

Jasserand-Breeman, Catherine. 'Reprocessing of biometric data for law enforcement purposes: Individuals' safeguards caught at the Interface between the GDPR and the 'Police' directive?' PhD diss., University of Groningen, 2019.

Lebois v Bulgaria, App No 67482/14 (ECHR, 19 October 2017).

Luyten, Katrien and Voronova, Sofija. 'Interoperability between EU border and security information systems', EPRS (June 2019) 1–12.

Máté Szabó and Beatrix Vissy v Hungary App No 37138/14 (ECtHR, 12 January 2016).

Milaj, Jonida. 'Privacy, surveillance, and the proportionality principle: The need for a method of assessing privacy implications of technologies used for surveillance' (2016) 30(3) *International Review of Law, Computers & Technology.*

Notices from the Member States, List of designated authorities which have access to data recorded in the Central System of Eurodac pursuant to Article 27(2) of Regulation (EU) No 603/2013, for the purpose laid down in Article 1(1) of the same Regulation [2015] OJ C237/1.

Notices from Member States List of competent authorities which are authorised to search directly the data contained in the second generation Schengen Information System pursuant to Article 31(8) of Regulation (EC) No 1987/2006 of the European Parliament and of the Council and Article 46(8) of Council Decision 2007/533/JHA on the establishment, operation and use of the second generation Schengen Information System [2019] OJ C222/01.

Opinion 1/15 (EU-Canada PNR Agreement) [2017] EU:C:2017:592.

Proposal for a Regulation of the European Parliament and of the Council on the European Border and Coast Guard and repealing Council Joint Action 98/700/JHA, Regulation (EU)1052/2013 of the European Parliament and of the Council and Regulation (EU)2016/1624 of the European Parliament and of the Council, COM (2018) 631 final.

Quintel, Teresa, 'Interoperability of EU Databases and Access to Personal Data by National Police Authorities under Article 20 of the Commission Proposals.' (2018) 4 *European Data Protection Law Review.*

Quintel, Teresa. 'Interoperable Data Exchanges Within Different Data Protection Regimes' (2020) *European Public Law* (forthcoming).

Quintel, Teresa. 'Why Should We Care about the Privacy of Asylum Seekers?' – Migration Policy Centre – MPC.

Regulation (EC) No 1987/2006 of the European Parliament and of the Council on the establishment, operation and use of the second generation Schengen Information System (SIS II) [2006] OJL381/4.

Regulation (EC) No 767/2008 of the European Parliament and of the Council of 9 July 2008 concerning the Visa Information System (VIS) and the exchange of data between MS on short-stay visas (VIS Regulation) [2008] OJ L218/60.

Regulation (EU) No 603/2013 of the European Parliament and of the Council of 26 June 2013 on the establishment of 'Eurodac' for the comparison of fingerprints for the effective application of Regulation (EU) No 604/2013 establishing the criteria and mechanisms for determining the MS responsible for examining an application for international protection lodged in one of the Member State by a third-country national or a stateless person and on requests for the comparison with Eurodac data by Member State law enforcement authorities and Europol for law enforcement purposes, and amending Regulation (EU) No 1077/2011 establishing a European Agency for the operational management of large-scale IT systems in the area of freedom, security and justice (recast) [2013] OJ L180/1.

Regulation (EU) 2016/679 of the European Parliament and of the Council of 27 April 2016 on the protection of natural persons with regard to the processing of personal data and on the free movement of such data, and repealing Directive 95/46/EC (General Data Protection Regulation) [2016] OJ L119/1.

Regulation (EU) 2016/794 of the European Parliament and of the Council of 11 May 2016 on the European Union Agency for Law Enforcement Cooperation (Europol) and replacing and repealing Council Decisions 2009/371/JHA, 2009/934/JHA, 2009/935/JHA, 2009/936/JHA and 2009/968/JHA [2016] OJ L135/53.

Regulation (EU) 2017/2226 of the European Parliament and of the Council of 30 November 2017 establishing an Entry/Exit System (EES) to register entry and exit data and refusal of entry data of third-country nationals crossing the external borders of the MS and determining the conditions for access to the EES for law enforcement purposes, and amending the Convention implementing the Schengen Agreement and Regulations (EC) No 767/2008 and (EU) No 1077/2011 [2017] OJ L327/20.

Regulation (EU) 2018/1240 of the European Parliament and of the Council of 12 September 2018 establishing a European Travel Information and Authorisation System (ETIAS) and amending Regulations (EU) No 1077/2011, (EU) No 515/2014, (EU) 2016/399, (EU) 2016/1624 and (EU) 2017/2226 [2018] OJ L236/1.

Regulation (EU) 2018/1725 of the European Parliament and of the Council of 23 October 2018 on the protection of natural persons with regard to the processing of personal data by the Union institutions, bodies, offices and agencies and on the free movement of such data, and repealing Regulation (EC) No 45/2001 and Decision No 1247/2002/EC [2018] OJ L295/39

Regulation (EU) 2018/1860 of the European Parliament and of the Council of 28 November 2018 on the use of the Schengen Information System for the return of illegally staying third-country nationals [2018] OJ L312/1.

Regulation (EU) 2018/1861 of the European Parliament and of the Council of 28 November 2018 on the establishment, operation and use of the Schengen Information System (SIS) in the field of border checks, and amending the Convention implementing the Schengen Agreement, and amending and repealing Regulation (EC) No 1987/2006 [2018] OJ L312/14.

Regulation (EU) 2018/1862 of the European Parliament and of the Council of 28 November 2018 on the establishment, operation and use of the Schengen Information System (SIS) in the field of police cooperation and judicial cooperation in criminal matters, amending and repealing Council Decision 2007/533/JHA, and repealing Regulation (EC) No 1986/2006 of the European Parliament and of the Council and Commission Decision 2010/261/EU [2018] OJ L312/56.

Regulation (EU) 2019/817 of the European Parliament and of the Council of 20 May 2019 on establishing a framework for interoperability between EU information systems in the field of borders and visa and amending Regulations (EC) No 767/2008, (EU) 2016/399, (EU) 2017/2226, (EU) 2018/1240, (EU) 2018/1726 and (EU) 2018/1861 of the European Parliament and of the Council and Council Decisions 2004/512/EC and 2008/633/JHA [2019] OJ L135/27.

Regulation (EU) 2019/818 of the European Parliament and of the Council of 20 May 2019 on establishing a framework for interoperability between EU information systems in the field of police and judicial cooperation, asylum and migration and amending Regulations (EU) 2018/1726, (EU) 2018/1862 and (EU) 2019/816 [2019] OJ L135/85.

Regulation (EU) 2019/816 of the European Parliament and of the Council of 17 April 2019 establishing a centralised system for the identification of Member States holding conviction information on third-country nationals and stateless persons (ECRIS-TCN) to supplement the European Criminal Records Information System and amending Regulation (EU) 2018/1726 [2019] OJ L135/1.

Regulation (EU) 2019/1896 of the European Parliament and of the Council of 13 November 2019 on the European Border and Coast Guard and repealing Regulations (EU) No 1052/2013 and (EU) 2016/1624 [2019] OJ L295/1.

Sajfert, Juraj and Quintel, Teresa. 'Data Protection Directive (EU) 2016/680 for Police and Criminal Justice Authorities' in Mark Cole and Franziska Boehm (eds) *GDPR Commentary* (Edward Elgar Publishing (Forthcoming)).

Speech by Marit Hansen at CPDP 2020: DPAs, Policing and Law Enforcement; www.youtube.com/watch?v=0tJ0WV3sdU0.

S.W. v the United Kingdom, App No 20166/92 (ECHR, 22 November 1995).

Zakharov v Russia App No 47143/06 (ECtHR, 4 December 2015).

Vavoula, Niovi. 'Is Processing Biometric Data of Turkish Nationals in a National Database Lawful under the EEC-Turkey Agreement? Reflections on the Judgment in A, B and P (C-70/18).' Blogpost for EU Immigration and Asylum Law and Policy (December 2019); eumigrationlawblog.eu/is-processing-biometric-data-of-turkish-nationals-in-a-national-database-lawful-under-the-eec-turkey-agreement-reflections-on-the-judgment-in-a-b-and-p-c-70-18/.

VIS Supervisory Coordination Group, 'Activity Report 2015-2016.'

Projecting Privacy and Data Protection in a Responsible, Sustainable Future

Brussels, 30 June 2020

WOJCIECH WIEWIÓROWSKI*

The concluding chapter of the CPDP book is usually the transcript of the EDPS' closing speech. The EDPS' concluding remarks at CPDP 2020 were intended to relate to the EDPS' strategy for the mandate 2019–2024. Since the delivery of the speech, the world has changed significantly. The Covid-19 pandemic also changed the EDPS' planning for the future. In this regard, this year, in a break with tradition, the closing chapter of the CPDP book will be the transcript of the EDPS' speech given in June, during the presentation of the EDPS' strategy for 2019–2024. The speech pertains to the strategy mandate but also includes reflections on the Covid-19 crisis.

Ladies, Gentlemen, good afternoon,

I am delighted to address you on this special day for the EDPS and I wish you a warm welcome from Brussels.

When I had the honour of being appointed as the European Data Protection Supervisor, I was picturing a very different setting and atmosphere for the launch of my strategy.

Surely, the reality we have been through challenged some of my convictions, for example, the necessity to have a stylish reception to digest the declamation of policy statements.

The EDPS has grown over the years as a strong and mature institution, a stronghold/fortress of independent and courageous thinking. Credits go to my predecessors Peter Hustinx and Giovanni Buttarelli, the giants behind such a huge endeavour, and to whom I wish to pay tribute to.

The Strategy intends to set the priorities and line of actions, marking the mandate for the four years and a half to come. Do join me on this journey for the following 8 minutes.

The GDPR was a global turning point for privacy and personal data protection. The European data protection law provided a solid basis for a human-centric data

* European Data Protection Supervisor.

economy. As a result, the EU has been a source of inspiration for many countries worldwide.

This process will endure and Europe should keep the leading role not only in legislating but also – or rather first of all – in its implementation.

Europe should not rest on its laurels, as the success of the European approach to data protection will constantly be assessed. For example, in our ability to scrutinise growing complexities in digital systems, pervaded by business models relying on tracking and (too much) powerful controllers.

The new decade will see the crusade for industrial data, where Europe wants to play a leading role.

We will see a proliferation of inter-connected devices, extending the risk surface for criminal and state-sponsored hacking, to gain access to protected information and disrupt services.

We will also see biometric technologies, facial and automatic recognition systems, Artificial Intelligence, Augmented/Virtual Reality, increasingly deployed in the spaces and facilities of public utility.

We are not questioning any technology per se. But, we oppose some untested and particularly invasive applications of certain technologies.

This is why, the EDPS expressed, in a recent opinion on the European Commission's White Paper on AI, our support for the idea of a moratorium on the deployment, in the EU, of automated recognition in public spaces of human features. Not only of faces but also of gait, fingerprints, DNA, voice, keystrokes and other biometric or behavioural signals, so that an informed and democratic debate can take place.

Security risks will be growing and cyber security will become more and more complex. Ensuring the security and fair competition throughout the electoral process will be of critical importance for democracies.

The crisis has revealed, even more so, the importance of ensuring that the privacy and personal data of people are protected. Epidemiological surveillance may pave the way for participatory and 'under the skin' surveillance, whose repercussions may be long-lasting.

I am preoccupied that the economic impact of the crisis will increase the pressure on organisations to maximise their efficiency, in ways, which may sacrifice the rights and freedoms of individuals.

We must all engage in an informed debate around what shall constitute 'public good', whether in times of crisis, or not.

The 'new normal' shall not give way to the permanent erosion of rights we have fought so long and hard to promote.

I want EU data protection norms to be solid road signs on the EU's road to recovery.

I want to engage with the EU industrial policy to boost privacy enhancing technologies, designed in the EU and exported around the world. Europe should also use taxation and international trade to foster a fairer and more sustainable digital Europe.

We do not want artificial geographical borders, but we do have a preference for data being processed by entities sharing European values.

I stand by the European efforts on 'digital sovereignty', where data generated in Europe is converted into value for European companies and individuals, and, processed in accordance with European values.

I am also convinced that, as much as we need digital sovereignty, the EU also needs digital solidarity.

Digital solidarity would refuse to replicate the business model of constant surveillance and tracking, which have been damaging the trust in the digital society. This would allow for technology to work for all people in Europe, and especially for the most vulnerable.

And please remember that for me – a Polish man born in 70s – the word Solidarity has also a historical meaning of changing the world together.

We want to have foresight. But, above all – we want to implement practical actions.

This is how I intend to achieve the EDPS' goals, built around the following three main pillars: foresight, action, and solidarity.

A Smart Digital Future

My institution will further expand as a hub of excellence.

We want to contribute to the understanding of the impact that digital technology has and *will have* on our rights.

Rest assured, we will use the best of our expertise to secure a fairer digital future.

I aim to achieve this through different actions: by continuing our contributions to data protection cases before the Court of Justice; monitoring the measures taken by EUI during this current health emergency, making sure that they are temporary; educating the new generation of EU staff on privacy and data protection matters.

I will also strengthen our engagements with NGOs and Civil Society, as they represent a pillar for advancing the understanding of complex systemic problems in our world.

Master Trends in Technology and Innovation

We shall be constructive, positive and forward-looking to appreciate the opportunities new technologies hold for humanity, and make sure that data protection is embedded, by design and by default, in innovation.

We will monitor developments in the areas of freedom, security and justice, via our supervision of Europol, Eurojust, EPPO, Frontex, EASO or eu-LISA.

We will focus on areas where data protection interacts with technology, for example by closely monitoring and forecasting emerging technologies and giving the alert when technology is deployed in such a way that does not respect the essence of the fundamental rights to personal data protection.

Naturally, we will also prioritise areas where data protection interplays with other fields. We recognise the synergies between the enforcement of data protection and other rules applicable to the digital economy, especially concerning consumer and competition law, and will carry on our work to ensure that they are mutually reinforced.

Use the Tools We Have and Develop New Ones

The EU administration relies on external digital service providers to carry out some tasks.

We have witnessed how this is susceptible to exacerbate risks for data protection, particularly where there is a lack of alternatives to companies that, in some cases, may have questionable standards on privacy and transparency.

The EU has leverage to inject a real change in the market, and transform business models which depart from EU values and rights. Developing a strong oversight for technologies and tools, which are increasingly 'endemic' to our digital ecosystem, will be key.

We shall aim to minimise our reliance on monopolies, avoid the EU lock-in syndrome, and explore free and open source software and solutions.

Ensure Coherence While Protecting Human Beings

We will pursue efforts to guarantee the coherent application of laws throughout the digital European Union.

As a member and provider of the EDPB secretariat, we will strengthen the cooperation between national authorities for high profile and resource-heavy enforcement cases, by creating a Pool of Experts within the EDPB.

The Pool of Experts shall be the expression of stronger European solidarity, burden sharing and common approach to ensure the enforcement of our data protection rules.

We aim to provide support in adopting a strategic approach to enforcement for a fairer Digital Single Market based on human rights, promote joint enforcement actions and active mutual assistance.

We want the GDPR to work as a model for all democracies around the world, to boost trust and respect for the digital society.

Promote Justice and the Rule of Law

The EU should promote digital justice and privacy for all.

Individuals should be given control, however in complex scenarios, 'consent' is not a panacea, as it will suffer from power imbalances between the controller and the individual.

Data protection is one of the last lines of defence for vulnerable individuals, such as migrants and asylum seekers, therefore we will make sure that their rights are preserved.

Moreover, privacy and data protection are an integral part of the rule of law and should never be treated in isolation. To this end, I wish to take action, when, for example, the independence of other DPAs is compromised.

Foster Solidarity and Sustainability

We will be an even stronger socially-responsible organisation, to promote responsible data processing, vis-à-vis the environmental crisis, growing inequalities and geopolitical tensions.

As a data distribution policy measure, access to privately held data by non-profit stakeholders to foster social and solidarity innovation and scientific research in the public interest, deserves attention, and we will engage in such a debate.

The EU needs to be smart in its approach towards new technologies. We should embrace those technologies that respect the principle of human dignity, which is the cornerstone of our Charter of Fundamental Rights.

Only then, will we inhabit a prosperous and sustainable future, which is fair and just to everyone. The EDPS stands ready to assist other EU institutions and other relevant stakeholders in this European project of shaping a safer, prosperous and sustainable digital future.

The breakdown of our future actions is in the text of the published Strategy, which I warmly invite you to consult and to comment.

Ladies, and Gentlemen,

Thank you for your attention and I look forward to further engaging with you all in the Q&A session after listening to our distinguished speakers Commissioner Reynders and Chairwoman Andrea Jelinek.

INDEX

www.ingramcontent.com/pod-product-compliance
Lightning Source LLC
Chambersburg PA
CBHW061144220326
41599CB00025B/4344